Social influences and
socialization in
infancy.

Social Influences
and Socialization
in Infancy

Genesis of Behavior

Series Editors: MICHAEL LEWIS
Robert Wood Johnson Medical School
New Brunswick, New Jersey

and LEONARD A. ROSENBLUM
Downstate Medical Center
Brooklyn, New York

Volume 1   *The Development of Affect*

Volume 2   *The Child and Its Family*

Volume 3   *The Uncommon Child*

Volume 4   *Beyond the Dyad*

Volume 5   *The Socialization of Emotions*

Volume 6   *Social Influences and Socialization in Infancy*

Social Influences and Socialization in Infancy

Edited by

Michael Lewis
Robert Wood Johnson Medical School
New Brunswick, New Jersey

and

Saul Feinman
University of Wyoming
Laramie, Wyoming

PLENUM PRESS • NEW YORK AND LONDON

Library of Congress Cataloging-in-Publication Data

Social influences and socialization in infancy / edited by Michael
  Lewis and Saul Feinman.
        p.   cm. -- (Genesis of behavior ; v. 6)
     Includes bibliographical references and index.
     ISBN 0-306-43632-9
     1. Infant psychology--Social aspects. 2. Child psychology--Social
  aspects. 3. Socialization.   I. Lewis, Michael, 1937 Jan. 10-
  II. Feinman, Saul. III. Series.
     [DNLM: 1. Child Development. 2. Family. 3. Infant.
  4. Socialization.   W1 GE275 v. 6 / WS 105.5.S6 S678]
  BF720.S63S623 1990
  305.23'2--dc20
  DNLM/DLC
  for Library of Congress   90-14308
                                                                  CIP

846 24284

ISBN 0-306-43632-9

© 1991 Plenum Press, New York
A Division of Plenum Publishing Corporation
233 Spring Street, New York, N.Y. 10013

Printed in the United States of America

LEONARD A. ROSENBLUM, *Department of Psychiatry, SUNY Health Sciences Center, Brooklyn, New York 11203*

H. RUDOLPH SCHAFFER, *Department of Psychology, University of Strathclude, Glasgow, Scotland G1-IRD, United Kingdom*

INA Č. UŽGIRIS, *Department of Psychology, Clark University, Worcester, Massachusetts 01610*

EVERETT WATERS, *Department of Psychology, SUNY at Stony Brook, Stony Brook, New York 11794-2500*

Contributors

K. ALISON CLARKE-STEWART, *Program in Social Ecology, University of California, Irvine, California 92717*

JUDITH F. DUNN, *Department of Human Development and Family Studies, College of Health and Human Development, Penn State University, University Park, Pennsylvania 16802*

SAUL FEINMAN, *Child and Family Studies, Department of Home Economics, University of Wyoming, Laramie, Wyoming 82071*

JACOB L. GEWIRTZ, *Department of Psychology, Florida International University, Miami, Florida 33199*

VIRGINIA GUNDERSON, *Department of Psychology, University of Washington, Seattle, Washington 98195*

JAMES JACCARD, *Department of Psychology, State University of New York at Albany, Albany, New York 12222*

SHARON LANDESMAN, *Departments of Psychiatry and Psychology, Frank Porter Graham Child Development Center, University of North Carolina at Chapel Hill, Chapel Hill, North Carolina 27599*

MICHAEL LEWIS, *Institute for the Study of Child Development, Robert Wood Johnson Medical School, New Brunswick, New Jersey 08903-0019*

JOHN E. RICHTERS, *Child and Adolescent Disorders Research Branch, National Institute of Mental Health, Rockville, Maryland 20857*

BARBARA ROGOFF, *Department of Psychology, University of Utah, Salt Lake City, Utah 84112*

Preface

How are we to understand the complex forces that shape human behavior? A variety of diverse perspectives, drawing on studies of human behavioral ontogeny, as well as humanity's evolutionary heritage, seem to provide the best likelihood of success. It is in an attempt to synthesize such potentially disparate approaches to human development into an integrated whole that we undertake this series on the genesis of behavior.

In many respects, the incredible burgeoning of research in child development over the last two decades or so seems like a thousand lines of inquiry spreading outward in an incoherent starburst of effort. The need exists to provide, on an ongoing basis, an arena of discourse within which the threads of continuity among those diverse lines of research on human development can be woven into a fabric of meaning and understanding. Scientists, scholars, and those who attempt to translate their efforts into the practical realities of the care and guidance of infants and children are the audience that we seek to reach. Each requires the opportunity to see—to the degree that our knowledge in given areas permits—various aspects of development in a coherent, integrated fashion. It is hoped that this series—which brings together research on infant biology, developing infant capacities, animal models, and impact of social, cultural, and familial forces on development, and the distorted products of such forces under certain circumstances—serves these important social and scientific needs.

Each volume in this series deals with a single topic that has broad significance for our understanding of human development. Into its focus on a specific area, each volume brings both empirical and theoretical perspectives and analysis at the many levels of investigation necessary to a balanced appreciation of the complexity of the problem at hand. Thus, each volume considers the confluence of the genetic, psychological, and neurophysiological factors that influence the individual infant, and the dyadic, familial, and societal contexts within which development occurs. Moreover each volume brings together the vantage points provided by studies of human infants and pertinent aspects of animal behavior, with particular emphasis on nonhuman primates.

Just as this series draws on the special expertise and viewpoints of workers in many disciplines, it is our hope that the product of these labors speaks to the needs and interests of a diverse audience, including physiologists, ethologists, sociologists, psychologists, pediatricians, obstetricians, and clinicians and scientists in many related fields. As in years past, we hold to our original objectives in this series of volumes to provide both stimulation and guidance to all among us who are concerned with humans, their past, their present, and their future.

The current volume examines the various ways in which the development of very young children is facilitated and modified through social influence and socialization processes. Although this broad issue was not the most central topic of investigation during the formative years of infancy research, recent years have witnessed a rekindling of interest in the socialization of infants and toddlers. This volume is intended to serve as a reflection, an integration, and an expansion of such work.

The volume is organized into two main sections: Sources of Influence and Processes of Influence. However, it should be noted that the integration of processes with sources within natural contexts is a theme which can be found throughout the chapters. A wide range of sources is considered, ranging from the macro-level influences of social structure to the micro-level influences of the self. Similarly, the processes examined run the gamut from strikingly direct approaches, such as operant conditioning, to distinctly indirect methods, such as imitation and social guidance. The predominant disciplinary orientation of the contributors is that of developmental psychology, and the chapters of this volume are most strongly influenced by the thinking of that discipline. Nevertheless, other perspectives—primarily primatology, social psychology and sociology—are represented as well.

As one might expect, the social influence model which underlies and unites the diverse chapters of this volume emphasizes the socialization impact of such influences upon very young children. But this model also highlights the salience of individual variation among children in mediating the outcomes of influence. It is recognized that the characteristics and reactions of children play a major role in determining the socialization impact of such influence. Furthermore, underlying the chapters of this volume is the shared assumption that adult sensitivity to inter- and intra-individual variation in children serves to mediate and influence outcomes. In this light, there is just as much concern for variational patterns as for typologies and averages. Finally, very young children are viewed not only as receiving influence from others, but as giving influence as well. What we have here, then, is a collection of contributions integrated by their common focus upon how very young children are socially influenced and socialized in a social context characterized by sensitivity, individual variation, and mutuality of influence.

MICHAEL LEWIS
SAUL FEINMAN

Contents

1   *Influence Lost, Influence Regained*   1
    SAUL FEINMAN AND MICHAEL LEWIS

I. SOURCES OF INFLUENCE

2   *Family and Friends in Primate Development*   23
    LEONARD A. ROSENBLUM

3   *A Home Is Not a School: The Effects of Environments on Development*   41
    K. ALISON CLARKE-STEWART

4   *The Family Environment: The Combined Influence of Family Behavior, Goals, Strategies, Resources, and Individual Experiences*   63
    SHARON LANDESMAN, JAMES JACCARD, AND VIRGINIA GUNDERSON

5   *Sibling Influences*   97
    JUDITH F. DUNN

6   *Self-Knowledge and Social Influence*   111
    MICHAEL LEWIS

II. PROCESSES OF INFLUENCE

7   Social Influence on Child and Parent via Stimulation
    and Operant-Learning Mechanisms   137
    JACOB L. GEWIRTZ

8   The Mutuality of Parental Control in Early Childhood   165
    H. RUDOLPH SCHAFFER

9   Attachment and Socialization: The Positive Side
    of Social Influence   185
    JOHN E. RICHTERS AND EVERETT WATERS

10 The Social Context of Infant Imitation   215
    INA Č. UŽGIRIS

11 The Joint Socialization of Development by Young
    Children and Adults   253
    BARBARA ROGOFF

12 Bringing Babies Back into the Social World   281
    SAUL FEINMAN

    Author Index   327

    Subject Index   337

Influence Lost, Influence Regained

Saul Feinman and Michael Lewis

Infancy conforms to nobody; all conform to it
(Emerson, 1865/1883, p. 50)

Ralph Waldo Emerson would probably not be displeased with the state of research on human infancy. His extolment of the moral superiority of *Self-Reliance*, and his belief that this virtue is especially evident in the behavior of "children, babes, and brutes, . . . their mind being whole, their eye as yet unconquered" (Emerson, 1865/1883, p. 50), appears to be in tune, although admittedly in an exaggerated way, with the strong emphasis upon nonsocial forces and individual behavior in contemporary research on infant development. Clearly, Emerson's view was a most radical one that, in essence, completely dismissed the role and significance of social influence. Although not as markedly slanted as Emerson's perspective, modern research on infancy has been inclined to view the infant as a rather self-reliant organism and has played down the impact of social influence and socialization on development.

The apparent absence for some time of a social influence and especially a socialization tradition in infancy research seems to have come about during the formative years of the modern scientific study of infancy, beginning in the early-to-mid-1960s. At that time, two major theories guided the study of child socialization: behaviorism and psychoanalysis. Up until the mid-60s or so, we can still find a significant proportion of

SAUL FEINMAN • Child and Family Studies, Department of Home Economics, University of Wyoming, Laramie, Wyoming 82071.   MICHAEL LEWIS • Institute for the Study of Child Development, Robert Wood Johnson Medical School, New Brunswick, New Jersey 08903-0019.

studies on infants which focused on issues relevant to one or both of these theories. By the late 1960s and early 1970s, however, a rash of protest over the assumptions and philosophical implications of behaviorism and psychoanalysis had broken out, followed by a hasty retreat within infancy research not only from the then-extant versions of these particular theories, but indeed from a social influence and socialization perspective in general.

THE IRRESISTIBLE FORCE OF SOCIAL INFLUENCE

> I should like to go one step further now and say "Give me a dozen healthy infants, well-formed, and my own specified world to bring them up in and I'll guarantee to take any one at random and train him to become any type of specialist I might select—doctor, lawyer, artist, merchant chief and yes, even beggar-man and thief, regardless of his talents, penchants, tendencies, abilities, vocations, and race of his ancestors." (Watson, 1924, p. 82)

> In the space of a few years the little primitive creature must turn into a civilized human being . . . This is made possible by hereditary disposition; but it can almost never be achieved without the additional help of upbringing, of parental influence. (Freud, 1940/1949, p. 42) The influence of the parents dominates the child by granting proofs of affection and by threats of punishment, which, to the child, means loss of love, and which must also be feared on their own account. (Freud, 1933, p. 89)

Despite the differences in perspective between Watson and Freud, their theories of socialization, especially of very young children, had much in common. Both of their orientations viewed infancy as a critical time for the child to be controlled so as to meet the needs of adult society. Although these theories did differ as to the image each had of the essential character of the child and therefore the valence of socialization interaction, the basic vision of the function and nature of socialization was essentially the same. The child of Freud's model is an active child, seething with instinctive drives that place her or him in inherent opposition to society. With such a child, socialization is likely to be a struggle, a taming process in which resistance is to be expected. In contrast, Watson's child is a good child, a child who needs only to be exposed to the "right" regimen of socialization in order to become a productive and self-sufficient member of society. Thus, socialization of Watson's well-tempered infant is a relatively peaceful process. Despite these differences, both the conflict model espoused in Freud's psychoanalytic theory and the clay-molding model represented in Watson's behaviorist approach (Schaffer, 1984) share the common view that, ultimately, the socialization process will accomplish its intended goal, that of modifying and "civilizing" the infant's behavior.

There is virtually no sense of positive commitment by the infant to the socialization process in either model. In Watson's behaviorism, the child's willingness to be molded is more accurately conceptualized as the absence of resistance rather than as the presence of an active desire to be socialized. The child cooperates but does not collaborate. Commitment is even less evident in the classic psychoanalytic perspective, for here infants are viewed as often being openly antagonistic to the goals of the civilization process, wishing only to have their own way—somewhat reminiscent of the Calvinist view that infants are the embodiment of the "imps of darkness" (Radbill, 1980).

This model of socialization is a didactic one in which the parent, as the representative of society, is assumed to possess the "right" answers and to teach them to the child. Viewing socialization as a civilizing process implies that there is a correct standard for expected behavior, and that the adult's "job" is to modify the child's behavior so that it comes to meet these expectations. In this perspective, any influence that the child might have on the adult is, at best, of secondary interest and, at worst, a source of interference that threatens to detain the adult from the socialization task at hand. Mutuality of influence is very much a moot point within the Freud-Watson model of socialization.

Although, on the surface, these two approaches appear to utilize different methods for implementing socialization goals, in truth the methods are remarkably similar—a resemblance, in fact, that was noted by Watson himself (Watson & Rayner, 1920). Put simply, modification of behavior is driven by the power-dependence relationship (Emerson, 1962), in that the infant's dependency upon the adult for receiving rewards and avoiding punishments gives the adult power to modify the infant's behavior. In behaviorism, a wide range of rewards and punishments may be used; indeed, although Watson, in his businesslike approach to child rearing, recommended against using emotional rewards—"Never hug and kiss them, never let them sit on your lap" (1928, p. 81)—there is no conceptual reason why, in the context of behaviorism, hugs and kisses could not be utilized to reinforce desired behavior. Freud's psychodynamic and explicitly emotional approach emphasized the utilization of the infant's fear of the withdrawal of parental love to modify behavior. In both models, the child's dependency upon the adult is the cornerstone of socialization, enabling behavior to be shaped according to adult standards.

Furthermore, neither theory seems to be notably concerned about individual variation. With the exception of Freud's belief that socialization acts through different channels as the child grows older—first through the parents during infancy and toddlerhood, and later through the internalized parent within the superego—there seems to be an assumption that all children can be socialized through essentially the same procedures. The notion that effective socialization calls for sensitive responsiveness to the infant's desires, for the parent to take into account the child's developmental status, state, or wishes, is not a conspicuous feature of this perspective on child rearing.

When infancy began to emerge as a field of research, the investigation of child socialization was guided predominantly by this behaviorist-psychoanalytic perspective. Although some doubts had been expressed about particular aspects of the Freudian perspective (Caldwell, 1964; Orlansky, 1949; Sewell, 1952), these questions referred mostly to issues that arise later in childhood—for example, identification due to fear of castration—and did not seriously challenge the basic notion that infants' behavior could be modified through adult administration of reinforcement and through manipulation of the young child's fear of parental love withdrawal.

The synergistic integration of the behaviorist and psychoanalytic approaches to socialization can be seen, for example, in Sears, Maccoby, and Levin's classic work *Patterns of Child Rearing* (1957), which examined the impact of parental reinforcement upon the training and controlling of feeding, toilet training, sexual expression, and aggression. A few years later, although admitting that such studies only weakly supported the hypothesis that parental training techniques modified the behavior of young children, Caldwell (1964) still advocated the continuation of this sort of work—although she did suggest that better prediction of rearing outcomes probably could be achieved through consideration of the impact of individual differences and of parent-child interaction effects. The socialization-through-parental-reinforcement approach was still guiding research at the end of the 1960s, as indicated by Yarrow, Campbell, and Burton's (1968) study, *Child Rearing*, and by the fact the very first article that appeared in the new journal, *Developmental Psychology*, in 1969, presented a study of the impact of reinforcement upon school-aged children (Gewirtz, 1969b). Despite criticism and (perhaps because of) modification, the Watsonian-Freudian vision of child socialization was a powerful force during the 1960s—a force to which the emerging field of infancy research reacted rather negatively.

RESISTANCE AND REJECTION

> When Felix Mendelssohn's sister Fanny was born, her mother looked at the baby's hands. "Bach fugue fingers!" she delightfully exclaimed.
>
> (KVOD Guide, 1988, p. 24)

By the late 1960s and early 1970s, it was quite clear that the assumptions embraced by infant researchers were rather different from, and often diametrically opposed to, those of the Freudian-Watsonian vision of socialization. At first, confrontation was avoided, but as infant research matured in the latter half of the 1960s, it began to formulate its own unique view of infancy, which led to the rejection of the behaviorist-psychoanalytic model of socialization. Fundamentally, the opposition centered around three major interrelated themes: infant competence, individual differences in infancy, and mutuality of influence.

Competence

In many ways, behaviorism had envisioned the infant as incompetent, and as desperately in need of adult guidance and direction. The Freudian view did not see the infant so much as *un*directed but, rather, as *mis*directed, and thought of socialization as the procedure by which the infant would be set on the right path. In contrast, thinking and research which came to be guided by the competent infant paradigm took a diametrically opposite stance by considering the infant to be capable and skillful. This model relied to a significant degree upon the work of Piaget who, in his stage theory of cognitive development, informed us that children were not inferior and less developed versions of adults nearly as much as they were just different. Children—especially infants—had their own ways of processing and understanding information. In this perspective, children's answers were not wrong but merely at variance with those of adults (Piaget & Inhelder, 1966/1969). By encouraging a sense of what can perhaps be called "developmental relativism," Piaget legitimized the skills, thoughts, and competencies of young children. In this view, as Bruner (1983) noted, children at any stage of development can be perceived as fully-formed and capable versions of what they are at that moment.

In the competent infant paradigm, rather than being seen as existing in a blooming, buzzing confusion, infants came to be conceptualized as organized and skilled processors of information, differing from adults in perspective rather than in proficiency. In this spirit, infancy research began to investigate infants' capabilities, especially in the area of cognition, information processing, and problem solving (Stone, Smith, & Murphy, 1973). The emphasis of such research upon attention, patterns of looking, recognition, and discrimination implied a belief in the competence and even the *early* competence of infants.

A radical version of this belief in the precocity of infant competency was reflected particularly in the work of Bower: "A newborn thus begins life as an extremely competent social organism, an extremely competent learning organism, an extremely competent perceiving organism" (Bower, 1977, p. 35). Indeed, Bower suggested that infants could recognize their mothers at two weeks, that they formed attachments during the first few days of life, and that "right from the moment of birth the baby realizes he is a human being and has specific responses elicited only by other human beings" (Bower, 1977, p. 28). Such strong claims, as well as more modest beliefs about infants' cognitive and social capabilities, derive from the message that emerged from research on infant cognition that began in the 1960s; namely, that this was a competent infant.

The Influence of Individual Differences on Socialization Outcomes

Both the Freudian and the Watsonian approaches to socialization made fairly universalistic predictions which typically took the generic form of "If parental behavior X occurs, then consequence Y will be produced in the child." Other than taking age into account, there was little consideration of the possibility that particular socialization techniques might be more effective for some children than others. Indeed, many socialization studies in this theoretical mold (e.g., Baumrind, 1967; Goldberg & Lewis, 1969; Lewis & Goldberg, 1969; Sears, Maccoby, & Levin, 1957; Yarrow et al., 1968) tested simple hypotheses which predicted the general impact of specific parenting techniques upon children at a particular age. Fanny Mendelssohn's "Bach fugue fingers" would not have counted for very much within this view of socialization!

By the mid-60s, however, interest in individual differences and in how such variations might mediate the influence of socialization techniques had surfaced. Research and conceptual formulations about temperament (Carey, 1970; Thomas, Chess, & Birch, 1968) suggested that even very young children varied on a wide range of behavioral dimensions. Infant variation associated with gender also emerged as a major theme of research during the 1960s (e.g., Goldberg & Lewis, 1969; Korner, 1974; Moss, 1967). Furthermore, that decade also witnessed the appearance of considerable interest in intra-individual variation, as reflected by research on waking-sleeping state and arousal in infancy (Korner, 1969).

The idea that such variation might mediate socialization outcomes was also suggested by research and commentary beginning in the 1960s. It is not especially difficult to make the leap from Schaffer and Emerson's (1964) finding of individual variation in infant cuddliness to the possibility that such differences could modulate the impact of parental behavior. Similarly, the existence of considerable intra-individual variation in alertness and arousal readily implies that the impact of reinforcement will be mediated by the cyclical fluctuations of infant state (Sameroff, 1975). Indeed, there was a growing realization that the failure to acknowledge the importance of intra- and inter-individual variation in mediating socialization outcomes had severely impaired the predictive validity of child socialization research (Caldwell, 1964). Thus, during the 1960s, as infancy research emerged, there was a clear and growing awareness of the existence of individual variation and of the impact of such differences upon socialization outcomes.

The Infant as an Active Participant: Commitment and Mutuality

Not only did infants come to be seen as influencing socialization outcomes through the interaction of their own individual characteristics with adults' parenting actions but, in an even more active conceptualization, it was noted that they themselves instigate socialization episodes and "caregiving bouts" (Bell, 1968, 1974; Lewis & Rosenblum, 1974). In contrast to the Watsonian clay-molding view of the infant as a willing but disinterested party, or the Freudian assumption that the infant would even be actively resistant (although to no avail) of socialization, during the 1960s infants came to be seen as interested, active, and eager participants who had an enthusiastic commitment towards their own socialization (Richards, 1974). Of course, conceptualizing infants as active and competent leads to viewing them not only as earnestly involved in their own socialization, but as capable of resisting parenting actions as well. In this less helpless image, the infant becomes at the same time both a more actively cooperative and a more militantly defiant participant in socialization.

Beginning in the late 1960s, various commentators criticized the inclination of child development research to examine only the impact of adult upon child, ignoring the possibility that the child also might be affecting the adult's behavior (Bell, 1968, 1974; Gewirtz, 1969a; Sameroff, 1975). Thus, in addition to being able to mediate and even instigate the adult's socialization efforts, infants could have an independent impact upon adults. Reflecting this more active conceptualization, Lewis and Rosenblum's (1974) volume, The effect of the infant on its caregiver, firmly reinforced the notion that adult-infant interaction was characterized by mutuality of social influence: "Not only is the infant or child influenced by its social, political, economic, and biological world, but in fact the child itself influences the world in turn" (Lewis & Rosenblum, 1974, p. xv).

In the envisagement of socialization as a process in which the adult controls the infant's behavior, a process in which social influence flows unidirectionally, and in which the infant is neither a committed collaborator nor a respected resister, it is easy to think of adult-infant interaction as the encounter of unequal-status actors. On the other hand, socialization episodes that involve joint, active, and committed participation of mutually-influencing partners are more readily characterized as equal-status encounters. The equal-status conceptualization of infant socialization reinforces the message already conveyed by the competent infant paradigm—namely, that the infant is a capable partner in social interaction and socialization.

Implications for Socialization

Backing Away from the Study of Infant Socialization

The image of a committed and competent infant, a unique individual who can influence adults as well as be influenced by them, suggested a markedly different pattern of socialization than that envisioned in the Freudian-Watsonian model. Nevertheless, this reconstituted paradigm certainly need not have abandoned the view that socialization is still, fundamentally, a process in which the parent or other agent of socialization shapes the infant's behavior. Commitment, competence, and individuality do not mean that the infant cannot be socialized. Indeed, the infant's commitment to being guided may increase the likelihood that socialization goals will be met. That infants are more proficient than previously imagined implies not only that they may be able to resist some efforts to shape their behavior, but also that they can actively collaborate in their own socialization. The notion that each infant is a distinctive individual, whose personal qualities mediate the outcome of parenting, simply means that socialization must transpire in a sensitive and responsive fashion if positive results are to be achieved. And, although the assumption of mutuality acknowledges that the infant can have an impact on the adult, it in no way suggests that adults cannot influence the infant.

Furthermore, the realization that infants were competent, active, and unique individuals challenged but certainly did not deny entirely the assumptions of the Freudian-Watsonian paradigm. It is possible to believe that social interaction between infant and adult involves mutuality of influence while still comfortably accepting the idea that the adult remains the more potent force. Similarly, recognition of individual variation among infants does not, of logical necessity, deny the existence of powerful common forces that drive the behavior of most, if not all, infants. Certainly the concept of variation does not negate that of theme. Likewise, the idea that infants are committed to socialization does not deny the possibility that they may be disinterested or even openly antagonistic at times. And, the concept of a competent infant does not contradict the claim that infants depend upon adults for instruction and guidance. Indeed, the respective images of infancy promulgated in the late 1960s and in the earlier behaviorist-psychoanalytic paradigm complement more than contradict each other, together forming a fuller and more meaningful framework in which to study socialization. Thus, it is entirely reasonable to view the "Competent Collaborator" baby of the 1960s and the "Dependent Resister" baby envisioned by Freud and Watson as flip sides of the same coin.

Unfortunately, in rejecting the behaviorist-psychoanalytic envisagement of early socialization in particular, the emerging field of infancy research also backed away generally from the study of infant socialization. This backing-away can be seen as reflected in Foss's *Determinants of Infant Behaviour* volumes, which were published between 1961 and 1969, as the field of infancy research emerged. Volume I (Foss, 1961; based on a 1959 conference) included several contributions on social learning, reinforcement, and socialization (the piece on socialization per se, however, was about kittens rather than human infants), but there were even more chapters which examined patterns of interaction or the effects of presence/absence. By the time that Volume IV appeared (Foss, 1969; based on a 1965 conference), the pattern was even more firmly established: The index did not contain any listings of social learning, socialization, or reinforcement, and the contributions had swung almost entirely in the direction of examining matters of interaction, presence, attachment, and reactions to social stimuli.

Looking back, it seems likely that the newly emerging enterprise of infancy research objected to behaviorist-psychoanalytic assumptions about the nature of infancy—and not to the process of socialization itself. The path by which the field came, however inadvertently, to downplay for some time the study of infant socialization can be noted most strikingly in the introductory chapter of Martin Richards' (1974) volume *The Integration of a Child into a Social World*: "Early in the preparation of this volume, one of the publishers' representatives suggested that the word 'socialisation' should appear in the title. This was rejected—unanimously, I think—by the contributors. In doing this we were not trying to suggest that socialisation was not a central theme of the book but that the word itself had become associated with theoretical views of the topic which we did not share. . . . the word had tended to become the property of psychologists who adopt a neo-behaviorist approach to the study of development . . . where socialisation . . . is regarded as something that has to be imposed on the child . . . [and] that the child is mere putty to be worked on by external forces" (Richards, 1974, p. 4).

Child Socialization Research: A Different Response

Disillusionment with the Freudian-Watsonian model of socialization occurred not only in the infant research community, but also among those studying older children. Indeed, the criticisms aimed then at the extant behaviorist-psychoanalytic model often were expressed not only about infants in particular but about children in general (e.g., Bell, 1968; Caldwell, 1964; Richards, 1974). Unlike their colleagues in infancy research, childhood researchers responded, for the most part, by fine-tuning, expanding, and shifting the manner in which they studied child socialization while not diminishing their fundamental interest in the process.

Studies that were compatible, for the most part, with the older behaviorist-psychoanalytic approach to child socialization certainly did continue to appear past the mid-60s (Baumrind, 1967; Maccoby & Martin, 1983; Yarrow et al., 1968). But, in the spirit of the Competent Collaborator zeitgeist, new research on childhood socialization began to focus upon more indirect methods of influence as well, such as social learning, imitation, and vicarious learning. Although these were processes that modified the child's behavior so that it came to fall into line with societal expectations, the nature of the influence was such that the child had to play a more active role in being socialized. Thus, research on children managed to incorporate some of the elements of the newly emerging zeitgeist concerning the nature of children, while maintaining a basic orientation to the study of social influence and socialization.

Furthermore, the topical foci of this new research were central to the main thrust of everyday socialization, as indicated in studies of children's imitation of filmed aggression and prosocial behavior, sex role modeling, and the impact of teachers' expectations on pupils' academic performance. Thus, while investigating influence processes in which children participated more actively, childhood researchers managed to retain Freud's and Watson's emphasis upon studying socialization in the context of actual parenting issues that commonly arise in everyday life.

The rather different responses of the infancy and childhood research communities are understandable as a function of their disciplinary origins and allegiances. Infancy research came primarily from developmental psychology, reflecting its emphasis upon individual psychology, biological influences, and the centrality of the concept of development. In contrast, research about older children, although guided by the same developmental orientation as infancy research, was also affected by its intimate association with social psychology and by that discipline's investiture in the concept of social influence.

The bipartite nature of the study of older children is suggested by its sociological as well as psychological foundations, and by the association of the appellation "developmental social psychology" with such research. The strong linkage of the study of childhood socialization with the mainstream of social psychology is further suggested by the fact that children were the major empirical testing ground for several of the most significant theoretical developments in social psychology from the mid-60s to the mid-70s (e.g. expectation states, social learning). The publication of such results with virtually equal frequency in developmental journals and social psychology journals provides additional evidence that the study of childhood socialization truly drew from traditions in both developmental and social psychology. In contrast, these claims could not be made about the study of infancy during that period of time.

In developmental psychology, the key concept (not surprisingly) is *development*, a process of unfolding through which behavior and abilities emerge. For social psychology, the key concept is *social influence*, a process through which individuals, groups, and societies are affected by each other; socialization is one of the major forms of social influence which impact upon individuals. Infancy research, having little connection to the social psychological concepts of social influence and socialization, could comfortably respond to the challenge posed in the 1960s to the behaviorist-psychoanalytic model by downplaying the study of socialization. But those researchers studying children were driven to find more sophisticated and suitable ways in which to continue to embrace social influence and socialization. The investigation of more indirect methods of childhood socialization may very well have reflected the efforts of that research community to find a middle ground that could support key concepts of social influence as well as the newly emerging more active and respectful image of the character of childhood.

A major deficiency of the behaviorist-psychoanalytic model was its relative lack of concern for individual differences as to how children varied in their receptivity to particular socialization methods. Similarly, the failure of the model to consider the active participation of children in their own socialization also reduced that perspective's value in predicting and understanding socialization encounters. Clearly, this model needed to be revised and reformulated. Infancy researchers, with their feet firmly planted in the firmament of developmental psychology, and with little orientation towards social influence paradigms, probably were not inclined then to deal with the task of modifying and reformulating the existing model of socialization.

In contrast, social psychologists, including those who studied children, had by the 1960s accumulated a vast storehouse of information about the subtleties of social influence and socialization (Aronson, 1976,

Ch. 3). In social psychology, simple theoretical schemes of social influence had begun to fall out of favor in the late 1940s, so that by the 1960s influence was scrutinized within a sophisticated framework that took into account variation among target audiences, the credibility and trustworthiness of the source of the persuasive communication, and the degree to which the audience played an active role in seeking out influence. With this arsenal at their disposal, it was not difficult for developmental social psychologists to remedy the limitations and oversimplifications of the Freud-Watson model. In contrast, because their own developmental orientation provided little understanding of social influence and because of the lack of crosstalk between developmental and social psychology, infancy researchers were left with little to go on in reworking the behaviorist-psychoanalytic model of socialization.

RECENT STUDIES IN EARLY SOCIALIZATION

In the course of reacting to the Freudian-Watsonian assumptions about child rearing, infancy research not only dismissed these particular views, but also came, in a broader sweep, to depreciate the value of studying socialization. The downplaying of social influence and socialization came to pass while the contemporary study of infancy was in its formative stages and has characterized much of the work in that field of study for quite some time. More recently, however, infant researchers have begun to turn their attention to questions about socialization. The chapters of this volume are indicative of that enterprise.

The particular character of the approach reflected in this volume, as well as of other recent work on infant socialization, is a matter more of perspective than of substance. For example, there probably is no subject that has been investigated more intensively in infancy research than attachment, which typically has been studied in an interaction and relationship framework. In contrast, Richters and Waters' chapter in the present volume emphasizes the potency of attachment as a source of active socialization, and delineates a theory concerning how the attachment relationship may influence the formation of prosocial and antisocial tendencies. Gewirtz, in his chapter, directs our attention to what he calls "mutual tuning of responses," i.e., synchrony. Undeniably, and as has often been noted (e.g., Brazelton, Koslowski, & Main, 1974) these terms describe an interactional feature of adult-infant interchanges. But here Gewirtz considers the manner in which synchronic tuning facilitates social influence. Similarly, while much has been written about the interactional and relational qualities of infants' contact with older siblings, Dunn's chapter on siblings draws our attention to the manner in which the development of social understanding in infancy is influenced by such interaction. Thus, it is not a matter of *what* we are looking at but, rather, of *how* we are looking at it which constitutes the essence of this edited volume in particular, and of recent studies of early socialization more generally. And, it is the social psychological focus upon social influence and socialization that is the *how* of this perspective.

But our perspective on socialization is very different from that of the behaviorist-psychoanalytic paradigm of an earlier time. Here is an approach that takes into account parental sensitivity to individual differences, mutuality of influence, and the mediation of socialization outcomes by infants' characteristics and responses. This conceptualization of social influence allows for the existence of gentler, more indirect, and less conflicted mechanisms of socialization in which infants play a more active role as competent and involved participants who are committed to their own socialization.

In the Freudian-Watsonian model of socialization, parenting seems a rather stern, severe, and rude undertaking. But in the chapters of this volume, socialization has a softer, kinder feel to it. Thus, Schaffer's chapter indicates that even control-oriented socialization encounters are not necessarily driven by the *sturm und drang* of the psychoanalytic mode. When parents are sensitive to the infant's developmental status, mood, and situational motivation, then the control of behavior proceeds smoothly. Sensitivity of socialization is reflected also in Rogoff's chapter on how adults structure infants' cognitive development. That chapter provides clear narrative descriptions of adults' awareness of what the infant can and wants to do, and of gentle and supportive adult guidance. In all these chapters, it is obvious that adults shape the infant's behavior intentionally, but it is equally obvious that they do so sensitively.

This model also responds to the concern that the young child should be viewed neither as a passive recipient of adult input, for whom socialization is a process of "being made" rather than of "becoming made" (Richards, 1974), nor as resisting such socialization efforts consistently. Rather, it is assumed that infants are committed and active participants in their own socialization. This assumption is particularly evident in the chapters by Lewis, Rogoff, Schaffer, and Richters and Waters. Indeed, in Schaffer's account of control techniques, one gets the distinct impression that the infants are highly interested in cooperating with their parents' socialization efforts. Furthermore, Lewis proposes that very young children's active and collaborative involvement in their own socialization is greatly facilitated by the emergence of objective self-awareness and self-conscious emotions during the second year of life.

In the late 1960s and early 1970s, the notion that infant-adult interaction (even in socialization encounters) could be characterized by mutuality of influence (Bell, 1968; Lewis & Rosenblum, 1974; Richards, 1974) served as a contentious rallying cry for researchers who wished to envision the young child as an active and competent organism. In the present volume, this theme is found in virtually every chapter and is so noncontroversially accepted that there seems to be an attitude of, "Well, *of course,* there is mutuality in adult-infant interactions, how could there not be." Thus, Užgiris emphasizes the importance of conceptualizing imitative interchanges as encounters in which the infant influences as well as is influenced by the adult. Similarly, while examining the impact of families upon young children, Landesman, Jaccard and Gunderson imply that the infant, as part of the family system, can have an impact upon other family members. And, while making it abundantly clear, in his distinctly macroscopic examination of socialization, that social structure influences the developing infant monkey, Rosenblum also provides an account of how the infant's actions, in turn, perpetuate the social organization of the monkey troop. In the late 1960s, mutuality was an issue of dissension in the world of infancy research. In the present volume, it is a given, as are the assumptions that parenting will be sensitive to infants' characteristics and desires, that socialization outcomes will be a function of the infant as well as of the parent, and that infants are active, competent, and committed collaborators in their own socialization.

The directness with which influence is exerted in the Freudian-Watsonian model implies that it is something which is imposed on the infant. Although some of these fairly direct socialization methods are incorporated in the approach that this volume represents, indirect methods that call for the infant to participate more actively—methods that feel softer and gentler to the touch—are well represented here, as well. Rather than view socialization simply as a process in which adults control and regulate, the wider-ranging approach to social influence expressed in this volume also emphasizes the role of adults in helping, guiding, structuring, and assisting. Much of the work on social guidance, social referencing, scaffolding, and learning within the Zone of Proximal Development that is discussed in Rogoff's and Feinman's chapters reflects this conceptualization of adult influence. And the importance of the even more indirect influence of contextual effects is acknowledged within the chapters contributed by Clarke-Stewart, Rosenblum, and Landesman and her colleagues.

The approach incorporated in this volume reflects a belief in the importance of considering the entire gamut of social influences, from the direct to the contextual. Thus, the section of the book entitled "Processes of Influence" begins with the most direct methods and moves on to the consideration of ever-more indirect mechanisms. This wide-angle perspective allows us to envision a comfortable conceptual relationship between development and socialization. One of the concerns voiced by Richards (1974) about the neobehaviorist approach to socialization was that ". . the notion of development itself may be lost, . . . replaced by a very mechanical idea of change as a response to external pressure" (pp. 4–5). The modification of behavior imposed on the young child within the Freudian-Watsonian model of socialization would indeed challenge the image of development as a process of unfolding—an image intimated by the Old and Middle French etymology of this word, which first appeared as *desveloper*, the antonym of *voloper*, meaning to wrap up. The contextual and facilitative effects discussed in the present volume (e.g., by Clarke-Stewart, and by Rogoff) constitute forms of socialization that are very much in line with a conceptualization of development as an unfolding or unwrapping. On the other hand, the focus on more direct forms of socialization (as in the chapters by Schaffer, Gewirtz, and Richters and Waters) is consistent with the conceptualization of development as a process in which the actions of an external force educe and stimulate the infant's capabilities.

While our approach does respond affirmatively to concerns about the earlier behaviorist-psychoanalytic perspective on socialization, Freud and Watson have not been abandoned altogether. Thus, our model acknowledges the importance of the direct approach to behavior modification that they emphasized. The difference is that we assume that these direct methods must be employed in a sensitive and responsive manner if they are to be successful. As can clearly be seen in Gewirtz's and Schaffer's chapters, even the most direct of socialization methods are presumed to transpire with consideration for the infant's nature and inclinations. In general, the approach reflected in this volume takes the attitude that the Dependent Resister and the Competent Collaborator models of socialization provide valid complementary insights into the role of social influence in infancy, and that both need to be considered.

The behaviorist-psychoanalytic approach to socialization has two other features which have been incorporated into our working model. First of all, both Freud and Watson postulated specific mechanisms to account for the outcomes of infants' socialization contact with adults. Although some of the postulated mechanisms were later proven wrong, the general practice of delineating pathways through which influence is hypothesized to proceed keeps us from falling back on "black box" models of influence, and from assuming that presence, contact and interaction per se constitute influence. Insisting that process be considered, even in studies that are concerned primarily with sources of influence, provides a more integrated model of socialization, one that connects sources with processes.

Despite this conceptual integration, it seems appropriate to divide up the contributions to this volume into two sections—Sources of Influence and Processes of Influence—inasmuch as the chapters tend to be oriented one way or the other. Nevertheless, those authors who focus primarily upon sources of influence do not fail to consider possible mechanisms through which their chosen sources might be influencing the young child. Thus, Clarke-Stewart explores in depth the pathways through which various child-care environments affect cognitive development. Similarly, Landesman and her colleagues delineate in particular detail the mechanisms through which families influence development.

We also have retained the Freudian-Watsonian framework's ecologically valid emphasis upon the actual agents, contexts, and issues of everyday socialization. Infancy research has tended to operate within what could be criticized as an overly microanalytic perspective, emphasizing the intra- and inter-personal context of development while not paying enough attention to its broader social setting. The Sources of Influence section provides a expansive view of levels of influence, from the most macroanalytical (society) to the most microanalytical (the self). The macroscopic orientation of Rosenblum's chapter in examining how feeding ecology and social structure frame the behavior and development of infant monkeys, and Feinman's insistence in his chapter that we more faithfully examine the highly social nature of human infancy both serve to remind us of the broader context in which infants develop.

In addition, all of the chapters focus on real-world, socially relevant socialization outcomes, such as anti- and pro-social behavior (Richters and Waters), self-conscious emotions, e.g., shame (Lewis), social understanding (Dunn), the functioning of imitation in real social context (Užgiris), and the role of reinforcement in attachment and environmental deprivation (Gewirtz). The ecologically valid study of infant socialization requires that we investigate influence processes within the parameters of everyday outcomes and contexts. Thus, Uzgiris argues that because imitation has been examined, for the most part, outside of its actual social context, we really do not know what role it plays in socialization. Furthermore, as part and parcel of their rejection of the Freudian-Watsonian model of influence, infancy researchers became less concerned with the task of connecting processes with sources of influence, and less attuned to the importance of studying real life issues of socialization. In contrast, however, these principles provide considerable guidance within the present edited volume.

Some years ago, we suggested that a social-psychological perspective could describe and account for infants' social connections "Beyond the Dyad" (Feinman & Lewis, 1984). Our focus in the present volume is considerably broader and more ambitious, for here we are proposing that a sophisticated social-psychological model of socialization and social influence can provide valid insights into virtually the entirety of infant behavior and development. Over the last decade, infancy research has shown encouraging signs of its willingness to embrace the concept of socialization—a concept that it underestimated at an earlier time. In this volume, we have aimed to confirm the repatriation of the social influence perspective with the study of infancy. Furthermore, we have warmly embraced the orientation of earlier socialization research towards maintaining a close connection between sources and processes, and studying real life socialization outcomes, pathways, and contexts. We also have incorporated perspectives and assumptions from both the Dependent Resister model of the Freudian-Watsonian view of socialization and the Competent Collaborator paradigm of the 1960s. In this spirit, all of the chapters in the volume focus upon social influence processes in infant socialization within natural contexts. Indeed, it is this theme that is the essential factor that binds together these otherwise diverse works into an integrated whole.

REFERENCES

Aronson, E. (1976). *The social animal* (2nd ed.). San Francisco: Freeman.
Baumrind, D. (1967). Child care practices anteceding three patterns of preschool behavior. *Genetic Psychology Monographs, 75,* 43–88.
Bell, R. Q. (1968). A reinterpretation of the direction of effects in studies of socialization. *Psychological Review, 75,* 81–95.
Bell, R. Q. (1974). Contributions of human infants to caregiving and social interaction. In M. Lewis & L. A. Rosenblum (Eds.), *The effect of the infant on its caregiver* (pp. 1–19). New York: Wiley.
Bower, T. G. R. (1977). *A primer of infant development.* San Francisco: Freeman.
Brazelton, T. B., Koslowski, B., & Main, M. (1974). The origins of reciprocity: The early mother-infant interaction. In M. Lewis & L. A. Rosenblum (Eds.), *The effect of the infant on its caregiver* (pp. 49–76). New York: Wiley.
Bruner, J. (1983). *In search of mind.* New York: Harper & Row.
Caldwell, B. M. (1964). The effects of infant care. In M. L. Hoffman & L. W. Hoffman (Eds.), *Review of child development.* (Vol. 1, pp. 9–87). New York: Russell Sage Foundation.
Carey, W. B. (1970). A simplified method for measuring infant temperament. *Journal of Pediatrics, 77,* 188–194.
Emerson, R. M. (1962). Power-dependence relations: Two experiments. *American Sociological Review, 27,* 31–41.
Emerson, R. W. (1883). *Essays: First and second series.* Boston: Houghton Mifflin. (Original work published 1865)
Feinman, S., & Lewis, M. (1984). Is there social life beyond the dyad?: A social psychologi-

cal view of social connections in infancy. In M. Lewis (Ed.), *Beyond the dyad* (pp. 13–41). New York: Plenum Press.

Foss, B. M. (Ed.). (1961). *Determinants of infant behaviour I*. London: Methuen.

Foss, B. M. (Ed.). (1969). *Determinants of infant behaviour IV*. London: Methuen.

Freud, S. (1933). *New introductory lectures on psychanalysis*. London: Hogarth.

Freud, S. (1949). *An outline of psycho-analysis*. New York: Norton. (Original work published 1940)

Gewirtz, J. L. (1969a). Mechanisms of social learning: Some roles of stimulation and behavior in early human development. In D. A. Goslin (Ed.), *Handbook of socialization theory and research* (pp. 57–212). Chicago: Rand McNally.

Gewirtz, J. L. (1969b). Potency of a social reinforcer as a function of satiation and recovery. *Developmental Psychology, 1*, 2–13.

Goldberg, S., & Lewis, M. (1969). Play behavior in the year-old infant: Early sex differences. *Child Development, 40*, 21–31.

Korner, A. F. (1969). Neonatal startles, smiles, erections, and reflex sucks as related to state, sex and individuality. *Child Development, 40*, 1039–1053.

Korner, A. F. (1974). The effect of the infant's state, level of arousal, sex, and ontogenetic stage on the caregiver. In M. Lewis & L. A. Rosenblum (Eds.), *The effect of the infant on its caregiver* (pp. 105–121). New York: Wiley.

KVOD Guide. (1988). *3* (7). Denver, CO.

Lewis, M., & Goldberg, S. (1969). The acquisition and violation of expectancy: An experimental paradigm. *Journal of Experimental Child Psychology, 7*, 70–80.

Lewis, M., & Rosenblum, L. A. (Eds.). (1974). *The effect of the infant on its caregiver*. New York: Wiley.

Maccoby, E. E., & Martin, J. A. (1983). Socialization in the context of the family: Parent-child interaction. In P. H. Mussen (Ed.), *Handbook of child psychology* (4th ed., Vol. 4, pp. 1–101). New York: Wiley.

Moss, H. A. (1967). Sex, age, and state as determinants of mother-infant interaction. *Merrill-Palmer Quarterly, 13*, 19–36.

Orlansky, H. (1949). Infant care and personality. *Psychological Bulletin, 46*, 1–48.

Piaget, J., & Inhelder, B. (1969). *The psychology of the child*. New York: Basic Books. (Original work published 1966)

Radbill, S. X. (1980). Children in a world of violence: A history of child abuse. In C. H. Kempe & R. E. Helfer (Eds.), *The battered child* (3rd ed., pp. 3–20). Chicago: University of Chicago Press.

Richards, M. P. M. (1974). Introduction. In M. P. M. Richards (Ed.), *The integration of a child into a social world* (pp. 1–10). London: Cambridge University Press.

Sameroff, A. J. (1975). Transactional models in early social relations. *Human Development, 18*, 65–79.

Schaffer, H. R. (1984). *The child's entry into a social world*. London: Academic.

Schaffer, H. R., & Emerson, P. E. (1964). Patterns of response to physical contact in early human development. *Journal of Child Psychology and Psychiatry, 5*, 1–13.

Sears, R. R., Maccoby, E. E., & Levin, H. (1957). *Patterns of child rearing*. Evanston, IL: Row, Peterson.

Sewell, W. H. (1952). Infant training and the personality of the child. *American Journal of Sociology, 58*, 150–159.

Stone, L. J., Smith, H. T., & Murphy, L. B. (Eds.). (1973). *The competent infant*. New York: Basic Books.

Thomas, A., Chess, S., & Birch, H. G. (1968). *Temperament and behavior disorders in children*. New York: New York University Press.

Watson, J. B. 1924). *Behaviorism*. New York: Norton.

Watson, J. B. (1928). *Psychological care of the infant and child.* New York: Norton.
Watson, J. B., & Rayner, R. (1920). Conditioning emotional reactions. *Journal of Experimental Psychology, 3,* 1–14.
Yarrow, M. R., Campbell, J. D., & Burton, R. V. (1968). *Child rearing: An inquiry into research and methods.* San Francisco: Jossey-Bass.

Sources of Influence

I

2

Family and Friends in Primate Development

Leonard A. Rosenblum

The Social Nature of the Primates

It is clear that regardless of the perspective one brings to the task, any overview of the primate order would reflect one quality that characterizes the great majority, although not all, of the species within it: Primate species have evolved essentially socialized forms of living. Group sizes may vary from a few to a hundred or more, but most members of our primate order spend most of the hours of most of the days during most of their lives together with others of their species. We are still at a primitive level of understanding the basis of evolutionary selection for sociality and of the factors influencing the fitness of primate groups as a whole and the individuals within them. But we cannot escape the conclusion that virtually all the functional activities that we observe in the primates (ourselves obviously included) must be shaped by the nature of the social environment within which the individual was reared and now functions. In many respects, this statement is obvious, but serves to remind us that the propensities and constraints which the young primate brings into the world as genetic baggage—while perhaps rarely dictating outcome—make certain forms of sensitivities and responses to external stimuli understandable only within a broad evolutionary, developmental, and contemporaneous social context.

It is the purpose of this chapter to highlight some of the elements of

Leonard A. Rosenblum • Department of Psychiatry, SUNY Health Sciences Center, Brooklyn, New York 11203.

primate social structure as these influence the course of behavioral development. The size and composition of the social unit varies widely in
primates at least in part because of characteristics of their environment.
As we shall see, the feeding ecology has proven to be a particularly
salient aspect of the physical setting in shaping evolutionary history.
These environmental features and qualities of the social structure interact with the maturing, genetically determined characteristics of the
individual, and its own specific experiences, to shape behavior. This
basic interactive process is illustrated by the findings that species factors, sex differences, particular early life experiences, current social status of the individual and its kin, all coalesce to produce the individual
variations that typify the primate.

Factors Influencing Social Structure

Some aspects of the genotypic factors affecting behavior may be
readily apparent, such as the capacity to see color or hear sounds at
certain frequencies. One is not surprised to learn that rat pups communicate distress to their mothers at ultrasonic frequencies whereas humans do not—after all, they can hear such sounds and we cannot. But
as one moves away from these evident morphological features, the lines
between genotype and phenotype and those between genetically and
ontogenetically determined factors shaping adult patterns blur terribly.
For example, suppose we determined that a particular species was never
found in group sizes greater than N under natural conditions. Our understanding of the reasons for this group size limitation in a distal,
evolutionary sense might derive from our appreciation of the feeding
ecology in which the species lives, or of factors relating to predator/prey
relations, or of the relationship between kinship size and maturation
rates. Thus, for example, in smaller forms, if predation by large car-
nivorous birds has represented a strong selective pressure over evolutionary time, a social pattern sometimes called "mobbing,"—larger
groups responding together against a threatening predator—may have
evolved because a larger group can effectively turn away a predator that
could easily assault any individual when it is alone.

Similarly, consider the potential evolutionary impact of food availability. If food sources are widely dispersed and occur in small quantities
when they are found, it would be disadvantageous for the animals to
search for food in large groups because sharing of any given food source
would not be feasible. Moreover, large groups searching in a limited
area would leave many animals without food, whereas other areas of
potential food sources would go unexplored. Such an environment

might discourage the evolution of large group social structures. If, on the other hand, food is hard to find, but when located is found in large quantities (for example, large trees which bear fruit individually as op- posed to all trees of a given type fruiting simultaneously), there would be an advantage to foraging in larger groups, perhaps spreading out across a more limited area within which communication was possible. When this type of foraging strategy is employed, there are more indi- viduals available to find food in a given area and any individual who does can communicate the fact and share the spoils with others of its troop, or at the least share its find with other members of its kinship group. Thus, once again, the evolution of large group structures would be encouraged.

Obviously, not only would the evolution of group size be influenced by these ecological arrays, but the communicative repertoire of species foraging in a group manner would have to evolve in ways that permit the animals to exploit these resources in an effective manner. The con- trolling proximal factor might be the number of different individuals this species can remember at any one time, i.e., a memory storage limitation. Similarly, if their sensory apparatus does not permit them to distinguish more than a limited set of stimuli in a certain domain, their capacity to establish different relationships with large numbers of conspecifics as individuals might be limited. On the other hand, group size might be kept relatively small because the members of the species are too dis- tracted from efficient foraging for themselves when they must contend with, and be responsive to, "too many" others within a certain proxi- mity.

We must remember, however, that in theory, the elements regulat- ing group composition might not be anchored entirely within differen- tially evolved capacities, but might depend instead upon an interaction of some nascent characteristics and the individual's own developmental experiences with groups of a certain size as it matured. Although this particular effect has not been demonstrated experimentally, such on- togenetic factors must be considered. In any event, as these kinds of forces press against one another across evolutionary time, if the selective advantages to larger groups increase, the means to accomodate in- creased numbers of interactants, whether kin or not, would have to be acquired. More subtle distinctions could become perceptable, more dis- tinctive differentiating cues could emerge, or greater capacity to learn and retain such distinctions could evolve. In general, some change in capacity or responsivity in relations to the nature of the social milieu would have to appear. It is the current endpoint of such multiple forces that we confront in our studies of the clearly social world of most of the contemporary primates, including man.

NATURAL VARIATIONS IN THE SOCIAL STRUCTURE

The social milieu of the primates does indeed vary to a considerable degree, and notwithstanding the above, one of the great gaps in our information is that we still know very little about the developmental and genetic bases of these species-characteristic group patterns. Forms as different as the marmoset, a small South American prosimian, and the gibbon, a large old world ape, live in small, monogamous family units. Other species, such as the langur, form harems that include a single male and a protected group of breeding females and their young. We also see species with large groups of males and females living together in which the sexes interact frequently, e.g., the rhesus monkey, as well as species in which males and females are present but segregate themselves from one another most of the time (e.g., the Peruvian squirrel monkey; see Coe & Rosenblum, 1974). In this latter species, even during the breeding season—which lasts only several months each year— females and males remain in the vicinity of one another only within what we have termed a "sphere of potential interaction." The two sexes do not spend prolonged periods of time in close proximity even during periods of active copulation. Males leave the male subgrouping for brief intervals of courtship and copulation, then return to the company of the other males. When not in breeding condition, females either do not allow males to remain near them or are actively avoided by the males. It is interesting to note, in considering the variation in social structure among species, that even closely related subspecies of squirrel monkeys differ regarding the segregation pattern; some types of squirrel monkeys (e.g., those from Guyana) do not show sexual segregation. Although we know something of the biological substrate underlying this segregated pattern—it appears to be dependent upon gonadal hormone levels and breaks down following gonadectomy (Bromley, 1978)—we do not know why the pattern differs among subspecies, nor which adaptive functions are served by the pattern.

The contrasts in the range of primate social structures within which infants develop are really remarkable. There are relatively solitary forms of primates such as the orangutan, in which adults have relatively infrequent contact with one another. Infant orangs, as a consequence, do not interact with adults other than the mother for the first several years of life (although a juvenile sibling may be present). In the langur, on the other hand, not only is there a complex social group present but, within moments of its birth, an infant is handled and carried for considerable distances by a number of other females in its troop (Jay, 1963). This array of species-characteristic social patterns should provide a natural laboratory of extraordinary proportions regarding social influences on behavioral development. Thus far, however, we have been struck by this diversity but have deciphered neither the mechanisms that underlie their occurrence nor their varied roles in the origins of adult patterns. We can suggest from this material, however, that the size and composition of the human social unit at the point at which biological evolution ceased and sociocultural evolution took over is likely to have played a crucial role in shaping many characteristics of human behavior concerning us today. From dominance and aggression issues to concerns about patterns of sexual behavior and exclusivity of partners, from interests in patterns of maternal behavior to those regarding aging and senescence, we are likely to be dealing with the sequelae of the evolution of primate social structure in response to ancient ecological demands.

THE IMPACT OF THE PRESENCE OF OTHERS UPON DEVELOPMENT

We know from the experimental literature on primate development that many essential features of behavior, perhaps even those directly related to reproduction, may be markedly affected by the nature of the social milieu within which the infant is reared. Thus, the classic work on rhesus monkeys demonstrated the severe effects that individual housing devoid of social or maternal companionship can have on behavioral development (Mitchell, 1970). Rhesus infants raised under these conditions of deprivation are deficient, often hyperaggressive social partners, may be sexually inadequate (particularly true of deprivation-reared males) and may, with first-borns at least, be totally inadequate as mothers. While other species may not fare as poorly after this early deprivation (Sackett, Holm, Ruppenthal, & Fahrenbach, 1976), most forms of primates, when raised in the absence of others of their species, or even when unable to interact fully with others (Sackett & Ruppenthal, 1973), are simply grossly different animals than those raised with normal or even somewhat limited opportunities to interact with conspecifics.

But alterations in essential features of development are certainly not restricted to the "all-or-none" effects of severe social deprivation. More subtle shaping of development in primates may also occur as a function of particular features of the structure of the social conditions during rearing in primates.

In rhesus, for example, Goldfoot has shown important shifts in male and female behavior patterns as a function of the sexual makeup of the social group in which males and females are reared (Goldfoot, Wallen, Neff, McBair, & Goy, 1984). In bonnet macaques, a very gregarious species under normal circumstances, infants reared by their mothers in the absence of any other conspecifics fall far behind in learning to visually differentiate their mothers from strangers. Some of these single-dyad reared infants fail to show such differentiation at even one year of age whereas group-reared subjects generally are capable of this discrimination by 3 to 4 months of age (Rosenblum & Alpert, 1977). In the pigtail macaque, a comparatively close, congeneric species, unrelated females of a group are extremely protective of their young infants; the infants, as a consequence, have relatively little close contact with other adults even though the latter are present in the same area. Emergence of clear discrimination of mother from stranger proceeds more slowly in this species than in the more gregarious bonnet macaque. Thus, the comparative experimental data on these two closely related species suggest that an infant's early discrimination of the mother initially depends on seeing her in some form of close relation to others of similar type. Infants who had the opportunity to have close contact with mother and one other adult female became capable of differentiating the mother from this specific other female at the normal age, i.e., at about 3 months. Nonetheless, these same infants were not able to distinguish between the mother and complete strangers until several months later. Thus, initial discrimination of mother from nonmother is specific to particular nonmothers and only later, apparently as cognitive capacity matures and the development of "learning-set" capacities emerge (Zimmerman & Torrey, 1965), does the class distinction, "mother versus nonmother" enter the repertoire of the infant. We see quite clearly in this instance that a basic developmental feature essential to early survival depends not on the genetically timed development of particular capacities but also on the existence of a social context for development.

THE ROLE OF PARTICULAR COMPONENTS OF THE SOCIAL GROUP

From the very earliest moments of life, the altricial primate neonate, absolutely dependent on support from others for its very existence, confronts the interface between its genetic propensities and the concrete features of the social world into which it is born. Certainly the mother is, normally, always present, but who else may the infant gradually come to interact with? Will there be other mothers, or responsive females and juveniles, or a father who participates in caregiving? In some species, in particular the monogamous forms (where the male can be certain that his efforts are directed towards his own genetic offspring), paternal behavior may be quite pronounced. In the marmoset, for example—in which twins are commonly found and triplets occasionally noted—by the time the infants are two weeks old, the male begins to carry the infants on his back for most of the day; the infants are only returned to the mother for periodic nursing (Epple, 1975).

There is also variation with regard to the extent to which other close kin are available to the infant. In pigtail macaques, although the mother will drive away or flee from the attentions directed towards her young by unrelated females or males, she will seek out and maintain proximity and even physical contact with close kin (Rosenblum, 1974). As mentioned above, in some other species, such as the langur, there is considerable access to the newborn infant by others, including those lacking close kinship to the mother. In other species, mothers zealously guard their newborns and flee from, or attack, any nonkin who attempts even close inspection of the neonate. Still other species allows intermediate levels of interaction with others immediately following the birth and thereafter.

SOCIAL STRUCTURE AND THE ONTOGENY OF SEXUAL SEGREGATION

As we consider sex differences in development, we note that, in some species, infants may have prolonged contact with males as well as females, while in others infants may rarely interact with adult males during early life. Whether in the orangutan, where the mother lives essentially alone with her young, or in the squirrel monkey, where adult males and females of a troop are sexually segregated, low frequency of early contact with adult males affects development. And, in a broader sense, the social structure of the conditions of rearing are likely to play an important, although as yet poorly assessed, role in the development of sex-typical patterns.

The characteristics of sexual segregation in the squirrel monkey is an interesting case in point. We have carried out some experimental studies regarding the influence of social factors upon the course of the early development of the form of social structure which is observed in this species. As mentioned above, the segregated social structure of this species means that when adult male and female squirrel monkeys are placed together, distances between males and females are systematically greater throughout the year than spacing within each sex. Males and females generally avoid sitting together, feeding together or interacting other than sexually. (Reproductive behavior occurs only during a few months of the year.) As a consequence, under "natural" conditions, during the first 2 to 3 months of life, male and female infants do not interact with adult males. Some time after about 10 weeks, as the infants move away from their mothers more and more, male infants—who are, in general, more "adventuresome" (Rosenblum, 1974)—make more contacts with the adult male subgroup than do female infants, although the latter have some contacts as well. Over the next two years, males gradually shift to increasingly selective contact with the adult male subgroup while female young continue to remain close to the female subgroup to which their mother belongs.

Experimental studies have shown that several factors contribute to this development of sexual segregation in squirrel monkeys. First, it has been shown that when environments are inconstant and socially and physically complex, male infants move away from their mothers more than do females (Rosenblum, 1974). This occurs, incidentally, in spite of increased maternal efforts to restrain their male infants under such conditions. That is, there is something in the genetic makeup of the males that permits or encourages them to function more autonomously than the females under such environmentally unstable and enriched circumstances. Second, it has been shown what whereas preadult squirrel monkeys will not segregate when interacting only with peers, once a segregated adult group is also present, the adolescents soon segregate as well, with each sex joining their isosexual adult subgroup. Adults as well as the adolescents play their roles. The entire process appears to involve greater acceptance of same-sex adolescents coupled with some difference in the attraction of the adult subgroup of each sex to the young of each sex. Remove the adults and the adolescents return to an unsegregated grouping. The emergence of the adult patterns under wild conditions can be seen as an interaction of the genetically based male–female differences and the presence of a sexually segregated adult social context to which the infants can respond differentially. Furthermore, the sexual segregation pattern in the social structure of the adult generation influences the offspring in a manner that leads to the perpetuation of that pattern once they grow into adulthood. Thus, not only does social structure influence development of the offspring generation, it sometimes also acts to lay the foundations for its own replication.

SOCIAL STATUS AND BEHAVIORAL DEVELOPMENT

Other dimensions of the impact of the social milieu in shaping the development of social behavior have also been demonstrated in a number of monkey species. In many social groupings of nonhuman as well as human primates, some form of social status emerges among the members of the group. Status is generally signalled in a most readily discernable way, by the relative ease with which different members of the group have access to various resources. The precise nature of dominance hierarchies in primates, and factors controlling their evolution and contemporaneous functions, are neither clear nor generally agreed upon. Broad species differences and individual differences in motivation and experience, as well as the nature of the ecology in different times and places, may serve to prevent the emergence of a monolithic hierarchy of status that functions in the same way at all times in all primate groups. That is, different individuals may emerge as most dominant in the group at different times and in relation to different incentives. But nonetheless, it is fair to say that in many species, most individuals learn to "get out of the way" of certain others in their group at one time or another.

Because of the social structure of most primate groups, in addition to the mother's genotypic and phenotypic background and her own prior experiences, a mother's status in her current group may markedly affect the development of her offspring. Some years ago we conducted a unique experiment in our laboratory to assess the effects of a sudden change in maternal status on the behavior of her young infant (Stynes, Rosenblum, & Kaufman, 1968). For this purpose, groups were formed, each containing two bonnet macaque and two pigtail macaque mother-infant dyads. Because pigtail females are larger and more aggressive, when the females were together, the pigtails were relatively dominant. They occupied the best resting places and had freedom of movement around the pen. The bonnets, much more constrained in their behavior, spent most of their time on the floor of the pen. The infants of the study were between 3.5 and 12 months of age, with the bonnets averaging several months older than the pigtails.

The experimental manipulation involved introduction of either a pigtail adult male or a bonnet adult male. Once the adult male was introduced, and rapidly asserted his dominance over the females, the females of his species immediately rose in status to become the dominant females of the group. In the case of the pigtails, their existing dominance was enhanced; in the case of the bonnets, there was a dramatic reversal from their subordinate status in either the no-male or pigtail male condition. Thus, when the bonnet male was introduced, his females moved to the high shelves of the pen, displacing the fleeing pigtails.

The infants of these groups also showed rapid changes in their behavior that paralleled the changed status of their mothers. When the bonnet male was present there were significant increases in bonnet exploration and social (intraspecific) play. The latter change is particularly interesting because the bonnet infants, even though somewhat older than the pigtails, played considerably less than the pigtails under all conditions in which their mothers were subordinate. Pigtail infants, similarly, decreased the amount of time separated from their mothers, increased time on the nipple and reduced play when their mothers became subordinate in the presence of the bonnet male. This finding also suggests the possibility that the impact of status may not merely be limited to short-term changes in behaviors. Because of their greater mobility and freedom of movement, and their increased play and independence from mother, the offspring of more dominant females may well be elevated in their subsequent standing in their social groups through the "inheritance of dominance" that has been suggested in primate groups in the wild (Sade, 1967).

STATUS AND THE EMERGENCE OF SEXUAL BEHAVIOR

Another interesting and illuminating reflection of the impact of maternal status on the behavior of their offspring was observed during experimental tests of sexual behavior, in which estrogen-treated bonnet females were brought into the pen of individual males (Rosenblum & Nadler, 1971). The older males (4 to 5 years) in this study rapidly mounted any receptive female presented to them. In contrast, the 2-year-old males (puberty in such males is about 2 years away and full adult size will not develop for another 4 or 5 years), never made any attempt to approach, let alone mount sexually, a receptive adult female. This seemed surprising to us because these same males were very active sexually when presented with smaller, young females. Indeed, when a female much smaller than the male was presented, the young males were prodigious sexual performers, mounting and showing repeated ejaculatory patterns.

In addition to these active performances with the younger females in the test, we had often seen males as young as a year of age mount adult females when living with their mothers in one of our large social groups. It became clear that the problem was one of dominance, or to be precise, one of subordinance. Males will not respond sexually unless they are (i.e., perceive themselves to be and are perceived as) dominant over their potential sexual partner. The 4- and 5-year-old adult males in this study were clearly dominant over both the smaller and adult females, and mounted each quite readily. But, when tested by themselves, no 2-year-old male could be dominant over the larger and stronger adult females. Hence, no sexuality emerged in the young males in our experimental tests. But our repeated observations in the home pen reflected the fact that an infant's mother, if dominant over another female, confers some elements of her status to her offspring. This transferred dominant status then allows that infant to mount an otherwise undefeatable female with impunity.

Thus, the story grows more complex but convincingly indicates that social influences affect the course of development in a variety of interactive ways.

THE SOCIAL COGNITIVE NATURE OF STATUS RELATIONSHIPS: IMPLICATIONS FOR DEVELOPMENT

The role of social cognition in relation to the establishment and functioning of a dominance or status hierarchy is especially relevant to consideration of the impact of status upon the developing young primate. For it may be that the nature of that impact is mediated by the level of social cognition at which a particular immature individual is currently functioning. Although extant research on this issue is scarce, an examination of the ways in which social cognitive factors influence status relationships among adult individuals has clear implications for understanding the impact of status upon development *per se*.

Lewis (1983), in a recent essay on the role of the self in the process of knowing, examines in detail some of the same issues that have been involved in the debates regarding status hierarchy of primate groups: ". . . cognition, in general," Lewis suggests, "represents a continuum of involvement of the knower (or self) with what is known. Social cognition represents that part of the continuum where there is a marked relationship between the knower and the known." (p. 159) Later in this incisive work, Lewis, reflecting a view shared by others, makes it clear that, "Cognitions about self and other are not separate processes but rather are part of a duality of knowledge." (p. 165) The literature on the hierarchical nature of primate societies as well as the example presented above reflect the idea that each partner in an interaction involving status has some recognition of self (however primitive), other, and self in relation to other.

Thus, when two individuals are placed together for the first time, some potential dominance encounters are settled immediately, without either partner attacking or even making an overtly threatening gesture. This is almost always true when there is a large size disparity between the participants. One animal, seeing the other, evidently judging its own size in relation to that of the other, immediately, and without further behavioral testing, signals its subordinate status and may remain in that status thereafter. Each animal rapidly assumes the role it appears to interpret as appropriate. Once their relative status is settled, some apparent "contradictions" of that status may appear without altering their basic relationship. Indeed, at times the clearly dominant subject may "play the role of subordinate" briefly, by subordinance—presenting to an individual actually lower on the hierarchy. Or, in equally dramatic fashion, if injured, the more dominant partner may encourage a subordinate to groom the wound in spite of the pain being inflicted by the subordinate.

In spite of these "behavioral violations" of their social positions, the subordinate would never misinterpret this interaction to mean that the relative status of the two animals had actually changed. Thus, whereas each individual may not maintain a sense of its numerical place in the social hierarchy—being number 3 or number 7 in a group of 10, for example—each animal retains an understanding of its status relative to every other member of the social unit. Temporary "violations" of the usual patterns of interactions do not interfere with the stable relationship, nor does a given individual's temporary absence from view cause an immediate readjustment of the remaining members of the hierarchy. Individuals will, in general, maintain the general quality of their own status–influenced patterns and their deference or perogatives regarding others until specifiable behavioral events have occurred to change hierarchical relations.

Similarly, further reflections on the influence of social status on behavior have emerged in experimental studies of male dominance control over sexual access to a female in bonnet macaques. First, perhaps reflecting some feature of their phylogeny, and unlike males of many of the other species of the Macaque genus, adult male bonnets can live quite contentedly with one another so long as no conspecific females are present. When by themselves, they frequently sit together, groom with one another and rarely show agonistic behaviors. Introduction of a group of females from another species (a control for crowding and activity levels), if anything, enhances this gregarious pattern between the males. But following introduction of a group of bonnet females, most males cannot remain together, as agonistic and related patterns of dissociation rise dramatically (Coe & Rosenblum, 1984). These problems appear to arise not so much because of the efforts of the subordinate to gain access to the females, but rather seem to result from the increasing tension of the more dominant male.

If a single female is introduced to the pair of bonnet males for a short time, only the so-called "alpha male" will approach her. The subordinate avoids the whole situation. Is that because the more dominant male forces him away by threats or attacks? Not at all. The subordinate "knows his place" and does his best to avoid the situation. Thus, in keeping with the social cognition perspective suggested above, both of the males, once their status has been decided, enact their respective roles without further reenactments of their dominance struggle. Indeed, even if the alpha is locked into a clear Plexiglas box within the test chamber so that he can see but is not free to do anything to either the female or the beta male, beta acts as if the female were not even there. The status difference is, in a very real sense, maintained in the memory of both males. Perhaps the most suggestive and intriguing outcome of this set of studies emerged when alpha was completely removed. With alpha gone, beta did mate with the introduced female (the strength of a social stimulus in evoking otherwise inhibited behaviors should not be underestimated). However, compared to control trials when beta was alone while alpha was out, *beta showed more subordinant behaviors following alpha's return if he had previously been mating with the female.*

There is some support in all of these data for a view derived from Lewis's position that it is at least in part the way in which a given individual views itself in relation to some other(s) that generates what we see as a hierarchy. That hierarchy, having been interpreted in terms of the "rewards of status" is seen as a hierarchy of dominance, but as others have cogently pointed out, may well be a hierarchy of subordinance (Rowell, 1974). Regardless of how we choose to conceptualize the nature of the status relationships within a primate group, whether they are seen as linear or hierarchical at all, the process of attaining the social skills necessary to the establishment of those relationships are clearly critical in the life of the young primate. The perceptual and memorial capacities of a given species are therefore likely to characterize the nature of the hierarchical relationships that will emerge in social groups; with variations in discriminitive capacities in the social sphere and the different abilities to retain social information, we can expect group size and the clarity or uniformity of dominance/subordinance relations to differ as well as variation in the degree of social control which can be maintained in the absence of "face to face" contact between partners. Thus, in some species, there may be much more of a sense of "out of sight, out of mind" than in others. Similarly, we may expect that the developmental changes in these capacities within a species will affect the nature of relationships between young partners and between the young and adult members of the group. The acquisition of these abilities, and the opportunities to use them in the achievement of social skills, are likely to be key ingredients in the ontogeny of social functioning in primates. Within this social cognitive perspective, young primates cannot be expected to be involved fully in stable dominance and status ordering of relationships until they have achieved the level of social cognition needed to maintain such relationships.

THE SYMBIOTIC NATURE OF THE
MOTHER-INFANT RELATIONSHIP

In the material presented above, I have intentionally left out the obvious influences on development that result from the behavior directed at the infant by that most primary of primate caregivers, the mother. Perhaps because so much more has been written on this topic elsewhere, relatively little needs to be said here. Nevertheless, one dimension of the infant primate's interaction with the mother is too often neglected; the influence the infant has on its mother's biology and behavior. Although this symbiotic influence is as yet poorly studied in primates, it appears to range from prenatal alterations in the mother's behavior to postnatal influences on aspects of her contemporary and future social status.

It has been shown, for example, that when females are carrying a female fetus, they are more likely to be the recipient of bite wounds than when carrying a male fetus (Sackett, 1981). Similarly, it has been shown that in addition to the obvious increases in nutritional needs encumbent upon the lactating mother, the presence of a dependent infant adds to the thermal load of the mother, requiring a series of often subtle adjustments in her thermoregulatory behaviors (Schwartz & Rosenblum, 1983). In the social sphere, it has been shown that a mother's social status may actually increase, and the cluster of adult social partners with whom she interacts may be changed, when she delivers and carries her young infant (see Swartz & Rosenblum, 1981, for this and related references). Aside from the study of patterns of responses to infant vocalization, as in human research, concerns for other ways in which infants are influential partners for their mothers have been relatively slow to develop, although there has been some growing investment in the study of the "symbiosis in parent-offspring interactions" (Rosenblum & Moltz, 1983).

THE SPECIAL IMPORTANCE OF THE MOTHER'S
INFLUENCE UPON DEVELOPMENT

The special relationship that develops between an infant and its mother can be viewed as the *primary experiential basis* upon which behavioral development is built (Rosenblum & Alpert, 1977). I would like to suggest that one reason why this set of social interactions may be so important is that the effective mother repeatedly provides the infant with safe opportunities in which to engage in three basic types of interactive processes with the newfound world around it. These are: (1) those actions on the infant's part which produce rather fixed reactions; (2) those that produce one of a limited, but perceptably and predictably finite set of outcomes; and (3) those actions to which the response is unpredictable. Thus, the infant may find that striking the substrate always produces a characteristic sound, and that, in the same way, sucking the mother's nipple always produces an immediate infusion of milk into its mouth. On the other hand, a particular vocalization may produce one of a limited subset of responses ranging from tighter clasping to the ventrum to the onset of grooming. Finally, there are those behaviors, the responses to which exceed the infant's predictive capacity and appear (to the infant) to result in a random return from the social/physical environment.

Since the mother is the most prominent feature of the infant's environment, when an excessive amount of the infant's behavior with her falls into the third class, it is likely that the infant will have difficulty in dealing with subsequent adaptation. This effect may be due not only to the increased emotionality attendant upon a sense of nonpredictability regarding the environment (Levine, 1980), but also to the consequent effects of such disturbance on effective learning in complex situations. Thus, maternal failure to respond in a way that is contingently related to the infant's behavior during early development may be of crucial importance (Lewis & Goldberg, 1969) in the reduction of long term as well as short term adaptation.

On the other hand, exposure to a gradual increment in the range of response patterns to a given infant behavior, paced to the infant's developing cognitive capacities, enhances the infant's ability to respond adaptively to an expanding environment without loss of a sufficient level of predictability and control to permit effective functioning. In nonhuman primates at least, both the almost absolute predictibility found in isolation-rearing environments and the chaos of having a mother who is sometimes responsive and sometimes "unavailable" (e.g., as in the case of Harlow's "motherless mothers") result in deficient behavioral outcomes (e.g., Mitchell, 1970; Sackett & Rupenthal, 1973). Neither of these settings produces young that are as successful at coping with difficult situations as are infants who live in a caregiving situation that permits the gradual growth of autonomy, but in which the caregivers are more immediately and appropriately responsive to the infant's needs early in life. It would appear that it is the peculiar mix of responses provided by the normal socializing agent(s) that ultimately permits successful phenotypic forms to emerge.

SUMMARY AND CONCLUSION

Research on nonhuman primates under both laboratory and naturalistic conditions affirms the view that a given genetic structure (genotype) can serve only as the starting point from which individual behavioral development (phenotype) emerges. Even the most basic aspects of subsequent behavior, including reproduction, infant rearing, group structure and individual roles within groups, depend for their expression on the nature of the social milieu within which early development occurs.

ACKNOWLEDGMENTS

The research reported in this chapter was supported in part by USPHS Grant Mh#15965 and funds from the H. F. Guggenheim Foundation, and the State University of New York.

REFERENCES

Bromley, L. (1978). *Hormonal determinants of sexual segregation in squirrel monkeys*. Unpublished doctoral dissertation. City University of New York.
Coe, C. L., & Rosenblum, L. A. (1974). Sexual segregation and its ontogeny in squirrel monkey social structure. *Journal of Human Evolution, 3*, 551–561.
Coe, C. L., & Rosenblum, L. A. (1984). Male dominance in the bonnet macaque: Malleable relationship. In P. Rarchas & S. P. Mendoza (Eds.), *Social cohesion* (pp. 31–64). Westport, CT: Greenwood Press.
Epple, G. (1975). The behavior of Marmoset monkeys (Callithricidae) In L. A. Rosenblum (Ed.), *Primate behavior Vol. IV* (pp. 195–240). New York: Academic Press.
Goldfoot, D. A., Wallen, K., Neff, D. A., McBair, M. C., & Goy, R. W. (1984). Social influences on the display of sexually dimorphic behavior in rhesus monkeys: Isosexual rearing. *Archives of Sexual Behavior, 13*, 395–412.
Jay, P. (1963). Mother-infant relations in langurs. In H. L. Rheingold (Ed.), *Maternal behavior in mammals* (pp. 282–304). New York: Wiley.
Levine, S. (1980). A coping model of mother-infant relationships. In S. Levine & H. Ursin (Eds.), *Coping and health* (pp. 87–99). New York: Plenum Press.
Lewis, M. (1983). Newton, Einstein, Piaget, and the concept of self: The role of the self in the process of knowing. In L. S. Liben (Ed.), *Piaget and the foundations of knowledge* (pp. 141–177). Hillsdale, NJ: Erlbaum.
Lewis, M., & Goldberg, S. (1969). Perceptual-cognitive development in infancy: A Generalized expectancy model as a function of mother-infant interaction. *Merrill-Palmer Quarterly, 15*, 81–100.
Mitchell, G. (1970). Abnormal behavior in primates. In L. A. Rosenblum (Ed.), *Primate behavior, Vol. I* (pp. 195–249). New York: Academic Press.
Rosenblum, L. A. (1974). Sex differences, environmental complexity and mother-infant relations. *Archives of Sexual Behavior, 2*, 117–128.
Rosenblum, L. A., & Alpert, S. (1977). Response to mother and stranger: A first step in

socialization in primates. In C. Poirier & S. Chevalier–Skolnikoff (Eds.), *Socialization in primates* (pp. 463–478). New York: Aldine.

Rosenblum, L. A. & Moltz, H. (Eds.). (1983). *Symbiosis in parent-offspring interactions.* New York: Plenum Press.

Rosenblum, L. A., & Nadler, R. D. (1971). Ontogeny of male sexual behavior in bonnet macaques. In D. Ford (Ed.), *Influence of hormones on the nervous system* (pp. 388–400). Basel: Karger.

Rowell, T. E. (1974). The concept of social dominance. *Behavioral Biology, 11,* 131–154.

Sackett, G. P. (1981). Receiving severe aggression correlates with fetal gender in pregnant pigtailed monkeys. *Developmental Psychobiology, 14,* 267–272.

Sackett, G. P., & Ruppenthal, G. C. (1973). Development of monkeys after varied rearing experiences during infancy. In S. A. Barnett (Ed.), *Ethology and development* (pp. 52–87). Philadelphia: Lippincott.

Sackett, G. J., Holm, R. A., Ruppenthal, G. C., & Fahrenbach, C. E. (1976). The effects of total social isolation rearing on behavior of rhesus and pigtail macaques. In R. N. Walsh & W. T. Greenough (Eds.), *Environment as therapy for brain dysfunction* (pp. 115–131). New York: Plenum Press.

Sade, D. S. (1967). Determinants of dominance in a group of free–ranging rhesus monkeys. In S. A. Altmann (Ed.), *Social communication among primates* (pp. 99–114). Chicago University of Chicago Press.

Schwartz, G. G., & Rosenblum, L. A. (1983). Allometric influences on primate mothers and infants. In L. A. Rosenblum & H. Moltz (Eds.), *Symbiosis in parent–offspring interactions* (pp. 215–248). New York: Plenum Press.

Stynes, A. J., Rosenblum, L. A., & Kaufman, I. C. (1968). The dominant male and behavior within heterospecific monkey groups. *Folia Primatologica, 9,* 123–134.

Swartz, K. B., & Rosenblum, L. A. (1981). The social context of parental behavior. In D. J. Gubernick & P. H. Klopfer (Eds.), *Parental care in mammals* (pp. 417–454). New York: Plenum Press.

Zimmerman, R. R., & Torrey, C. C. (1965). Ontogeny of learning. In A. M. Schrier, H. F. Harlow, & F. Stolnitz (Eds.), *Behavior of nonhuman primates* (pp. 405–477). New York: Academic Press.

3

A Home Is Not a School
The Effects of Environments on Development

K. Alison Clarke-Stewart

Over the past 15 years, we have seen a dramatic shift in the environments in which young children spend their time. Whereas a decade and a half ago fewer than one third of the preschool-aged children in this country were in any kind of preschool program, now over half attend a nursery school, kindergarten, or day-care center. An even more striking rise has occurred for infants and toddlers; their participation in such programs has more than doubled in the same period. In addition, many thousands of children are now spending a significant portion of their time in other kinds of nonparental care environments—with a babysitter, a neighbor, an aunt, or a paid day-care home provider. Every year the number of young children in some form of "nontraditional" child care environment increases markedly.

A question that concerns parents, politicians, and psychologists is what effects these alternative environments have on children's development. Until quite recently, however, data about the effects of different child care environments were lacking. Although day care had existed in this country since at least 1838, when the first day nursery was opened in Boston (and for longer if informal arrangements between neighbors or with live-in housekeepers are included), the first systematic studies of

A version of this chapter was published in the *Journal of Social Issues*, 1990.

K. Alison Clarke-Stewart • Program in Social Ecology, University of California, Irvine, California 92717.

child care environments and effects did not appear until 1970. Since that time, a sizable number of studies have been undertaken, and now important evidence is beginning to accumulate. In the present chapter I review the available research, including my own, in an attempt to answer the question: "What are the effects of different types of child care environments on children's social and cognitive development?"

Differences between Children in Different Child Care Environments

In my research in Chicago (Clarke-Stewart, 1984; Clarke-Stewart & Gruber, 1984), we selected 150 2- and 3-year-old children in six different child care arrangements: (1) care at home by parents; (2) care by a sitter in the child's home; (3) care in a day-care home; (4) care in a center or nursery school part time; (5) care in a center full time; and (6) care in a center part time and with a sitter at home part time. No more than four children were selected from any child care setting, and all the children of nonparental child care environments were in their first such environment and had been there less than one year. We followed these children over a year-long period, observing them six times, in their family and child care settings and recording their moment-to-moment experiences. Children also were brought into a laboratory playroom on two occasions for extensive assessments of their social skills, and on one occasion were given standard assessments of social, emotional, and cognitive development at home. The assessment procedures in these visits included leaving the child alone in the observation room, asking the child to play with an unfamiliar peer, getting the child to cooperate with the examiner in tests and games, and testing language comprehension, verbal fluency, and memory. From the data collected in these assessments, we created a set of complex, empirically intercorrelated and conceptually meaningful variables. Table 1 describes seven of these variables which reflect children's social and intellectual competence. On all these variables, older children scored significantly higher than younger ones.

Differences among children in the six child care arrangements were estimated by analyzing differences in mean scores on the seven child development variables. The results of these analyses, presented in Table 2, are clear and consistent. On all these variables reflecting advanced social and intellectual skills—verbal ability, nonverbal cognition, social cognition, creativity with materials, cooperation with the examiner, cooperation with an unfamiliar peer, and overall social competence—there were no significant differences among the children in different home care environments (with mother, sitter, or day-care home provider), nor

TABLE 1. Child Competence Variables

Cognition (verbal)	Knowledge of concepts: Number of correct matches between pairs of pictures illustrating the same action or spatial relation
	+ Verbal fluency: Number of colors, foods, and animals child can name
	+ Memory span: Number of digits child correctly repeats after experimenter
	+ Language comprehension: Number of pictures correctly identified following experimenter's verbal descriptions
	+ Perspective recognition: Number of correct matches of photographs of objects taken from unusual perspectives with drawings of objects in usual perspective
Cognition (non-verbal)	Number of three-dimensional block designs child correctly copies after demonstration by experimenter
Creativity with materials	Number of 10-second intervals during free play in which child's play with toys is constructive, symbolic, or involves problem-solving
Social competence	Total score on examiner's ratings of child's friendliness, responsiveness, self-confidence, self-reliance, cooperativeness, awareness of social norms and conventions, and lack of hostility
	+ General social competence ratings assigned after observing child in 2 hours of tasks and free play, with mother, peer, and two examiners in laboratory playroom
	+ Competence in responding to examiner's requests (e.g., for a drink, to see child's toys, to ask mother to leave the room, and to teach mother a game)
Cooperation with examiner	Degree of cooperation in 10 tasks with examiner in the laboratory
	+ Degree of cooperation shown in tasks with examiner at the child's house
	+ Proportion of times child complies with examiner's requests to put materials away
	+ Degree of helpfulness when examiner drops toys or cannot complete task
	+ Willingness to leave room with examiner and, at examiner's request, walk across balance beam or jump from chair with eyes closed
	− Negative affect or hostility toward examiner in laboratory tasks and in transitions between tasks

(*continued*)

Table 1.   (*Continued*)

	−	Frequency of refusal to do tasks requested by examiner at home
Social cognition		Number of correct identifications of appropriate emotions and visual orientations in perspective-taking situations depicted by stories and cartoons
	+	Conceptual perspective-taking in a "secret game" in which child must determine who has knowledge of a secret and who does not
	+	Communication ability in which the child describes to mother line-and-dot patterns not visible to her
Cooperation with unfamiliar peer		Number of 30-second intervals in which child cooperates with peer while playing with blocks, coloring together, playing with a jack-in-the-box, and engaging in free play
	+	Level of cooperation during block play and coloring
	+	Level of cooperation during a game played with peer to win marbles
	+	Helpfulness toward peer in putting away blocks and coloring materials

were there differences among the children in different center environments (part time or full time). But the children in center care (child care arrangements 4, 5, and 6) performed at higher levels than the children in home care (child care arrangements 1, 2, and 3). Only 2 of the 15 analyses did not reveal a significant difference between children in home care and center care, and these two analyses (for creative play with materials and cooperation with the examiner on the first assessment) approached significance.

The difference between children in home and center environments did not occur, however, for a set of variables that did not so directly assess social or intellectual competence: security of the child's attachment to the mother, hostility toward the mother, sociability toward the examiner, gender-stereotyped use of toys, compliance with the mother's requests, positive interaction with a familiar playmate, and help or comforting directed toward the mother.

The findings from this study are consistent with the results of other research (see review by Clarke-Stewart & Fein, 1983, and more recent studies by Andersson, 1989; Burchinal, Lee, & Ramey, 1989; Robinson & Corley, 1989; Tietze, 1987; Wadsworth, 1986) which also suggests that children in day-care centers and preschool programs tend to be more socially skilled and intellectually advanced than children at home with

TABLE 2. Ranks on Competence Variables for Children in Six Child-Care Arrangements

Competence variables		Child-care arrangements					
		Home with parents (1)	Home with babysitter (2)	Day-care home (3)	Day-care center part time (4)	Day-care center full time (5)	Day-care center plus babysitter (6)
Cognition (verbal)	B	2	3	1	6	4	5
Cognition (nonverbal)	B	1	2.5	2.5	4	5	6
Creativity with materials	A	2	4	1	6	3	5
	B	2	3.5	1	5	6	3.5
Social competence	A	2	2	2	5	4	6
	B	2	2	2	5	4	6
	C	3	3	1	6	3	5
Cooperation with examiner	A	2	4	1	5	3	6
	B	3	2	1	6	4	5
	C	4	2	1	6	3	5
Social cognition	A	2	3	1	5	4	6
	B	1	3	2	6	4	5
	C	2.5	2.5	1	5	4	6
Cooperation with unfamiliar peer	A	1.5	3	1.5	5	6	4
	C	1.5	3	1.5	5.5	5.5	4

Note: Underscoring indicates significant ($p < .05$) contrasts between groups, in a multivariate analysis of covariance covarying out child's age and family SES. Rank 1 = low; Rank 6 = high. A = first assessment, in laboratory; B = second assessment, at home; C = third assessment, in laboratory.

their parents, sitters, or in day-care homes. Of course, significant differences favoring center attendees have not been found in all studies, in all samples, or with all indices of social or cognitive competence (e.g., Ackerman-Ross & Khanna, 1989; Lamb, Hwang, Broberg, & Bookstein, 1988; Scarr, Lande, & McCartney, 1988). But when differences have been found, they consistently favor children in center care.

In the social realm, there is evidence that children in center care are more self confident, self assured, and outgoing, less timid and fearful, more assertive, self sufficient, and independent of parents and teachers, yet more helpful and cooperative with peers, the mother, or the examiner when the situation requires it. They are more verbally expressive, more knowledgeable about the social world (e.g., know their own name, address, and birthday, dress themselves, brush their own hair, tie their shoes earlier), more comfortable in a new or stressful situation, and more competent to manage on their own (Cochran, 1977; Fowler, 1978; Kagan, Kearsley, & Zelazo, 1978; Lally & Honig, 1977; Rubenstein, Howes, & Boyle, 1981; Schwarz, Krolick, & Strickland, 1973). When they get to school, they are better adjusted, more task oriented and goal directed, and show more leadership and persistence (Fowler & Khan, 1974; Lally & Honig, 1977). In Sjolund's (1971) international review, only three of the available 56 studies showed no difference favoring the social skills of children in nursery school.

In the intellectual domain, of the more than twenty studies of child care that have included some measure of children's intelligence or intellectual development, only two have reported significantly higher scores for children reared at home than for children of comparable family backgrounds who were in day-care centers (Melhuish, 1990, for vocabulary only; Peaslee, 1976, for language and IQ). Other studies consistently show that children in day-care centers do at least as well as those at home with their parents, and often they do better, at least for a time (e.g., Cochran, 1977; Fowler, 1978; Golden, Rosenbluth, Grossi, Policare, Freeman, & Brownlee, 1978; Kagan et al., 1978; Ramey, Dorval, & Baker-Ward, 1983; Robinson & Robinson, 1977; Rubenstein & Howes, 1983; Winnett, Fuchs, Moffatt, & Nerviano, 1977). In Sjolund's (1971) review, 21 of the 36 studies assessing children's intellectual development showed advanced development in nursery school children compared to children not in nursery school; the other 15 showed no significant difference. Comparisons of children in day-care homes and day-care centers, similarly, have often revealed significant differences among children in these two types of day care, favoring the children in centers (e.g., Bruner, 1980; Robinson & Corley, 1989; Winnett et al., 1977).

In the assessments of particular kinds of intellectual abilities, differences favoring center-care children have been found in eye–hand coordination (Cochran, 1977; Kagan *et al.*, 1978), creative use of materials (Provost, 1980), memory (Ramey *et al.*, 1983), problem solving and reasoning (Fowler, 1978; Garber & Heber, 1980; Moss, Blicharski, & Strayer, 1987), and knowledge about the physical world (Stukat, 1969). Advanced language abilities have also been observed in children who are in center care (Fowler, 1978; Garber & Heber, 1980; Ramey *et al.*, 1983; Rubenstein & Howes, 1983; Rubenstein *et al.*, 1981; Scarr *et al.*, 1988; Stukat, 1969).

In brief, then, differences favoring children in center care appear across a range of intellectual abilities including both verbal and nonverbal skills. These differences are not permanent, but they have been observed to last for a year or two after "graduation" into elementary school (Haskins, 1989; Larsen & Robinson, 1989; Lee, Brooks-Gunn, Schnur, & Liaw, 1989; Tietze, 1987; Wadsworth, 1986). They are more likely to occur for children who have been in center care since infancy (Andersson, 1989).

CAUSES OF THE DIFFERENCE BETWEEN CHILDREN IN DIFFERENT CHILD CARE ENVIRONMENTS

More than simply documenting the differences among children in different child care environments, research offers some tentative suggestions about what causes these differences.

Differences in Amount of Attention and Stimulation

One reason that the development of children in center care is advanced might be that center programs simply provide *more* of the same kind of stimulation that predicts advanced development in other care environments. Perhaps centers are just like homes, but more so.

One piece of evidence that could be used to support this hypothesis would be the finding that the development of children in centers full time is more advanced than the development of children in centers part time. Available data, including the findings in Table 2, however, suggest that part-time programs have as large an effect as full-time programs (Lazar, Hubbell, Murray, Rosche, & Royce, 1977; Winnett *et al.*, 1977). This does not support the hypothesis that centers are just like homes but more so.

Another piece of evidence that would support the hypothesis that centers are like good homes would be the finding that centers offer children more space and materials than they have at home, and provide more physical stimulation of the same kind that is found in homes. Here again, however, the evidence offers no support for the hypothesis. Although extreme differences in the amount of space per child have indeed been related to children's behavior and development in child care environments (Prescott, 1973; Rohe & Patterson, 1974; Ruopp, Travers, Glantz, & Coelen, 1979; Smith & Connolly, 1980), because homes generally offer more space per child than centers, this relation cannot explain the advanced development of children in centers. There may be more play materials in centers than in homes (e.g., Golden et al., 1978), but this is probably not important in accounting for the difference in children's development either, because studies of the effects of the number of toys in children's environments suggest that toys alone are not a direct promoter of development (Golden et al., 1978; Rubenstein & Howes, 1979).

Another kind of evidence that could support the hypothesis that the difference between centers and homes is that centers offer children more stimulation would be the finding that caregivers in centers interact more with children than do caregivers at home. The social and intellectual development of individual children in day-care centers has indeed been positively related to the amount of adult attention they receive (Carew, 1980; Clarke-Stewart, 1984; Phillips, McCartney, & Scarr, 1987; Phillips, Scarr, & McCartney, 1987; Ruopp et al., 1979). But of the studies comparing the amount of caregiver attention in homes and in centers, the majority show that children at home receive more attention from the caregiver than do children in centers (Clarke-Stewart, 1984; Cochran, 1977; Golden et al., 1978; Hayes, Massey, Thomas, David, Milbrath, Buchanan, & Lieberman, 1983; Melhuish, 1990; Prescott, 1973; Tizard, Carmichael, Hughes, & Pinkerton, 1980; Tyler & Dittman, 1980). Once again, the available data do not support the hypothesis that the important difference between center and home environments is simply the amount of stimulation children receive.

Differences in Type of Attention and Stimulation

Perhaps, then, the important difference between homes and centers is not the amount of stimulation the child receives but the type. Center environments differ qualitatively from home environments in a number of ways. Perhaps most obvious, centers offer children the opportunity to interact with other children their age. It has been observed that playing with a peer raises the complexity and creativity of children's activities with materials (Rubenstein & Howes, 1983; Sylva, Roy, & Painter, 1980), that social play is more advanced with a familiar playmate (Doyle, Connolly, & Rivest, 1980; Rubenstein & Howes, 1979), and that this more complex level of play then generalizes to interaction with unfamiliar peers (Lieberman, 1977). However, interaction with agemates is less likely to have a direct effect on the child's language acquisition. Language development is facilitated by hearing a more advanced language model, not by listening to peer chatter (McCartney, 1984; Sjolund, 1971). It seems unlikely, therefore, that the presence of other children alone would account for the observed difference in intellectual development for children in different child care environments.

Results of studies comparing different types of child care support this suggestion. First, if peers were the critical factor, then all group programs, not just programs in centers, should show the effect. But, as we have already suggested, children in day-care homes do not generally show the same level of competence as children in centers—despite the fact that they interact with peers to much the same extent (Clarke-Stewart, 1984; Howes & Rubenstein, 1981). Second, more peer interaction occurs in more "open" preschool programs, but gains in cognitive development and achievement are typically lower in these programs than in less open programs (Miller & Dyer, 1975). Finally, measures of social and intellectual competence from my research in Chicago were not significantly positively correlated with the amount of peer interaction experienced by individual children (Clarke-Stewart, 1984).

Children's competence in the Chicago study was, however, correlated with the number of different children interacted with in the care setting. Thus, children may gain from exposure to a wider *variety* of other children. Dunn and Kontos's (1989) observation—that when there were more children in day-care homes children engaged in higher levels of play—would support this suggestion. But the advantage of diversity exists only up to a certain point. When the number of children becomes too large, a lower level of play and intellectual development is observed (Ruopp *et al.*, 1979; Smith & Connolly, 1980; Sylva *et al.*, 1980). Altogether, then, there seems to be little evidence to support the hypothesis that the important difference between center care and home care is simply the presence of other children or the amount of interaction with other children. The variety and diversity of peer contacts in centers may, however, be a significant contributor.

Similarly, the variety of different adults with whom the child has an opportunity to interact may contribute. In my study in Chicago, the number of adults children encountered in centers was, on the average, greater than in homes (see also Howes, 1983), and the number of adults so encountered was positively related to children's competence (Clarke-Stewart, 1984).

Another qualitative difference between home and center care is that, in centers, rules, lessons, and schedules are more likely to be fixed and based on the needs of the group rather than of the individual child. Thus, children in centers must learn to recognize and adapt to "abstract," arbitrary, general rules and to take in information presented formally. However, children at home operate in a concrete "hands-on" context, where rules and lessons, as such, are limited. Children who have been in day-care center programs for some time have indeed been observed to have a more advanced understanding of social rules than newly enrolled children (Siegal & Storey, 1985). It has been suggested (Cole, Gay, Glick, & Sharp, 1971) that "schooling" in this institutional sense facilitates the development of advanced intellectual skills. It is also plausible to expect that it would foster the social, language, and test-taking skills and knowledge in which center children are advanced.

Yet another possibility is that different kinds of physical equipment and materials are provided in day-care centers and homes that contribute to the observed differences in children's development. Within center settings, high-level, cognitively challenging and constructive activity with materials is more likely with building materials or during teacher-directed art or music sessions (Pellegrini, 1984; Sylva et al., 1980). These kinds of opportunities are likely to be more frequent in centers than in homes. In homes, the opportunities are greater for tactile exploration, i.e., with sand, water, dough, and soft objects, for cooking, messing around, and free play (Cochran, 1977; Prescott, 1973; Rubenstein & Howes, 1979). However, academic and construction materials are less common. Therefore, the physical materials and equipment in centers may encourage more frequent intellectual activities.

But the physical environment alone is unlikely to account for all the differences observed. Simply adding novel materials to preschool classrooms or having more varied material accessible does not lead to cognitive gains; it is only in combination with teacher behavior that materials are related to children's advanced development (Busse, Ree, Gatride, & Alexander, 1972; Ruopp et al., 1979). Moreover, toys and materials are not likely to account for observed differences in social competence; advanced social behavior involving cooperation, conversation, and complex interaction with peers is more common with dolls, dressups, dramatic props, and social toys like checkers and pickup sticks than with puzzles, art, books, or intellectual exercises (e.g., Howes & Rubenstein, 1981; Smith & Connolly, 1980; Quilitch & Risley, 1973; Sylva et al., 1980), and these materials are more common in homes than in centers (Rubenstein & Howes, 1979). Physical materials may make a contribution to children's development, but they alone do not account for the differences in competence observed in different child care environments.

Another possible reason for observed differences between children in homes and in centers is education instruction. Most home care providers, whether parents or paid professionals, do not have education as their primary goal. Nor do they follow a set curriculum. There are several hints that this may be an important distinction between home and center care.

For example, children in more educationally oriented programs—with more prescribed education activities such as lessons, guided play sessions, teaching of specific content, and more direct teacher instructions—do better than those in less educationally oriented programs. They do more constructive and complex play with materials and with peers and score higher on intelligence and achievement tests (Clarke-Stewart, 1984; Ferri, 1980; Fowler, 1978; Johnson, Ershler, & Bell, 1980; Lazar et al., 1977; McCartney, 1984; Miller & Dyer, 1975; Sylva et al., 1980; Tizard, Philips, & Plewis, 1976; Winnett et al., 1977). In correlational analyses, the more direct teaching children receive, the greater their competence (Clarke-Stewart, 1984; McCartney, 1984). There may even be a match between the particular content taught and the outcomes exhibited. For example, children in a program stressing problem solving in visual-spatial skills showed superior performance on the Griffith's visual-spatial scale (Fowler, 1978); children in a program stressing social skills were advanced only in social competence (Miller & Dyer, 1975). Most telling, when care in day-care homes was enriched by the experimental addition of a structured educational curriculum, the intellectual competence of the children reached the level of children in day-care centers (Goodman & Andrews, 1981). An educational curriculum, then, seems to be a likely candidate for contributing to the advanced development of children in centers.

Another benefit of having a curriculum is that it can ensure "equal opportunities" in the child-care environment for boys and girls. Gunnarsson (1977), for example, suggested that the reason that boys in centers did better than boys in homes on the Griffiths personal-social scale, whereas girls in centers did better than girls in homes on the fine-motor scale, was that boys and girls are ordinarily given fewer opportunities at home to perform these kinds of nongender-stereotyped activities. This may be another way in which the curriculum contributes to the advanced development of children in centers.

Qualitative differences between the kinds of teaching that occur in center environments and in home environments may also be involved. In homes, "teaching" is likely to be casual and informal; children have more free time and time alone, and learn from exploring household objects, helping the caregiver, performing real-life tasks, and seeing real live role models—not from explicit lessons (Cochran, 1977; Prescott, 1973; Tyler & Dittman, 1980). Conversations are longer, include more complex utterances, offer children more opportunities to ask questions and express opinions, and are more "inductive" (Cochran, 1977; Fiene, 1973; Prescott, 1973; Tizard et al., 1980; Tyler & Dittman, 1980): "What would you like for lunch?" might lead to a long discussion about people's food preferences, the time it takes to prepare food, what foods are nutritious, and so on. In centers, conversations are more likely to be "deductive" and convergent, taking the form of the teacher's questions and the children's answers (Cochran, 1977; Fiene, 1973; Prescott, 1973; Tyler & Dittman, 1980; Wittmer & Honig, 1989). The parallel question in a center would be "What are we having for lunch today?" and it might lead to a discussion of peas as vegetables, other vegetables the children can name, what colors and sizes they are, and so on. It seems reasonable that the kinds of conversations occurring in centers are just the kind that would prepare children to do well on standardized tests of intelligence. They may not be designed to enhance practical problem solving or sensitivity to human needs, but they are directed toward the kinds of school skills that are assessed in tests of intellectual development.

One reason for the difference in the educational emphasis of homes and centers is that center caregivers are more likely to have been trained in child development (Clarke-Stewart, 1984; Goelman & Pence, 1987). The level of training caregivers have is correlated with their interaction with the children. Caregivers with more training are more interactive, helpful, talkative, and didactic (Fosburg, Hawkins, Singer, Goodson, Smith, & Brush, 1980; Kinney, 1989; Lazar et al., 1977; Tyler & Dittman, 1980), and the children in their care make more cognitive gains (Clarke-Stewart, 1984; Ruopp et al., 1979). When teachers are trained to use more cognitively demanding, abstract representational "distancing" strategies in talking to the children in their preschool classes, the children exhibit advanced achievement in reading and mathematics in elementary school (Sigel, 1986).

Perhaps because of their training, center caregivers as compared to home caregivers (whether mothers or sitters) are less directive and authoritarian, more likely to help, to explain, to make tasks into games, and to respond to children's initiation of play (Bryant, Harris, & Newton, 1980; Cochran, 1977; Hess, Price, Dickson, & Conroy, 1981; Howes & Rubenstein, 1981; Prescott, 1973; Rubenstein & Howes, 1979; Tyler & Dittman, 1980). Since we know that authoritarian discipline is related to children's lower intellectual development and social competence (see Clarke-Stewart & Apfel, 1979), it seems reasonable that this difference between homes and centers is another part of the explanation for the observed difference in children's development.

In sum, it appears that differences in the kinds of attention and stimulation in home and center environments account for many of the differences observed in children's competence. In particular, the educational emphasis and nonauthoritarian style of center caregivers, combined with the availability of stimulating educational materials, the presence of a variety of adults and other children, and the influence of institutional regulations, create a school-like environment that facilitates the development of social skills and intellectual competencies for both boys and girls.

Differences in Quality of Stimulation

It has been suggested recently (e.g., by Lamb *et al.*, 1988), however, that observed differences in children's development in centers and homes are the result of differences in the quality of child care rather than the type of child-care environment. Lamb and his associates found that the social skills of preschool children in Sweden were related to the observed quality of their experiences in child care rather than whether the children were in home care or centers. In this study, the day-care centers observed were of lower quality than the homes (more negative events occurred). In a study in England in which children in centers did not show advanced intellectual development, similarly, the centers observed were of generally poor quality (Melhuish, 1990). It makes sense that children would do better in a high quality home than in a poor quality center. But perhaps in the real world of child care in America, or at least in the centers and homes that have been the targets of study, centers, on the average, offer care and stimulation of higher quality than do homes. Perhaps quality and type of care are confounded. Differences between children in different child care environments are most marked when the centers are of high quality and/or the children come from disadvantaged families (Andersson, 1989; Fowler & Khan, 1974; Robinson & Robinson, 1971; Scarr *et al.*, 1988). Differences are least when the homes are of high quality. For example, in research by Goelman and Pence (1987), although the competence of children in *unregulated* day-care homes in Canada was inferior to that of children in centers, the competence of children in *regulated* homes was equivalent. We do not have a clear answer to the question of whether the differences observed between children in homes and in centers are due to the quality or the kind of stimulation. Center environments may have unique benefits so that some things may be easier to accomplish in centers. There may be subtle differences among environments that are glossed over by an emphasis on global quality. Or it may be that, although typical practice in centers is often more educational than typical practice in homes, this is not a *necessary* difference between the two environments. Untangling these possibilities remains for future research.

Differences in Children and Families

Before we conclude that children's competence is solely the result of differences in their child-care experiences, however, we must examine the contributions of the family and the child to the advanced competence of children in center care. Although socioeconomic differences had been statistically controlled in the reported analyses of the Chicago study, there is always the possibility that family variables contribute to the observed pattern of advanced development in center children.

Parents of children in centers may provide more stimulation and education for their children than the parents of children in home care. In well-controlled studies in which center- and home-care families have been matched (e.g., on SES), there are large areas of overlap where no differences among the groups of parents are observed. But, when differences are observed, they are in the direction of greater verbal stimulation and play and less authoritarian discipline for mothers using center care than for mothers using only home care (Garber & Heber, 1980; Clarke-Stewart, 1984; Ramey et al., 1983; Rubenstein, Howes, & Boyle, 1981).

In some cases, this difference may be the result of self-selection: most parents who send their children to centers value education and tend to be most satisfied with the type of care they have selected when they think the child is receiving an education (Clarke-Stewart, 1984; Hess et al., 1981). Moreover, when parents think that the purpose of the center program is educational, their children spend relatively more time there engaged in educational activities (Meadows, Philips, Weaver, & Mably, 1977).

In other cases, the difference may be the result of the child's influence on the parents. It has been observed that children who are in preschool programs affect their mothers' behavior by asking them to watch, read, play, and answer questions, and, as a result, their mothers give more information and are more stimulating and responsive (Garber & Heber, 1980; Vandell, 1979).

The difference is less likely to be the result of changes in the parents' behavior as a result of learning about child development from center staff. Although one study did show that parents whose children were attending a model day-care center program in which they were encouraged to visit and participate became more child centered and more like the teachers in the program (less likely to ignore, scold, refuse, or coax the child) than a matched sample of parents whose children were not in the program (Edwards, Logue, Loehr, & Roth, 1986), in most centers communication between parent and teacher occurs spontaneously, and, when it does, it does not lead to more agreement (Powell, 1978). Moreover, even when a formal parent education component is part of the day-care program, this does not ensure that the parents' behavior will change (e.g., Fowler, 1978; Lally & Honig, 1977). It is unlikely, therefore, that parent education at the center is a strong contributor to the difference observed between parents using center and home care.

There is, however, always the possibility that there are certain qualities present in the children who are placed in centers which account for their advanced development. Perhaps they are selected for center care (by staff or by parents) because they are already more competent. This possibility cannot be ruled out. It is a fact that many centers only accept children who are toilet trained. This would force mothers who must work to use day-care homes or babysitters for care of less mature toddlers. But, once the child is toilet trained, center staff would be unlikely to select on the basis of maturity or competence without more screening than is commonly done. Moreover, advanced development in center children was also observed in studies in which children were matched on IQ at the beginning of their child-care experience (Fowler, 1978) or in which self-selection was eliminated by randomly assigning children to center or home care (Garber & Heber, 1980; Ramey et al., 1983). Therefore, although self-selection may magnify the differences in children's development, it is unlikely to be the most significant contributor.

CONCLUSION AND IMPLICATIONS FOR FUTURE RESEARCH

Child-Care Environments

In sum, children in center child-care environments are, on the average, socially and intellectually advanced over their peers at home. This advanced development is likely to arise from a combination of factors, not a single critical cause. For one thing, experiences at home, including those initiated or evoked by the child, may contribute to the advanced development of children whose parents have chosen to put them in centers. Even more important, the advanced development of children in centers is likely to be the result of lessons to foster social and intellectual skills, instructions in recognizing and following rules, opportunities to practice skills and follow rules with a variety of peers and nonparental adults, and encouragement of independence and self-direction by nonauthoritarian teachers. These experiences of children in centers are substantially different from those of children at home—with parents, babysitters, or day-care home providers. Home is where the heart is, but a home is not a school. Both quantitatively and qualitatively, center environments differ from home environments, and these differences are likely to have significant effects on the development of children growing up in them.

The test of just how significant these effects are remains for future researchers. In the past, researchers took an overly simple approach to defining and assessing child care, as if "child care" were a single uniform condition rather than an enormous variety of environments, programs, and settings. They did not study the full range of home and center care, for the whole range of children. They did not observe and compare children's experiences in home and center environments. They did not analyze the relations between child care and family factors. They sidestepped the issues of causal direction and extent.

To investigate more fully the effects of child-care environments on children's development, researchers need to overcome these limitations. They need to examine in detail the nature of children's experiences in different kinds of child-care environments, paying particular attention to the educational content of those experiences and attempting to identify intellectually and socially valuable dimensions. They then need to experimentally probe the implications of their descriptive observations, by controlling the dimensions of programs in centers and by supplementing the dimensions of experiences in homes. Only by systematically enriching home care with the educationally focused opportunities more typically found in centers, and only by unconfounding quality and type of care, will we find out with any degree of certainty whether a home is not—and cannot be—a school.

Environments at Large

In this chapter we have focused on just one example of how environments affect children's behavior and development. Many other examples could have been discussed: noisy homes, crowded classrooms, barren, boring play areas, adventure playgrounds, small schools, well-defined activity areas stimulating social milieux—to name a few. But the research on child-care environments illustrates findings and issues that are common to all research on how environments affect children's development.

Like other research on the psychological effects of different environments, the research on child-care environments suggests that people adapt to their environments, that environments elicit behavior that is congruent with features and demands of the setting, and that both environments and their effects are multidimensional. The research demonstrates how for understanding the effects of surroundings on development there are advantages to observing features of the environment itself rather than just comparing mean levels of children's development in different environments. It suggests something about what kinds of analyses of the environment might be most informative, namely, analyses that go beyond global unanalyzed terms like "child care," "home care," "quality care," or even "environment" itself, and relate individual children's development to specific dimensions of their environments.

This does not necessarily mean that the best kind of analysis is to break down the environment into its smallest component parts and look for variable-by-variable links between environmental input and developmental output (e.g., Wachs & Gruen, 1982). Life is not a master factorial design in which every variable is crossed with every other. In life, as naturalist John Muir observed, everything is hooked to everything else. The way things are hooked up and hang together also needs to be examined. The analysis of the research on child care presented here illustrates an approach in which environmental effects are assessed at the broader level of the overall ecology of different environmental settings. This approach shows how complex and intricately integrated environments really are. Environments include both physical and social components, acting both together and separately, forming both quantitatively and qualitatively different configurations. Environments both act upon and are acted on by their inhabitants. They act on people both directly and indirectly.

Although the data on child-care environments were far from adequate to perform this kind of analysis well, even this preliminary effort at ecological analysis was useful for understanding why children in daycare centers might be different from children at home. Ecological analyses produce an appealing sense of reality; they feel as if one is examining the "real world." They fit, too, with the contemporary trend in environmental research, away from the analysis of the immediate effects of isolated units of the environment toward the analysis of broad environmental contexts and macrosystems (Bronfenbrenner, 1979; Stokols, 1982; Stokols & Altman, 1986).

Another issue raised by the study of child-care environments, which will not be resolved even by taking a more comprehensive and integrated approach to analyzing environments, is the issue of cause and effect. This issue is best investigated by systematic experimentation. Analyses of the sort we have tried to do here provide a description of different environments and an abundance of hypotheses about their different effects—hypotheses that need to be tested experimentally and ecologically. In ecological experiments, as in ecological descriptions, researchers must find levels of analysis that combine both specificity and generality. What should be varied experimentally is neither isolated bits of behavior nor global chunks of the environment, but specific dimensions or clusters of dimensions in the environment. To carry out and evaluate "blunderbuss" experimental interventions is wasteful; to vary only highly specific components like types of toys, without looking at what the implications of the specific changes are for other components, like teaching methods, is shortsighted. We have a long, complicated, tedious way to go before we will fully understand the effects of real environments on human behavior and children's development. But we do know which direction to go.

References

Ackerman-Ross, S., & Khanna, P. (1989). The relationship of high quality day care to middle-class 3-year-olds' language performance. *Early Childhood Research Quarterly, 4,* 97–116.

Andersson, B.-E. (1989). Effects of public day care: A longitudinal study. *Child Development, 60,* 857–866.

Bronfenbrenner, U. (1979). *The ecology of human development.* Cambridge: Harvard University Press.

Bruner, J. (1980). *Under five in Britain.* London: Grant McIntyre.

Bryant, B., Harris, M., & Newton, D. (1980). *Children and minders.* London: Grant McIntyre.

Burchinal, M., Lee, M., & Ramey, C. (1989). Type of day care and preschool intellectual development in disadvantaged children. *Child Development, 60,* 128–137.

Busse, T. V., Ree, M., Gatride, M., & Alexander, T. (1972). Environmentally enriched classrooms and the cognitive and perceptual development of Negro preschool children. *Journal of Educational Psychology, 63,* 15–21.

Carew, J. (1980). Experience and the development of intelligence in young children. *Monographs of the Society for Research in Child Development, 45* (6–7, Serial No. 187).

Clarke-Stewart, K. A. (1984). Day care: A new context for research and development. In M. Perlmutter (Ed.), *The Minnesota Symposium on Child Psychology* (Vol. 17, pp. 61–100). Hillsdale, NJ: Erlbaum.

Clarke-Stewart, K. A., & Apfel, N. (1979). Evaluating parental effects on child development. In L. S. Shulman (Ed.) *Review of research in education* (Vol. 6, pp. 47–119). Itasca, IL: Peacock.

Clarke-Stewart, K. A., & Fein, G. G. (1983). Early childhood programs. In P. H. Mussen, M. Haith, & J. Campos (Eds.), *Handbook of child psychology* (Vol. 2, pp. 917–1000). New York: Wiley.

Clarke-Stewart, K. A., & Gruber, C. P. (1984). Day care forms and features. In R. C. Ainslie (Ed.), *The child and the day care setting* (pp. 35–62). New York: Praeger Special Studies.

Cochran, M. M. (1977). *Group day care and family childrearing patterns in Sweden.* Unpublished report to the Foundation for Child Development, Cornell University, Ithaca, NY.

Cole, M., Gay, J., Glick, J. A., & Sharp, D. W. (1971). *The cultural context of learning and thinking: An exploration in experimental anthropology.* New York: Basic Books.

Doyle, A., Connolly, J., & Rivest, L. (1980). The effect of playmate familiarity on the social interactions of young children. *Child Development, 51,* 217–223.

Dunn, L., & Kontos, S. (1989, April). *Influence of family day care quality and childrearing attitudes on children's play in family day care.* Paper presented at the biennial meeting of the Society for Research in Child Development, Kansas City, MO.

Edwards, C. P., Logue, M. E., Loehr, S., & Roth, S. (1986). The influence of model infant-toddler group care on parent-infant interaction at home. *Early Childhood Research Quarterly, 1,* 317–332.

Ferri, E. (1980). Combined nursery centres. *Concern,* National Children's Bureau, No. 37.

Fiene, R. J. (1973). *The differential structural characteristics of sentences formed by preschool children in family and group day care centers.* Stony Brook, New York: State University of New York. (ERIC ED 094 849)

Fosburg, S., Hawkins, P. D., Singer, J. D., Goodson, B. D., Smith, J. M., & Brush, L. R. (1980). *National Day Care Home Study.* Cambridge: Abt Associates.

Fowler, W. (1978). *Day care and its effects on early development: A study of group and home care in multi-ethnic, working-class families.* Toronto: Ontario Institute for Studies in Education.

Fowler, W., & Khan, N. (1974). *The later effects of infant group care.* Toronto: Ontario Institute for Studies in Education.

Garber, H., & Heber, R. (1980, April). *Modification of predicted cognitive development in high-risk children through early intervention.* Paper presented at the annual meeting of the American Educational Research Association, Boston, MA.

Goelman, H., & Pence, A. R. (1987). Effects of child care, family, and individual characteristics on children's language development: The Victoria Day Care Research Project. In D. A. Phillips (Ed.), *Quality in child care: What does research tell us?* (pp. 89–104). Washington, D.C.: National Association for the Education of Young Children.

Golden, M., Rosenbluth, L., Grossi, M. T., Policare, H. J., Freeman, H., & Brownlee, E. M. (1978). *The New York City Infant Day Care Study.* New York: Medical and Health Research Association of New York City.

Goodman, N., & Andrews, J. (1981). Cognitive development of children in family and group day care. *American Journal of Orthopsychiatry, 51,* 271–284.

Gunnarsson, L. (1977, August). *The Swedish childrearing study: A longitudinal study of children in different childrearing environments.* Paper prepared for the Conference on Research Perspectives in the Ecology of Human Development, Cornell University, Ithaca, NY.

Haskins, R. (1989). Beyond metaphor: Efficacy of early childhood education. *American Psychologist, 44,* 274–282.

Hayes, W. A., Massey, G. C., Thomas, E. A. C., David, J., Milbrath, C., Buchanan, A., & Lieberman, A. (1983). *Analytical and technical report of the National Infant Care Study.* San Mateo, CA: The Urban Institute for Human Services.

Hess, R. D., Price, G. G., Dickson, W. P., & Conroy, M. (1981). Different roles for mothers and teachers: Contrasting styles of child care. In S. Kilmer (Ed.), *Advances in early education and day care* (Vol. 2, pp. 1–28). Greenwich, Ct.: JAI Press.

Howes, C. (1983). Caregiver behavior in centers and family day care. *Journal of Applied Developmental Psychology, 4,* 99–107.

Howes, C., & Rubenstein, J. L. (1981). Toddler peer behavior in two types of day care. *Infant Behavior and Development, 4,* 387–394.

Johnson, J. E., Ershler, J., & Bell, C. (1980). Play behavior in a discovery-based and a formal-education program. *Child Development, 51,* 271–274.

Kagan, J., Kearsley, R. B., & Zelazo, P. R. (1978). *Infancy: Its place in human development.* Cambridge: Harvard University Press.

Kinney, P. F. (1989). *Antecedents of caregiver involvement with infants and toddlers in group care.* Unpublished doctoral dissertation, University of Maryland, Baltimore.

Lally, J. R., & Honig, A. S. (1977). *The Family Development Research Program* (Final Report, No. OCD-CB-100). Syracuse: University of Syracuse.

Lamb, M. E., Hwang, C-P., Broberg, A., & Bookstein, F. L. (1988). The effects of out-of-home care on the development of social competence in Sweden: A longitudinal study. *Early Childhood Research Quarterly, 3,* 379–402.

Larsen, J. M., & Robinson, C. C. (1989). Later effects of preschool on low-risk children. *Early Childhood Research Quarterly, 4,* 133–144.

Lazar, I., Hubbell, R., Murray, H., Rosche, M., & Royce, J. (1977). *The persistence of preschool effects: A long-term follow-up of fourteen infant and preschool experiments.* Final Report to Office of Human Development Services (Grant No. 18-76-07843). Ithaca: Cornell University Press.

Lee, V. E., Brooks-Gunn, J., Schnur, E., & Liaw, F-R. (1989). *Are Head Start effects sustained? A longitudinal followup comparison of disadvantaged children attending Head Start, no preschool, and other preschool programs.* Unpublished paper, University of Michigan, Ann Arbor.

Lieberman, A. F. (1977). Preschoolers' competence with a peer: Relations with attachment and peer experience. *Child Development, 48,* 1277–1287.

McCartney, K. (1984). Effect of quality of day care environment on children's language development. *Developmental Psychology, 20,* 244–260.

Meadows, S., Philips, J., Weaver, J., & Mably, S. (1977, December). *Adults' and children's views on education and their behavior at home and in nursery school.* Paper presented at the annual meeting of the British Psychological Society, London.

Melhuish, E. C. (1990). Research on day care for young children in the United Kingdom. In P. Moss & E. C. Melhuish (Eds.), *Day care and young children: Research and policy implications.* London: Department of Health.

Miller, L. B., & Dyer, J. L. (1975). Four preschool programs: Their dimensions and effects. *Monographs of the Society for Research in Child Development, 40* (5–6, Serial No. 162).

Moss, E., Blicharski, T., & Strayer, F. F. (1987, April). *Daycare experience and problem-solving tactics during the second year.* Paper presented at the biennial meeting of the Society for Research in Child Development, Baltimore, MD.

Peaslee, M. V. (1976). *The development of competency in 2-year-old infants in day care and home reared environments.* Unpublished doctoral dissertation, Florida State University, Tallahassee.

Pellegrini, A. D. (1984). The social cognitive ecology of preschool classrooms: Contextual relations revisited. *International Journal of Behavioral Development, 7,* 321–332.

Phillips, D. A., McCartney, K., & Scarr, S. (1987). Child-care quality and children's social development. *Developmental Psychology, 23,* 537–543.

Phillips, D. A., Scarr, S., & McCartney, K. (1987). Dimensions and effects of child care quality: The Bermuda study. In D. A. Phillips (Ed.), *Quality in child care: What does research tell us?* (pp. 43–56). Washington, D.C.: National Association for the Education of Young Children.

Powell, D. R. (1978). The interpersonal relationship between parents and caregivers in day care settings. *American Journal of Orthopsychiatry, 48,* 680–689.

Prescott, E. (1973). *A comparison of three types of day care and nursery school-home care.* (ERIC ED 078 910)

Provost, M. A. (1980). The effects of day care on child development. *Canada's Mental Health, 28,* 17–20.

Quilitch, H., & Risley, T. (1973). The effects of play materials on social play. *Journal of Applied Behavior Analyses, 6,* 573–578.

Ramey, C. T., Dorval, B., & Baker-Ward, L. (1983). Group day care and socially disadvantaged families: Effects on the child and the family. In S. Kilmer (Ed.), *Advances in early education and day care* (Vol. 3, pp. 69–106). Greenwich, CT: JAI Press.

Robinson, H. B., & Robinson, N. M. (1971). Longitudinal development of very young children in a comprehensive day care program. *Child Development, 42,* 1673–1683.

Robinson, J., & Corley, R. (1989, April). *The effects of day care participation: Sex differences in early and middle childhood.* Paper presented at the biennial meeting of the Society for Research in Child Development, Kansas City, MO.

Rohe, W., & Patterson, A. H. (1974). The effects of varied levels of resources and density on behavior in a day care center. In D. H. Carson (Ed.), *Man-environment interaction.* Washington: EDRA.

Rubenstein, J. L., & Howes, C. (1979). Caregiving and infant behavior in day care and in homes. *Developmental Psychology, 15,* 1–24.

Rubenstein, J. L., & Howes, C. (1983). Social-emotional development of toddlers in day care: The role of peers and of individual differences. In S. Kilmer (Ed.), *Advances in early education and day care* (Vol. 3, pp. 13–45). Greenwich, CT: JAI Press.

Rubenstein, J. L., & Howes, C., & Boyle, P. (1981). A two-year follow-up of infants in community based infant day care. *Journal of Child Psychology and Psychiatry, 22,* 209–218.

Ruopp, R., Travers, J., Glantz, F., & Coelen, C. (1979). *Children at the center.* Cambridge: Abt Associates.

Scarr, S., Lande, J., & McCartney, K. (1988). Child care and the family. In J. Lande, S. Scarr, & N. Gunzenhauser (Eds.), *Caring for children: Challenge to America.* Hillsdale, NJ: Erlbaum.

Schwarz, J. C., Krolick, G., & Strickland, R. G. (1973). Effects of early day care experience on adjustment to a new environment. *American Journal of Orthopsychiatry, 43,* 340–346.

Siegal, M., & Storey, R. M. (1985). Day care and children's conceptions of moral and social rules. *Child Development, 56,* 1001–1008.

Sigel, I. (1986). Early social experience and the development of representational competence. In W. Fowler (Ed.), *Early experience and the development of competence: New directions for child development* (No. 32, pp. 49–66). San Francisco: Jossey-Bass.

Sjolund, A. (1971). *The effect of day care institutions on children's development: An analysis of international research.* Copenhagen: Danish National Institute of Social Research.

Smith, P. K., & Connolly, K. J. (1980). *The ecology of preschool behaviour.* Cambridge: Cambridge University Press.

Stokols, B. (1982). Environmental psychology: A coming of age. In A. G. Kraut (Ed.), *The G. Stanley Hall Lecture Series.* Washington: American Psychological Association.

Stokols, D., & Altman, I. (Eds.). (1986). *Handbook of environmental psychology.* New York: Wiley.

Stukat, K. G. (1969). Lekkskolans inverkan pa barns utveckling (The influence of preschool on the child's development). Cited in Berfenstam, R., & William-Olsson, I. (1973). *Early child care in Sweden.* London: Gordon & Breach.

Sylva, K., Roy, C., & Painter, M. (1980). *Child watching at playgroup and nursery school.* London: Grant McIntyre.

Tietze, W. (1987). A structural model for the evaluation of preschool effects. *Early Childhood Research Quarterly, 2,* 133–153.

Tizard, B., Carmichael, H., Hughes, M., & Pinkerton, B. (1980). Four-year-olds talking to mothers and teachers. In L. A. Hersov & M. Berger (Eds.), *Language and language disorders in childhood.* London: Pergamon Press.

Tizard, B., Philips, J., & Plewis, I. (1976). Play in preschool centres—II. Effects on play of the child's social class and of the educational orientation of the centre. *Journal of Child Psychology and Psychiatry, 17,* 265–274.

Tyler, B., & Dittman, L. (1980). Meeting the toddler more than halfway: The behavior of toddlers and their caregivers. *Young Child, 35,* 39–46.

Vandell, D. L. (1979). Effects of a playgroup experience on mother–son and father–son interaction. *Developmental Psychology, 15,* 379–385.

Wachs, T. D., & Gruen, C. E. (1982). *Early experience and human development.* New York: Plenum Press.

Wadsworth, M. E. J. (1986). Effects of parenting style and preschool experience on children's verbal attainment: Results of a British longitudinal study. *Early Childhood Research Quarterly, 1,* 237–248.

Winnett, R. A., Fuchs, W. L., Moffatt, S., & Nerviano, V. J. (1977). A cross-sectional study of children and their families in different child care environments. *Journal of Community Psychology, 5,* 149–159.

Wittmer, D., & Honig, A. (1989, April). *Convergent or divergent? Teachers' questions to three-year-old children in day care.* Paper presented at the biennial meeting of the Society for Research in Child Development, Kansas City, MO.

4

The Family Environment

The Combined Influence of Family Behavior, Goals, Strategies, Resources, and Individual Experiences

SHARON LANDESMAN, JAMES JACCARD, AND
VIRGINIA GUNDERSON

Considerable research has been conducted on families—how families create, experience, and respond to the world in which they live. The purpose of this chapter is to describe a conceptual framework for studying the family environment which (1) incorporates recent advances in understanding multiple social influences on behavior, (2) recognizes both common and idiosyncratic characteristics of families as social units, (3) identifies research strategies to assess families, and (4) generates hypotheses about the reasons families vary in their functioning. The framework derives from theories and research in psychology, ethology, sociology, anthropology, and demography. We rely most heavily on empirical work in social ecology and in decision making, incorporating elements from existing theories and combining them operationally in our formulation of the family environment.

Studies of social influences on young children have tended to focus on a selected dyadic relationship (usually between a parent and child, sometimes between siblings or parents), a single aspect of family behav-

SHARON LANDESMAN • Departments of Psychiatry and Psychology, Frank Porter Graham Child Development Center, University of North Carolina at Chapel Hill, Chapel Hill, North Carolina 27599.   JAMES JACCARD • Department of Psychology, State University of New York at Albany, Albany, New York 12222.   VIRGINIA GUNDERSON • Department of Psychology, University of Washington, Seattle, Washington 98195.

ior (e.g., communication patterns, parental teaching style, allocation of responsibilities), or parental attributions and subjective ratings (e.g., understanding of normative development, ratings of parenting self-esteem, perceived family stress, adequacy of social support, satisfaction with the family). The results of these studies, especially those that are longitudinal, are relevant to understanding the social influences that operate within families and, in turn, that contribute to differential child outcomes. Organizing the numerous and diverse findings into a cohesive view of the *family environment* and *family effects*, however, is difficult, because the central theme or level of analysis is rarely the family unit per se. Although developmental psychologists share many implicit assumptions about the family environment, they seldom provide an explicit framework that defines the family unit, addresses the mission and commitment of families, considers how families are organized (from their inception through various life stages, including possible dissolution), and offers hypotheses about the *combined influence* of family environment variables on the young child.

Several recent trends in developmental psychology have yielded useful insights into the nature of the family environment. Investigators increasingly recognize that social relationships within the family are complex and can be described in terms of their bidirectionality, reciprocity, complementarity, situational sensitivity, indirect or second order influences, and integration within larger social-ecological contexts (e.g., Belsky, 1981; Bronfenbrenner, 1979; Clarke-Stewart, 1978; Dunn, 1983; Feinman & Lewis, 1984; Lewis, 1984; Lewis & Rosenblum, 1974, 1978, 1979; Maccoby & Martin, 1983; Parke, Power, & Gottman, 1979). The fervent period of microanalytic observation of mother-infant relationships has evolved to accommodate a broader conceptualization of the child's social network that recognizes the role of fathers, siblings, grandparents, and peers (e.g., Brody & Stoneman, 1986; Dunn & Kendrick, 1981; Lewis & Feiring, 1979, 1981; Lewis & Weinraub, 1976; MacDonald & Parke, 1984; Tinsley & Parke, 1984). Developmental psychologists often write about the family as a "system," borrowing heavily from the basic concepts of general systems theory (von Bertalanffy, 1968; Miller, 1965). For discussions and selected applications of a systems or multidimensional perspective to the family environment, see Belsky (1981), Bronfenbrenner (1979), Feiring and Lewis (1984), Lewis (1982), Parke (1986), Patterson (1982), Ramey, MacPhee, and Yeates (1983), Sameroff (1983), Sigel (1982), and Turnbull, Summers, and Brotherson (1986), among others. A systems framework also appears in the literature on clinical assessment and treatment of families (e.g., Bateson, Jackson, Haley, & Weakland, 1956; Epstein & Bishop, 1981; Gurman & Kniskern, 1981; Minuchin, 1974; Reiss, 1971a; Terkelsen, 1980). The theme "beyond the dyad" (Feinman & Lewis, 1984; Lewis, 1984) captures the spirit of present inquiry about social influences on young children.

Sociologists, in contrast to developmental psychologists, tend to approach the family as a social unit. Sociological literature is replete with theories about the nature of families and their role in societies (e.g., Beavers & Voeller, 1983; Elder, 1984; Epstein, Bishop, & Baldwin, 1982; Holman & Burr, 1980; Nye & Berardo, 1966; Olson, 1985; Olson, Russell, & Sprenkle, 1983; Olson, Sprenkle, & Russell, 1979). Such large-scale theories have contributed valuable concepts about the missions of families (e.g., intergenerational transmission of cultural information, efficient distribution of workload and management of resources) and the dimensions along which families may differ (e.g., family cohesion and adaptability, control orientation, expressive style, affective involvement, structural arrangement). Rarely, however, do sociologists study how the development of individual family members relates to variations in the family unit, even when within-family differences are studied (e.g., discrepancy in family members' perceptions, satisfaction, or behavior).

After reviewing the recent literature on families, we realized the potential value of proposing a system that would help facilitate the integration of principles and findings across disciplines. In this chapter, we begin by discussing basic issues in conceptualizing the family and its behavior as a unit. We then identify major domains of family functioning to underscore the importance of assessing the family environment in terms of its potential contribution to diverse aspects of development. Next, we present our conceptual framework designed to account for variation in the ways that families function across these domains. Four major elements relevant to family functioning are central in our thinking: *goals, strategies for attaining goals, resources,* and *individual life experiences.* We refer to this conceptual framework as GSRI, an acronym for the four elements. After describing the model, we consider the types of variables needed to apply the GSRI framework to a contextual analysis of family functioning and mention some related methodological issues. Finally, we compare GSRI to three other approaches—the confluence model (Zajonc, 1976, 1983; Zajonc & Markus, 1975; Zajonc, Markus, & Markus, 1979), the circumplex model (Olson *et al.*, 1983), and dimensional analyses of parenting behavior (e.g., Baumrind, 1966).

We recognize that in proposing such a conceptual framework, psychologists may criticize us for being too broad and ambitious, whereas sociologists and anthropologists may view us as too narrow. We hope, nonetheless, that a framework linking major family concepts and research from these diverse disciplines will further our ability to under-

stand the effects of families on children. Many concepts in our model are
similar to those in other frameworks, but we have tried to use general
words (rather than technical or theory-specific terminology) to describe
them. If a single theme underlying our conceptual framework must be
stated, it would be a rather obvious one—that the family environment is
multivariate in nature and a host of variables operate in a complex
fashion to influence family behavior and individual development. However, rather than waving the magic wand of "this is a complex multivariate phenomena" and then proceeding to focus on one or two variables,
we shall describe directly the multivariate complexity of the issues.

The Family: A Unit or a Collection of Subunits?

One dilemma investigators encounter when studying an individual's development within the family context is how to treat the concept of family. Is the family somehow more than the sum of its parts?
Can the family be studied as a unit without negating the significance of
specific dyadic relationships within it? Do family members, including
young children, have a concept of "family" or a collective "we" that is
distinct from their independent relationships with individual family
members? If so, to what extent do family members' notions of "family"
and their subjective experiences of their family influence actual family
behavior and individual child outcomes?

In a scholarly review of anthropological attempts to derive a "scientific, correct, and useful definition of the family," Yanagisako (1979) con-
cludes that we should abandon efforts to discover "the irreducible core
of the family and its universal definition" and instead "seek out the
functions of the family in each society" (p. 200). Accordingly, in our
conceptual framework, we define the family as: *a collection of individuals
who have a commitment to the general well-being of one another and who label
themselves a "family."* This definition is sensitive to the many structural
and demographic changes in American families. It implicitly recognizes
that criteria such as biological relatedness, a common place of residence,
anticipated stability of the unit, and focus on childrearing activities are
inadequate for purposes of identifying the diversity of families today.
Because our primary interest is how families function and what aspects
of the family environment have significant and pervasive effects on children, we have settled for a non-restrictive definition of the family. In
fact, this definition permits the possibility that individuals may belong
to more than one family at a time (Landesman, 1986).

Level of Analysis

Within a family, three levels of analysis are possible: (1) analysis at the level of individuals, (2) analysis at the level of social subunits (all combinations of two or more individuals), and (3) analysis at the level of the group as a whole. Ideally, an analysis of how a family functions would incorporate all three. In this conceptual framework, a family is described at the *individual level* by examining all family members' behavior, as well as their individual goals, strategies, resources, and experiences which pertain to family functioning. At the individual level of analysis, the family is equated with the composite obtained by considering each family member separately (i.e., the family equals the sum of its parts).

At the *social subunit level*, the nature of each dyad, triad, etc. is considered, including quantitative and qualitative descriptions of the similarities and differences of family members in each subunit. The subunits are viewed as having a valid existence that is distinct from, and not entirely predicted by, data concerning individuals. For example, when considering the parental dyad, a mother may have different goals or aspirations for her children than does the father. Or both parents may share the same goals, but select alternative strategies to help achieve them. For a given subunit, when family members have differing goals, strategies, resources, and/or individual experiences, these can be characterized as "conflicting" (i.e., the attainment of one person's goals would prevent the attainment of the other person's goals), "non-implicative" (i.e., one person's goals, if realized, would not affect the achievement of another's goals), or "complementary" (i.e., success in reaching one person's goals fosters the attainment of the other person's goals). We hypothesize that social subunits have effects on how the family actually behaves, above and beyond those attributable to the individuals within these subunits. These effects represent *relativistic* or *relational* properties that theoretically have significant social influences in their own right. Two mothers from different families, for example, may have identical goals, similar strategies for attaining them, comparable resources, and equivalent individual life experiences relevant to their functioning as mothers. Yet, these maternal variables may have significantly different meaning and consequences in the two families depending on the degree to which other family members have goals that are similar, conflicting, non-implicative, or complementary to the mother's.

At the *level of the family as a whole*, the objective is to describe the family as a single unit. To achieve this, one approach involves a contextual analysis that simultaneously considers the GSRI profiles of all family members. This then yields a single characterization of the entire family unit. A second approach treats the family as a single subject. For instance, an investigator might observe the activities of family members, which then are converted to a single code to describe the entire family. Similarly, judgments can be made about a family's overall or collective strategies to achieve goals. Finally, a third approach is to use "family" as a conceptual entity. This approach recognizes that most family members have and use a concept of the collective unit (i.e., "we are a family") which may mediate aspects of their behavior. (For an excellent discussion of this topic, see Reiss, 1971a, 1971b.) Theoretically, the collected statements and ratings by family members about their perceptions of their family "as a whole" may not be a simple function of component analyses at the individual and subunit levels. In essence, an abstracted conception of "family" can be created, by a variety of empirical methods, and used to study changes over time and effects of the "family" on children's outcomes. (Note: Effects of family members' notions of "our family" may be studied at the individual and the social subunit levels as well as at the collective level.)

Investigators frequently overlook the context-dependent nature of a family member's goals, strategies, resources, and individual life experiences or characteristics. Investigators often measure such variables for only one family member at a time and then relate these data to child outcomes. Even when measures for multiple family members are obtained, the data rarely are treated in a contextual manner. Rather, the relative contributions of each set of variables tend to be explored in a main effects regression model. In contrast, we hypothesize that family functioning and, in turn, how the family environment contributes to different child outcomes, will be influenced not only by the *content* of each family member's behavior, goals, strategies for attaining goals, resources, and experiences, but also by the *context* in which these are expressed. That is, *the functional consequences of the GSRI elements and family behavior will be relativistic rather than absolute.* For example, the consequences of parental punishment on a child will be influenced, in part, by contextual variables such as the frequency of punishment, the meaning family members attach to the punishment, the responses of other family members to the child's punishment, and the extent to which other family members are treated similarly for their transgressions.

Although we emphasize the importance of assessing each family member's goals, strategies, resources, and individual life experiences, we do not assume that the GSRI profiles of family members are independent of one another. For example, the goals of individual family members frequently emerge through discussions and interactions with other family members. The elements of GSRI (described below) are viewed as dynamic and interdependent.

FAMILY BEHAVIOR AND FUNCTIONAL DOMAINS

In our model, *family behavior* is defined as: *the overt behavior of family members, generally enacted so as to realize the goals for the family unit.* The behavior of family members outside the family realm is not included in this definition, although this can affect family functioning. For instance, a child's school adjustment is not considered part of family behavior, even though this may influence the family. Similarly, a parent's activities at work are not viewed as family behavior, but these may influence the parent's behavior toward other family members or may change the parent's goals or resources related to the family.

We categorize family behavior into six major functional domains: (1) physical development and health, (2) emotional development, (3) social development, (4) cognitive development, (5) moral and spiritual development, and (6) cultural and aesthetic development. Table 1 describes these goal-related domains. Each corresponds to a major area of research in child development and represents a realm in which the family environment theoretically can influence a child. We do not limit social influence analysis, however, to the children in a family. Physical development and health, emotional development, social development, cognitive development, moral development, and cultural and aesthetic development are ongoing enterprises at all ages. Most families consider these domains important for all family members throughout the family's lifetime.

For a given family or family member, the relative emphasis on different goal-related domains is determined, in part, by variables such as the ages of family members (e.g., relatively more emphasis may be placed by the parent on physical development and health when children are infants than when they are adolescents), the family's value system (e.g., parents who value formal education highly are likely to spend more time and resources related to cognitive development than parents who do not), and the society in which the family lives (e.g., a family in a communal or cooperative society may be more concerned about social and moral development than is a typical family in an individually competitive society). Families also differ in how much family members agree with one another regarding the relative priorities for these broad developmental domains.

TABLE 1.   Six Major Goal-Related Domains of Family Functioning

Domain 1: Physical development and health
Concerns meeting basic needs for survival, such as providing food, housing, and
clothing; promoting good health (medical and dental care, good nutrition, personal
hygiene); arranging for child care (responsible adult supervision when children do not
have minimal self-care skills); and insuring safety (protection from potential physical or
social harm, procedures for handling emergencies).

Domain 2: Emotional development and well-being
Refers to acquiring emotional self-regulation, fostering positive expression of emotional
states, encouraging constructive ways to deal with emotions (especially negative states),
developing the capacity to give and receive love (both within and outside the family
context), learning to assess the emotional needs of other people, and maintaining good
mental health.

Domain 3: Social development
Refers to developing positive interaction skills to initiate and maintain relationships,
acquiring the ability to avoid and/or resolve social conflict, and recognizing the role of
the individual in group contexts, both within and outside the family unit.

Domain 4: Cognitive development
Encompasses activities that foster intelligence and academic skills (e.g., formal
education), daily living skills (e.g., money management, transportation use), and future
vocational competence; learning to think critically and creatively, and understanding
how to evaluate one's own thought processes.

Domain 5: Moral and spiritual development
Includes efforts to help family members acquire beliefs and values about ethical
behavior and a philosophy of life. Examples of activities that foster the acquisition of
such beliefs and values are religious education and practices, discussion of basic values,
and reasoning about moral dilemmas.

Domain 6: Cultural and aesthetic development
Includes activities that foster an appreciation of one's own and others' cultural heritage,
folklore, and traditions, as well as help one develop a personal sense of beauty and art.

Because families are hypothesized to show unevenness in how skillfully they function across the six domains, we view any attempt to
generate a global or unidimensional assessment of a family (e.g., as
more or less "successful," "supportive," "normal," or "cohesive") as
limited in value and likely to be misleading. Multidimensional study, in
contrast, permits identifying a family's domain-specific strengths and
weaknesses and yields a family profile suitable for making precise predictions about the effects of family environments on selected aspects of
development. Different combinations of environmental variables will
facilitate or hinder "success" (i.e., achievement of goals) in the various
functional domains. Family behavior is expected to change over time
and across situations, as a direct result of shifts in the family's goals,

strategies and plans, resources, and individual experiences relative to the six functional domains. We further recognize the potential for cross-domain conflicts or cross-domain enhancement in family functioning. That is, a family's behavior at a given time may serve multiple functions: An activity that enhances functioning in one domain may also advance, or restrict, functioning in other domains. Similarly, individuals or sub-units within the family may benefit from certain behavioral decisions or activities, while others within the same family may be adversely affected.

THE FAMILY ENVIRONMENT

We define the *family environment* as: the family's behavior (see above) and the combined goals, strategies, resources, and individual life experiences of family members. This definition includes physical and behavioral features of the environment, as well as the subjective experiences and emotions of family members. The family environment is not thought of as something that influences family behavior. Rather, family behavior is part of the environment. What is important to study is how different aspects of the family environment relate to one another (e.g., how goals relate to family behavior; how family behavior affects a family member's emotions or moods) and, in turn, how these jointly contribute to child and family outcome variables.

The characterization of the family environment is expected to vary depending on the level of analysis—individual, subunit, or the "family as a whole"—and the perspective of the informants and the investigator. These different views of the family environment can be powerful tools in studying the impact of the family environment on children.

THE GSRI ELEMENTS

We view the behavior of families in each of the functional domains as the product of four primary elements: (1) their goals, (2) their strategies or plans to attain those goals, (3) their resources, and (4) their individual life experiences. These GSRI elements are related, but distinct. We define each separately, then suggest ways that the elements influence one another and combine to affect family functioning and child outcomes. When discussing each element, we usually will characterize it from the perspective of an individual family member, typically the parent. However, consistent with our previous comments, the analysis of each element should be undertaken at all three levels within the context of the family unit.

Element 1: Goals

Goals are central to understanding family functioning. Goals reflect a family's ambitions, hopes, and values. A goal is a desired end state (e.g., good health, happiness, educational achievement) or a desired mode of conduct (e.g., honest, respectful of others, creative). Families are goal oriented in that they function to achieve desired end states and desired modes of conduct for family members and for the family unit as a whole. Goals of family members may be grouped according to the functional domains listed in Table 1.

Goals may be characterized in a variety of ways. Here, we mention some characteristics of family goals that we posit are important to consider when studying differences across families. First, goals may be classified as (a) universal (i.e., shared by almost all families across cultures and over time), (b) culture-specific (i.e., prevalent in a given culture), and (c) family-specific (i.e., operative for a particular family unit). An example of a universal family goal is providing adequate food and protection; a culture-specific goal in the United States is schooling for children until 16 years of age; and a family-specific goal may be having children who are athletic or musical. Second, goals may be explicit or implicit (i.e., more or less recognized by family members). A family member may think consciously about the best way to attain a goal and, hence, explicitly consider it when deciding how to behave. By contrast, implicit goals sometimes reflect societal values which are so fundamental that family members consider them only when the goals are blocked or others question them. Third, goals differ in their importance or centrality to a family. The importance assigned to family goals may be influenced by available resources, current needs of family members, prior experiences, and individuals' basic values and preferences. Fourth, goals are developmental and not static. Families often assess and modify their goals. As families progress in their life courses, both chronologically and experientially, re-evaluation of goals and their priorities is expected. Fifth, goals may be either short term or long term. Short-term goals are frequently "steps" toward attaining long term goals. Sixth, many family goals are interrelated or mutually dependent, although some may be independent. This means that choices related to a given family goal may have implications for other goals. Seventh and finally, goals may differ for family members. A family's goals thus may be characterized by the extent to which they are shared by family members and whether there are conflicts among the family goals of individuals. Careful delineation of the interdependence among a family's implicit and explicit goals is important for evaluating how effectively a family functions in each domain and for understanding why certain aspects of family behavior are associated with differential success in meeting goals.

To understand differences in family or child outcomes, it is useful to study family members' goals. A comprehensive profile for a family would include goals relevant to each functional domain (see Table 1). After listing domain-specific goals, their relative importance, stability, etc. may be considered. For example, one family's goals for moral development may include having the children adopt the parents' religious practices wholeheartedly, encouraging compassion and helpfulness towards those whose lives are less fortunate, and adopting high standards for self-performance in all aspects of their lives. This family's goals might be characterized further as follows: highly conventional within their community, only moderately explicit, judged of very high importance by the family, relatively stable over the years, highly compatible with this family's goals in other domains, and agreed upon by the parents but not necessarily by the children. A second family, in contrast, may hold moral development goals that are the same in content, but less normative within this family's community. Further, compared to the first family, the second family's goals may be far less explicit, judged by the family as less important than are goals in other domains, more fluctuating and vulnerable to external influences, somewhat at odds with other family goals, and less agreed upon by individual family members. In sum, goals need to be described in terms of their actual content, their form (e.g., the characteristics identified above), and their contextual aspects.

Element 2: Strategies and Plans

Family members need to devise strategies and plans that will enable them to attain their goals. A family, in general, is hypothesized to function better if good decision making and problem solving strategies are present. Thus, decision making skills are hypothesized to be an important mediator of the effects of external variables on family functioning. Families in which members are better decision makers or problem solvers, and are able to follow through behaviorally, are predicted to be more likely to achieve their goals and to be more satisfied with their families.

We define a *family problem* as the failure to realize a goal or to make satisfactory progress toward goal attainment. How well a family functions is determined partially by family members' abilities to solve problems as well as to make decisions that maximize achieving family goals. In some cases, goal conflict itself can create problems for a family. In this section, we discuss a range of activities individuals can engage in during decision making and problem solving, and factors that characterize "good" decisions and "effective" solutions. Our primary focus is on decisions that the individual actively thinks about, in which the individual considers such issues as the alternative courses of action available and their probable consequences. We recognize that many behavioral decisions related to a family's everyday life are not of this character. However, when family members perceive that an issue or problem is important, they are likely to reflect on the matter. Their future behavior then may be affected by these reflections, even though the individual may not be engaged in active thought or evaluation each time the behavior is performed.

Activities in Behavioral Decision Making and Problem Solving

Research concerning decision making and problem solving has identified multiple activities that an individual can engage in during decision making or problem solving (e.g., Abelson & Levi, 1985; Jaccard & Wood, 1986) Table 2 describes eight primary activities. Not all of these activities necessarily are performed by an individual in making a given decision or solving a particular problem. Nor must the activities be performed in the sequence described. Each activity, however, is important to consider when evaluating the decision making or problem solving strategies operative within a family.

Optimal Strategies for Decision Making and Problem Solving

The identification of good decision makers/problem solvers is difficult and requires value judgments. Decision theorists typically distinguish between "good" decisions in terms of outcome or process. From an outcome perspective, an optimal decision is one in which the "best" option is chosen, where "best" is defined on the basis of external criteria (e.g., successfully attaining a goal with no detrimental effects). From a process perspective, the focus is not on the option that is chosen, but rather, on the process that the individual engages in. Certain decision making activities usually yield better decisions or solutions. An optimal decision from a process perspective is one that follows these prescribed activities. Theoretically, an individual can make a good decision in terms of outcome without engaging good decision making processes. Conversely, good strategies do not guarantee good outcomes.

Good planning strategies, decision making orientations, and problem solving methods can be elaborated for the eight activities in Table 2. For (1) problem recognition, good decision makers show sensitivity to cues in their environment which suggest a decision needs to be made. Additionally, they anticipate and try to prevent problems from developing, and confront problems directly, when appropriate. For (2) goal

TABLE 2. Strategic Activities in Family Decision Making/Problem Solving

1. *Recognizing the need for active decision making or problem solving*
The individual determines that a decision is needed or a problem state exists; therefore, a strategy or plan to correct the situation must be considered. Families vary considerably in how sensitive they are in detecting certain family problems and in recognizing that a thoughtful choice at a given time may foster achievement of their own family goals.

2. *Defining the desired outcomes*
The individual specifies a priori what an ideal solution or decision would be, making explicit his or her goals and values as well as the criteria for "success."

3. *Generating options*
The individual thinks of multiple ways that potentially could solve the issue or help realize the goal.

4. *Gathering information*
The individual seeks information, either about what additional strategies or solutions might be available (e.g., approaches other families have used or professionals recommend) or about properties of one or more of the options (e.g., how time consuming, expensive, or difficult a given strategy might be to enact) under consideration.

5. *Assessing relevant option information*
The individual consciously considers the information he or she has about the different strategies and their probable outcomes. The term "information" is used in a general sense and refers to any anticipated consequences or characteristics subjectively associated with a given behavioral option or strategy. Based on this information, the individual forms preferences for some options or alternative solutions.

6. *Selecting a strategy or making a choice*
The individual selects one of the decision options or problem solutions for the purposes of future behavioral enactment.

7. *Behavioral translation*
The individual transforms the decision choice or proposed solution into overt behavior.

8. *Post-decision evaluation*
The individual reflects on the decision after the strategy option has been enacted, then evaluates the choice (and the decision making process) in light of the outcomes that have resulted. The individual's subjective feelings are often as important as are objective criteria in this evaluative stage.

---

identification, good strategizers explicitly identify the criteria and goals that they want to use to evaluate their decision options. Concerning (3) option identification, good decision makers initially consider a wide range of solutions or plans, and are able to generate creative strategies to the problem or situation. For (4) information assessment and search, good strategies depend on an individual's recognition of the limits of the information he/she has initially and his/her ability to identify expert and reliable sources for gathering additional information. Understanding how much information is necessary is important as well, because excessive information gathering can be as problematic as an inadequate search. Regarding (5) option evaluation, effective problem solvers base their preferences on careful consideration of all relevant information, including short-term and long-term consequences and anticipated effects on others. Decision making frequently requires that a person "trade-off" advantages and disadvantages. Good decision makers recognize the trade-offs they make, and judge these in terms of the variables they deem important. For (6) the choice process per se, individuals ideally should choose options they feel most positively towards, all things considered. For (7) behavioral translation, good problem solvers explicitly consider conditions that may interfere with effective behavioral performance (e.g., their own emotional reactions, responses of other family members, adequacy of resources) and develop strategies to deal with these. Finally, (8) good decision makers and problem solvers continue reflecting on their decisions and solutions after they have enacted them. These individuals evaluate new information that becomes available, both from firsthand and vicarious experience, and modify their behavior when appropriate.

Strategies within the Family Context

Family members may differ in their decision making and problem solving skills. One family member might be adept at one decision making or problem solving activity (e.g., recognition of the need for a decision or problem solution), but poor with respect to another activity (e.g., information gathering). Furthermore, the individual's ability to make a good decision, either in terms of process or outcome, can vary across functional domains. A parent may be good in deciding how to foster a child's cognitive development but not as competent in solving interpersonal conflicts that arise within the family. Similarly, a young child may be able to participate in some types of family planning activities, but may lack the minimal skills needed to contribute in other areas. Families thus may be described in terms of the decision making abilities or problem solving strategies of individual family members relative to each functional domain. When considering analysis of the family at the social subunit level or the family as a whole, in some situations, decision skills will be *compensatory,* such that one family member's weaknesses can be offset by another family member's strengths. In other situations, a family's ability to cope with a problem will be *non-compensatory,* with performance either a function of the level of the "best" decision maker or the "worst" decision maker, depending on the roles they play in the family.

Thus, overall family functioning will be influenced not only by the independent decision making abilities of individual family members, but also by such variables as who has primary responsibility for decision making related to particular goals, how family members resolve conflict, and who monitors the consequences of particular decisions. Finally, the decision making abilities of family members may be influenced by current family goals and their priorities, by the available social and financial resources, and by changes in the individuals' life experiences. For example, emotional states (such as anger or depression) and personality orientations (e.g., impulsiveness) may adversely affect the decision making process.

Element 3: Resources

Family resources consist of the social, physical, and financial means available to achieve family goals. Social resources include immediate family members, the extended family, friends, neighbors, and local groups (e.g., church, community mental health center, cooperative nursery). Physical resources consist of the family's residence and its contents, as well as outside objects and services related to family functioning (e.g., means of transportation, telecommunication, recreation, education, home maintenance). Financial resources include cash, savings, and assets that are available to (or will become available to) the family. The family's resource inventory may be characterized in part by the number, arrangement, accessibility, and functional use of resources. These resources are integrally related to many aspects of family functioning. Family members clearly help shape their social and physical environments. At the same time, the resources available to families influence their activities. Environmental variables outside the family unit also may exert indirect effects on family functioning (e.g., economic climate, availability of housing, quality of public schools).

Regarding social support, we adopt a fourfold dimensionalization that derives from extensive empirical research (e.g., Brownell & Shumaker, 1984; Gottlieb, 1981). Specifically, the four major types of social support are (1) instrumental (i.e., direct help), (2) informational, (3) emotional/personal, and (4) companionship/recreational. To obtain an overview of a family's social resources, an inventory can be compiled of the individuals whom each family member perceives to be available to provide different types of social support, how often the family member seeks such support from each person, how satisfied he or she is with the support provided, and whether there are any problems associated with receiving such support (independent of level of satisfaction).

In our framework, resources do not have absolute or inherent value;

rather, they must be evaluated in a contextual manner. To judge the adequacy of a family's resources, each resource must be considered in terms of its potential to facilitate achieving specific family goals. Resources may be characterized by their type (e.g., social, physical, financial), their relevance to each domain of family functioning (Table 1), their frequency of use by different family members, and their perceived adequacy by family members. Like behavior, a single resource may serve multiple purposes. Furthermore, both social and non-social resources can be used in different ways by different family members, and may be judged as more or less adequate at different times or in different situations.

Element 4: Individual Life Experiences

For each family, the life experiences of its members contribute in diverse—and obviously complex—ways to family functioning. Although the concept of life experiences is broad and theoretically could encompass a person's entire developmental history, we use the concept more restrictively to study family functioning. Generally, an individual's life experiences, coupled with genetic and biological factors, manifest themselves in the form of cognitive, affective, and behavioral orientations to one's current environment. The GSRI framework focuses on those select aspects of past and/or present life experiences that are hypothesized to affect family functioning. We group these individual variables into four categories (1) personality-based orientations, (2) emotional and affective reactions, (3) cognitive and intellectual abilities, and (4) beliefs and attitudes pertaining to the family, family behavior, and family roles. Each category consists of some features that remain relatively stable over time and others that are more transitory or related to immediate environmental stresses and opportunities.

Personality-Based Orientations

Useful taxonomies of personality-based orientations have been presented by Cattell (1965), Eysenck (1953), Jackson (1967), and Norman (1963), among others, and include such constructs as extroversion, empathy, impulsiveness, conscientiousness, and locus of control. Such variables may relate to family behavior, goals, strategies, and resources, as well as to child and family outcome variables. For example, locus of control may affect goal setting: Individuals who perceive having little control over their lives may set fewer goals and engage in less purposive achievement strategies than do those who sense having more influence. Eysenck and Eysenck (1977) have identified impulsiveness, risk-taking, planfulness, and decision ease as personality dimensions that affect decision making. Numerous personality-like variables also may impinge on joint decision making in families and on the interaction that occurs when making such decisions. Examples include emotional expressiveness, the sex role orientation of the participants, dominance, flexibility, and social and empathic skills. Finally, given equal resources, families may vary in their use of those resources as a function of individual difference variables and their previous experiences. For example, individuals who are extroverted may be more willing to seek out certain types of social support than are comparatively introverted individuals. See Hamilton (1984) for a useful discussion of personality variables in a cognitive context.

Emotional and Affective Reactions

Emotional and affective variables can range from feelings about one's self-worth and satisfaction with one's life situation to emotional responses triggered by other family members and general mood stability. This category also includes the more traditional conceptualizations of emotional states. Useful taxonomies of adult emotions have been presented by Daly, Lancee, and Polivy (1983) and Buck (1985). Lewis and Michalson (1983) have provided valuable speculations about the development of children's moods and emotions. Hamilton (1984) describes the concept of emotions from a cognitive perspective. Recently, Gottman and Levinson (1986) have reported on long-term consequences associated with couples' patterns of emotional interaction.

Emotional states and degree of satisfaction with others or oneself clearly can affect a family member's goals, strategies, and resources as well as their everyday behavior. For example, a parent who is emotionally distressed in his or her marriage may be less likely to make the effort required to confront certain family problems. He or she also may be less inclined to consider the implications of his or her decisions for others or may be less sensitive to family problems when they occur. This may make matters worse, thereby leading to greater dissatisfaction and a situation of reciprocal causality.

Cognitive and Intellectual Abilities

Cognitive and intellectual abilities refer to both general intelligence and more specialized cognitive abilities of the individual (e.g., Gardner,

1984; Sternberg, 1986).[1] Such variables are relevant in our framework. For example, one variable that affects goal setting and goal orientations is the extent to which an individual can engage in both concrete and abstract thinking. To reflect on long-term goals, or those that cannot be realized until much later, requires a certain degree of abstract thought. A person who tends to think only in "here-and-now" terms generally will have a different goal structure (e.g., more short-term goals) than will someone who thinks more futuristically. An individual's intelligence also may contribute to how thoroughly and effectively decision making or problem solving activities are conducted. A child's characteristics, such as reasoning ability and interest in learning, may influence the availability of certain types of resources (e.g., quantity and developmental level of games and educational materials, extracurricular lessons, and time invested by parents in joint learning activities).

Beliefs and Attitudes Pertaining to the Family

This category encompasses perceptions of the family as a unit, beliefs about the different roles that family members should have, and interpretations of family members' behavior (including one's own behavior) in the context of the family. The beliefs that a family member holds about the proper functioning of the family and why family members behave as they do can have a powerful influence on the family's behavior, goals, strategies for attaining goals, and use of resources. Such belief systems will shape one's interpretation of family problems and family successes. Thus, we posit that parents' beliefs may exert an influence on children both directly (e.g., creating an interpretative framework for children) and indirectly, via parental behavior (e.g., providing models, setting limits on the children). For interesting approaches to the analysis

---

[1]Technically, problem solving and decision making skills, discussed in the context of the second GSRI element, are largely "cognitive" and can be considered an "individual characteristic" which belongs in this fourth component of GSRI. We distinguish between decision making activities (element 2 of GSRI) and decision making skills. The former refers to the decision making process per se and how the individual enacts the eight different components of decision making (i.e., the decision making activities of the individual). In contrast, problem solving and decision making skills refer to characteristics of the individual that promote effective performance of the various decision activities. These skills obviously will have a strong impact on decision making and problem solving activities. To avoid confusion and because of its natural relation to the decision making process in the family, the notion of decision making skills is treated in the second GSRI element. This is analogous to the distinction between "intelligence" and "intelligent behavior."

of parental belief systems, see Mancuso and Handin (1983) and Sigel and Laosa (1983).

Family belief systems derive, in part, from one's own family of origin. Many aspects of family functioning show an almost routine pattern. To the extent that parents select strategies based on their own childhood experiences—re-enacting positive behavioral solutions and correcting or eliminating negative ones—then parents' prior life experiences mediate an *intergenerational effect* on their children. Similarly, older siblings may display behavior that is the result of their personal history of interaction with their parents, which in turn creates an altered behavioral environment for the younger siblings.

The above four categories of individual variables are neither mutually exclusive nor exhaustive. They are interrelated and operate interactively. As emphasized earlier, when life experience variables are analyzed in relation to the family environment, it is important to keep in mind their context-dependent nature. Two mothers may be equally high in intelligence, for example, but the level of intelligence will take on quite different meaning in the context of the family if one is a single parent whereas the other is married to a spouse of much lower intelligence.[2]

In sum, within any given family, there is a context of personalities, emotions, cognitive and intellectual abilities, and family belief systems within which family behavior is enacted. This aspect of the family environment is a critical element to include in the analysis of family functioning and family success.

FAMILY OUTCOMES AND SUCCESSFUL FAMILIES

Family success may be measured in terms of how well a family functions relative to achieving family goals. The family goals used in judging success may be identified either by family members (i.e., self-defined) or by external sources (e.g., community, investigator). In this framework, the merit of particular parenting beliefs, values, and practices or the effects of different family resources are evaluated by measuring the degree to which these foster or hinder achieving particular family goals. We do not endorse an a priori notion of what constitutes optimal family

---

[2]We recognize that the above statements are general and provide little guidance as to exactly what life experiences and orientations an investigator should focus on when applying GSRI. This is because the relevant individual characteristics and experiences will depend upon the functional domain of interest and the specific hypotheses being tested.

functioning or an ideal family environment, except to state generally that "good" families will engage in activities that will maximize realizing specified family goals or child outcomes. Conclusions about how successfully a family functions in particular domains may differ depending on whether a family's own criteria or external standards are used. Further, simple measures, such as the number of achieved goals or the number of important unmet goals, convey only limited information, because families differ in the number of goals they set, how explicit their goals are, the proportion of goals shared or recognized by family members, and whether their goals are long versus short term.

The definition of family "success" as the achievement of (or satisfactory progress towards) family goals places the concept of "optimal family functioning" within a relativistic framework. For one family member, the family might be highly "successful," whereas for another family member, it may not be. If a father places high priority on the goal that his child be religious, and if the child is not, then from the father's perspective, a "problem" exists (in this case, in the moral and spiritual development domain). In contrast, the mother may be indifferent about the religiosity of her child, and the fact that the child is not religious does not constitute a family failure from her perspective.

Relationship of GSRI Profiles to Family Behavior and Family Outcomes

Figure 1 depicts postulated relationships among GSRI, family behavior, and outcome variables. Outcomes are conceptualized as being a direct result of the family environment, including the elements of GSRI and family behavior. In addition, GSRI and family behavior have reciprocal causal relations: Family behavior is influenced by the goals, strategies, resources, and individual life experiences of family members. Conversely, the GSRI elements can be modified in light of the behavior of family members. Family outcomes at any given point in time are hypothesized to influence GSRI at later times vis-à-vis its reciprocal (but lagged) influence on the GSRI elements. Thus, the GSRI framework explicitly recognizes the importance of feedback mechanisms within the family cycle. By using the GSRI framework to assess families longitudinally, developmental processes can be studied. Consistent with the relativistic perspective, a family's cumulative GSRI history is predicted to influence later outcomes (i.e., both present and past GSRIs contribute to child and family outcomes). Further, a child's age and individual characteristics are hypothesized to interact with the family environment, so

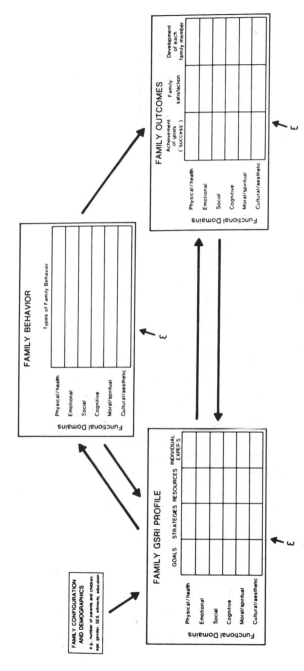

Fig. 1. Schematic representation of the GSRI conceptual framework for studying family behavior and outcomes. ε indicates exogenous influences.

that what comprises an optimal environment will vary with a child's stage of development and temperament.

EXTERNAL AND DEMOGRAPHIC INFLUENCES ON THE FAMILY ENVIRONMENT

Sociologists and psychologists have studied extensively the impact on child development of such variables as social class, family size, birth order, parental age and education, religion, and life transitions. Although this research has yielded interesting findings, it can be criticized for failing to identify important variables that mediate the influence of these variables on child development. In our view, it is not sufficient to say, for example, that birth order "influences" the intelligence of the child. Rather we want to obtain a better understanding of why these two variables are related and the processes that account for the relationship. The GSRI framework is designed to identify combinations of variables that may mediate the effects of "static" or "distal" variables. Thus, differences in children's intelligence associated with the above "static" variables must be related to identifiable differences in family behavior and in the goals, strategies for attaining goals, resources, and individual life experiences for differing types of families.[3] By applying GSRI, a more comprehensive picture of how such external variables combine to affect children's development can be obtained. This is especially important from the standpoint of social interventions. For example, if the objective is to improve children's academic motivation and performance, variables such as social class, birth order, and parental age are not amenable to ready change. In contrast, selected elements within the GSRI framework which vary with such external variables may be suitable for change (e.g., encouraging parents to modify their goals or adopt more effective problem solving strategies).

In this section, we briefly consider two major classes of variables that are external to the GSRI model, but whose effects on child develop-

---

[3]We fully recognize that for almost every interesting child outcome, biological factors are operative, even though the model is not designed to assess their precise contribution. In the above example, we realize that intergenerational health effects could be mediated via non-genetic routes, such as a mother's nutritional status at time of puberty affecting the prenatal nutritional status of her offspring, which in turn could affect vulnerability to certain health problems in childhood. Similarly, we do not discount the importance of heredity in determining a child's academic and intellectual performance. Rather, the GSRI model focuses on those aspects theoretically amenable to change via the social environment of the family.

ment are hypothesized to be mediated, in large part, by the GSRI elements.

Historical, Structural, and Intergenerational Variables

Numerous variables will affect the components of GSRI. One class of such variables is that related to historical, structural, and intergenerational phenomena. Consider a person's family of origin. We posit that the type of family (configuration) in which an individual grew up will influence his or her later behavior as a parent, as well as feelings about the type of family he or she creates. A single mother, for example, who grew up in a single parent home may be more satisfied with this type of family and is more likely to have a wide range of experiences relevant to functioning as a single parent than does a woman who grew up in a traditional two parent family. In two parent families, similarities and differences between a mother's and father's family of origin experiences may be important influences on how their present family functions. Other important classes of external variables considered here are cohort effects and family structural features.

Environmental and Psychological Demands on the Family

A second class of variables for which GSRI analysis might prove fruitful are those concerning environmental and psychological demands on the family. For example, if a child is identified as a "slow learner" and "highly inattentive" pupil in school, the parents might experience additional external demands related to having the child (and perhaps the entire family) evaluated, participating in the development and conduct of behavioral programs to help the child, and cooperating with the school in more frequent monitoring of their child's progress. Such a situation may create changes that affect many other aspects of that family's functioning, based on increased demands related to parents' time with the target child and the school, emotional involvement (or withdrawal) from the child and/or other family members, the cost of diagnostic and treatment services, etc. Other examples of environmental and psychological demands include change in parental employment status, parental needs to assume caretaking responsibility for their elderly parents, or the onset of physical or mental health problems in a family member. In a longitudinal framework, the adaptation strategies used by families when under such external constraints can be identified and evaluated in terms of their relative effectiveness.

Using GSRI to Profile Families: Variables and Methods

Variables

A family profile may be generated by evaluating a family's goals, strategies and plans for attaining goals, resources, and individual life experiences across different functional domains. Table 3 suggests some of the variables that might be assessed for each aspect of GSRI. The

TABLE 3.   Examples of Variables Relevant to Generating Family Profiles[a]

Goals
Number of goals; qualitative content of goals; relative importance of goals; relationships between goals; long term and short term goals; stability of goals; communality of each of the above among family members, including the delineation of conflicting goals and different points of emphasis.

Strategies and Plans
Ability to perceive and anticipate problems; acceptance of responsibility for making decisions; awareness of the criteria or goals that are to be considered when making a choice; ability to generate a range of options to consider when approaching a problem or decision, and to do so in a creative fashion; ability to recognize limited information and to gather necessary information in an efficient fashion; awareness of the trade-offs made in choosing an option; ability to consider a wide array of information when evaluating options; logical consistency in preference formation; anticipation and the ability to circumvent obstacles to carrying out the decision; evaluating one's decision, especially in light of new information and self-knowledge (e.g., recognizing emotional or irrational factors that will influence decision choice or ability to implement a decision); receptivity to feedback; dynamics of joint decision making, including interaction patterns with others during the decision making process and how conflicting preferences and beliefs are resolved.

Resources
Within each of the following major categories, resources can be distinguished in terms of their nature, frequency of use, and the family members' satisfaction with the resource, as derived from different sources: social support (e.g., types = emotional, instrumental, informational, and companionship support; sources = extended family, friends, spouse/partner, etc.); economic resources; features of the home environment (e.g., number of books, presence of television, toys, safety); features of the community (e.g., day care alternatives, public transportation, quality of public schools, health care); availability of each of the above resources to individual family members (e.g., some members may have access to certain types of social support, while other members do not).

Individual Life Experiences
Personality orientations (e.g., locus of control, impulsiveness, authoritarianism); emotional states (e.g., depression, anxiety, self-esteem, life satisfaction, marital satisfaction, family satisfaction); intelligence and cognitive abilities; parenting attitudes; communication experiences between family members, including emotional tone; attributions about the causes and meaning of others' behavior, beliefs about family roles and role expectations; perceptions about the family as a unit.

[a] The variables listed should be assessed separately for each functional domain under study.

focus in this table is on variables that could apply to all six functional domains. Domain-specific variables have been excluded, but may need to be added, depending on the topic of the research. In addition, some of the variables listed will serve as outcome variables for some researchers (e.g., family satisfaction, children's intelligence), in which case, these obviously would not be treated as independent variables. The variables listed are intended to guide researchers in considering the kinds of measures that may be informative when investigating the relationship of family functioning to outcomes, such as the behavioral development of individual children.

Methods

Application of the GSRI framework is usefully conceptualized in the context of etic versus emic distinctions in cross cultural psychology (Jaccard & Choi, 1986). Etic constructs or measures are those which hold across different cultures or groups of individuals. For example, the concept of a "goal" or "family role" is meaningful in many cultures. Emic constructs or measures, in contrast, are culture or group specific. GSRI combines both etic and emic features. First, GSRI delineates a set of variables that are assumed to be etic in character (goals, plans for attaining goals, resources, and individual life experiences). The content of these etic constructs, however, will be emic in character. For example, although families in different cultures or ethnic groups may have goals that vary on some of the dimensions discussed in Table 3 (e.g., number of goals, interelatedness of the goals), the content of the goals may be quite different. Similarly, even though the concepts may be identical in diverse cultures, different measurement techniques may be needed to yield valid and reliable assessment of these concepts. For a discussion of etic-emic issues in measurement and theory construction, see Jaccard and Choi (1986), Poortinga (1975) and Malpass (1977).

In addition to traditional nomothetic analyses, we ultimately hope to apply GSRI at the idiographic level in which the dynamics of a given family are evaluated within the context of that family, and not with reference to other families. For example, nomothetic analyses (using means or correlations across individuals) of the relationship between paternal intelligence and child development assess the relationship using different families as a reference point. With such a strategy, it is impossible to state how a father's intelligence in a given family affects child development. One can only state that relative to families with fathers who are more or less intelligent, child development is affected in a more or less positive fashion. Such relative statements are unsatisfactory when attempting to understand the dynamics of a specific family. A useful direction for future methodological approaches is the development of scientifically acceptable methods of idiographic analysis. (For an example of an idiographic based research program in the decision making area, see Jaccard & Wood, 1986.)

COMPARISON OF THE GSRI CONTEXTUAL MODEL WITH OTHER MODELS

The interpretations afforded by the GSRI contextual model of the family environment are interesting to compare with those offered by other theoretical frameworks. Our discussion is intended to highlight (briefly) aspects of GSRI that are complementary to other frameworks and to juxtapose some of our assumptions to those in other frameworks. The discussion is admittedly scant and is intended only to point out selected similarities and differences.

Confluence Model

Zajonc (1976, 1983; Zajonc et al., 1979) has developed the confluence model to quantify the influences upon intellectual growth that occur within the family context. The "birthorder puzzle" is pieced together in this theory by considering the following variables—the target child's birthorder, the number of children in the family, the chronological spacing between children, and the opportunity for the target child to teach a younger sibling. Used collectively, these variables have demonstrated reasonably good efficacy in estimating children's intellectual ability, based on analysis of large data sets. The model is assumed to provide confirmation of the fundamental axiom that children's intellectual performance is a function of the general intellectual environment (i.e., the sum of the absolute levels of intelligence in the home) and the opportunity to be an intellectual resource for others (i.e., only children and last-born children show intellectual decrements consistent with this disadvantage hypothesis because they lack the opportunity to teach a younger sibling).

The confluence model does not attempt to identify the functional components of the family's "intellectual environment." Generally, the model fits population data reasonably well, but cannot account for variation at the level of individual families (e.g., Grotevant, Scarr, & Weinberg, 1977). Gathering data about what types of behavior and experiences occur in families with relatively higher and lower absolute levels of intelligence would be important for understanding the mediating influences within these families. Do parents of first versus later borns simply differ in the amount of time they spend with each child? Or are there important qualitative differences in the ways parents interact with first and later borns? Similarly, how much time do siblings actually spend together and what proportion of that time are they engaged in activities that theoretically could influence cognitive competencies? If differential family functioning is associated with birth order and other family configurational effects, then more precise predictions could be achieved at the individual family level rather than aggregate levels. Once functional differences are specified, the GSRI model can be used to locate the specific reasons why parents, for example, may spend different amounts of time with children or why they engage in different types of social exchange. How much of the observed variance can be accounted for by changes in family goals and/or family resources over successive children? Thus, the GSRI framework complements the confluence model by specifying mediating variables that are otherwise unaddressed.

Circumplex Model

Olson and colleagues (Olson *et al.*, 1983) have developed a model of family functioning that is distinct from the confluence model. Their circumplex model originally was designed to describe marital and family dynamics in ways that would be clinically useful. The circumplex model deals with three primary family processes: cohesion ("emotional bonding of family members"), adaptability ("ability to change in response to situational and developmental stress"), and communication ("a facilitating dimension" for the other two processes). Family cohesion is characterized by four levels, from disengaged (very low), to separated, to connected, to enmeshed (very high). Family adaptability is dimensionalized into rigid (very low), structured, flexible, and chaotic (very high). For both areas, the two intermediate levels are considered good and are assumed to relate to positive family outcomes, while the extreme levels are predicted to cause problems and pathology. The model does recognize the possibility of exceptions to this rule of balanced moderation—namely, when family members' expectations endorse extreme levels, the family may function well as long as all family members accept these expectations. The circumplex model also considers communication styles within the family. According to the model, certain communication styles foster balanced levels of cohesion and adaptability, while others mitigate against such balanced states.

Applying the circumplex model to the example of birthorder and family size effects illustrates some limitations of the approach in accounting for family and child outcome variables. One problem is that both positive and negative outcomes have been associated with particular birth positions and family sizes, depending on the domain of interest (e.g., social vs. cognitive). The circumplex model treats family processes as general orientations, having trait-like qualities assumed to operate similarly across functional domains. For academic achievement, the circumplex model would predict that families of first borns show more balance in their family cohesiveness and adaptability, associated with relatively more positive communication styles than do families of later borns. However, the circumplex model then would offer little insight into the occurrence of negative child outcomes in other domains as a function of birthorder, or of being an only child. In contrast, the GSRI framework would hold that a family's communication behavior can differ in the domain of cognitive development from that in other domains, or that the cohesiveness of family members can vary from one area to another, and so on. Assessment of each GSRI component in each of the six domains of family functioning would offer considerable insight into across-domain consistencies and the different family environments experienced by first versus later-born children.

Parenting Behavior

Another popular approach to the study of families and their impact on child development has been the analysis of dimensions of parental behavior (e.g., Baumrind, 1966; Becker & Krug, 1965; Schaefer, 1965). Although theorists focus on somewhat different components (see Maccoby & Martin, 1983), two broad parenting dimensions that have been studied extensively are: (1) parental control and demands for compliance and (2) parental acceptance and warmth. Considerable research has attempted to relate such dimensions to child outcomes, such as social interaction skills, creativity, and cognitive competence. As a conceptual approach to studying the effects of families on child outcomes, parenting styles can be interpreted in the context of GSRI as follows:

First, if alternative parenting styles relate significantly to differential patterns of child development, then the processes involved can be explored. GSRI provides some insights into what the mediating variables might be. For example, parents who are warm and permissive may have different goals for their children than do parents who are judged less affectionate and more controlling. Or when trying to solve a problem (such as motivating a child to do well in school), parents who vary in their general permissiveness toward childrearing also may differ in their decision making strategies (e.g., the types of solutions they consider and why they choose the options they do).

The GSRI framework recognizes that parents' orientations and behavior toward raising children can vary from child to child. A parent might be relatively warm and controlling for one child but less so for another child. Many (but not all) of the current measures of parenting styles do not permit such differentiation. Parents are expected to show some consistency in their behavior toward children. Yet a parent's GSRI profile relative to one child might be quite different from that for another (e.g., for first vs. later borns, for boys vs. girls). A contextual analysis of parents' similarity of parenting style and each parent's effectiveness with individual children may reveal general principles about how parenting techniques (a) affect different types of children, (b) vary depending on the developmental stages of the family members, and (c) reflect reciprocal influences (i.e., are adapted to the behavior and perceived needs of individual family members).

Our framework also allows for the possibility that parenting style may differ depending on the domain of family functioning. For cognitive, social, and emotional development, a parent may adopt one parenting style, whereas in the domain of moral development, he or she may rely on a different parenting style. Rarely do studies of parenting style differentiate the functional realms being considered. Seemingly conflicting results may indicate domain-specificity in parenting behavior. That is, certain parenting styles that may be "good" (i.e., highly effective in achieving specified goals) for some developmental outcomes may be "unsuccessful" or even detrimental to facilitating development in other domains.

The literature on parenting styles has tended to ignore social context effects on the outcome of parenting styles. In contrast, the GSRI framework emphasizes the importance of such perspectives. The parenting style of a given parent can have different implications and meaning in the context of a family, depending upon the GSRI profiles of other family members. For example, how a child perceives and interprets a given parental action will have important implications for how that child behaves with respect to that action. In turn, the GSRI framework posits that the collective family environment will contribute to the child's behavior and will mediate the effects of particular parenting styles.

CONCLUSION

The family environment is inherently multidimensional, dynamic, and complex. The responses of children to their families, and the contribution children make to the functioning of their families, have been related to many variables, ranging from microbehavioral observations of interaction patterns to broad classes of exogoneous factors. To create a

cohesive picture of the role of the family environment in the development of children, from birth on, we have proposed the use of a conceptual framework that is designed to be multipurpose. Specifically, we
have defined the family as a functional unit of individuals identified by
two features: their self-definition as a "family" within their culture and
their commitment to the general well-being of family members. This
commitment may be dimensionalized into broad domains of family
functioning that operate concurrently and apply to all family members:
(1) physical development and health, (2) emotional development, (3)
social development, (4) cognitive development, (5) moral and spiritual
development, and (6) cultural and aesthetic development. A fundamental axiom in this framework is that family environments are not inherently good or bad, but that select aspects of the environment potentially
have differential effects on each domain of family functioning. Accordingly, multivariate assessment of the family environment is needed to
account for the complex child outcomes observed, and to provide data
relevant to understanding the processes that mediate both child and
family outcomes.

Despite the logistical and statistical difficulties inherent in treating
the family as a single unit (although continuing to recognize the potential contribution of individuals and dyads), we are optimistic about the
merit of developing procedures to permit *contextual* and *relativistic* assessment of family environments. Abstract judgments of family "success" and family "problems" must be related to family goals and priorities. These may be defined from multiple perspectives (e.g., family
members, the investigator, society). Theoretically, these different perspectives are hypothesized to lead to different conclusions about the
significance of particular family environment variables.

We have presented a framework for analyzing family functioning as
well as for predicting family and child outcomes. We describe the family
environment as the product of four major classes of variables—family
goals, strategies and plans for attaining goals, social and physical resources, and individual life experiences. We believe it is important to
consider each class of variables when evaluating family outcome measures. At the very least, an investigator who studies a single type of
variable (e.g., emotions) should recognize that its effects will operate, in
natural contexts, in combination with the other classes of variables specified in our framework. To ignore these other variables may result in a
failure to understand key aspects of how a single or a few variables
influence family outcomes. We hope investigators will find our framework useful in that we provide a multidimensional context within which
research findings can be interpreted. More importantly, potential mediating and moderating variables are identified in a manner that facilities

understanding how one or two variables may impinge on child development or family functioning. Thus, our intent has been to explicate a framework that can guide data collection efforts and can serve as a useful diagnostic tool for analyzing the effects of a wide array of distal (external) and proximal (internal) variables on family and child outcomes. We believe that studying the combined effects of the GSRI elements, and their natural interdependence will advance our understanding of both normative and exceptional families. We (Landesman & Jaccard) are conducting a large-scale home-based study of 500 families with young children to evaluate the utility of this framework. In the process, we have developed and are gathering measures pertinent to each of the GSRI elements, based on the perspective of all family members, as well as direct behavioral observations of the family as a whole. Through this empirical effort, we hope to refine and extend perspectives on the influence of the family environment on child development.

REFERENCES

Abelson, R., & Levi, S. (1985). Decision making and decision theory. In G. Lindzey and E. Aronson (Eds.), *Handbook of social psychology* (Vol. 1, pp. 231–309). Hillsdale, NJ: Erlbaum.

Bateson, G., Jackson, D. D., Haley, J., & Weakland, J. H. (1956). Toward a theory of schizophrenia. *Behavioral Science, 1,* 251–264.

Baumrind, D. (1966). Effects of authoritative control on child behavior. *Child Development, 38,* 291–327.

Beavers, W. R., & Voeller, M. N. (1983). Family models: Comparing and contrasting the Olson Circumplex Model with the Beavers Systems Model. *Family Process, 22,* 85–98.

Becker, W., & Krug, R. (1965). Parent attitude research instrument: A research review. *Child Development, 36,* 329–365.

Belsky, J. (1981). Early human experience: A family perspective. *Developmental Psychology, 17,* 3–23.

Bertalanffy, Von L. (1968). *General systems theory.* New York: Braziller.

Brody, G. H., & Stoneman, Z. (1986). Contextual issues in the study of sibling socialization. In J. J. Gallagher & P. M. Vietze (Eds.), *Families of handicapped persons: Research, programs, and policy issues* (pp. 197–217). Baltimore: Paul H. Brookes.

Bronfenbrenner, U. (1979). *The ecology of human development.* Cambridge, MA: Harvard University Press.

Brownell, A., & Shumaker, S. (1984). Social support: An introduction to a complex phenomenon. *Journal of Social Issues, 40,* 1–10.

Buck, R. (1985). Prime theory: An integrated view of motivation and emotion. *Psychological Review, 92,* 389–413.

Cattell, R. (1965). *The scientific analysis of personality.* Baltimore, MD: Penguin.

Clarke-Stewart, K. A. (1978). And daddy makes three: The father's impact on mother and young child. *Child Development, 49,* 466–478.

Daly, E., Lancee, W., & Polivy, J. (1983). A conical model for the taxonomy of emotional expression. *Journal of Personality and Social Psychology, 45,* 443–457.

Dunn, J. (1983). Sibling relationships in early childhood. *Child Development, 54,* 787–811.

Dunn, J., & Kendrick, C. (1981). Social behavior of young siblings in the family context: Differences between same-sex and different-sex dyads. *Child Development, 52,* 1265–1273.

Elder, G. H. (1984). Families, kin, and the life course: A sociological perspective. In R. D. Parke (Ed.), *Review of child development research Vol. 7: The family* (80–136). Chicago: University of Chicago Press.

Epstein, N. B., & Bishop, D. S. (1981). Problem centered systems therapy of the family. *Journal of Marital and Family Therapy, 7,* 23–31.

Epstein, N. B., Bishop, D. S., & Baldwin, L. M. (1982). McMaster model of family functioning: A view of the normal family. In F. Walsh (Ed.), *Normal Family Processes* (pp. 115–141). New York: Guilford.

Eysenck, H. J. (1953). *The structure of human personality.* New York: Wiley.

Eysenck, S. & Eysenck, H. (1977). The place of impulsiveness in a dimensional system of personality description. *British Journal of Social and Clinical Psychology, 16,* 57–68.

Feinman, S., & Lewis, M. (1984). Is there social life beyond the dyad?: A social-psychological view of social connections in infancy. In M. Lewis (Ed.), *Beyond the dyad* (pp. 13–41). New York: Wiley.

Feiring, C. & Lewis, M. (1984). Changing characteristics of the U.S. family: Implications for family networks, relationships, and child development. In M. Lewis (Ed.), *Beyond the dyad* (pp. 59–89). New York: Plenum Press.

Gardner, H. (1984). *Frames of mind.* New York: Basic Books.

Gottlieb, B. (1981). *Social networks and social support.* Beverly Hills: Sage.

Gottman, J. M., & Levinson, R. W. (1986). Assessing the role of emotion in marriage. *Behavioral Assessment, 8,* 31–48.

Grotevant, H. D., Scarr, S., & Weinberg, R. A. (1977). Intellectual development in family constellations with adopted and natural children: A test of the Zajonc and Markus model. *Child Development, 48,* 1699–1703.

Gurman, A. S., & Kniskern, D. P. (Eds.). (1981). *Handbook of family therapy.* New York: Brunner/Mazel.

Hamilton, E. (1984). *Cognitive analysis of emotions and personality.* New York: Academic Press.

Holman, T. B., & Burr, W. R. (1980). Beyond the beyond: The growth of family theories in the 1970s. *Journal of Marriage and the Family, 42,* 729–741.

Jaccard, J., & Choi, W. (1986). Cross-cultural methods for the study of behavioral decision making. *Journal of Cross-Cultural Psychology, 17,* 123–149.

Jaccard, J., & Wood, G. (1986). An idiothetic analysis of behavioral decision making. In D. Brinberg & R. Lutz (Eds.), *Methodological perspectives in consumer behavior* (pp. 67–106). New York: Springer-Verlag.

Jackson, D. (1967). *Personality research form manual.* Goshen, NY: Research Psychologists Press.

Landesman, S. (1986). Toward a taxonomy of home environments. *International Review of Research in Mental Retardation, 14,* 259–289.

Lewis, M. (1982). The social network systems model: Toward a theory of social development. In T. Field, A. Huston, H. C. Quay, L. Troll, & G. E. Finley (Eds.), *Review of human development* (pp. 180–214). New York: Wiley.

Lewis, M. (1984). *Beyond the dyad.* New York: Plenum Press.

Lewis, M. & Feiring, C. (1979). The child's social network: Social object, social functions and their relationship. In M. Lewis & L. A. Rosenblum (Eds.), *The child and its family* (pp. 9–27). New York: Plenum Press.

Lewis, M., & Feiring, C. (1981). Direct and indirect interactions in social relationships. In L. Lipsitt (Ed.), *Advances in infancy research* (Vol. 1, pp. 131–161). New York: Ablex.

Lewis, M., & Michalson, L. (1983). *Children's emotions and moods.* New York: Plenum Press.

Lewis, M., & Rosenblum, L. A. (Eds.). (1974). *The effect of the infant on its caregiver.* New York: Wiley.

Lewis, M., & Rosenblum, L. A. (Eds.). (1978). *The development of affect.* New York: Plenum Press.

Lewis, M., & Rosenblum, L. A. (Eds.). (1979). *The child and its family.* New York: Plenum Press.

Lewis, M., & Weinraub, M. A. (1976). The father's role in the child's social network. In M. E. Lamb (Ed.), *The role of the father in child development* (pp. 157–184). New York: Wiley.

Maccoby, E. E., & Martin, J. A. (1983). Socialization in the context of the family: Parent-child interaction. In P. H. Mussen (Ed.), *Handbook of child psychology* (4th ed., Vol. 4, pp. 1–101). New York: Wiley.

MacDonald, K., & Parke, R. D. (1984). Bridging the gap: Parent-child play interaction and peer interactive competence. *Child Development, 55,* 1265–1277.

Malpass, R. (1977). Theory and method in cross-cultural psychology. *American Psychologist, 32,* 1069–1079.

Mancuso, J. C., & Handin, K. H. (1983). Prompting parents toward constructivist caregiving practices. In I. Sigel and L. Laosa (Eds.), *Changing families* (pp. 167–202). New York: Plenum Press.

Miller, J. G. (1965). Living systems: Basic concepts. *Behavioral Sciences, 10,* 193–237.

Minuchin, S. (1974). *Families and family therapy.* Cambridge MA: Harvard University Press.

Norman, W. (1963). Toward an adequate taxonomy of personality attributes: Replicated factor structure in peer nomination personality ratings. *Journal of Abnormal and Social Psychology, 66,* 574–583.

Nye, F. I., & Berardo, F. M. (Eds.). (1966). *Emerging conceptual frameworks in family analysis.* New York: Macmillan.

Olson, D. H. (1985). Commentary: Struggling with congruence across theoretical models and methods. *Family Process, 24,* 203–207.

Olson, D. H., Russell, C. S., & Sprenkle, D. H. (1983). Circumplex model of marital and family systems: VI. Theoretical update. *Family Process, 22,* 69–83.

Olson, D. H., Sprenkle, D. H., & Russell, C. S. (1979). Circumplex model of marital and family systems: I. Cohesion and adaptability dimensions, family types, and clinical applications. *Family Process, 18,* 3–28.

Parke, R. D. (1986). Fathers, families, and support systems: Their role in the development of at-risk and retarded infants and children. In J. Gallagher & P. Vietze (Eds.), *Families of handicapped persons: Research, programs, and policy issues* (pp. 101–113). Baltimore: Paul H. Brookes.

Parke, R. D., Power, T. G., & Gottman, J. M. (1979). Conceptualizing and quantifying influence patterns in the family triad. In M. E. Lamb, S. J. Suomi, & G. R. Stephenson (Eds.), *Social interaction analysis: Methodological issues* (pp. 231–252). Madison, WI: University of Wisconsin.

Patterson, G. R. (1982). *Coercive family process.* Eugene, OR: Castalia.

Patterson, G. R., & Reid, J. B. (1970). Reciprocity and coercion: Two facets of social systems. In C. Neuringer and J. L. Michael (Eds.), *Behavior modification in clinical psychology.* New York: Appleton-Century-Croft.

Poortinga, Y. (1975). Some implications of three different approaches to intercultural comparisons. In J. Berry & W. Lonner (Eds.), *Applied cross-cultural psychology.* (pp. 327–332). Amsterdam: Swets & Zeitlinger.

Ramey, C. T., MacPhee, D., & Yeates, K. O. (1983). *Preventing developmental retardation: A general systems model.* Hanover, NH: University Press of New England.

Reiss, D. (1971a). Varieties of consensual experience: I. A theory for relating family interaction to individual thinking. *Family Process, 10,* 1–27.

Reiss, D. (1971b). Varieties of consensual experience: II. Dimensions of a family's experience of its environment. *Family Process, 10,* 28–35.

Sameroff, A. J. (1983). Contexts and development: The systems and their evolution. In W. Kessen (Ed.), *History, theories and methods* (Vol. 1, pp. 237–294) of P. H. Mussen (Ed.), *US handbook of child psychology.* New York: Wiley.

Schaefer, E. (1965). Children's reports of parental behavior: An inventory. *Child Development, 36,* 413–424.

Sigel, I. E. (1982). The relationship between parental distancing strategies and the child's cognitive behavior. In L. M. Laosa & I. E. Siegel (Eds.), *Families as learning environments for children* (pp. 47–86). New York: Plenum Press.

Sigel, I. E., & Laosa, L. (1983). *Changing families,* New York: Plenum Press.

Sternberg, R. J. (1986). *Beyond IQ: A triarchic theory of human intelligence.* New York: Cambridge University Press.

Terkelson, K. G. (1980). Toward a theory of the family life cycle. In E. A. Carter & M. McGoldrick (Eds.), *The family life cycle: A framework for family therapy* (pp. 21–52). New York: Gardner.

Tinsley, B., & Parke, R.D. (1984). Grandparents as support and socialization agents. In M. Lewis (Ed.), *Beyond the dyad* (pp. 161–194). New York: Plenum Press.

Turnbull, A., Summers, J. D., & Brotherson, M. J. (1986). Family life cycle: theoretical and empirical implications and future directions for families with mentally retarded members. In J. Gallagher & P. Vietze (Eds.), *Families of handicapped persons: Research, programs, and policy issues* (pp. 45–65). Baltimore: Paul H. Brookes.

Yanagisako, S. J. (1979). Family and household: The analysis of domestic groups. *Annual Review of Anthropology, 8,* 161–205.

Zajonc, R. B. (1976). Family configuration and intelligence. *Science, 192,* 227–236.

Zajonc, R. B. (1983). Validating the confluence model. *Psychological Bulletin, 93,* 457–480.

Zajonc, R. B., & Markus, G. B. (1975). Birth order and intellectual development. *Psychological Review, 82,* 74–88.

Zajonc, R. B., Markus, H., & Markus, G. B. (1979). The birth order puzzle. *Journal of Personality and Social Psychology, 37,* 1325–1341.

5

Sibling Influences

JUDITH F. DUNN

About 80% of children grow up with siblings—individuals with whom they are deeply and often uncomfortably familiar, who share the daily intimacies, pleasures, and problems of family life, and who are competitors for the affection and attention of their parents. Siblings do not choose to live together; they are forced to do so. Tension and hostility, as well as affection, are engendered by this combination of intimacy and familiarity, as the extremely uninhibited aggression and affection expressed by young siblings reveals. It is a "no-holds-barred" relationship.

On commonsense grounds it appears quite likely that such a relationship would have some influence on a child's personality and well-being. Indeed, psychologists from a wide variety of backgrounds have proposed that siblings influence each other's development.[1] First, clinicians from Freud on have emphasized the importance of rivalry between siblings as an influence on personality (Adler, 1928, 1959; Levy, 1934, 1937; Winnicott, 1977). Second, behavior geneticists have drawn attention to the marked differences between siblings in personality, psycho-

---

[1]This chapter was written in 1985, when this volume was first conceived. Since then, much relevant research on siblings has been presented, particularly on the issues of differential experiences of siblings within the sibling relationship (see Dunn & Plomin, 1990, for an overview), and on siblings in middle childhood (see, for example, Brody, Stoneman, & Burke, 1987; Hetherington, 1988; Raffaelli & Larson, 1987; Rowe, Rodgers, Meseck-Bushey, & St. John, 1989; Stocker, Dunn, & Plomin, 1989). The main theoretical points made in the chapter are further supported by this more recent research, to which the reader is referred.

JUDITH F. DUNN • Department of Human Development and Family Studies, College of Health and Human Development, Penn State University, University Park, Pennsylvania 16802.

pathology, and intellectual development (Rowe & Plomin, 1981; Scarr & Grajek, 1982). Siblings who share 50% of their genes and the same family environment nevertheless differ from one another almost as much as unrelated children growing up in different families do. It is a striking finding and one that has major implications for our views on the nature of family influence. As Maccoby and Martin (1983) point out, it shows us how little of the variation in individual development is explained by the parental variables that we have assumed to be important. Siblings have these parental variables in common, yet they develop to be very different individuals. In attempting to explain these differences, the possible direct influence of siblings upon one another must be taken into account. Differential parental treatment, and selection of differing aspects of the family environment by different siblings may well, of course, contribute to these differences between siblings as well. The point is that either directly, by their behavior towards one another, or indirectly, by their very presence and relationship with the parents, siblings may influence one another's development and contribute to striking differences between them.

Third, the arguments that many psychologists put forward to explain the important influence of peers on children's development (Piaget, 1965; Sullivan, 1953; more recently, Berndt & Ladd, 1989; Hartup, 1983) imply that if peers are important, then siblings are too. It is argued that the reciprocal nature of interaction between peers is of central importance in the development of social sensitivity, of understanding of self and other, and of moral understanding. If this argument is plausible, then the familiarity and intimacy of siblings with one another, and the extent to which they understand each other's interests and motivation, suggest that siblings may be particularly important in the development of social understanding.

On theoretical grounds, therefore, it seems quite plausible that siblings influence each other's development (Dunn, 1983). What evidence is there from empirical research on the nature or extent of such influence? The traditional approach to the issue of sibling influence has been to look for relationships between personality and birth order or sibling status—the sex and spacing of siblings. A large literature makes comparisons between only children and those with siblings (Falbo, 1984), between children of differing ordinal position, or between children with siblings of different gender or age spacing (for a review see Wagner, Schubert & Schubert, 1979). From such studies it has been argued that while firstborn children are primarily influenced by their parents, later-born children are importantly affected by their siblings; processes of identification, deidentification, modelling and imitation are invoked to explain the pattern of results that are found (Sutton-Smith & Rosenberg,

84624284

1970). However, this birth order and sibling status literature has yielded conflicting and inconsistent results, and it does not help us to get very far in understanding the nature of sibling influence. There are a number of different reasons why it has been relatively unilluminating. First, much of the birth order research suffers from methodological shortcomings, as Schooler pointed out in 1972. His review indicates that most birth order associations are spurious. More recently Ernst and Angst (1983), on the basis of a thorough review of the literature and an empirical study, came to the conclusion that birth order and sibling status do not have a strong impact on personality. A number of different studies have now shown, for instance, that only children do not differ from those with siblings once the over-representation of only children in single-parent families is controlled for (Falbo, 1984). Second, as Scarr and Grajek (1982) show, the constructs of sibling spacing, birth order, and gender are inadequate to explain the magnitude of the differences between siblings. Scarr and Grajek (1982) point out that there is little theoretical basis for interpreting the sibling constellation research. Processes of modelling, deidentification, or identification are applied to explain whatever results are achieved, and it is evident that with the two processes of identification and deidentification *any* result can be explained. It is hardly an explanatory model of great power.

Does the lack of consistent findings from the sibling constellation research imply that siblings have no influence? We certainly should not draw that conclusion yet. Let us look at the evidence on what in fact happens between children, their siblings and their parents within the family. We will consider first one of the most important indirect effects of a sibling—the effects on a child's relationships with his or her parents.

INDIRECT EFFECTS: THE IMPACT OF SIBLINGS UPON PARENT-CHILD RELATIONSHIPS

The arrival of a second child has marked effects on the relationship between first children and their mothers. Increases in dependent behavior, in demanding and naughty behavior, and in confrontation between child and mother, as well as decreases in maternal play, attention, and warmth have now been documented in a number of studies employing different methodologies, including home observations, maternal interviews, and laboratory observations (Dunn & Kendrick, 1982; Feiring & Lewis, 1984; Taylor & Kogan, 1973; Trause, Voos, Rudd, Klaus, Kennell, & Boslett, 1981). In the Dunn and Kendrick study, the observations of children at home showed that the balance of responsibility for starting communicative exchanges also changed. Mothers became much less likely to initiate conversation with their firstborn, and were also much less likely to return the gaze of their firstborn, after the birth of a sibling. Some of these changes in the relationship appear to be relatively short term. In the Dunn and Kendrick study the marked increase in confrontation between mother and firstborn and dependent behavior of the firstborn had disappeared by the time the second child was 8 months old. However, the level of maternal attention and play did not regain the level it had been before the birth of the sibling.

In each of the studies cited, the firstborn children also showed signs of disturbance after the birth of a sibling. Sleep problems, feeding and toilet problems, excessively demanding behavior, withdrawn behavior, and marked misery were relatively common. In these ways, the arrival of a sibling had a profound impact on the firstborn. It is important to note that individual differences among the children in the form and extent of the disturbed behavior were striking, a point to which we will return. It is also interesting to note that over half the children in two studies were also reported to show developmental advances—primarily increases in independent behavior—followed the sibling birth.

As the siblings grow up together, the complex pattern of associations between the different family relationships suggests that indirect effects of the sibling upon the mother-child relationship continue to be important. In our first study, for instance (Dunn & Kendrick, 1982), we found that firstborn children responded promptly to interaction between their mother and their sibling when the secondborn child was 8 months old. Frequently, this response took the form of demanding or difficult behavior directed at the mother, or quite explicit protest. In other families, the firstborn child responded to interaction between mother and sibling by joining in the play in a friendly fashion. The individual differences in the firstborns' response were marked and were related to the temperament and gender of the children. The general point of importance is that the first child's relationship with the mother continued to be coloured in a very obvious way by what was happening between mother and secondborn. The extent to which first children continue to feel that they are "unfairly" treated by their mothers, in comparison with their younger siblings, highlights this point (Koch, 1960). And in adolescence, a recent study reports that a third of the sample studied felt that they had been treated differently from their siblings by their parents (Daniels & Plomin, 1985). If we regard the parent-child relationship as an important influence in development, then we should take seriously the impact of siblings upon that relationship. The complexity of mutual influences within the family is clear, too, in the ways in which the first child's behavior towards the sibling is apparently influenced by the mother. It is this interaction with the sibling that we examine next.

DIRECT EFFECTS

To assess the possible direct influence of siblings in childhood we must first consider the nature of the relationship between the children. Studies of young siblings at home show that interaction between the children is frequent, though individual differences among families are very marked. For instance, in a current study of siblings, we find that 2-year-olds were spending on average 20% of the observation time in interaction with their older siblings, but that there was a range from 10 to 63% of observation time among the different families. These interactions between siblings were frequently marked by intense emotion—positive and/or negative. On average, 20% of the interactions involved intense emotions expressed by the younger sibling. In non-Western cultures, interactions between siblings are very frequent indeed (Barry & Paxon, 1971; Weisner & Gallimore, 1977; Whiting & Whiting, 1975) and, even in the U.S., Bank and Kahn (1975) report from a study of 4 to 6-year-olds that the children spent over twice as much time in only each other's company as with their parents.

The children's interest in each other is revealed not only in the frequency of their interaction, but in the nature of that interaction. Imitation, for instance, is often observed. In the home observation study by Abramovitch and her colleagues (Abramovitch, Pepler, & Corter, 1982), 27% of all interactions between 20-month-old secondborn children and their older siblings were imitative. Laboratory studies of siblings also report high frequencies of imitation of older siblings by younger (Lamb, 1978). With the prominence assigned to "modeling" in theoretical discussion of sibling influence, it is important to find that imitation is indeed so common.

Aggression between siblings is also relatively common. In Abramovitch's Canadian study (Abramovitch et al., 1982), 29% of the acts of the 20-month-olds and their older siblings were antagonistic; in our Cambridge study we found a similar figure of 25% of interactions between 18-month-olds and their siblings that involved conflict. And play between siblings is, of course, frequent as well as distinctive in character. The nature of the collaborative pretend play that a 2-year-old engages in with his or her sibling is, for instance, very different from joint play with the mother (Dunn & Dale, 1984). In middle childhood these features of frequent emotionally loaded interaction, aggression, and imitation apparently continue to be prominent in the relationship between siblings, though we have relatively little good systematic information on this age period. Self-comparison and disparagement of the other become increasingly obvious, and it seems plausible that these aspects of the relationship may be developmentally important, especially as the children become more conscious of self, self-worth and of the opinion of peers.

These characteristics of the relationship between siblings—frequent imitation and aggression, intense hostility and affection, wild excitement in joint play—all suggest that the exchanges with the sibling may well influence a child's behavior and development. Moreover, in the context of the sibling relationship, children show powers of understanding the other child remarkably early in their development (Dunn, 1988). They are able, for instance, to tease and to provoke in a manner that demonstrates a clear understanding of what will annoy and upset *this person*, as well as to comfort, well before they are 2 years old (Dunn & Munn, 1985). It appears that the emotional urgency of the sibling relationship, and the close familiarity with the other child, provides a forum in which children develop powers of understanding another person far earlier than has been assumed from the research in which children are presented with perspective-taking tasks in an experimental setting.

INDIVIDUAL DIFFERENCES AND SIBLING INFLUENCE

Do we have any other direct evidence that such interactions do influence the future course of the sibling relationship or, more broadly, the development of a child's personality, self-esteem or emotional well-being? In each of the aspects of the sibling relationship that have been studied, a strikingly wide range of individual differences are found. It is the analysis of these individual differences that allows us to examine the question of sibling influence in detail.

Longitudinal studies indicate that there is considerable continuity in the quality of sibling relationships. In one study following 2-year-old firstborn children from the birth of the second child until four years later, we found correlations between the firstborn children's initial reaction to the birth—his or her positive interest in the newborn sibling at two weeks after the birth—and the quality of the relationship between the siblings four years later (Stillwell & Dunn, 1985). The correlations were between measures of observed behavior of the firstborn children and maternal interview at the early time points, on the one hand, and measures from the interviews with the children themselves as 6-year-olds and maternal interviews at the later time points, on the other. The pattern of correlations between very different measures over an extensive time period is striking, and suggests that the continuity cannot be simply the result of a stability in maternal perception of the siblings. A second example is the study by Lamb (1978) of sibling interaction in a laboratory playroom. Lamb found that the behavior of firstborn children towards their siblings was better predicted by the behavior of the infant siblings at an earlier time point than by the firstborn children's own behavior at the earlier time point.

This pattern of association between early and later behavior is particularly evident in physically aggressive behavior. In a study of secondborn children followed from 18 months to 36 months, we found that the frequency of physical aggression from older children at the 18 month visits was correlated with the frequency of physical aggression from the younger child six months later (Dunn & Munn, 1986). And in a series of meticulous fine-grain studies of aggressive behavior within the family Patterson and his colleagues have shown that siblings are the "prime shapers" of aggressive behavior in both hyper-aggressive boys and boys from a non-clinical population (Patterson, 1986).

Epidemiological studies, which approach these questions on a much broader scale, confirm the point that poor relations between siblings are associated over time with the development of behavior problems. Richman, Stevenson and Graham (1982), in their large-scale study of 955 children from one London borough, followed from 3 years to 8 years, report that poor sibling relations at 4 years were correlated with clinical ratings of disturbance at 8 years in the control group of children who were not initially disturbed.

When siblings get into disputes, they do more than just hit each other. They also make attempts to conciliate and resolve the conflict, show concern at the other's distress, tease and provoke in a way that reflects understanding of what will annoy or upset the other, and refer to social rules in justification for their own actions. All these behaviors reflect some understanding of the feelings or intentions of the other child, or of the social rules of the family. The individual differences among preschool-aged children in the likelihood that they will demonstrate such skills of social understanding in the course of conflict with the sibling are striking (Dunn & Munn, 1985). These differences raise the question of whether the behavior of the sibling over time influences the development of social understanding.

The answer from one longitudinal study of siblings is that there are indeed some patterns of association over time linking the actions of older siblings to the early development of behaviors that depend upon some grasp of feelings and social rules. For instance, in families in which the older sibling showed relatively frequent prosocial behavior towards the child at 18 months—sharing, comforting, helping, and cooperating—the younger child by 24 months not only showed more frequent prosocial behavior him or herself, but also was more likely to tease or conciliate in conflict (Dunn & Munn, 1986). There were also correlations between the frequency with which the older sibling cooperated in pretend play when the younger child was 18 months and the frequency with which the second child cooperated in pretend play six months later. And, particularly striking, there were significant correlations between the proportion of the older sibling's conversational turns that were concerned with feelings and the proportion of the second child's conversation turns that were concerned with feelings six months later.

We cannot, of course, draw causal inferences from these correlations over time. Nevertheless, they indicate that individual differences in sibling behavior may well be part of a pattern of family interaction that influences the development of social understanding. This claim is supported by analyses of the development of another aspect of the children's behavior—the ability to participate in joint pretend play. In each of two studies of young siblings, we have found that about a third of the children took part in joint role play with their older siblings at a strikingly early age—by 18 or 24 months (Dunn & Dale, 1984). The pretend play was almost always initially organized by the older siblings, who assigned roles to the younger child and gave instructions about the course of the play. However, the younger siblings not only acted appropriately for the assigned role, but also made innovatory contributions to the fantasy play, and referred explicitly to their "pretend" role. "I a Daddy" announced one 2-year-old, explaining his role to the observer. This is remarkably mature behavior for a 24-month-old, involving a transformation of identity, and the understanding that the pretend world is a shared world.

This play was observed only in families in which the siblings were very friendly. There was a clear link between the affectionate quality of the relationship and the frequency of joint pretend play. In those families in which the older sibling was interested in and affectionate towards the younger, the younger was being initiated into a world of pretend in which social rules and roles were explored and exploited. While we do not know what the long-term significance of such experiences may be, it is clear that here the influence of the sibling was very different from that of the mother. Mothers were never observed to engage in joint role play with their two year olds. Their interest in pretend-play took the form of didactic suggestions rather than joint participation.

The question of how far siblings influence each other's behavior during middle childhood—either within the family or in the world of school and peers—remains relatively unexplored, though the quality of the relationship in this period is now better understood (see, for example, Furman & Buhrmester, 1985). Bryant and Crockenberg (1980) examined the relationship between the prosocial and aggressive behavior of 6- to 7-year-old girls and the behavior of their mothers and siblings in a game-playing situation, and showed that while the mothers' behavior was the best predictor of comforting and sharing, it was the siblings' behavior rather than that of the mothers that predicted refusal to share or help, accept help, anger and boasting. This was especially true for the younger siblings. One important feature of this study was that it highlighted the complex pattern of connections between the different relationships in the mother-child-sibling triad. For instance, the relationship between a mother's behavior and that of her children towards each other depended in part on how each child was treated relative to the other. When either child had his or her needs met while their sibling did not, "discomforting" behavior was high for both children. And in families in which the mother ignored the children frequently, both siblings were likely to ask each other for help. There is a parallel here with the finding from the cross-cultural study of Whiting and Whiting (1975) which showed that in cultures in which the social system encouraged siblings to take responsibility for one another, their social development was apparently fostered.

Perhaps the most striking studies of sibling influence in middle childhood are those of Patterson (1986), which explore the origins and sequelae of aggressive behavior and conflict within the family. In one study of boys from 4th, 7th, and 10th grade, he showed that the quality of the relationship between the siblings was systematically related to delinquency and antisocial behavior outside the home, thus linking what he termed the "microsocial training" of sibling interaction to these developments. That poor sibling relationships are associated with the development of antisocial or disturbed behavior has been shown in the large-scale epidemiological study of Richman and her colleagues, already cited (Richman et al., 1982). Although no causal link can be inferred from Patterson's study, his methodology allows the researcher to examine the processes of family interaction specifically, and his results certainly suggest that sibling aggression plays a formative part in the pattern of later disturbance.

With the exception of Patterson's work there is little systematic research examining directly the links between sibling interaction and children's behavior outside the home. The issue of how far the experience of growing up with a sibling influences a child's behavior in the outside world remains wide open. It has been suggested that there are links between children's sociability towards peers and their experiences with a sibling. Some studies report that laterborn children are more sociable than firstborn when first entering nursery school, and this is attributed to the previous interaction with their sibling. However, such findings are open to all the ambiguities of other birth-order findings. Are the differences between the firstborn and laterborn attributable to the direct influence of siblings? Or do they arise because of differential parental treatment? While it seems extremely plausible that parents treat their first and laterborn children differently, and that these differences in parental behavior are important developmentally, there have been very few studies which examine this issue carefully. In two studies that do examine the behavior of the same mother to her successive children when they are the same age, the mothers were found to be remarkably consistent in their behavior towards their two children, even though the time period between the observations of the mother with her first and her second child was, on average, 35 months (Dunn, Plomin, & Daniels, 1986; Dunn, Plomin, & Nettles, 1985). One implication of this maternal consistency is that the striking differences found within sibling pairs in this study (the Colorado Adoption Project, Plomin, DeFries, & Fulker, 1988) and in other sibling studies cannot be attributed solely to differential parental treatment. It reinforces the argument for studying sibling interaction and the role that such interaction may play in contributing to the individual differences between the children.

To tease apart the relative influence of parent and sibling upon developing children, it is increasingly clear that our research strategy must take serious account of two issues. The first is the complexity of mutual influences within the family. We must study not just the interaction and relationship between siblings, but also the interaction between each parent and each sibling, and the response of each child to the interaction among the others in the family. We must examine the differences in the behavior of each parent to the different children, and we must include assessments of the children's perceptions of such differential treatment, as well as more "objective" measures of parental behavior.

The second issue concerns the wide range of individual differences in the affective quality of sibling relationships. For some children, growing up with a sibling means growing up with an exciting playmate, an affectionate, supportive comforter. For others, it means daily intimacy with a hostile, aggressive child who disparages, teases and bosses relentlessly. The question we should ask is not, Does growing up with a sibling influence a child's development? Or, How do only children differ from children with siblings? Rather, we should ask, How does growing up with a rivalrous, hostile sibling influence a child's development? How does an affectionate relationship with a sibling influence the way a child grows up? It seems very probable that the lack of illumination we have achieved with the sibling constellation research is attributable in part to the failure to take account of this most important feature of the sibling relationship—its affective quality.

One question that remains to be explored is how far heredity affects these individual differences in sibling behavior. The importance of this issue is highlighted in research showing that the association between environmental measures and measures of development can be mediated genetically (Plomin, Loehlin, & DeFries, 1985). By comparing environment-development relationships in adoptive and non-adoptive homes, it was found that "the genetic components of these 'environmental' correlations are fully as large as the environmental components" (Plomin et al., 1985). Although the major influences on family relationships are nearly always assumed to be environmental, it is clear from the ubiquity of genetic effects on behavior that we should seriously consider the possibility that there are also genetic influences on family relationships. It is a possibility that we can examine by studying sibling relationships in adoptive homes, in which the members share family environment but not heredity, as well as in non-adoptive families. Only when we consider sibling constellation variables *and* the affective quality of the sibling relationship *and* the relationship between each sibling and the parents in both non-adoptive and adoptive families will we begin to tackle the question of why siblings growing up within the same family become such different people.

REFERENCES

Abramovitch, R., Pepler, D., & Corter, C. (1982). Patterns of sibling interaction among preschool-age children. In M. Lamb & B. Sutton-Smith (Eds.), *Sibling relationships: Their nature and significance across the lifespan* (pp. 61–86). Hillsdale, NJ: Erlbaum.

Adler, A. (1928). Characteristics of the 1st, 2nd and 3rd child [Special issue]. *Children, 3,* (5).

Adler, A. (1959). *Understanding human nature.* New York: Premier.

Bank, S., & Kahn, M. D. (1975). Sisterhood-brotherhood is powerful: Sibling subsystems and family therapy. *Family Process, 14,* 311–337.

Barry, H., & Paxon, L. M. (1971). Infancy and early childhood: Cross-cultural codes 2. *Ethnology, 10,* 466–508.

Berndt, T. J., & Ladd, G. W. (1989). *Peer relationships in child development.* New York: Wiley.

Brody, G., Stoneman, Z., & Burke, M. (1987). Child temperaments, maternal differential behavior, and sibling relationships. *Developmental Psychology, 23,* 354–362.

Bryant, B. K., & Crockenberg, S. B. (1980). Correlates and dimensions of prosocial behaviors: A study of female siblings and their mothers. *Child Development, 51,* 529–544.

Daniels, D., & Plomin, R. (1985). Differential experience of siblings in the same family. *Developmental Psychology, 21,* 747–760.

Dunn, J. (1983). Sibling relationships in early childhood. *Child Development, 54,* 787–811.

Dunn, J. (1988). *The beginnings of social understanding.* Cambridge, MA: Harvard University Press.

Dunn, J., & Dale, N. (1984). I a Daddy: Two-year-olds' collaboration in joint pretend with sibling and with mother. In I. Bretherton (Ed.), *Symbolic Play: The development of social understanding* (pp. 131–158). New York: Academic Press.

Dunn, J., & Kendrick, C. (1982). *Siblings: Love, envy and understanding.* Cambridge, MA: Harvard University Press.

Dunn, J., & Munn, P. (1985). Becoming a family member: Family conflict and the development of social understanding in the second year. *Child Development, 56,* 480–492.

Dunn, J., & Munn, P. (1986). Sibling quarrels and maternal intervention: Individual differences in understanding and aggression. *Journal of Child Psychology and Psychiatry, 27,* 583–597.

Dunn, J., & Plomin, R. (1990). *Separate lives: Why siblings are so different.* New York: Basic Books.

Dunn, J., Plomin, R., & Daniels, D. (1986). Consistency and change in mothers' behavior towards two-year-old siblings. *Child Development, 57,* 348–356.

Dunn, J., Plomin, R., & Nettles, M. (1985). Consistency of mothers' behavior towards infant siblings. *Developmental Psychology, 21,* 1188–1195.

Ernst, L., & Angst, J. (1983). *Birth order: Its influence on personality.* Berlin: Springer-Verlag.

Falbo, T. (1984). *The Single-Child Family.* New York: Guilford Press.

Feiring, C., & Lewis, M. (1984). Only and firstborn children: Differences in social behavior and development. In T. Falbo (Ed.), *The single-child family* (pp. 25–62). New York: Guilford Press.

Furman, W., & Buhrmester, D. (1985). Children's perceptions of the qualities of sibling relationships. *Child Development, 56,* 448–461.

Hartup, W. W. (1983). Peer relations. In P. H. Mussen (Ed.), *Handbook of child psychology: Vol. IV. Socialization, personality and social development* (4th ed., pp. 903–963). New York: Wiley.

Hetherington, E. M. (1988). Parents, children, and siblings: Six years after divorce. In R. A. Hinde & J. Stevenson Hinde (Eds.), *Relationships within families: Mutual influences* (pp. 311–331). Oxford: Oxford University Press.

Koch, H. (1960). The relation of certain formal attitudes of siblings to attitudes held towards each other and towards their parents. *Monographs of the Society for Research in Child Development, 25* (4, Serial No. 78).

Lamb, M. E. (1978). The development of sibling relationships in infancy: A short-term longitudinal study. *Child Development, 49,* 1189–1196.

Levy, D. M. (1934). Rivalry between children of the same family. *Child Study, 11,* 233–261.

Levy, D. M. (1937). Studies in sibling rivalry. *American Orthopsychiatric Association Research Monographs, 2.*

Maccoby, E. E., & Martin, J. A. (1983). Socialisation in the context of the family: Parent-child interaction. In P. H. Mussen (Ed.), *Handbook of child psychology*: Vol. IV. Socialization, personality, and social development (4th ed., pp. 1–101). New York: Wiley.

Patterson, G. (1986). A microsocial analysis of the contribution of siblings to antisocial process in the family. In D. Olweus, J. Block, & M. Radke-Yarrow (Eds.), *Development of antisocial and prosocial behavior: Research issues and theories* (pp. 235–261). New York: Academic Press.

Piaget, J. (1965). *The moral judgement of the child.* New York: Free Press.

Plomin, R., Loehlin, J. C., & DeFries, J. C. (1985). Genetic and environmental components of "environmental" influences. *Developmental Psychology, 21,* 391–402.

Plomin, R., DeFries, J. C., & Fulker, D. W. (1988). *Nature and nurture during infancy and early childhood.* Cambridge: Cambridge University Press.

Raffaelli, M., & Larson, R. (1987, April). *Sibling interaction in late childhood and early adolescence*. Paper presented at the Biennial Meeting of the Society for Research in Child Development, Baltimore, MD.

Richman, N., Stevenson, J., & Graham, P. (1982). *Preschool to school: A behavioural study*. London: Academic Press.

Rowe, D. C., & Plomin, R. (1981). The importance of nonshared (E1) environmental influences in behavioral development. *Developmental Psychology, 17*, 517–531.

Rowe, D., Rodgers, J. L., Meseck-Bushey, S., & St. John, C. (1989). Sexual behavior and non-sexual deviance: A sibling study of their relationship. *Developmental Psychology, 25*, 61–69.

Scarr, S., & Grajek, S. (1982). Similarities and differences among siblings. In M. E. Lamb & B. Sutton-Smith (Eds.), *Sibling relationships: Their nature and significance across the lifespan* (pp. 357–381). Hillsdale, NJ: Erlbaum.

Schooler, C. (1972). Birth order effects: Not here, not now! *Psychological Bulletin, 78*, 161–175.

Stillwell, R., & Dunn, J. (1985). Continuities in sibling relationships: Patterns of aggression and friendliness. *Journal of Child Psychology and Child Psychiatry, 26*, 627–637.

Stocker, C., Dunn, J., & Plomin, R. (1989). Sibling relationships: Links with child temperament, maternal behavior, and family structure. *Child Development, 60*, 715–727.

Sullivan, H. C. (1953). *The interpersonal theory of psychiatry*. New York: Norton.

Sutton-Smith, B., & Rosenberg, B. G. (1970). *The sibling*. New York: Holt, Rinehart and Winston.

Taylor, M. K., & Kogan, K. L. (1973). Effects of birth of a sibling on mother-child interaction. *Child Psychiatry and Human Development, 4*, 53–58.

Trause, M. A., Voos, D., Rudd, C., Klaus, M., Kennell, J., & Boslett, M. (1981). Separation for childbirth: The effect on the sibling. *Child Psychiatry and Human Development, 12 (1)*, 32–39.

Wagner, M. E., Schubert, H. J. P., & Schubert, D. S. P. (1979). Sibshipconstellation effects on psychosocial development, creativity and health. In H. C. Reese & L. P. Lipsitt (Eds.), *Advances in child development and behavior* (Vol. 14, pp. 57–148). New York: Academic.

Weisner, T. S., & Gallimore, R. (1977). My brother's keeper: Child and sibling caretaking. *Current Anthropology, 18*, 169–190.

Whiting, B. B., & Whiting, J. (1975). *Children of six cultures: A psychosocial analysis*. Cambridge, MA: Harvard University Press.

Winnicott, D. W. (1977). *The piggle*. London: Hogarth Press.

6

Self-Knowledge and Social Influence

Michael Lewis

> Don't yell, just tell me what you want!
> (Overheard from a 4-year-old child to his mother)

Socialization and the uses of social control involve the parent as the agent of the distribution of social rules, ideas, and action, and the child as an agent of receipt. Adaptive significance requires the wish to become a conspecific. It is not a struggle between child and parent, but a mutual learning experience. To be socialized does not involve, for the child, a passive role but an active one. The infant's development of consciousness or objective self-awareness facilitates this process.

Two general world views of human nature predominate in our theories of social influence and development. In the first view, the child is acted on by a variety of forces; as such, this perspective has been called a mechanistic view. In the second, the child acts on these forces; it has been called a constructivist view (Lewis, 1979). The reactive, passive, or mechanistic view, in turn, generates two major theoretical paradigms, the biological or maturational and the social control. The active view, on the other hand, has generated the constructivist or development-cognitive theoretical paradigm. Each of these world views and the paradigms which follow have important implications for our theories about social influences and development.

In both the biological/motivational and social control paradigms,

Michael Lewis • Institute for the Study of Child Development, Robert Wood Johnson Medical School, New Brunswick, New Jersey 08903-0019.

the cause of the child's behavior, in this case the child's social behavior and its developmental change, are forces which act on the infant. Internal biological forces, particular features of the species, are one example. Since we are interested in social influences, we will not deal further with these forces, except to say that the degree to which these forces are known by others—caregivers of infants, for example—is the degree to which they can and most likely do affect social influences. For example, if a parent knows that prematurity results in slower development, at least to begin with, they are likely to alter their expectations as well as their behavior toward their child. Thus, not only do biological factors directly influence development, but adult knowledge of them also may affect the child's development. Moreover, to the degree that these forces are known to the children themselves, they, too, may exert a social influence on the self. Thus, the 4-year-old who knows that "small children cannot run as fast as big ones because their legs are shorter" may not try to run fast because of this knowledge of growth differences.

Social control or socialization forces also act on the passive child, although the characteristics of the infant, including its age, sex, temperament, etc., do have a modifying effect. It is these forces, usually described by such terms as reinforcement or shaping, which will occupy our attention. In the case of social control, the infant is acted upon and its behavior shaped or formed. When we view this control, from the notion of personal freedom, a child, passive and restricted by action, presents an image that is abhorrent to us. This is especially so from the viewpoint of individualization. Although the restriction of personal freedom as a metaphor for socialization comes readily to mind, consideration of alternatives leads us to realize that any other perspectives may not be reasonable. First, the view of individual freedom implies that there exists, in the infant, behavior patterns, ideas, and desires, which are already formed and do not need socialization to bring about. This reflects the idea of "natural person," one in which culture plays only a negative role. Second, such a view of personal freedom denies the adaptive significance of the human child's long period of infancy, a period in which the survival of the child is only possible inasmuch as it is cared for and raised by others.

I think it safe to assume, therefore, that the infant, by its nature, needs to be acted upon, and that this action has as its consequence the creation of a conspecific, another member of the group, one who shares similar beliefs, customs, and patterns of thought. Although the model of being acted upon appears pejorative from the point of view of individual freedom, it is a necessity borne out of adaptive processes.

Returning to our example of sex role, we find that behavior is both biologically determined by gender (e.g., the effects of hormones), and/or by the shaping effect of the social environment. The differential rewards and punishment of our parents, siblings, friends and teachers vis à vis behavior deemed to be sex role-appropriate clearly affects how we think and behave.

Not only are our behaviors determined by differential rewards and punishments, but also by how the environment shapes the child's world. For example, it would be foolish for parents to buy a doll for a boy child and then punish him for playing with it. Rather, they shape his behavior by not letting him play with a doll through not making it available to begin with (Rheingold & Cook, 1975). This refers to structuring rather than reinforcement.

Either of these processes highlight how the infant's behavior and development is determined by the social environment into which it is born. The environment determines the goals, the actions necessary to reach these goals, and the change in goals as a function of development. The setting of these goals and their change, the rewards and punishments, are generated by the adults and they are imposed on the child (although under proper socialization, the individual characteristics of the infant are taken into account). The source of these goals and the processes of change are to be found outside the organism in the social structures and "ideas" that exist in the social world surrounding the child.

Parenthetically, it should be kept in mind that the social world which surrounds the child consists of more than the mother. In two volumes, *Beyond the Dyad* and *The Child and its Family*, we have tried to indicate that the social world of the infant is inhibited by fathers, siblings, aunts, uncles, family friends, peers and others (Lewis, 1984; Lewis & Rosenblum, 1979). Each plays an important role and each may have separate functions vis à vis outcomes or areas of competence. Thus, for example, we see peer and sibling relationships having powerful effects on friendship patterns whereas paternal relationships impact on social performance (Lewis, 1987; Lewis & Feiring, 1979).

The contrast to this passive view (the child acted upon), is the constructivist position. The basis of this position is the belief that even children interact with their environments. Children participate in, are influenced by, and in turn influence those forces that determine their development. From the point of view of social influences, we see little difficulty. Certainly adults' socialization practices take into account the child and are influenced by the child's behavior and reaction (Lewis & Rosenblum, 1974). Such a view, therefore, does not necessitate the rejection of either the biological imperatives or the social control of behavior. However, the constructivist view does allow us to modify the idea of socialization as a passive process.

Most socialization models rely upon a metaphor of force. Consider the psychoanalytic position. Here, the child's impulses direct its behavior, and the role of socialization is to modify and alter these impulses. It is in this struggle that the personality of the child is formed. The metaphor, therefore, is of struggle, conflict, and resolution; in particular, the socialization of the child's sexual impulses and its Oedipal desires (Freud, 1959).

We can assume that although biological imperatives affect particular goals, these goals are of a most general nature. Moreover, given the adaptive significance of these biological needs and the role of the social environment in meeting them, our metaphor should be one where conflict is not the major force in development. In some sense, we see the role of the child as an *active participant in its socialization*. Rather than the infant in struggle with rules, we see the infant trying to adapt to the rules. One important species-specific way of adaptation is through the processes of learning and understanding.

Social control and the socialization process becomes both the material for understanding and a motive for action. Such a view allows for the active participation of the infant in its socialization. In our example of sex role behavior, the effects of social control both inform the child that certain behaviors are approved while others are not, and at the same time become the material for self-generation of the rules others are using. Thus socialization provides both *motives* for particular action and *knowledge* about structure and rules.

In our model of social influences, the environment exerts part of its effect through the structures *within* the infant. It is preferable for us to think of the biological and social forces as the material for the construction of cognitive and affective structures located within the child. Thus, while biological and social forces act on children and are the material children use to construct their world, these forces do not correspond in any simple one-to-one relationship with the structures so created. An example may clarify this distinction: Although a loud noise has the biological capacity to force us to turn toward the sound source and to startle, it is the construction of the interpretation of our action that is important for psychological inquiry. Any inquiry has to be both the study of the action (loud noise → startle) and the interpretation of that action. In the study of emotional behavior, this distinction has been emphasized because it is both the action and interpretation that characterize emotion (James, 1890; Lewis & Michalson, 1983). Within the domain of socialization, an example would be the study of the effect of the parent's action on the child's behavior and the child's understanding of the parental action and its own response (Baumrind, 1989).

The model of a child, active in its own socialization by developing plans, motives, and cognitive structures, requires that we consider the self. If we both hold to a world view of an active organism and one that participates in its development including its socialization, we must logically hold to a belief in the self. It does not appear possible to believe in plans, intentions, and hypothesis testing without a belief in the child's possession of some type of self. "I wish to please my parents," "What is it I am to do in this situation?" "How do these go together?"—all imply some active agent. Holding to a world view of an active child necessitates an implicit belief in self-knowledge and the child's participation in development. A mechanistic or reactive view makes no such premise— machines have no self—and therefore we insist on the sine qua non of a constructivist view, the notion of self.

The study of social influence is not merely the study of action directed toward the child, but the child's interpretation of the meaning of the events, including its own action in reaction to the behavior of adults. The developmental task for the young child is to make sense of the variety of events that occur, some of which are external, and some of which are internal to it. If, indeed, the developmental task is such, then it must follow that the task of perceiving, ordering, and interpreting social events, including the rewards and punishments of others, involves the development of self. Assuming this to be the case, it is of interest to note that the study of the ontogenesis of the self in the socialization process has received little attention. Part of the difficulty lies in the models employed by most theorists. These models usually have contrasted the two passive paradigms: that is, social control and biological determinism. Still another difficulty is the inability to specify what is meant by the term self. Such terms as self-awareness, self-consciousness, and self-concept are often used interchangeably, giving rise to some confusion (Wylie, 1968). Nevertheless, theoretical attempts have been made by Mischel (1966), Lewis (1987, 1989, in press a, b; Lewis & Brooks-Gunn, 1979a), and Bandura (1982) to consider the role of self in social behavior. From a developmental perspective, social knowledge and behavior require and must include a study of the development of self.

In the comments that follow, we will offer first a definition of the features of self and next determine the early development of these features. Having argued for the development of the knowledge of self within the first two years, we will address the more general issue of the role of the self in social development; in particular, in knowing, feeling, and relating to others.

WHAT WE MEAN BY SELF

The relationship of self-knowledge and self-awareness is particularly important to first consider (see Duval & Wicklund, 1972). When organisms are preverbal, such as infants, or unable to speak, such as non-human primates, it is not possible to explore the issue of awareness, because the organism cannot be easily questioned and the self, as a phenomenological event, is not easily studied without access to the internal processes of the organism. Because of this, we must make inferences about self-awareness. Although we can study self-knowledge, we cannot explore, at least in infancy, the epistemological issue of knowledge of the knowledge of self (or what we have called self-awareness). Moreover, knowledge can precede knowledge of knowledge, and therefore self-knowledge precedes self-awareness.[1] For example, by eight months, infants know—that is, will search for—a hidden object, but cannot tell us if they have knowledge of their knowledge of object-permanence. We can accept their behavior as demonstrating knowledge but do not ask about knowledge of knowledge. In the same way, we may speak of a cat's knowledge of spatial properties when it goes around an object rather than trying to go through it. Although we have no idea as to the form this knowledge takes—what is the nature of thought in the young infant or cat?—we do infer and act on the assumption that their knowledge exists.

By referring to adult behavior in this regard, we can consider this issue more readily. We would agree that adults have self-awareness, citing as evidence their use of self-referents, their ability to recognize themselves, and their use of self-directed behavior. Moreover, most languages inform us of the self-awareness. For example, in French, the verb to wash differs depending on if it refers to oneself, "je me lave," or our washing of something else, "je lave les vêtements." The reflexive use of language by adult users informs us that adults have self-awareness. Although adults have self-knowledge at all times, they do not always have self-awareness. Much knowledge does not involve any consideration of self. Much of our behavior occurs rapidly, with little or no self-reflective thought: for example, driving a car to and from our homes to a familiar site such as our offices. However, during times of decision-making, when action requires a choice between goals, we are likely to reflect on the self: I could do X or Y, what should I do? Moreover, when we have made an error and need to rethink an action, or when we socially transgress some rule, self-awareness and self-conscious emotions occur (Mandler, 1975; Lewis & Brooks-Gunn, 1979a; Lewis, Sullivan, Stanger, & Weiss, 1989).

The absence of self-awareness does not reflect the absence of self-involvement in ongoing behavior, but suggests that the self-awareness

---

[1]We use the term self-knowledge to refer to what the self knows and self-awareness to refer to knowledge of self-knowledge.

has an executive role, leaving for other self processes the mechanics of action. It is reasonable to suppose that goal setting, intentions, and evaluation involve self-awareness while specific behaviors can be executed through other process levels of knowledge including association, learning, or even over-learning of response patterns. Schank (1982) has linked some of these different level processes to scripts which guide behavior. Scripts as a metaphor are useful since they assume the organization and maintenance of complex behavior without evoking such executive functions as self-awareness, thinking, or planning. In brief, self knowledge and self-awareness may be considered as somewhat separate, and their development and assemblage in need of study.

THE SELF CREATED IN THE SOCIAL NEXUS

In our consideration of the meaning of self we have emphasized, as have others, the duality of the self. The distinction is between the self as object and as subject (Wylie, 1961). Recently, we have articulated three levels of self development. These have been called self-other differentiation, conservation of self across time and place, and self-awareness (Lewis, 1989, in press a,b,c). We will not detail this developmental sequence here but only add that others as well have recently attempted to trace the development of self across the first 2 years of life (Emde, 1983; Sanders, 1980; Stern, 1985).

However, in all cases, it has been suggested that differentiation of self-other occurs within the context of the social interactions between the infant and others. In particular, these others include the primary caregivers, and may be mothers, fathers, or even parent substitutes. In a sense, the first social influence to affect the infant is in the realm of self-other differentiation. The development of the self occurs as more mature conspecifics interact with it. From this perspective, both psychoanalytic and sociological theories agree, the self grows out of its social connectedness. Let us consider first the sociological theories regarding the origins of the self.

Cooley and Mead were interested in the self, believing that self-awareness (what they called knowledge of self) and other awareness developed simultaneously, both being dependent on social interaction. Indeed, neither could exist without the other, since both originated through social interaction. Cooley (1909/1962, 1912), in developing a theory regarding the social nature of humans and social organization as a whole, posited a reflective or "looking glass" self. The self is reflected through others, thus other people are one's "looking glass." In addition, Cooley stressed that self and society are a common whole, with neither existing in the absence of the other. Cooley believed that infants are not conscious of themselves or the "I," nor are they aware of society or other people. Infants experience a simple "stream of impressions," impressions that gradually become discriminated as the young child differentiates self, or "I," from society, or "we."

Mead (1934/1972), drawing upon Cooley's theory of a "looking-glass" self as well as William James's distinction between the "me" (self as known) and the "I" (self as knower) (James, 1892/1961), provided the first systematic description of the development of the self. Heavily influenced by Darwin, Mead believed that the human infant is active rather than passive, selectively responding to the stimuli rather than indiscriminately responding to all events. Mead further believed that the infant actively constructs the self. He stated:

> The self has a character which is different from that of the physiological organism proper. The self is something which has a development; it is not initially there at birth but arises in the process of social experience and activity. That is, develops in the given individual as a result of his relations to that process as a whole and to other individuals within that process. (1934, pg 43)

Mead believed that the self is dependent upon language development, developing after the child has the communicative ability to interact verbally with others, can take the role of others, can perceive itself as an object, and can differentiate between itself and others through play and games. Thus, interaction with others is crucial for self-development.

Although Freud wrote extensively on the self, the contributions were broad but at the same time limited. Two major aspects of classic psychoanalytic theory that have influenced current notions of the self are the construct of the unconscious and the tripartite division of the personality. Freud's theory of the unconscious emphasized aspects of the self that, until the turn of the century, were not considered to be part of a person's self. The unconscious explains behavior by relying upon the existence of feelings, thoughts, and even knowledge that are not readily available to the person. Dreams, slips of the tongue, and accidents, rather than being random events, are a reflection of the self. For example, dreams provide a way of fulfilling hidden wishes or ridding oneself of painful experiences. Also, the unconscious, even though based on a theory of sexual or libidinal energy, plays a role in self-expression (Freud, 1900/1954, 1959, 1965).

The tripartite division of personality into the id, ego, and superego was Freud's attempt to account for and differentiate among aspects of the self. Believing that the self develops in the opening years of life as a result of the infant's active interaction with the world, Freud also theorized about the development of ego control and defenses. The ego functions by mediating among instinctual needs (the id), external relations, and the conscience (the superego); it aids in the gratification of instincts, while transforming and restraining these instincts to cope with the social world. Erikson eloquently described the role of the ego in Freudian theory:

> Between the id and the superego, then, the ego dwells. Consistently balancing and warding off the extreme ways of the other two, the ego keeps tuned to the reality of the historical day, testing perceptions, selecting memories, governing action, and otherwise integrating the individual's capacities of orientation and planning. To safeguard itself, the ego employs "defense mechanisms." (1963, p. 193)

A functioning ego requires the differentiation of self and other and requires knowledge of the social world; the ego arises out of the awareness that the mother and the self are separate and that the mother does not fulfill the infant's every need (Freud, 1900/1954). Let us note that such theorizing has some relation to our distinction between self knowledge (id and some ego function—the unaware aspects of action, plans, feelings and thought), and self awareness (ego and superego functions—the aware aspect of personality).

Although Freud believed that the development of the self (or personality) is accomplished in the first six or eight years of life, Erikson theorized that each individual progresses through a series of eight stages of development. However, it is Erikson's first three stages which involve us here. The first stage involves *basic trust versus basic mistrust*. In order for ego identity to emerge, the infant must develop a sense of trust in the self and in the world. Such trust is predicated on the continuity and predictability of familiar objects and people and on the maternal provision of comfort and care. The quality of the maternal relationship, not the overall amount of food or love provided, is of importance, as is the transmission of the belief that the child's actions have a meaning. If the infant feels deprived, a sense of trust, of being "all right" with the world, will not emerge.

The second stage, *autonomy versus shame and doubt,* arises when the toddler begins to have control over his or her body. Experimenting with free choice, the toddler practices holding on to and letting go of objects and bodily functions. At the same time, the toddler needs some protection from shame and doubt through parental guidance. As Erikson (1963) states, "Where shame is dependent on the consciousness of being upright and exposed, doubt, so clinical observation leads me to believe, has much to do with a consciousness of having a front and a back and especially a 'behind' " (p. 253); hence, the need for protection. The third stage, *initiative versus guilt,* occurs in early childhood. The child moves about with direction, accomplishing tasks, even "attacking and conquering" them. At the same time, the child moves from being dependent on the parent to being more independent and powerful.

Just as Erikson described each self-identity stage as a struggle between two poles of a dimension, so does Mahler (Mahler, Pine, & Bergman, 1975) describe the development of self as a struggle between separateness and relatedness, terming this the separation-individuation process. Mahler's hypothesis is that healthy functioning requires a sense of separateness as well as relatedness to the world. As she states, "Consciousness of self and absorption without awareness of self are the two polarities between which we move, with varying ease, with varying degrees of alternation of simultaneity" (Mahler et al., 1975, p. 129). This task reoccurs throughout the life span as new tasks are confronted. However, the major period of development involves the first five years of life, because during this time the child needs to emerge from the symbiotic relationship with the mother (separation) and acquire individual characteristics (individuation) in order to develop an independent and autonomous sense of self (Mahler, 1968).

At the beginning of this process, the newborn is like a chick in an egg who has no need for awareness of the world or for individuation. As the several-month-old infant becomes dimly aware of the fact that another person is meeting his or her needs, this "oneness" with the mother ends. Not until four to five months of age does the infant actually differentiate between the self and the mother. In Mahler's terms, the infant is "hatching" from the mother-infant symbiotic orbit (Mahler et al., 1975), which is evidenced by the onset of the social smile and recognition of the mother (Spitz, 1954). Not until six months of age is the separateness of mother and self firmly established, as evidenced by increased play with the infant's own and the mother's body parts. The infant investigates the mother's face, hands, hair, clothing, and jewelry in what has been called "customs inspection." When the child recognizes the mother, inspection of others begins, sometimes with astonishment, sometimes with apprehension. From 12 to 18 months, the infant refines his own knowledge about self-other differentiation, body boundaries, and emotional separation. One of the major milestones is the ability to move away from the mother:

> Walking seemed to have great symbolic meaning for both mother and toddler; it is as if the walking toddler had proved by his attainment of independent upright locomotion that he had already graduated into the world of fully independent human beings. The expectation and confidence that mother exudes that her child is now able to "make it" out there seems to be an important trigger for the child's own feeling of safety and perhaps also the initial encouragement for his exchanging some of his magic omnipotence for pleasure in his own autonomy and developing of self-esteem. (Mahler et al., 1975, p. 74)

After locomotion and autonomy, the child begins a "love affair with the world" (Greenacre, 1956). As the 12- to 18-month-old moves further and further away from the mother, he or she also returns periodically, and so enjoys both the safety of her presence and the excitement of independent exploration.

The next stage (the last half of the second year), involving an increased awareness of self, resulting in a heightened concern with the mother. Mahler *et al.* (1975) suggest that the child "now seems to have an increased need, a wish for his mother to *share with him* every one of his new skills and experiences" (pp. 76–77). In addition, both empathy and understanding, what it means to be separate and autonomous, emerge between 18 and 24 months of age. The "love affair with the world" becomes tempered as the child learns about frustrations and limitations. In the third year, individuality is consolidated, separations from the mother become easier to bear, and the ability to take another's role becomes more pronounced. Thus, self-identity emerges through the first years of life; the child has developed a self that is separate from but also related to others.

One last group of theories is considered. These we can call genetic epistemology. The writings of the epistemologists are exemplified by Merleau-Ponty (1964), Wallon (1949), and Piaget (1936/1963, 1937/1954). For them, as well as for Cooley and Mead, knowledge of self may not be considered apart from knowledge of others; both develop through interaction with the social world. As Merleau-Ponty states, "If I am a consciousness turned toward things, I can meet in things the actions of another and find in them a meaning, because they are themes of possible activity for my own body" (1964, p. 113).

Piaget's main concern was not knowledge of the social world but knowledge of the logical and physical world. However, he does address the question of self, albeit somewhat obliquely, believing that society has a unique role in the child's development: "Society, even more, in a sense, than the physical environment, changes the very structure of the individual" (1947/1960, p. 156). For Piaget, self-knowledge is not thought to occur until the end of sensorimotor period, and is dealt with in terms of egocentrism and decentering. Although Piaget believes that this process only starts after two years, it is interesting to note that the process of decentering is similar to that discussed by Mead.

We have argued that the self develops from consistency, regularity, and contingency of the infant's action and reaction in the world of *both* objects and people, although the contingency of the social world is viewed as the primary factor (Lewis, 1982, 1986, 1989). Contingency feedback provides for the generalized expectancies about infants' control of their worlds and such expectancies should help differentiate infants' actions from others' actions. The consistency, timing, and quality of the caregiver's responses create expectancies about control and competence. If infants' demands are reinforced, they are, in a sense, controlling their environment. Moreover, since other-interaction always involves the other's relating to a specific locus in space, the interactive nature of social experience should facilitate the schema of self.[2]

It seems evident that the social world provides the context and, therefore, influences self-development, and more so when we realize that the categories by which we refer to ourselves are of social origin. These categories, even their names, reflect the influence of the social environment. For example, in regard to the category of age, Edwards and Lewis (1979) found that 3-5-year-old boys were equally likely to classify themselves as "big" boys or "babies" while girls were more likely to classify themselves as "babies." Likewise, at 9 years of age, girls are less likely to classify themselves as athletic while boys are less likely to classify themselves as physically attractive.

In considering the role of social influences on all aspects of self-development, it makes little sense to consider self without socialization. It might be the case, if we would set up such a condition, that the self-awareness might develop independently of a social context. But what kind of self-awareness might that be? Certainly not a human or social self. The socialization and the influences of social others, their goals, structures, and beliefs are what become part of the self, both as self-knowledge and self-awareness.

[2]While one might argue that particular features of caregiving, for example, responsivity, may be responsible for the emergence of self-other distinction, it is possible that other factors are also at work. Improper caregiving, where the child is stressed, may actually facilitate self-other discrimination. Infants who are more challenged by their environments and less protected from environmental perturbations may need to copy at earlier ages and, thus, form self-other differentiation more easily (Lewis, Brooks-Gunn, & Jaskir, 1985). While the infant's interactions with its object-world also lead to a sense of self, we suspect that self-object interactions are less important because (1) object interactions are apt to be less regular than social interaction, at least very early in life; and (2) one learns less about the social human self through the interaction with non-animate things. Self-object interactions are less contingent early in life because the self's agency or permanence is not established and, therefore, there is little intended connection between the child's action and outcome. This is not so in the social realm where social objects, usually caregivers, intend for their actions to be contingent on those of the child. Under these conditions, the pairing of action-social response is much more likely to lead to contingency learning for the child. Moreover, although in self-object interaction the infant may learn about such dimensions as movement and shape, in self social interactions the infant learns about people. Given the need to learn about features of selves (the categorical self), self social interactions supply the child with more information about the human self.

EMPIRICAL SUPPORT OF AN EMERGING SELF-AWARENESS

Empirical support for the emergence of self-awareness comes from a variety of sources. By 2 years of age, children use a self-referent such as "me" or "mine." Observation of a child taking a toy from another, bringing the toy toward their own bodies and saying "mine" provides strong evidence for the development of self-awareness. The terrible twos—a period when children's clear differentiation from their care-givers is most evident—also serves to mark the active self and aware self in social behavior (see Mahler et al., 1975, for a complete discussion of individuation). At earlier ages, the evidence becomes more problematic; we believe that while other aspects of self develop, it is awareness which emerges in the last half of the second year of life (Lewis, in press a, b).

One way to explore the concept of self awareness in a nonverbal child is through the study of self-referential behavior (Lewis & Brooks-Gunn, 1979b). One form of self-referential behavior is self-recognition, in particular, using the reflected self to guide one's action or to touch oneself. We have chosen to use self-recognition. The only adults who would have difficulty recognizing their faces visually are psychotic pa-tients and those suffering from certain central nervous system dysfunc-tions (Cornielson & Arsension, 1960; Frenkel, 1964). However, self-rec-ognition (usually of the face) and self-awareness are not synonymous, because it is possible to have a self-awareness and not be able to visually recognize oneself. Nevertheless, it is hardly possible to recognize oneself and not have self-awareness. Thus, the use of self-recognition provides a simple and straightforward way of exploring the develop-ment of awareness.

In choosing to investigate visual self-recognition as a method for exploring self-awareness, three different procedures, each related to nat-urally occurring situations and using three different types of self-im-ages, have been studied (Lewis & Brooks-Gunn, 1979a). Infants' re-sponses to mirrors, videotapes, and pictorial representations of the self were explored since each of these procedures presents the child with different dimensions of self-recognition—contingent and/or feature rec-ognition. Contingency cues allow the infant to learn that the self image "acts like me," while feature cues allow the infant to learn that a self representation "looks like me." Both contingent and feature recognition contribute to the differentiation of self and other: A contingent image reproduces one's own actions, whereas others only do so sometimes (as in the case of imitation); and a self representation always has the fea-tures of the self, while others only have similar features (as in the case of a same-sex and same-age person). Mirror images, videotapes, and pic-torial representations of the self may be described in terms of contingency and feature recognition. The findings from the different procedures reveal how infants utilize contingent and feature cues.

The knowledge that a reflection in the mirror is oneself and not another involves contingent as well as feature recognition. Mirrors possess special and unique properties: They are three dimensional, are relatively distortion-free, and reproduce one's actions immediately. The one-to-one correspondence of one's actions and the reflection of these actions is naturally present in light-reflecting surfaces. Such contingencies give infants valuable feedback as they learn that other people do not produce behavior sequences identical to their own and that only a reflected image of self does so. An infant must discover the contingent nature of mirrors, making the inference that a reflection is not another, but is oneself. With this knowledge, the special features unique to oneself are learned.

Infants' responses to mirrors have been observed in experimental situations. The most commonly used situation was first used by Amsterdam (1968) and developed by Lewis and Brooks-Gunn (1979a), and by Gallup (1970) for chimpanzees. In the procedure we use, the infant's face is marked by rouge and the infant's response to seeing the marked face in a mirror is observed. The operational definition of self-recognition is self-referential behavior—that is, touching the mark on their faces because the infants must recognize that the image in the mirror is, in fact, themselves, and that the mark resides not on the image's face, but on their own. Non-contingent self-recognition can be studied through the use of either photographs or videotape feedback. In the former, the infant can be shown a variety of photographs and his or her affective, attentional, and verbal responses measured. In the case of videotape feedback, a variety of procedures have been used, including the delay feedback of the child's own image. In both types of procedure, the use of verbal response, "That's me," or the subject naming its own name, as well as differences in attention and affect, are used as a means of distinguishing images of self from images of others. Finally, in order to ensure that the infant is responding to its own image, rather than to a class (such as male, blond, etc.), the contrasts for comparison are carefully selected. The results of these studies have already been reported elsewhere and appear to suggest that at about 15/18 months of life infants begin to show self-referential behavior, which is for us the measure of the emergence of self awareness.

SELF SOCIALIZES ITSELF

Socialization acts on the infant. Prior to the development of an active self, the social influences are direct, shaping and molding the child's behavior with minimum participation from the infant itself. As we have suggested, this process should not necessarily be viewed as a struggle. However, prior to an active self, the infant can be of relatively little help. In some sense, it cannot join into the process because such active participation involves self-awareness: an agent who is trying to understand the rules and generate the goals himself. If the data on self-recognition reflects self-awareness, then somewhere around the beginning of the second half of the second year of life, the infant itself can participate in the socialization process.

Could not the infant participate before self-awareness occurs? Since self-knowledge occurs prior to self-awareness (Lewis, in press), we have no reason not to believe that the child can be active at an earlier time. What is important at this point in development is that the child can represent itself as well as others, both people and "rules or goals" and it is this joint representation of self and others which becomes critical for the socialization process. For example, we will consider two specific tasks. The first has to do with the child's social relationships. We do not believe that the socialization of relationships can be actively joined by infants until they have developed self-awareness. This is pursued further especially because it has to do with attachment relationships and "working models" of relationships.

Emotional life and intentionality also is affected by the emergence of self-awareness. Although goal-directed behavior exists earlier, in particular, determined by the socialization of actions with the primary emotions, much more goal generation can only occur once the infant develops self-awareness. Until such time as awareness emerges, infants are not capable of generating evaluation of their own actions (Kagan, 1984), and therefore not capable of such motivating emotions as pride (achievement of socially-specific goals), shame (failure of the self vis à vis the other's goals) and guilt (the attempt to correct one's action in order to adhere to socially determined goals). Until such time, the motivating and self-correcting processes related to children's active participation in socialization cannot be supported by their self-conscious emotions. In the following discussion, each of these issues is considered.

THE ROLE OF SELF-AWARENESS IN RELATIONSHIPS

Levels of Social Relationships

A social relationship requires a variety of abilities that have not been well studied. Hinde (1976, 1979) has articulated six dimensions that can be used to characterize a relationship. These are (1) goal structures, (2) diversity of interactions, (3) degree of reciprocity, (4) meshing of interactions, (5) frequency, and (6) patterning and multidimensional qualities of interactions.

These six features of interaction define lower levels of relationships. Young human infants and their mothers, as well as other social creatures, can be said to have acquired this lower level of relationship. While this is one level, a human adult relationship needs to be characterized by a higher level. I find it difficult to accept that a rat and her pups have the same level of a relationship as a human mother and her 3-year-old child. Hinde suggests two further features of a relationship that allow us to conceptualize a higher level for the human child and mother and to differentiate relationships of humans from those of animals. These features include (7) cognitive factors, or those mental processes that allow members of an interaction to think of the other member as well as of themselves, and (8) something which Hinde calls penetration, which I would interpret as something having to do with ego boundaries.

Notice that interactions alone (features 1–6) are insufficient to describe a higher level human relationship. Although interactive patterns may describe the nature of the relationship between mother and the very young infant, unless these patterns also have something to do with awareness of self, they are not descriptive of adult relationships. In other words, uniquely human relationships require self-awareness (Lewis, 1987). Such a view was suggested by Sullivan (1953). For him, a relationship is by necessity the negotiation of at least two selves. Higher level abilities are vital for a relationship since, without two selves (one has only an I–it not an I–thou), there can be no relationship (Buber, 1958). Emde (1988) makes reference to the "we" feature of relationships, and in support of the timetable of consciousness (self-awareness), points to the second half of the second year of life for its appearance.

Interactions and Relationships

Our model of mature human relationships requires that we consider different levels in the development of a relationship of time, rather than seeing it existing in its adult form from the first. Uniquely mature human relationships arise from interactions only after the development of self-awareness. An interaction can lead to a relationship through the mediation of cognitive structures, in particular the development of awareness (Lewis, 1987). Only after the acquisition of self-awareness can a higher level, specifically human, relationship occur. Higher level human relationships require self-awareness. Animal relationships do not need this skill and neither may relationships in infancy that occur prior to the acquisition of awareness. The meaning of the term "relationship," therefore, is not the same across levels. As with the problem of imitation, the meaning of the terms we use (even when we use the same term) are not necessarily equivalent without considering the issue of level.

What we mean when we refer to mature human relationships is the level that usually includes what the organism thinks about its self and the other, the desire to share, and the use of empathy to regulate the relationship. Moreover, the issue of ego boundaries, as discussed by Hinde, also needs to be considered. When we consider ego boundaries we need to make reference to the child's growing understanding of privacy, as well as its need to become a "we." Without these skills, we may talk about a lower level relationship, but not a mature human one.

From this point of view, the achievement of adult human relationships has a developmental progression. This progression involves, first, interactions (which may be similar to those shown by all social creatures), second, cognitive structures, including awareness and such skills as empathy (the ability to place the self in the role of others), and finally, third, the mature human form of relationships (Lewis, 1987). The relationships of 1-year-olds do not contain these cognitive structures and, therefore, may only approximate that of adults. By 2 years most children have identity and the beginning of such skills as empathy (Borke, 1971; Zahn-Waxler & Radke-Yarrow, 1981). Their relationships now approximate more closely those of the mature level. Mahler's concept of individuation is relevant here, for as she has pointed out, only when the child is able to individuate can it be said that a more mature relationship exists (Mahler *et al.*, 1975).

Such an analysis raises the question of the nature of the child's relationships prior to awareness. For me, a pre-awareness level relationship is a complex social species-patterned process, which is imposed by the caregivers and which, through adaptive processes, may be wired in the human infant. This imposed (or socialized) complex patterned system—a lower level relationship—gives way to a mature relationship in which the child joins the socialization process. The nature of the higher level relationship is dependent on many factors. These include the nature of the socialization practices (the initial interactions imposed on the infant), self awareness, and the cognitions about the interactions of self and other, that is, the meaning given to them by the selves involved (Bowlby, 1980).

Attachment as Representation

Recently, Main and colleagues (Main, Kaplan, & Cassidy, 1985) and Bretherton (1987) have returned to a more cognitive view of attachment, as suggested by Bowlby (1980), that of a "working model." By a working model, these authors suggest a schema concerning the mother as a secure base. By focusing attention on the child's cognitive construction rather than on just the interactive patterns of the dyad, the theory of attachment and relationships moves toward a greater realization that an attachment relationship involves the self and the representation of the self, what I have called self-awareness. For example, Bowlby (1973) states, "The model of the attachment figure and the model of the self are likely to develop so as to be complementary and mutually nonconforming. Thus, an unwanted child is likely not only to feel unwanted by his parents, but to *believe that he is essentially unwanted*" (emphasis added, pg. 208).

Such a view of relationships is much more similar to the one that we posit assumes an adult like form. The level of representation of relationship, including the self, is far different from relationships formed by simple interactions. Notice that in Bowlby's quote, children believe that they—their selves—are unwanted. Such a representation must involve a child capable of self-reflection (awareness). Moreover, it may even be the case that the simple interactions themselves are not the only material the representation of a relationship is based on. Other forms of knowledge may affect these representations. For example, two fathers have little interactive time with their children, one because he likes to play golf with his friends, the other because he works all the time to earn a living for his family. The children's representation of their fathers should differ since it will be based upon both the interactive time and the reasons for that time.

As soon as we come to consider relationships in terms of representations, something also suggested by Hinde, we need to return to the child's capacity to reference itself (self-awareness). This, we believe, occurs after the first year of life, somewhere toward the middle of the second. If this is so, then our observation of the attachment relationship at 1 year reflects (1) the interactions based on socialization patterns that the child will subsequently use to form a working model of the relationship, and (2) the adult caregivers' relationship, which includes the adults' working model of their attachment relationship with their parents.

To summarize, socialization determines the pattern of parent-infant interactions. For example, boys are reinforced less for crying than girls, presumably because of the socialization of sex role differences in the expression of emotion (Brooks-Gunn & Lewis, 1982; Malatesta & Haviland, 1982). These interaction patterns provide the social context which facilitates self-development and ultimately self-awareness. The emergence of self-awareness allows for the representation of self and other and for the representation of the affective "good" or "safe" mother as well as her actions (Bowlby, 1980). These representations in turn help transform the behaviors of interaction into goals and rules. Thus, parental goals and rules generate specific patterns of behavior which in turn develop structures (self and representations) enabling the child to reconstruct the parental goals and rules. The socialization of relationships provides the material for the generation of relationships; its influence is on both *structures and content.*

Self-Awareness, Emotional Life, and Self-Socialization

The proposition we wish to entertain here is that socialization helps create self-awareness. Awareness, in turn, gives rise to emotional states unavailable before this development. These emotions, called self-conscious emotions, include pride, shame, and guilt (Lewis *et al.*, 1989). Because these emotions have to do with goals, standards, and rules, the child becomes able to reward/punish itself, independent of the parent. The influence of socialization in this regard, has to do with the creation of self awareness first, and in articulating through action and words, goals, rules and standards. Having done so, the socialization process of the parent is joined by the child who, having developed self-awareness and standards/rules and goals now serves as an active reinforcer of these practices.

Identity and Secondary Emotional Attainment

The development of self-awareness provides the cognitive underpinning for the emergence of emotional states absent in the young child in the first year and a half of life. Although the child exhibits the primary emotions, including joy, anger, sadness, interest, disgust, and fear, it is not until the acquisition of awareness that the child acquires such emotions as embarrassment, envy, empathy, pride, guilt, and shame (Lewis *et al.*, 1989; Lewis in press a). These latter emotions, often called secondary emotions (as opposed to the primary ones), should be relabeled as self-conscious emotions. Lewis *et al.* (1989) have presented a model of development of emotional states. The first set of states, called primary emotions, occur early and, as states, are independent of self-awareness. The second set of states, called secondary emotions, occur later and *only after* the attainment of self-awareness. Let us consider the emotions of pride, shame, and empathy.

Pride occurs when the child evaluates its own action against a standard and finds it successful. The emergence of pride appears only after self-awareness and is related to achievement motivation (Heckhausen, 1984). Because of this emotion, the child seeks out action which is likely to lead to this feeling. Although the infant expresses joy in achievement, we have called this efficacy (Lewis & Goldberg, 1969). Not until the onset of awareness can we see pride. Happiness is reflected in facial behavior but pride can be seen both in facial and bodily action (See Gepphart, 1986).

Shame, guilt, and embarrassment emerge only after self-awareness (Lewis *et al.*, 1989; Zahn-Waxler, in press). The responses of these three emotions are quite different, but all have to do with the child's evaluation of its action against a standard. Failure results in one of these negative emotions, depending upon socialization factors (Dweck & Leggett, 1988), as well as dispositional ones (DiBiase & Lewis, 1989). Children will focus on the self's action or the self's action toward another or they will focus on themselves. The distinction between self-action and self is one of global versus specific evaluation. Focus on the self's action—as in, "I should not have said that to Mom"—leads to guilt which is characterized by reparation; that is, action to correct the failure, "I shall not say that again." Focus on the self leads to shame and to such statements as, "I am no good." Shame is characterized by wanting to hide or disappear. Notice there is not corrective action save this desire to disappear.

In each of these emotions, self-awareness relative to some goal, standard, or rule is necessary for the emotional state to occur. Thus, self-awareness is directly related to the emergence of these emotions. But how does the emergence of these emotions facilitate the socialization of the child and how are they related to social control? As we pointed out earlier, the child joins in its own socialization. In order for the child to be able to do so, it needs to develop structures that allow it to generate the social order without the moment-to-moment control of others or without the others being present. One way in which this can be done is to "incorporate" the rules, standards, and goals of the socializing others. Incorporation is not simply the storage and organization of specific parental behaviors, although this is necessary. Incorporation requires that the child represent itself as well as others. This representation is seen as self-awareness. However, having done so, it is still unclear as to why the child behaves in a particular manner. At a simpler level they do so because of the fear or anxiety of punishment (Freud, 1959). However, incorporation cannot be said to exist until the child incorporates *both the information and the motives for behaving*. The motives for behaving also grow out of the development of self-awareness. The self-conscious emotions of pride, shame, and guilt cannot occur until self-awareness emerges. Once present, the generation of pride or shame, guilt and embarrassment serve as *self* motivators. Thus, as before, self-awareness, itself a function of socialization, gives rise to information and motives that promote the socialization process itself.

SUMMARY

In the example we used at the start of this discussion, we overheard a 4-year-old boy say, "Don't yell, just tell me what you want!" This example was meant to convey several aspects of our belief about the role of self in socialization. Let me state them in a more propositional form.

Proposition I. Socialization is a joint effort of parents (and others) and child to teach the child the rules, values, standards, goals, and actions of the social nexus.

Proposition II. Socialization is both the *process* and *material* which the child uses to become a conspecific.

Proposition III. Infants learn simple rules through passive learning until self-awareness emerges and active joining occurs.

Proposition IV. Self-awareness occurs within the context of social behavior and socialization.

Proposition V. Self-awareness gives rise to representation of self, parents, and primary emotions which, in turn, give rise to relationships.

Proposition VI. Representations give rise to standards, rules, and goals and the evaluation of these by the self.

Proposition VII. Self conscious emotions are the motives for the child's active joining in the socialization of itself.

In our example, the child knows that the mother wishes him to do something. There is a socialization of rule occurring. The child wishes to do what the mother wants him to and will do so when he is able to understand her rule or request. Perhaps parents would do better in socializing their children if at some point in the child's development they simply informed them about the goals, standards, or rules. This might allow the child to incorporate the standards (identification with the parent already taken place) and to generate his or her own socialization through his or her own self-conscious emotions. If we viewed socialization as a joint task, one in which the child, early in life, is an active self-participant, such a possibility in regard to "training" becomes possible.

REFERENCES

Amsterdam, B. K. (1968). *Mirror behavior in children under two years of age.* Unpublished doctoral dissertation. Chapel Hill: University of North Carolina.

Bandura, A. (1982). The self and the mechanisms of agency. In J. Suls (Ed.), *Psychological perspectives on the self* (Vol. 1, pp. 3–40). Hillsdale, NJ: Erlbaum.

Baumrind, D. (1989). The permanence of change and the impermanence of stability. *Human Development, 32,* No. 3–4, 187–195.

Borke, H. (1971). Interpersonal perception of young children: Egocentrism or empathy. *Development Psychology, 5,* 263–269.

Bowlby, J. (1973). *Attachment and loss. Vol 2: Separation.* New York: Basic Books.

Bowlby, J. (1980). *Attachment and Loss. Vol 3: Loss, sadness and depression.* New York: Basic Books.

Bretherton, I. (1987). New perspectives on attachment relations: Security, communication and internal working models. In J. D. Osofsky (Ed.), *Handbook of infant development, 2nd ed.* New York: Wiley.

Brooks-Gunn, J., & Lewis, M. (1982). Affective exchanges between normal and handicapped infants and their mothers. In T. Field & A. Fogel (Eds.), *Emotion and early interaction* (pp. 161–188). Hillsdale, NJ: Elrbaum.

Buber, M. (1958). *I & thou* (2nd ed.). Translated by Ronald Gregor Smith. New York: Charles Scribner.

Cooley, C. H. (1912). *Human nature and the social order.* New York: Charles Scribners' Sons.

Cooley, C. H. (1962). *Social organization: A study of the larger mind.* New York: Schocken Books. (Originally published 1909)

Cornielson, F. S., & Aresnian, J. (1960). A study of the responses of psychotic patients to photographs of self-image experience. *Psychiatric Quarterly, 34,* 1–8.

DiBiase, R., & Lewis, M. (1988). *Temperament and emotion.* Paper presented at International Conference on Infant Studies meeting, Washington, DC

Duval, S., & Wicklund, R. A. (1972). *A theory of objective self awareness.* New York: Academic Press.

Dweck, C. S., & Leggett, E. L. (1988). A social-cognitive approach to motivation and personality. *Psychological Review, 95,* 256–273.

Edwards, C. P., & Lewis, M. (1979). Young children's concepts of social relations: Social functions and social objects. In M. Lewis & L. Rosenblum (Eds.), *The child and its family: The genesis of behavior, 2.* New York: Plenum Press.

Emde, R. N. (1983). The prerepresentational self and its affective core. *The Psychoanalytic Study of the Child, 38,* 165–192.

Emde, R. N. (1988). Development terminable and interminable II. Recent psychoanalytic theory and therapeutic considerations. *International Journal of Psychoanalysis, 69,* 283–296.

Erikson, E. H. (1963). *Childhood and society.* New York: Norton

Frenkel, R. E. (1964). Psychotherapeutic reconstruction of traumatic amnesic period by the mirror image projective technique. *Journal of Existentialism, 17,* 77–96.

Freud, S. (1954). *The interpretation of dreams.* New York: Basic Books. (Originally published 1900)

Freud, S. (1959). *Instincts and their vicissitudes. Collected papers.* New York: Basic Books. (Originally published 1915)

Freud, S. (1965). *New introductory lectures on psychoanalysis.* New York: Norton.

Gallup, C. G., Jr. (1970). Chimpanzees: Self-recognition. *Science, 167,* 86–87.

Gepphart, U. (1986). A coding system for analyzing behavioral expressions of self-evaluative emotions (Technical Manual). Munich: Max Planck Institute for Psychological Research.

Greenacre, P. (1956). Experiences of awe in childhood. *Psychoanalytic Study of the Child, 11,* 9–30.

Heckhausen, H. (1984). Emergent achievement behavior: Some early developments. In J. Nicholls (Eds.), *The development of achievement motivation* (pp. 1–32). Greenwich, CT: JAI Press.

Hinde, R. A. (1976). Interactions, relationships, and social structure. *Man. 11,* 1–17.

Hinde, R. A. (1979). *Towards understanding relationships.* London: Academic Press.

James, W. (1890). *The principles of psychology.* New York: Holt.

James, W. (1961). *Psychology: The briefer course.* Edited by G. Allpert. New York: Harper & Row. (Originally published 1892)

Kagan, J. (1984). *The nature of the child*. New York: Basic Books.

Lewis, M. (1979). The self as a developmental concept. *Human Development, 22,* 416–419.

Lewis, M. (1982). The social network systems model: Toward a theory of social development. In T. Field, A. Huston, H. Quay, L. Troll, & G. Fritz (Eds.), *Review of human development* (pp. 180–214). New York: Wiley.

Lewis, M. (Ed.). (1984). *Beyond the dyad.* New York, NY: Plenum Press.

Lewis, M. (1986). Origins of self-knowledge and individual differences in early self-recognition. In A. G. Greenwald & J. Suls (Eds.), *Psychological perspective on the self, 3* (pp. 55–78). Hillsdale, NJ: Erlbaum.

Lewis, M. (1987). Social development in infancy and early childhood. In J. Osofsky (Ed.), *Handbook of infant development* (2nd ed., pp. 419–493). New York: Wiley.

Lewis, M. (1989). Thinking and feeling—The elephant's tail. In C. A. Maher, M. Schwebel, & N. S. Fagley (Eds.), *Thinking and problem solving in the developmental process: International perspectives.* Hillsdale, NJ: Erlbaum.

Lewis, M. (1990). Social knowledge and social development. *Merrill-Palmer Quarterly, 36,* 93–116.

Lewis, M. (in press b). Self-knowledge and social development in early life. In L. A. Pervin (Ed.), *Handbook of social psychology.* New York: Guilford.

Lewis, M. (in press c). *The exposed self.* New York: Free Press.

Lewis, M., & Brooks-Gunn, J. (1979a). *Social cognition and the acquisition of self.* New York: Plenum Press.

Lewis, M., & Brooks-Gunn, J. (1979b). Towards a theory of social cognition: The development of self. In J. Uzgiris (Ed.), *New directions in child development: Social interaction and communication during infancy.* (pp. 1–20). San Francisco: Jossey-Bass.

Lewis, M., Brooks-Gunn, J., & Jaskir, J. (1985). Individual differences in early visual self recognition. *Developmental Psychology, 21,* 1181–1187.

Lewis, M., & Feiring, C. (1979). The child's social network: Social object, social functions and their relationship. In M. Lewis & L. Rosenblum (Eds.), *The child and its family: The genesis of behavior* (Vol. 2, pp. 9–27). New York: Plenum Press.

Lewis, M., & Goldberg, S. (1969). The acquisition and violation of expectancy: An experimental paradigm. *Journal of Experimental Child Psychology, 7,* 70–80.

Lewis, M., & Michalson, L. (1983). *Children's emotions and moods: Developmental theory and measurement.* New York: Plenum Press.

Lewis, M., & Rosenblum, L. A. (1974). *The effect of the infant on its caregiver: The origins of behavior, 1.* New York: Wiley.

Lewis, M., & Rosenblum, L. (Eds.). (1979). *The child and its family: The genesis of behavior, 2.* New York: Plenum Press.

Lewis, M., Sullivan, M., Stanger, C., & Weiss, C. (1989). Self development and self conscious emotions. *Child Development, 60,* 146–156.

Lewis, M., & Weinraub, M. (1976). The father's role in the infant's social network. In M. Lamb (Ed.), *The role of the father in child development* (pp. 157–184). New York: Wiley.

Mahler, M. S. (1968). *On human symbiosis and the vicissitudes of individuation: Infantile psychosis* (Vol. 1). New York: International Universities Press.

Mahler, M. S., Pine, F., & Bergman, A. (1975). *The psychological birth of the infant.* New York: Basic Books.

Main, M., Kaplan, K., & Cassidy, J. (1985). Security in infancy, childhood and adulthood. A move to the level of representation. In I. Bretherton & Waters (Eds.), Growing points of attachment theory and research. *Monographs of the Society for Research in Child Development, 50* (1–2, Serial No. 209), 66–104.

Malatesta, C., & Haviland, J. (1982). Learning display rules: The socialization of emotion expression in infancy. *Child Development, 53,* 991–1003.

Mandler, G. (1975). *Mind and emotion.* New York: Wiley.

Mead, G. H. (1972). *Mind, self, and society.* Chicago: University of Chicago Press. (Originally published 1934)

Merleau-Ponty, M. (1964). *Primer of perception.* Edited by J. Eddie & translated by W. Cobb. Evanston, IL: Northwestern University Press.

Mischel, W. (1966). A social-learning view of sex differences in behavior. In E. E. Maccoby (Ed.), *The development of sex differences* (pp. 56–81). Stanford: Stanford University Press.

Piaget, J. (1954). *The construction of reality in the child.* Translated by M. Cook. New York: Basic Books (Originally published 1937)

Piaget, J. (1960). *The psychology of intelligence.* Translated by M. Piercy & D. E. Berlyne. Paterson, NJ: Littlefield, Adams & Co. (Originally published 1947)

Piaget, J. (1963). *The origins of intelligence in children.* New York: Norton (Originally published 1936)

Rheingold, H. L., & Cook, K. V. (1975). The content of boy's and girl's rooms as an index of parents' behavior. *Child development, 46,* 459–563.

Sanders, L. (1980). New knowledge about the infant from current interactions. *Journal of the American Academy of Child Psychiatry, 3,* 231–264.

Schank, R. C. (1982). *Dynamic memory. A theory of reminding and learning in computers and people.* Cambridge, MA: Cambridge University Press.

Spitz, R. A. (1954). Infantile depression and the general adaptation syndrome: On the relation between physiologic model and psychoanalytic conceptualization. In P. Hoch & J. Zubin (Eds.), *Depression.* New York: Grune & Stratton.

Stern, D. N. (1985). *The interpersonal world of the infant.* New York: Basic Books.

Sullivan, H. S. (1953). *The interpersonal theory of psychiatry.* New York: Norton.

Wallon, H. (1949). *Les origines du caractère chez l'enfant: les préludes du sentiment de personalité* (2nd ed.). Paris: Presses Universitaires de France.

Wylie, R. C. (1961). *The self concept.* Lincoln: University of Nebraska Press.

Wylie, R. C. (1968). The present status of self theory. In E. F. Borgatta & W. E. Lambert (Eds.), *Handbook of personality theory and research* (pp. 728–787). Chicago: Rand McNally.

Zahn-Waxler, C. (in press). The origin of guilt. In R. Thompson (Ed.), *Nebraska Symposium on emotion.*

Zahn-Waxler, C. J., & Radke-Yarrow, M. R. (1981). The development of prosocial behavior: Alternative research strategies. In N. Eisenberg-Berg (Ed.), *The development of prosocial behavior.* New York: Academic Press.

II

Processes of Influence

Social Influence on Child and Parent via Stimulation and Operant-Learning Mechanisms

Jacob L. Gewirtz

Patterns of stimuli for behavior can represent social influence on child or parent on the occasion of presentation. Through the mechanisms of operant learning, that influence may carry over to subsequent occasions. Social-stimulus effects on behavior and, in particular, those that can be organized under the operant-learning paradigm and derivative paradigms, including pervasive imitation (identification) and attachment, are examined in this chapter as salient mechanisms of social influence. In early socialization settings, these operant mechanisms can influence readily not only the behavior of the child, but the behavior of parents and other environmental agencies as well. Operant processes denoting mutual influence can operate in the concurrent (often simultaneous) conditioning of the behavior of the child and of its caregiving environment. This chapter presents a survey of the diverse ways social influence on offspring behavior can be implemented via operant-learning and derivative processes that are effected through patterns of environmental conditions provided by the behavior of parents/caregivers. In addition, the survey considers the ways in which influence on parent/caregiver behavior can be effected by stimulation patterns provided by child behavior. Prior to presentation of the survey, however, the concepts of operant learning and of environment will be examined in the next two sections.

Jacob L. Gewirtz • Department of Psychology, Florida International University, Miami, Florida 33199.

OPERANT LEARNING

The open-ended conception of learning ordinarily refers to behavior-change processes wherein proximate, antecedent, environmental-event patterns systematically modify the units of an individual's behavior. The behavior modification produced is the result of the influence of the effective antecedent conditions operating. There are diverse paradigms of learning, and it is also realized that some behavior changes can be influenced by environmental events that are not readily organized by the operant-learning paradigm. Even so, in this chapter that most useful paradigm is emphasized because it can efficiently put into relief the social-influence determinants of adaptive behavior, and its antecedents and consequents, in both contemporaneous (proximate) and evolutionary (ultimate) frames (Petrovich & Gewirtz, 1985). Further, operant learning is ubiquitous in the animal world, occurring throughout life. In humans, such learning has been noted in neonates and infants when they detect changes in environmental events that are contingent on their own behavior and can adapt to such changes.

The paradigm of operant learning is employed in this chapter as an exemplar of the social-influence process. Under the operant-learning paradigm, acquisition and its reversal via extinction, differential reinforcement of other behavior (DRO), and reversal learning epitomize adaptive processes within the frame of evolution (Skinner, 1966, 1981). In operant learning, *acquisition* is denoted by a systematic increase in the rate of occurrence (or some other measure, such as amplitude) of a behavior effected by its environmental consequence or contingency (e.g., food or some visual or auditory display); conversely, *extinction* is denoted by a systematic decrease in rate (or some other measure) of the behavior effected by removing the contingent event that maintains it. (This rate decrease may also be effected in the context of a DRO or reversal-learning treatment.) Investigators have shown in human infants, children, and adults that diverse behaviors that ordinarily enter social interchanges can be conditioned readily under the operant paradigm, often with social-reinforcing stimulus consequences. For instance, operant learning has been demonstrated in neonates or infants for sucking (Lipsitt & Kaye, 1964), head turns (Caron, 1967; Papousek, 1961; Siqueland & Lipsitt, 1966), vocalizations (Poulson, 1983; Routh, 1969), eye contacts (Etzel & Gewirtz, 1967), and smiles (Brackbill, 1958; Etzel & Gewirtz, 1967). On this matter of early learning, see also Hulsebus (1973), Millar (1976), and Papousek (1977).

Responses here are characterized not topographically (in terms of their isolated characteristics as movements) but functionally (in terms of the discriminative cues and consequences that control the particular movements). Responses having the same topographic content often may serve entirely different ends (e.g., whistling a catchy tune vs. whistling in the dark) and, conversely, those having manifestly different topographies may be functionally equivalent (e.g., whistling in the dark vs. hiding under the covers). Thus, the functional approach requires the specification in parallel detail of both the target responses to be fostered and their influencing stimulus determinants. A functional analysis examines the co-relation between observable responses and stimuli specified in equivalently grained units.

The operant-learning conception provides a useful system for studying generic influence processes, for heuristic analyses, and for analyzing and designing new environmental settings. It affords a ready means of focusing simultaneously on the functional elements of the environment and of the child behavior affected by them. In the analysis of operant learning in any behavior arena, numerous definitions are possible for stimuli and responses. A functional analysis examines the relations, if any, between particular sets of definitions of the terms stimulus and response, focusing on systematic changes in some attribute (e.g., rate) of the behavior that has an environmental event contingent upon it, compared with when the environmental event is not presented. The conditioning denoted confirms the functional utility of the category definitions developed and leads to the contingent event being termed the *reinforcing stimulus* (or *reinforcer*) for the behavioral event that is termed the *response*. The reinforcement concept implies only that there exist environmental events which, when made contingent upon responses, will change the rates of some of these responses systematically. That is, if the occurrence of a response is followed by the presentation of a (reinforcing) stimulus, there is an increase in response "strength," typically indicated by response rate. Aversive stimuli comprise another class of events that, when provided contingently, decrease response rate.

Reinforcing stimuli need not exist under all conditions for every potential response; a contingent event that can reinforce one response need not serve as a reinforcer for that response under all other contextual-setting conditions or for another potential response. Furthermore, the fact that an event functions as a reinforcing stimulus in one context does not preclude its functioning in different stimulus roles in other contexts (Catania, 1973; Gewirtz, 1971a, 1971b, 1972d).

Social learning labels a category of adaptive behavior that involves stimuli provided by a member of a social unit, but otherwise appears to follow the same principles as does nonsocial learning. Because it is involved in human interaction and is the product of such exchanges, social learning accounts for many of the distinctive behavioral qualities of humans. Much of the influence effected by the cueing and reinforcement of behavior in complex human learning situations is of a social nature, e.g., discriminative settings for parental, teacher, or peer approval. If social stimuli have not acquired discriminative and reinforcing value for children's behavior, the learned skills of those children might not attain satisfactory levels. Individuals who have a deficiency in the experience base underlying social learning may be unable to fend for themselves in society. For these reasons, it is important to mount a functional analysis of the social-stimulus environment, social responses, and the learning processes organizing them. Those learning processes result from and denote social influence.

THE ENVIRONMENT

The terms "environment" and "stimulation" occur often in everyday discourse and have been used more intuitively than precisely. Often characterized as "wholesome" or "rich," these terms may be invoked as influence conditions, as presumed causes of certain patterns of behavioral development, and occasionally as labels for experimental or remedial treatments. Environment, stimulation, and their derivatives, such as "love" or "warmth," however, have neither universal definition nor consensually-defined operational indices. Objects and events (including people and their behavior) in the child's vicinity have often been termed the child's environment whether or not those objects and events have actual or potential relevance for influencing the child's behavior. This gross conceptualization of "environment" has but limited utility. In an analysis of influence, environment can be a meaningful summary term only for those events that actually or potentially function as *stimuli* directly to influence aspects of the individual's behavior. Under this functional conception, emphasis must be placed simultaneously on both the influencing environment and the behavior influenced, with the units of analysis—stimuli and responses—codetermined. At no analytic level is one analytic unit meaningful without the other.

A corollary of the functional-environment notion is that the "quality" of an influencing environment can be assessed. An abundance of events (physical objects, people, and their behavior) does not necessarily imply a "rich" environment unless it is known that those events are available and function as stimuli for (i.e., influence) child behavior. Thus, a jungle gym that a handicapped child cannot climb is only an ecological constraint, whereas play blocks that the child can manipulate could provide functional stimuli for some ongoing behavior. The quality of an environment cannot be revealed by assessing only the availability or the abundance of events. Such assessment requires, instead, an analysis of the events and a determination of whether they actually affect behavior. In this frame, the social environment consists of those functional stimuli that are provided by others, and social behaviors are those under the actual or potential control of social stimuli with regard to their acquisition, maintenance, or both. The term social stimuli tends to denote stimulus classes occurring in social interchange in natural settings (Gewirtz, 1968a, 1968b, 1971c).

FACILITATORS AND CONSTRAINTS FOR BEHAVIOR

Both the infrahuman and the human infant come into the world with facilitators and constraints on their behavior—some unlearned and biological, others ecological (Fitzgerald & Brackbill, 1976; Gewirtz, 1961, 1972d; Hinde & Stevenson-Hinde, 1973; Seligman & Hager, 1972). Thus, physical and chemical events, as monitored by the infant's sensory receptors and processors, can either limit or facilitate behavioral development for such behaviors as sucking and grasping.

There are occasionally instances where, at some point along an ordered temporal or contextual dimension, a behavior (or learning) fails to be manifested and where, at a later (or second) point along that ordered dimension, that behavior (or learning outcome) is shown. The concept of *preparedness* has occasionally been used in such instances to explain response occurrence after routine nonoccurrence in early life (Seligman, 1970). Where a dimension of time is involved in a molar approach, there is an implicit appeal in the usage of unindexed endogenous mechanisms of *maturation* to "explain" the differential. Such explanation is more apparent than real.

Social behavior and learning may be qualified and constrained by the physical and social ecology of a setting and can be facilitated or limited by the manipulation of ecological factors. In this frame, the term *ecology* stands for the gross conditions of an environment that determine which events and behaviors can occur in a setting, and specifically whether or not a child can detect a stimulus, emit a behavior, and have that behavior be reinforced by a contingent stimulus. Ecological conditions include the available space, the type and number of materials positioned in that space, and the type and number of peers and adults there. Similarly, the rules and regulations governing a setting can represent social facilitators or constraints for behavior systems. Thus, ecological conditions can insulate a young organism against, or cause the organism to be exposed to, adults, subadults, or their specific activities. In that way, those conditions can determine whether or not the organism can emit particular responses and have responses maintained by particular consequences.

A SURVEY OF SOCIAL INFLUENCES DUE TO OPERANT LEARNING

A good number of types of social influence can be interpreted within the operant learning paradigm. Within the context of the survey which makes up the rest of the chapter the following influences are discussed: (1) social referencing; (2) environmental deficiency; (3) attachment learning; (4) concurrent influence processes; and (5) pervasive imitative learning.

SOCIAL REFERENCING

The tendency of an infant to seek out and use the information, including affective cues, in the facial, vocal, and/or gestural expression of another (most often the mother) to provide a basis for its behavior in the context of an ambiguous event or person has been termed "social referencing." Thus, 1-year-olds, who had to cross the apparent deep side of a reduced visual cliff to reach an attractive toy, looked to their nearby mothers for cues, and tended to cross the visual cliff when their mothers posed a joyful or interested facial expression but not to cross when their mothers posed a fearful or angry expression. In the same way, 1-year-olds approached or avoided approaching a strange remote-control toy depending on their mothers' facial expression (Klinnert, Campos, Sorce, Emde, & Svejda, 1983). The authors cited have emphasized the communication of emotion involved in the phenomena of social referencing (see also Campos, 1983).

Because maternal facial-expressive cues provide the basis for the child's response in social-referencing phenomena, affective communication is clearly involved. But to stop with that observation overlooks what is a salient and even more interesting facet of the social-referencing paradigm under the influence-via-stimulation and operant-learning conception of this chapter and under other influence conceptions (Feinman, 1982, 1983). That is, maternal influence over the child's responses appears to be focally involved, and it is constructive to attempt to understand the process whereby maternal expressive behaviors acquire cue value for infant responses.

The history assumed to underlie maternal expressive-response cues acquiring social influence to modify the instrumental infant behavior of the social-referencing paradigm is that, across numerous ambiguous settings, responses (locomotor in the case of the visual cliff), cued by different maternal expressions, would have been reinforced differentially by successful and unsuccessful consequences. Thus, maternal face/body expressive cues denoting positive affect like those provided by smiles or positive nods would have become discriminative for positive reinforcement, while expressive cues denoting fear or anger would have become discriminative for aversive consequences. In this way, when in ambiguous situations the infant would look to (i.e., reference) its nearby mother/caregiver for expressive-response cues that would determine its behavior in those contexts. In ambiguous contexts later on, the increasingly-complex older child could request verbal information from such reference persons, to guide its behavior there.

To date, research on social referencing has focused on delineating the phenomenon, with little thought of the origins of the process. Results of an experiment support the assumption detailed above that the social-referencing response pattern can be trained/conditioned in interaction within infant–mother dyads during the first year. Thus, originally meaningless, one maternal hand–face "expression" came to predict *positive* (light music) auditory consequences for the infants, and a second hand-to-face "expression" came to predict *aversive* (harsh) auditory consequences, of the infants' approaches to each one of a series of ambiguous stimulus objects (hidden by a cloth until referencing occurred) that were placed in front of them. As a result of the differential conditioning procedure, all of the 20 nine-month-old infants showed that they learned, while manifesting the social-referencing response, which maternal hand-to-face cue denoted which consequence. Each infant was reliable in approaching positive-consequence, and avoiding negative-consequence, ambiguous objects before those consequences could occur contingent on his approach (Gewirtz, Pelaez-Nogueras, Diaz, & Villate, 1990). In the frame of our earlier discussion of social referencing, it is plausible that the social-referencing phenomenon in nature is acquired via a similar process of learning.

Environmental Deficiency as Social Influence: Privation, Deprivation, and Shift Conditions

The environment-deficiency conceptions of *privation* and *deprivation* have been centrally involved in earlier formulations that relate deficiency conditions of stimulation in early childhood, as antecedents, to aberrations in later child-behavior patterns, as consequences (Bakwin, 1942, 1949; Bowlby, 1940, 1951, 1953; Gewirtz, 1961, 1972c; Goldfarb, 1945a, 1945b, 1955; Levy, 1937; Spitz, 1945, 1946a, 1946b, 1949, 1954; Yarrow, 1961). As such, patterns of stimulus provision constituting deficiency may be conceived to represent influence conditions.

Privation

In keeping with previous analyses (Gewirtz, 1961, 1978) the term stimulus privation is reserved for the limited availability, through lengthy time spans, of all or particular classes of events that could function as stimuli, usually early in a child's life when such stimuli would ordinarily support basic learning. Abundant potential stimuli may be available but nonfunctional because of an absence of appropriate setting or context conditions or because they are provided ineptly, i.e., so that they are noncontingent on behavior. If social events are not made discriminative for behavior, they do not acquire cue or reinforcer value and hence could not influence behavior. The child developing under these conditions of social-stimulus privation may become generally responsive to nonsocial stimuli but unresponsive to discriminative and reinforcing stimuli for social sources.

Deprivation

The term stimulus deprivation refers to conditions involving gross shifts in maintaining environments, both long- and short-term, brought about by the removal or decreased availability of cue and reinforcing stimuli that had become functionally significant for, and frequently influenced key child-behavior systems, such as those provided during routine interaction patterns with the main attachment figure. These conditions include (1) a reduction in the accustomed rate of stimulation, (2) changes in the quality or patterning of stimulation, (3) removal of contextual conditions that can enhance the efficacy of key stimuli, and/or (4) direct interference with responses controlled by such stimuli. Examples of such conditions include a child's physical separation from, or the unavailability of, its principal caregiver, or that person's sudden and continuing rejection of the child.

In such situations, the child may first behave as in the initial phase of extinction effected by contingency removal, that is, the response rate may initially increase, then decrease, compared to the rate exhibited under reinforcement, and/or emotional responses may further disrupt the response pattern and preclude the learning of new adaptive behavior. Further, at least short-term disorganization in many behavior realms, including play, sleep, eating, and toileting, may result from stimulus deprivation due to short-term separations from a parent (Field, 1985, in press). The concept of stimulus deprivation involves the unavailability of stimuli, mostly conditioned, in a setting in which these stimuli have been maintaining selected behavior systems, and differs from the usually short-term stimulus impoverishment termed *sensory deprivation* (as described, e.g., by Bevan, 1967).

The Deficiency-Motivation Conception

The assumed consequences of privation and deprivation have often been explained by a deficiency-motivation conception, underlying which is the assumption that the short-term homeostatic drive model, ordinarily used to order periodic, reversible requirements for appetitive stimuli (food, water), can also order long-term, irreversible "hungers" or "needs" for such nonappetitive commodities as stimulation, affection, or love. The long-term deficiency-motivation conception generally emphasizes a "need for stimuli" that can build up through time and, if unrequited, result in aberrant, sometimes irreversible, behavior outcomes. Thus, if a child receives an inadequate supply of typically-unspecified essential stimuli from its caregiving environment over a lengthy period, it is thought that systematic changes occur in some behavior related to the deprived stimulus commodities. Moreover, the "need" that builds up may result in the child's later exhibiting seemingly insatiable requirements for the earlier-deficient stimulus commodities, as in extreme forms of dependence and attachment, or in total disinterest in social and nonsocial stimuli, as in developmental arrest, apathy, depression, and/or "shallowness of affect."

One explicit motivational analog of the deficiency model often used to explain the above outcomes is hunger. Thus, Spitz (1949) wrote of "emotionally starved" children. The conventional hunger model, however, cannot possibly order the reported conditions and results of regular, long-term deprivation. The hunger model operates only through hours, or at most a very few days, and it implies complete satiability (reversibility) after periodic deprivation, with no residual effects that cumulate in time to manifest themselves in systematic changes in behavior maintained by the events of which the organism was earlier deprived.

In contrast, the deficiency model described here has been used to order through months and years, not periodic and reversible but cumulating effects of recurring conditions of deprivation in the early life of the child, that result in systematic changes in behavior with reference to the withheld stimulus commodities. This model thus emphasizes a "need for stimuli" that can build up through time if unrequited, that is, if less than some unspecified "adequate" level is supplied to the child through the longer term. The "need" that builds up in this way may lead later to the child's exhibiting apparently insatiable requirements for (even the hoarding of) the stimulus commodities earlier provided in deficient supply. Or sometimes it may lead to apathy or other such affective behavior outcomes. In addition to the inherent difficulties of attempting to order long-term phenomena according to short-term models, the drive concept inherent in these models is further limited by the irrelevant and even misleading excess meaning that derives from using the short-term homeostatic drive model in contexts quite different in their essential properties from those in which the term *childhood depriva-tion* has been applied.

Despite the inadequacy of the short-term deficiency model for or-dering longer-term phenomena, it is still often used implicitly by many. Under the short-term deficiency model, a frequent solution for dealing with a history of inadequate or insufficient conditions is to provide nu-merous potential stimuli, but with no explicit concern for how they could influence the child's behavior. If this prescription were followed to the letter, the infrequent contingencies between responses and stimuli would affect response acquisition only minimally, but could change the long-term maintenance level for stimulation in proportion to the rate of stimulus provision.

However, in this frame, it is unlikely that a caregiver or therapist would ignore the child's behavior when providing stimuli. Rather, the caregiver is likely often to provide the stimuli in some functional relation to particular response classes of the child, with the identities of the response classes potentially reinforced in this manner varying from one caregiver to another. Without a predetermined specification of the de-sired responses, many behavioral outcomes are possible. If the stimuli intended to constitute "sufficient" attention and love are provided con-tingent upon the child's disruptive or attention-seeking behavior, those responses would be strengthened and the result might be a response pattern that precludes the learning of more appropriate adaptive behav-ior. On the other hand, if the caregiver provides those stimuli contingent upon socially-valued responses, such as those typical of the child's age group or oriented toward autonomy and achievement, these responses would be strengthened and the outcome would be more favorable.

Ironically, both of these behavior shifts can be used by advocates of the deficiency model to index the inadequacy of the previous setting. A high or increased incidence of attention-seeking behavior or disruptive emotional responses could be taken to validate that the child has a "hunger" for stimuli believed to have been inadequately provided pre-viously, and to require even more stimulation to satiate/reverse the "need." The opposite outcome, the relative increase in appropriate be-havior, may lead to the assumption that the new, more adequate en-vironment has satisfied the child's hunger for the stimuli, because the child no longer appears to "need" as much attention and love and, therefore, appears more "secure"—a result also interpreted as valida-tion for the deficiency model.

One cost of the routine use of a deficiency model, whether for appetitive or nonappetitive (including social) conditions, is to discour-age close attention to environmental stimuli and behavior at the level of detail required by a differentiated operant-learning-as-influence analysis. Under both normal and deficiency conditions of stimulation, it is not sufficient to focus simply on which or how many potential stimuli are provided to the child. Rather, one must take account of the circumstances under which stimuli are made available and, in particular, whether these stimuli are functional and enter into effective contingencies with the child's behavior. Thus, an operant-learning analysis first specifies the conditions of stimulus control over responses existing before the removal of stimulus classes in deprivation, as well as the changed contingencies between the child's behavior and the stimuli in the new setting. The outcomes of environmental shifts are regarded in a learning analysis as reflecting an adjustment of the child's behavior to the changed conditions of stimulus provision in the new setting, which includes new learning by the child resulting from changed response-reinforcement contingencies.

Environmental-Shift Conditions

A situation functionally similar to deficiency-stimulation conditions can occur in the absence of apparent deprivation. Such a situation might be introduced by a shift in the stimulus conditions that maintain the child's behavior, as when a child enters a day care or nursery school. Because such shifts can involve change in the stimuli controlling the child's behavior, the pattern of the child's responses will often change. The greater the functional similarity between the stimuli provided in the former environmental setting and the new one—in terms of caregiving routines and behavior, response definitions for reinforcement and reinforcement schedules—the easier it will be for behavioral adjustment to the new environment to occur. The stimulus similarity between environments, including gender, facial, and other features of caretakers, will also facilitate adjustment of the child's behavior to the new setting.

On the other hand, if stimuli like those that had been maintaining the child's responses are unavailable in the new setting and functionally similar stimuli are not provided, the responses controlled by those stimuli would severely decline in frequency. It is axiomatic that a child will bring to a new setting those behavior systems maintained by the stimuli in the prior setting. The child's initial responses to stimuli in a new setting will be a function of the similarity between the new stimuli and those that controlled behavior in the earlier context. The rate at which some responses (e.g., those denoting "fear," avoidance) habituate to novel stimulus conditions (sometimes a slow process with disruptive effects when abundant startle and noxious stimuli are present) will also affect the incidence and pattern of the child's initial behavior in the new setting. Thus, previously stable behavior patterns may be disrupted due to environmental shifts. The issue can be especially important when a child begins school, because this involves both a large-scale initial shift and routine smaller daily shifts from the family-home setting. It is best that caregivers in the new setting be aware of the degree to which a child's behavior can rely on particular environmental stimuli and of the difficulties that can occur when maintaining conditions are changed abruptly (Gewirtz, 1972c).

In essence, a child's adjustment in a new environment will depend on (1) the new caregivers recognizing the relevant discriminative and reinforcing stimuli controlling the child's social responses and providing them effectively; and (2) stimuli in the new setting acquiring discriminative and reinforcing value to maintain appropriate responses or to enable the learning of new response patterns. If caregivers in the new setting are not cognizant of these factors and are not flexibly responsive to the child, they may fail to shape behavior appropriate to the new setting. As a consequence, the child may not acquire an acceptable response repertory there. Further, a caregiver who does not consider the child's present level of functioning may respond purely in terms of expectations for children of that age group. A vicious cycle may result: The responses of the caregiver would not be appropriate to those of the child, and the child would drop farther behind in behavioral development. These conditions could result in the child being labeled "unteachable." Another possible outcome is that nonreinforcement of formerly reinforced responses may lead to tantrums or other such emotional "maladaptive" behaviors. If the latter are reinforced by the well-intentioned caregiver's attention, they may increase in frequency in the new setting. Because they may be incompatible with new adaptive learning, another vicious cycle could then be set in motion that might result in the child's being labeled "untrainable," but this time due to "emotional disturbance."

Multiple Environments

A special case of changes in stimulus control involves independent but often overlapping environmental settings that differ in their discriminative and reinforcing stimulus conditions for subsets of the child's responses, as in "multiple mothering" or mother's versus father's interaction or caregiving. Each parent/caregiver provides a different setting for the child's behavior, as defined by the unique discriminative and reinforcing stimuli presented to the child the identities of the child responses reinforced there. Difficulties may arise initially when a certain response is considered appropriate by one caregiver but inappropriate by another. The child, however, usually learns readily to discriminate between the caregivers and caregiving roles of the functionally-different environments, emitting responses appropriate to each. In the section to follow on the acquisition of attachment(s) it is seen that under an operant-learning analysis several concurrent stimulus-control patterns denoting attachments, as with mother and father and others, are to be expected routinely (Gewirtz, 1961). Such discriminative control is important for the child who, in a residential institution, nursery school, or day-care center, is concurrently and/or sequentially in the charge of several persons. It is relevant also in the understanding of the child's differential behavior to mother and father, or of the child reared jointly by several persons in a household (e.g., parent, older sibling, grandparents, and/or maid).

ATTACHMENT LEARNING VIA PARENTAL INFLUENCE

In many species, parent-offspring interactions may be initiated prior to hatching or birth and continue throughout the early social development of the offspring (e.g., Hess, 1973; Hinde, 1974; Roy, 1980). *Precocial* species mature rapidly and are capable of highly-adaptive complex perceptual-motor integration, orientation and locomotion soon after hatching. *Altricial* species are helpless for extensive periods after birth, but can engage in synchronous interaction with parents and others during that period. Precocial-species newborns, such as chicks, ducklings, goslings, kids, and lambs exposed to a moving social object (usually the biological mother) soon after hatching will learn to follow it and emit biologically-prepared species-typical filial responses which mitigate against predation and facilitate access to food and shelter. Further, the sexual orientation of precocial species adults is to objects of the class involved in the imprinting process. In contrast, altricial-species newborn, such as pigeons, doves, cats, dogs, monkeys, other infrahuman primates, and humans, possess at birth a repertoire of nonlocomotor responses (e.g., sucking, clinging in some) that are ultimately exploited in attachment learning. Other properties of the focal object may function eventually as discriminative and reinforcing stimuli mediated for the most part by distance (particularly visual) receptors, thereby facilitating the attachment learning.

Different terms have been applied in precocial and altricial species to the influence process wherein, through systematic early exposure, offspring filial responses acquire initially a social-object focus, ordinarily the biological mother. Typically the influence process has been termed "imprinting" in precocial species and "attachment" in altricial species (Petrovich & Gewirtz, 1985). The ways responses denoting infant imprinting/attachment became focused and restricted to a discriminated social object in precocial birds and in such altricial-like mammals as infrahuman and human primates appear similar and functionally analogous. It is assumed in this analysis that the same generic influence process that operant learning represents underlies both imprinting and attachment.

Imprinting

The German metaphor *Prägung* ("stamping in," "coining") was applied by Lorenz (1935) to the influence process wherein the newly born of many precocial avian species (e.g., the chicken, Greylag goose, jackdaw, mallard, pheasant, partridge) relatively rapidly form a social bond, or attachment, to a biologically appropriate conspecific or, in its absence, to some available object, even a human. The imprinting metaphor of a bond, tie, or attachment, has been applied to the pattern of close reliance of the behavior (e.g., locomotor following) of the young animal on stimuli provided by its parental figure, and is often denoted by the young animal's cued-response patterns to that parent. The notions of preparedness, biological constraints, species-specific behavior, and that the imprinting appears to promote the young individual's survival, as well as determine subsequently the mating-object class of the animal when mature, are implicit in the imprinting conception (Lorenz, 1935, 1969; Hess, 1959, 1964, 1973).

Concurrently, several investigators approached imprinting as a process involving various learning paradigms of influence, and they viewed social bonds or relationships as the outcomes of that learning (Bateson, 1966, 1971; Cairns, 1966; Gewirtz, 1961; Hoffman & DePaulo, 1977; Hoffman & Ratner, 1973). As did Scott (1960, 1968), those investigators emphasized the similarities between the imprinting process in precocial species and the processes involved in the formation of primary social bonds in such altricial species as the dog, monkey, and human. Of course, species exploit different sensory modalities for the development of the attachment bond, ranging from chemical to auditory, visual, tactile, and thermal.

Attachment

In his theoretical endeavors, Freud (e.g., 1938, 1953) attended to libidinal "object relations" in humans, as between mother and child, and suggested etiological determinants of such fundamental relations in life. In approaches to the social behavior of infrahumans and humans, diverse others have dealt with this topic in research and theory (Ainsworth, 1972; Ainsworth, Blehar, Waters, & Wall, 1978; Bowlby, 1958, 1969; Cairns, 1972, 1978; Gewirtz, 1961, 1972a, 1972b; Sears, 1972; Yarrow, 1972). Much of the contemporary flavor of the attachment concept derives from the work of Bowlby (1958, 1969) and Ainsworth (1972; Ainsworth *et al.*, 1978).

In the social-conditioning approach (e.g., Gewirtz, 1961, 1972a), attachment has served as a convenient label for a process involving the acquisition of a close reliance (typically concurrent) of one individual's behavior upon the appearance and behavior cues of another, expressed in a variety of cued-response patterns. The metaphoric term attachment has served to label the influence process wherein a complex of child-response patterns comes to be cued and reinforced by stimuli provided by the appearance and behavior of an attachment figure/object—in early life, usually the mother. The child-response pattern might maintain contact proximity, produce attention, or the like. The label "attachment behavior" designates concurrent reflections of the above process, such as the child's differential responding favoring the maternal attachment figure, distress when separated from her, protests upon preparations for her departure, and even increases in child exploration in her presence (Gewirtz, 1972b). These cued-response patterns denoting attachment are pervasive and may occur in any segment of the life span, from infancy onward, and with any interaction partners, for instance, mother and child, wife and husband, person and animal, as well as peers or lovers. Upon disruption by separation or rejection, the child's behavior can become highly disorganized, and may be accompanied by intense emotional (affective) responding.

In this social-conditioning account, the dyadic functional relations between the cue and reinforcing stimuli from the attachment figure/object and the child's responses that connote attachment of the child to the attachment figure may involve several object persons concurrently, as well as concurrent influence patterns—mother-to-child and child-to-mother—as is described in the next section. Moreover, initiations need not be reciprocated on an occasion by an attachment figure. The discriminated operants denoting attachments are not to be conceived as traits. Because, by definition, they are controlled by particular cue and reinforcing stimuli, as well as by contextual stimuli (including setting conditions), their occurrence will vary across situations.

Crying, Cued Responding, and Attachment

The influencing of caregiver behavior by an infant does not always have constructive implications, as illustrated by caregiver responses to high-rate instrumental crying. Because an infant's crying has strong aversive qualities, most adults will attempt to stop it in various ways (Gewirtz, 1961). These attempts can sometimes have undesirable consequences, as when a caregiver interrupts some activity (such as the care of another infant in a day-care facility) to attend to the crier. Moreover, the successful caregiver response that is (negatively) reinforced by the cessation of the infant's crying increases the likelihood the caregiver will attend to that child in the same way when the child again cries. Such attention can (positively) reinforce the infant crying responses. Thus, although the caregiver attains momentary relief on each crying occasion by responding to the crying, the long-range effect is to foster the very crying response that is aversive to the caregiver. An analysis of the "vicious cycle" inherent in this mutual conditioning process has been presented elsewhere (Gewirtz, 1968b). This influence/control pattern over parent/caregiver behavior, and a similar influence pattern in which the child cries/protests when the parent/caregiver makes preparations for distancing/departure/separation from the child, have both been discussed in the context of attachment indices (Gewirtz, 1977, 1978).

On the assumption that contingent maternal responding provides effective reinforcing stimuli for various infant responses, an infant's protests— or other cries that denote distress (Ainsworth & Wittig, 1969)—may come to be influenced/controlled by cues from the mother's preparations for departure (and by the ensuing short- or long-term separations) because of their association with the mother softening and responding, thereby delaying her departure, or otherwise hesitating or vacillating before departing. Similarly, particular types of cries may be shaped differentially under the control of cues denoting departure or absence (e.g., by a mother who responds only to her infant's plaintive cries but not other types of cries). Likewise, an infant's cries may come under the influence/control of cues from the mother's actual absence when those cries occasionally result in her return to the vicinity (reinforcement). In such instances, the infant's cries overcome physical and distance barriers, in addition to the mother's need to be away, to evoke a response from her. Those reinforced emitted cries that come to be cued by that attachment figure's absence, therefore, may often be lengthy or intense.

For infants in the early weeks of life, crying can be modified/reinforced by caretaker attention, such as is provided by hovering over, smiling, talking to, and/or picking up the child (Etzel & Gewirtz, 1967). Diverse other operant responses, which have also served occasionally as bases for attachment indices, can be effected by actual or simulated social-behavior contingencies in the first 3 months of life (well before the time some would expect that an attachment could have been acquired). Those responses include eye contacts, smiles, vocalizations, and cries (Hulsebus, 1973). If a single attachment index is used, therefore, a researcher working outside of an influence/learning approach would do well to take account of the possibility that the attributes of the cued response on which it is based might reflect only a history in which the child's display of that behavior had been routinely reinforced in the same situation (e.g., crying cued by the mother's preparations to leave the child's vicinity). A nonlearning approach, therefore, would often find it necessary to address directly the issue of possibly-learned behavior systems serving as its criterion indices.

The present concern can be illustrated with a widely cited report by Schaffer and Emerson (1964) of the age course and onset of focused attachments in infancy. They used several measures based on what was essentially a single cued-response-based index of attachment, derived form maternal reports. Those measures summarized the incidence, intensity, and direction of infant protests after seven types of separations from their mothers and others. Protests at separation may involve, in younger children, fussing, whimpering, whining, crying, or screaming, and in older children, grabbing the parent's body or clothing and pleading, in addition to fussing, whining, crying, or screaming. Schaffer and Emerson (1964, p. 50) concluded that the intensity of attachment-to-mother at 18 months (measured by the characteristic intensity of protests at separation) was a positive function of the frequency and speed with which a mother responded to her infant's crying.

One possible basis for these results is that the infants who protested/cried most intensely at separation were largely those whose mothers attended immediately (therefore contingently) to their protests/cries, either directly or by hesitating or vacillating before departing. Thus, the contingent responding of those mothers might have reinforced protests/cries, so that cues provided by a mother's preparations for departure became discriminative for reinforcement of those responses. Schaffer and Emerson (1964, p. 51) raised this possibility in discussing the relation between attachment intensity and the frequency and speed of maternal responding to infant crying, but discounted it by stating that cause and effect could not be disentangled in the context studied. At the same time, they suggested that the result could just as likely have reflected a mother's learning to "give in" to her infant's persistent crying. But this appears simply to be another way of saying the same thing, namely that contingent maternal responding can reinforce infant crying. Even so, an issue may till remain. The composite of the various measures of protests-in-separation situations used to index the child's attachment to the mother might have reflected only what the Schaffer and Emerson theory would take to be a limited fact: that mothers had systematically reinforced the protests/cries of their babies on some schedule, particularly when preparing to leave them (Gewirtz, 1976, 1978).

A series of experiments was carried out on the effects of contingent maternal responding on cued infant protests (cries, fusses, whimpers, and/or whines) during mothers' departures and, separately, during mothers' separations from their children. It was found that the cued protest rates of each one of the 6- to 9-month-old infants studied (both in departure and in brief separation contexts) increased when followed by contingent maternal responding and remained low or decreased when followed by *non*contingent maternal responding. This dramatic and reliable result pattern provides strong support for the conception detailed above that cued infant protests can be conditioned in everyday settings, trained (most likely, inadvertently) by the contingencies provided by the caregiver responding in the very departure and separation contexts in which infant protests are found (Gewirtz & Pelaez-Nogueras, 1991).

Cued Responding and the Enduring Features of an Attachment

Stimulus influence/control can account for much infant responding at separations and reunions, and during absences. Hence, the marked decrease in responses denoting attachment in the absence of the attachment figure appears due simply to the removal of the discriminative and reinforcing stimuli supporting those responses. When the controlling stimuli for orienting, smiling, and similar responses are again present after reunion, those responses should again be displayed to the attachment figure (Gewirtz, 1961).

Stimulus control accounts routinely for responses under close discriminative control not occurring in the absence of their controlling stimuli, but that reoccur when those controlling stimuli reappear. This concept also provides bases for understanding some types of delays occasionally noted at reunion after separation, before attachment responses are again exhibited to the reunited attachment figure: It may take some time before the controlling stimuli are presented effectively enough to be functional. A response under close stimulus control (like that denoting an attachment) will routinely diminish markedly in the absence of stimuli (like those from the attachment figure). Just as routinely, it will increase markedly when the attachment figure providing the controlling stimuli reappears. Hence, it is the axiomatic in an operant-learning framework that discriminated operants denoting attachment will endure undiminished in strength in the absence of an attachment figure, precluding the requirement to postulate an inner structure. Indeed, absence of the stimulus means that its function is unavailable for modification: thus, its absence insulates its function, preserving its strength undiminished for controlling responses.

In summary, patterns of crying cued by a mother's departures, separations, or absences might be understood as plausible outcomes of routine discriminated operant-learning procedures generated by the pattern of that mother's responding to her infant's cued crying. Such cued crying has been a common index of a baby's attachment to the mother and, on occasion, has been the only index. Using such a single index (or very few indices) under some attachment conceptions involves some risks. At the same time, the drastic diminution of cued responses denoting an attachment in the absence of the attachment figure and their equally marked reoccurrence upon the reappearance of that figure is explained by the concept of discriminated responding. In a functional framework, a concept of inner structure underlying attachment that endures in the absence of the attachment figure is gratuitous.

Concurrent (Mutual) Influence Processes

It is clear that caregiver-child interactions provide myriad occasions for stimulation and reinforcement of each other's behavior. That is, each of the two interactors provides stimuli that can influence the responses of the other. In recent years, there has been increasing emphasis on how the behavior of socializing agents can adapt to that of their charges (Bell, 1968; Bell & Chapman, 1986; Gewirtz, 1961; Gewirtz & Boyd, 1976). Just as the caregiver can condition the child's behavior by providing reinforcing consequences, so also can the child's behavior mediate reinforcing stimuli that condition responses of the caregiver (Gewirtz & Boyd, 1977). In this way, the influencing environment is influenced in turn and the socializing environment socialized.

Specifically, an infant's head turns, eye contacts, smiles, and cries, while being reinforced and maintained by a mother's systematic responding to them, might, in that very same context, be reinforcing/maintaining these very responses of the mother when contingent upon them. Often these concurrent conditioning processes might occur even without the mother's awareness that her own responses were changing systematically under the influence of her child's behavior (Gewirtz, 1961, 1969, 1972a, 1978). The efficacy of the synchrony, or mesh, among sequential infant and maternal stimuli and behavior might vary for mother-infant pairs, although the modal intrapair acquired-control pattern denoting the attachment of each actor to the other would ordinarily be a synchronous one. This conception is not unlike that of "psychological attunement" (Field, 1985).

Infants in the care of busy or ambivalent parents/caregivers, as in some institutional and family settings, might benefit from a program that strengthened those responses in their repertoires (e.g., eye contact, smiles, selected vocal responses) likely to provide effective reinforcers for caregiver responses and to facilitate the occurrence of lengthy interaction sequences. Such infants would be in a position to compete more effectively for the caregiver's limited attention, and a fertile basis could be established for the mutual acquisition of constructive interactions between child and caregiver responses (Gewirtz, 1968a).

A series of paradigmatic experiments on these reciprocal-influence processes was reported by Gewirtz and Boyd (1977). Compatible with the theoretical focus on potential conditioning mechanisms underlying infant attachment, Gewirtz and Boyd illustrated the influence, via a conditioning mechanism, of infant behavior on maternal responses. Specifically, they demonstrated that, in interaction, mothers' vocal, expressive, and smile responses of various types were conditioned by contingent head turns and vocalizations attributed to their infants, without the mothers' awareness that their own behaviors were being, or had been, influenced.

The approach to imprinting/attachment employing a routine operant-learning influence paradigm for the simultaneous acquisition of behavioral attachment of mother to infant and of infant to mother was detailed in an earlier section of this chapter, as well as elsewhere (Gewirtz, 1961). This influence approach assumes that both mother and infant respond differentially and synchronously to the other's behaviors and that the discriminative stimuli and responses provided by the appearance and behavior of each could come to function concurrently to cue and reinforce (i.e., to condition) the responses of the other. Thus, as the caregiver can condition/maintain child responses by providing reinforcing or aversive consequences, so also can the child's behavior concurrently provide reinforcing or aversive stimulus consequences to condition caregiver responses. On this basis, "baby talk" or outlandish grimaces can enter the caregiver's repertory as a function of contingencies provided by the infant. As indicated in the preceding section, the responses of the caregiver that are cued and reinforced by aspects of her child's appearance and behavior can index her attachment to her charge on the same conditioning basis that the responses of the child cued and reinforced by aspects of the caregiver's appearance and behavior can index the attachment of that child to its caregiver. In sum, these concurrent influence processes denote the acquisition by each of an attachment to the other. The underlying learning-as-influence approach recognizes the operation of unconditioned stimuli (releasers) for species-specific responses, as identified in animal-behavior research lore and by Bowlby (1958), in shaping the particular form that attachment behavior takes.

Pervasive Imitative Learning

Pervasive imitation refers to the selective process (sometimes termed identification) whereby a child acquires the range of the behavior repertory (including behaviors connoting values and standards) of a parent, usually the parent of the same gender as the child. The phenomena of identification can be reduced parsimoniously to the concept of conditional responding, with the imitation a functional matching-response class comprised of diverse responses matched to a parent-model's behaviors. Such conditional responses could be emitted after lengthy delays or in the model's absence, and would be acquired and maintained by extrinsic reinforcing stimuli usually provided by a parent's or other adult's response to the child (Gewirtz, 1969, 1971a, 1971b; Gewirtz & Stingle, 1968).

Acquisition of the imitative response class is thought to follow operant-learning principles of influence (Skinner, 1938), in particular that diverse responses leading to equivalent consequences are functional members of the same class—in this case a matching-response class—and that the matching-response class can become conditional (i.e., focused) on a particular parent (typically of the same gender) whose presence sets the occasion for extrinsic reinforcement of instances of that matching-response class. Moreover, because the matching-response class is ordinarily followed only intermittently by extrinsic reinforcement from the model or from other adults, such matching responses will often occur in the apparent absence of reinforcing contingencies. To those unaware of the conditioning history of the matching-response class in a child, such nonreinforced imitations may appear to be instances of the "observational learning" for which Bandura (1969) has argued. An extensive analysis of such considerations has been presented elsewhere (Gewirtz, 1971a).

Relation between Pervasive Imitation and Attachment

An early framework for focusing on the phenomena characterizing both attachment and identificatory processes and their outcomes was provided by psychoanalytic theory (Freud, 1920, 1933, 1938, 1953). Freud early on emphasized (a) the libidinal object relationship (attachment) of the child to its mother, (b) the identification of the child with its same-gender parent, and (c) the sequential order of appearance of these two processes/behavior systems in the course of the child's development, with the object relationship/attachment preceding the identification. And, while Freud (1933) dealt with identification in a scattered way and with many variations through decades of his writing, he employed the term both for a process and for the behavior-similarity outcomes of that process. In one writing, Freud's (1920) index of the outcome of identification was the imitation of the model's behaviors. When assumed in Freud's approach to result from complete instrumental dependence upon, and an emotional tie (attachment) to, the model (typically the parent), identification has been termed "anaclitic." At the same time, it was assumed that "defensive" or "aggressive" identification resulted from fear of punishment from the model figure, with the child avoiding the punishment by becoming like the model.

James Mark Baldwin (1906, 1906-1911) and Kohlberg (1966), following Baldwin's lead, have proposed that the process of pervasive imitation/identification plays a central role in early human social development, and that it precedes that of attachment in the course of early human development. Hence, their proposal as to the sequencing of the two processes is the reverse of Freud's, for whom the attachment process precedes selective pervasive imitation.

Imitative-identificatory and attachment-dependence phenomena typically have been approached at a gross level of conceptual analysis that obscures the identities and roles of the behavior classes and of the discriminative, contextual, and maintaining stimuli involved. In that frame, the question of the order of appearance in the course of early human development of the processes denoting attachment and pervasive imitation (identification) is regarded to be a pseudo issue from a behavioral view, as the two processes can be conceived to be orthogonal (Gewirtz, 1969, 1972a; Gewirtz & Stingle, 1968). In life settings, the social behaviors denoting the attachment and imitative-identificatory systems may be acquired concurrently or sequentially in identical or very similar stimulus contexts, as both behavior classes are emitted in the presence of many of the same parent-provided discriminative and maintaining reinforcing stimuli. Even so, one behavior class need not be the basis for the acquisition of the other. Attachment and identification involve separate behavior systems that can be represented by distinct paradigms, interdependent only insofar as they involve some of the same stimulus elements in their acquisition and maintenance.

The matching response class in pervasive imitation is ordinarily defined more in terms of similarity to the model's behavior (cue) than in terms of the social stimuli that cue and maintain-reinforce those matched responses. For our behavioral analysis, therefore, the imitative process involves a response class that is under the same type of stimulus control that is implied in, and summarized by, the concept of attachment. Both the matching responses in pervasive imitation and the responses to parents in attachment are cued and maintained/reinforced by the same classes of parent-provided stimuli. In this sense, the pervasive imitative-learning process that involves numerous matching-to-parent model behaviors cued and maintained by the same parent-provided stimuli may be conceived to constitute a subset of attachment-behavior outcomes under the attachment process.

Although the two processes, pervasive imitation and attachment, are conceived to be independent, very different determinants of the two processes may prevail in subsamples of the population. Hence, in some subsamples pervasive imitation may be influenced/fostered earlier than attachment and, in others, attachment may be influenced/fostered earlier than pervasive imitation. While such etiological-factor and outcome distribution patterns could be of occasional interest—for instance, in differences between demographically-defined population subgroups— they are incidental to the process analysis of influence that is the fundamental objective of a behavioral approach.

EPILOGUE

Processes of social influence on child and parent behavior were examined and surveyed, through the media of stimulation and operant-learning and derivative paradigms. These derivative paradigms included attachment and pervasive imitation (identification). In this endeavor, illustrations were provided of how operant processes denoting mutual influence operate when the stimuli provided facilitate the concurrent conditioning of both child and parent behavior. Emphasis was placed throughout on how patterns of presentation of potential or actual stimuli for behavior could represent social influence on child or parent on the presentation occasion per se and, through the mechanisms of operant learning, carry that influence over to subsequent behavior occasions.

REFERENCES

Ainsworth, M. D. S. (1972). Attachment and dependency: A comparison. In J. L. Gewirtz (Ed.), *Attachment and dependency* (pp. 97–137). Washington, D.C.: Winston.

Ainsworth, M. D., Blehar, M. C., Waters, E., & Wall, S. (1978). *Patterns of attachment.* Hillsdale, NJ: Erlbaum.

Ainsworth, M. D. S., & Wittig, B. A. (1969). Attachment and exploratory behavior of one-year-olds in a strange situation. In B. M. Foss (Eds.), *Determinants of infant behaviour IV* (pp. 111–136). London: Methuen.

Bakwin, H. (1942). Loneliness in infants. *American Journal of Diseases of Children, 63,* 30–40.

Bakwin, H. (1949). Emotional deprivation in infants, *Journal of Pediatrics, 35,* 512–521.

Baldwin, J. M. (1906). *Social and ethical interpretations in mental development.* New York: MacMillan.

Baldwin, J. M. (1906-1911). *Thoughts and things, or genetic logic* (Vols. 1–3). New York: MacMillan.

Bandura, A. (1969). *Principles of behavior modification.* New York: Holt, Rhinehart & Winston.

Bateson, P. P. G. (1966). The characteristics and context of imprinting. *Biological Review, 41,* 177–220.

Bateson, P. P. G. (1971). Imprinting. In H. Moltz (Ed.), *The ontogeny of vertebrate behavior* (pp. 369–387). New York: Academic Press.

Bell, R. Q. (1968). A reinterpretation of the direction of effects in studies of socialization. *Psychological Review, 75,* 81–95.

Bell, R. Q., & Chapman, M. (1986). Child effects in studies using experimental or brief longitudinal approaches to socialization. *Developmental Psychology, 22,* 595–603.

Bevan, W. (1967). Behavior in unusual environments. In H. Helson & W. Bevan (Eds.), *Contemporary approaches to psychology* (pp. 385–418). Princeton, NJ: Van Nostrand.

Bowlby, J. (1940). The influence of early environment in the development of neurosis and neurotic character. *International Journal of Psychoanalysis, 21,* 154–178.

Bowlby, J. (1951). Maternal care and mental health. *Bulletin of the World Health Organization, 3,* 355–534.

Bowlby, J. (1953). Some pathological processes set in train by early mother-child separation, *Journal of Mental Science, 99,* 265–272.

Bowlby, J. (1958). The nature of the child's tie to his mother. *International Journal of Psychoanalysis, 39,* 350–373.

Bowlby, J. (1969). *Attachment and loss: Vol. 1. Attachment.* New York: Basic Books.

Brackbill, Y. (1958). Extinction of the smiling response in infants as a function of reinforcement schedule. *Child Development, 29,* 115–124.

Cairns, R. B. (1966). Attachment behavior in mammals. *Psychological Review, 73,* 409–426.

Cairns, R. B. (1972). Attachment and dependency: A psychobiological and social-learning synthesis. In J. L. Gewirtz (Ed.), *Attachment and dependency* (pp. 29–80). Washington, DC: Winston.

Cairns, R. B. (1978). *Social development: The origins and plasticity of behavior.* San Francisco: Freeman.

Campos, J. J. (1963). The importance of affective communication in social referencing: A commentary on Feinman. *Merrill-Palmer Quarterly, 29,* 83–87.

Caron, R. F. (1967). Visual reinforcement of head-turning in young infants. *Journal of Experimental Child Psychology, 5,* 489–511.

Catania, A. C. (1973). The nature of learning. In J. A. Nevin & G. S. Reynolds (Eds.), *The study of behavior* (pp. 31–68). Glenview, IL: Scott, Foresman.

Etzel, B. C., & Gewirtz, J. L. (1967). Experimental modification of caretaker-maintained high rate operant crying in a 6- and 20-week old infant (*Infans tyrannotearus*): Extinction of crying with reinforcement of eye contact and smiling. *Journal of Experimental Child Psychology, 5,* 303–317.

Feinman, S. (1982). Social referencing in infancy. *Merrill-Palmer Quarterly, 28,* 445–470.

Feinman, S. (1983). How does baby socially refer? Two views of social referencing: A reply to Campos. *Merrill-Palmer Quarterly, 29,* 467–471.

Field, T. (1985). Attachment as psychobiological attunement: Being on the same wavelength. In M. Reite & T. Field (Eds.), *The psychobiology of attachment and separation* (pp. 415–454). Orlando, FL: Academic Press.

Field, T. (in press). Separation distress and attachment. In J. L. Gewirtz & W. Kurtines (Eds.), *Intersections with attachment.* Hillsdale, NJ: Erlbaum.

Fitzgerald, H. E., & Brackbill, Y. (1976). Classical conditioning in infancy: Development and constraints. *Psychological Bulletin, 83,* 353–376.

Freud, S. (1920). *A general introduction to psychoanalysis.* Garden City, NY: Garden City Publishing Co.

Freud, S. (1933). *New introductory lectures on psychoanalysis.* London: Hogarth.

Freud, S. (1938). *An outline of psychoanalysis.* London: Hogarth.

Freud, S. (1953). In J. Strachey (Ed. and Trans.), *The Standard edition of the complete psychological works of Sigmund Freud.* London: Hogarth.

Gewirtz, J. L. (1961). A learning analysis of the effects of normal stimulation, privation, and deprivation on the acquisition of social motivation and attachment. In B. M. Foss (Ed.), *Determinants of Infant behaviour* (pp. 213–229). London: Wiley.

Gewirtz, J. L. (1968a). On designing the functional environment of the child to facilitate behavioral development. In L. L. Dittmann (Ed.), *Early child care: The new perspectives* (pp. 169–213). New York: Atherton Press.

Gewirtz, J. L. (1968b). The role of stimulation in models for child development, In L. L. Dittmann (Ed.), *Early child care: The new perspectives* (pp. 139–168). New York: Atherton Press.

Gewirtz, J. L. (1969). Mechanisms of social learning: Some roles of stimulation and behavior in early human development. In D. A. Goslin (Ed.), *Handbook of socialization theory and research* (pp. 57–212). Chicago: Rand McNally.

Gewirtz, J. L. (1971a). Conditional responding as a paradigm for observational, imitative learning and vicarious reinforcement. In H. W. Reese (Ed.), *Advances in Child Development and Behavior, 6* (pp. 273–304). New York: Academic Press.

Gewirtz, J. L. (1971b). The roles of overt responding and extrinsic reinforcement in "self-" and "vicarious-reinforcement" phenomena and in "observational learning" and imitation. In R. Glaser (Ed.), *The nature of reinforcement* (pp. 279–309). New York: Academic Press.

Gewirtz, J. L. (1971c). Stimulation, learning, and motivation principles for day-care settings. In E. H. Grotberg (Ed.), *Day care: Resources for decisions*(OEO Pamphlet, pp. 173–226). Washington, D.C.: U.S. Office of Economic Opportunity.

Gewirtz, J. L. (1972a). Attachment, dependence, and a distinction in terms of stimulus control. In J. L. Gewirtz (Ed.), *Attachment and dependency* (pp. 139–177). Washington, D.C.: Winston.

Gewirtz, J. L. (1972b). On the selection and use of attachment and dependence indices. In J. L. Gewirtz (Ed.), *Attachment and dependency* (pp. 179–215). Washington, D.C.: Winston.

Gewirtz, J. L. (1972c). Deficiency conditions of stimulation and the reversal of their effects via enrichment. In F. J. Monks, W. W. Hartup, & J. de Wit (Eds.), *Determinants of behavioral development* (pp. 349–375). New York: Academic Press.

Gewirtz, J. L. (1972d). Some contextual determinants of stimulus potency. In R. D. Parke (Ed.), *Recent trends in social learning theory* (pp. 7–33). New York: Academic Press.

Gewirtz, J. L. (1976). The attachment acquisition process as evidenced in the maternal conditioning of cued infant responding (particularly crying). *Human Development, 19,* 143–155.

Gewirtz, J. L. (1977). Maternal responding and the conditioning of infant crying: Directions of influence within the attachment-acquisition process. In B. C. Etzel, J. M. LeBlanc, & D. M. Baer (Eds.), *New developments in behavioral research: Theories, method, and application* (pp. 31–57). Hillsdale, NJ: Elrbaum.

Gewirtz, J. L. (1978). Social learning in early human development. In A. C. Catania & T. A. Brigham (Eds.), *Handbook of applied behavior analysis: Social and instructional processes* (pp. 105–141). New York: Irvington.

Gewirtz, J. L., & Boyd, E. F. (1976). Mother-infant interaction and its study. In H. W. Reese (Ed.), *Advances in child development and behavior, 11* (pp. 141–163). New York: Academic Press.

Gewirtz, J. L., & Boyd, E. F. (1977). Experiments on mother-infant interaction underlying mutual attachment acquisition: The infant conditions the mother. In T. Alloway, P. Pliner, & L. Krames (Eds.), *Advances in the study of communication and affect: Vol. 3. Attachment behaviour* (pp. 109–143). New York and London: Plenum Press.

Gewirtz, J. L., & Palaez-Nogueras, M. (1991). The attachment metaphor and the conditioning of infant separation protests. In J. L. Gewirtz & W. Kurtines (Eds.), *Intersections with attachment.* Hillsdale, NJ: Erlbaum.

Gewirtz, J. L., Pelaez-Nogueras, M., Diaz, L., & Villate, M. (1990, August). *Infant learning of the social-referencing pattern.* Paper presented at the annual meeting of the American Psychological Association, Boston, MA.

Gewirtz, J. L., & Stingle, K. (1968). The learning of generalized imitation as the basis for identification. *Psychological Review, 75,* 374–397.

Goldfarb, W. (1945a). Effects of psychological deprivation in infancy and subsequent stimulation. *American Journal of Psychiatry, 102,* 18–33.

Goldfarb, W. (1945b). Psychological privation in infancy and subsequent adjustment. *American Journal of Orthopsychiatry, 15,* 247–255.

Goldfarb, W. (1955). Emotional and intellectual consequences of psychologic deprivation in infancy: A re-evaluation. In P. H. Hoch & J. Zubin (Eds.), *Psychopathology of childhood* (pp. 105–119). New York: Grune & Stratton.

Hess, E. H. (1959). Imprinting. *Science, 130,* 133–141.

Hess, E. H. (1964). Imprinting in birds. *Science, 146,* 1128–1139.

Hesse, E. H. (1973). *Imprinting: Early experience and the developmental psychobiology of attachment.* New York: Van Nostrand.

Hinde, R. A. (1974). *Biological bases of human social behavior.* New York: McGraw-Hill.

Hinde, R. A., & Stevenson-Hinde, J. (Eds.), (1973). *Constraints on learning.* New York: Academic Press.

Hoffman, H. S., & DePaulo, P. (1977). Behavioral control by an imprinting stimulus. *American Scientist, 65,* 58–66.

Hoffman, H. S., & Ratner, A. M. (1973). A reinforcement model of imprinting: Implication for socialization in monkeys and man. *Psychological Review, 80,* 527–544.

Hulsebus, R. C. (1973). Operant conditioning of infant behavior; A review. in H. W. Reese (Ed.), *Advances in child development and behavior, 8* (pp. 111–158). New York: Academic Press.

Klinnert, M., Campos, J. J., Sorce, J., Emde. R. N., & Svejda, M. J. (1983). Social referencing: An important appraisal process in human infancy. In R. Plutchik & H. Kellerman (Eds.), *The emotions* (Vol. 2, pp. 57–86). New York: Academic Press.

Kohlberg, L. (1966). A cognitive-developmental analysis of children's sex-role concepts and attitudes. In E. E. Maccoby (Ed.), *The development of sex differences* (pp. 82–173). Stanford CA: Stanford University Press.

Levy, D. M. (1937). Primary affect hunger. *American Journal of Psychiatry, 94,* 643–652.

Lipsitt, L. P., & Kaye, H. (1964). Conditioned sucking in the human newborn, *Psychonomic Science, 1,* 29–30.

Lorenz, K. (1935). Der Kumpan in der Umwelt des Vogels. *Journal fur Ornithologie, 83.* 137–213.

Lorenz, K. (1969). Innate bases of learning. In K. H. Pribram (Ed.), *On the biology of learning.* New York: Harcourt, Brace & World.

Millar, W. S. (1976). Operant acquisition of social behaviors in infancy: Basic problems and constraints. In H. W. Reese (Ed.), *Advances in child development and behavior, 11* (pp. 107–140). New York: Academic Press.

Papousek, H. (1961). Conditioned head rotation reflexes in infants in the first months of life. *Acts Paediatrica, 50,* 565–576.

Papousek, H. (1977). Entwicklung der Lernfahigkeit im Sauglingsalter [The development of learning ability in infancy]. In G. Nissen (Ed.), *Intelligenz, Lernen und Lernstorungen.* Berlin: Springer-Verlag.

Petrovich, S. B., & Gewirtz, J. L. (1984). Learning in the context of evolutionary biology: In search of synthesis. *The Behavioral and Brain Sciences, 7,* 160–161.

Petrovich, S. B., & Gewirtz, J. L. (1985). The attachment-learning process and its relation to cultural and biological evolution: Proximate and ultimate considerations. In M. Reite & T. Field (Eds.), *The psychobiology of attachment* (pp. 257–289). New York: Academic Press.

Poulson, C. L. (1983). Differential reinforcement of other-than-vocalization as a control procedure in the conditioning of infant vocalization rate. *Journal of Experimental Child Psychology, 36,* 471–489.

Routh, D. K. (1969). Conditioning of vocal response differentiation in infants. *Developmental Psychology, 1*, 219–226.

Roy, M. A. (Ed.). (1980). *Species identity and attachment: A phylogenetic evaluation.* New York: Garland STPM Press.

Schaffer, H. R., & Emerson, P. (1964). The development of social attachments in infancy. *Monographs of the Society for Research in Child Development, 29*, (3, Serial No. 94).

Scott, J. P. (1960). Comparative social psychology. In R. H. Waters, D. A. Rethlingshafer, & W. E. Caldwell (Eds.), *Principles of comparative psychology* (pp. 250–288). New York: McGraw-Hill.

Scott, J. P. (1968). *Early experience and the organization of behavior.* Belmont, CA: Brooks/Cole.

Sears, R. R. (1972). Attachment, dependency, and frustration. In J. L. Gewirtz (Ed.), *Attachment and dependency* (pp. 1–27). Washington, D.C.: Winston.

Seligman, M. E. P. (1970). On the generality of laws of learning *Psychological Review, 77*, 406–418.

Seligman, M. E. P., & Hager, J. L. (1972). Introduction. In M. E. P. Seligman & J. L. Hager (Eds.), *Biological boundaries of learning.* N.Y.: Appleton-Century-Crofts.

Siqueland, E. R., & Lipsitt, L. P. (1966). Conditioned head-turning behavior in newborns. *Journal of Experimental Child Psychology, 3*, 356–376.

Skinner, B. F. (1938). *The behavior of organisms.* New York: Appleton-Century-Crofts.

Skinner, B. F. (1966). The phylogeny and ontogeny of behavior. *Science, 153*, 1205–1213.

Skinner, B. F. (1981). Selection by consequence. *Science, 213*, 501–504.

Spitz, R. A. (1945). Hospitalism: An inquiry into the genesis of psychiatric conditions in early childhood. *The psychoanalytic study of the child, 1* (pp. 53–74). New York: International Universities Press.

Spitz, R. A. (1946a). Anaclitic depression. In R. S. Eissler, A. Freud, H. Hartmann & M. Kris (Eds.), *The psychoanalytic study of the child, 2* (pp. 313–342). New York: International Universities Press.

Spitz, R. A. (1946b). Hospitalism: A follow-up report. In R. S. Eissler, A. Freud, H. Hartmann & M. Kris (Eds.), *The psychoanalytic study of the child, 2* (pp. 113–117). New York: International Universities Press.

Spitz, R. A. (1949). The role of ecological factors in emotional development in infancy. *Child Development, 20*, 145–156.

Spitz, R. A. (1954). Unhappy and fatal outcomes of emotional deprivation and stress in infancy. In I. Galdston (Ed.), *Beyond the germ theory.* New York: Health Education Council.

Yarrow, L. J. (1961). Maternal deprivation: Toward an empirical and conceptual re-evaluation. *Psychological Bulletin, 58*, 459–490.

Yarrow, L. J. (1972). Attachment and dependency: A development perspective. In J. L. Gewirtz (Ed.), *Attachment and dependency* (pp. 81–95). Washington, DC: Winston.

8

The Mutuality of Parental Control in Early Childhood

H. Rudolph Schaffer

Introduction: Socialization and Social Influence

In what way do children change as a result of their encounters with other people and how is such change brought about? These questions pose a basic problem for developmental psychology; they form the core of the socialization issue.

There are three kinds of phenomena to which any complete account of socialization must address itself:

1. The end products of socialization (conscience, impulse control, sex role formation, etc.)
2. The intra-psychic mechanisms underlying these products (identification, role learning, internalisation, etc.)
3. The interactive experiences in the course of which children first encounter the expectations that other people have of them, as well as the means used to induce them to meet such expectations

The last mentioned of the three represents, of course, the first step in the sequence that eventually results in a fully socialized individual. It refers to the children's initial encounter with the aims and intentions that their social partners have with respect to the course of their behavior and it is here that a social influence orientation is applicable. Yet, curiously, this step has usually been omitted from direct empirical inves-

H. Rudolph Schaffer • Department of Psychology, University of Strathclyde, Glasgow, Scotland G1-IRD, United Kingdom.

tigation. By and large socialization research has been preoccupied with long-term changes and with end-products and has paid little attention to the beginnings of the sequence. Socialization studies, that is, have not been firmly tied to a social interaction context.

MODELS OF SOCIALIZATION

The reason for this failure is to be found in the various theoretical models of the socialization process which have prevailed in the recent past and dominated our thinking. Each of these made certain assumptions about the role of children's original encounters with other people and the way these shaped their further development of socially acceptable modes of behavior. Although these assumptions differed radically from one model to the next no attempt was made to check them by means of empirical investigation. Indeed, each arbitrarily asserted that the child's crucial formative experiences were of a particular kind and then at once proceeded to the study of end-products and their underlying psychic processes. Three such models have been particularly influential (see Schaffer, 1984, for a more extensive discussion):

1. *Laissez-faire model.* According to this view, the precise nature of social encounters with caretakers plays little part in shaping the child's development. Basing their ideas on a belief in preformationism, proponents of this model (who included Rousseau and Gesell) asserted that adults ought to avoid all interference with the wholly natural and spontaneous process of development; if they played a more vigorous part they were likely to disturb the orderly unfolding of inherent capacities and prevent the processes of self-regulation and maturation from taking place. The task of parents is thus to provide a maximally permissive atmosphere in which children are allowed to grow as their nature dictates; any more active role in socialization is denied to caretakers.

2. *Clay molding model.* Rather than seeing children as preformed, this model views them as formless and passive. It is as though the child arrives in the world as an amorphous lump of clay which is then molded into any shape that caretakers arbitrarily decide upon. The end product is thus wholly explicable in terms of the adults' behavior: It is their schedules of rewards and punishment, their ways of habit training and the examples they set that wholly account for the course of the child's development. This view found its most extreme expression in the writings of J.

B. Watson (1928), with his faith in the wholly deterministic role of experience; it influenced much subsequent work that examined child-rearing practices from a behavioristic approach (Bijou & Baer, 1962). Socialization, according to Bijou (1970), is simply the product of the individual's reinforcement history. It follows that the child is regarded merely as a passive recipient of other people's stimulation and that the key influences which will account for the end result of socialization are to be found in the nature of that stimulation and the manner whereby it is applied.

3. *The conflict model.* This is probably the most prevalent view, powerfully backed as it was by Freud. Children, it is agreed, are not passive. From the beginning they are equipped with desires and response tendencies that impel them to behave in certain ways. These ways, however, are antithetical to the requirements of society; inevitably they will bring the child into conflict with caretakers, whose task it is to compel him or her to give up egoistic preferences and adopt the unnatural modes of behavior that they insist upon. Development is thus a painful process, for it requires the resolution of the basic antagonism between the child and the social group. The key experiences are thus conflict situations. Parent and child are seen as having different aims but, by virtue of being the more powerful partner, the parent is generally able to resolve the conflict by imposing her will on an antagonistic and resentful child. Hoffman's (1977) description of the way in which parents bring about the child's conformity to the moral requirements of society is one recent and influential expression of this view; in his account of the "discipline encounter" as the prototypical socialization situation the conflict element in the relationship between an egoistic child and a powerful parent is given prominence and is seen as providing the motive power for the child's eventual conformity.

Each of these three models makes assertions about the nature of early social interactions, but in each case these are based more on a priori considerations (derived respectively from the global theories of preformationism, learning theory and psychoanalysis) than from empirical study of those interactions. However, in the last 20 years a considerable amount of research has begun to shed light on the nature of early social development, and two general conclusions that are particularly relevant here have emerged:

1. Even in the earliest social encounters the child is by no means a passive recipient of adult stimulation; both parent *and* child play an active part in determining the nature and course of their in-

teractions. The influence process is a bi-directional and not a
unilateral one.

2. Mutual adaptation, not conflict, is the basic theme that runs
   through the course of parent-child interaction. The child arrives in
   the world preadapted for social encounters; from infancy on, both
   partners jointly construct their interactions. Conflicts occur, of
   course, but there is no indication that they constitute the key
   socialization episodes in a child's life. Rather than seeing the parent-child relationship as a never-ending battle investigators have
   come to be impressed by the "fit" of the two individuals' sets of
   behavior patterns. Far from starting off as an antisocial being who
   must be coerced into sociability, children share a common
   heritage with their caretakers that impels them to adopt the same
   social goals.

A model of socialization based on *mutuality* is thus indicated. Such
mutuality is not an end-result to which children are driven by coercive
pressures. Rather, it is a prerequisite without which the adult could not
produce any effects in the first place. How this works out in practice has
begun to be clarified in recent years.

Parental Control Techniques

Socialization does not begin with attempts to convey abstract values—of right and wrong, of the importance of honesty and respect for
others, and of all those other qualities that one may regard as the hallmark of the "properly" socialized individual. It begins instead with
adults' efforts to induce children to comply with requests referring to the
ordinary, practical, very concrete minutiae of everyday living: to put a
toy back into a box, do up a button, give the baby a kiss, refrain from
shouting or from touching a valuable vase—in short, with any of those
constantly occurring situations where a caretaker considers it necessary,
for one reason or another, to change the ongoing course of the child's
behavior. We refer to these efforts as *control techniques*, using the term to
describe all those behaviors employed by one person to channel another's activity in certain directions, inhibiting some tendencies but en-
hancing others. The emphasis is primarily on immediate and not long-
term consequences, and though the controls used may be based on
certain abstract values, the focus is on their overt content and not the
underlying moral principles that they express. The interest for the investigator thus lies in the way in which a caretaker sets about the task of
conveying an aim in her mind in such a way that the child comes to
comply with it.

Control techniques take many forms. They are by no means confined to parade-ground commands but may be applied in indirect and subtle ways. They are also not to be considered in purely negative terms—as prohibitions, refusals, punishment, and discipline. There has been a tendency in the child-rearing literature to single out such didactic and negative techniques as though they were the only or at any rate the most effective means of dealing with young children, thus neglecting the many subtle and positive means parents have at their disposal for obtaining compliance from a child. Indeed, the first task confronting the investigator is to describe the range of control techniques parents and others use in their interactions with children of different ages and in various settings. Further tasks include relating the use of particular techniques to the child's condition and individuality, determining the circumstances under which controls are effective in obtaining the child's compliance, and investigating how, in the course of development, other-control gradually gives way to self-control.

One overriding conclusion that emerges from the relevant studies conducted so far (detailed in Schaffer, 1984) refers to the essentially interactive nature of control techniques. Controls, that is, are not to be understood as the arbitrary imposition of the will of one person upon another. By no means do they invariably take a bolt-out-of-the-blue form that descends on an unsuspecting and unprepared child. On the contrary, controls are to be understood in the same dialogic terms that are used for unstructured interactions in which neither partner is attempting to achieve any specified goal. Mutual influence, i.e., the effects of *both* partners upon each other, is just as evident in the one situation as it is in the other, even though one partner is more powerful and even though it may be the intention of that individual to induce the other one to conform to his wishes. This is seen particularly in the way in which the parent's control strategy is adapted to the characteristics of the child; the child's nature, that is, helps to determine the parent's behavior. We can illustrate this by referring to three kinds of child characteristics, namely the momentary state, the developmental level, and the individuality of the child.

Child's Momentary State

The now quite voluminous literature on adult-child interaction—whether concerned with face-to-face encounters or with object-centered interchanges, whether referring to infants in the very early months of life or to children in later years, and whether the adult involved is the mother or a less familiar individual—all points to one overriding conclusion, namely that the interactive quality of such encounters is largely derived from the sensitivity with which the adult integrates her behavior with the child's (Schaffer, 1977, 1984). Sensitivity takes many forms and subsumes a variety of phenomena (Ainsworth, Bell, & Stayton, 1971; Lamb & Easterbrooks, 1981; Schaffer & Collis, 1986)—it refers in particular to the *awareness* by the adult of the child's cues and communications, to the *appropriateness* of the nature of the adult's response to the child's behavior, and to the fineness of the *timing* of that response. With very young infants, interactions are largely brought about by virtue of the adult's willingness to accept any action on the part of the infant as though it were a message that required some sort of reply. A dialogue is thus set up—or to be more precise, a pseudo-dialogue, in so far as the interaction tends to be of an asymmetrical character, with one partner assuming major responsibility for converting the encounter into an interaction. Only with growing age will children gradually participate on a more equal basis; only with increasing cognitive capacity will they become capable of intentionally provoking the other person's behavior and of understanding the reciprocity that underlies all social exchanges (Schaffer, 1979).

These conclusions are largely derived from microanalytic studies of early social interaction. Much of the to-and-fro of any exchange between two individuals tends to take place at a split-second level: speaker-switch pauses, for instance, in adult conversations have been found to be around 0.6 sec. in duration (Jaffe & Feldstein, 1970); in the vocal interchanges of mothers and one-year-olds they are also frequently less than one second. Similarly, the integration of other interactional cues: of looking with vocalising (Schaffer, Collis, Parsons, 1977), of looking and vocalising with gestures (Murphy & Messer, 1977), of verbal labelling with manipulation (Messer, 1978) and with looking (Collis, 1977), and so forth. Both interpersonal and intrapersonal synchrony of responses tend to be so fine that videotaping or filming are required to record them, so that subsequent frame-by-frame or slow motion analysis may highlight the speed and precision of that synchrony.

This picture originally emerged from studies that placed adult and child in one particular context, namely in situations that were entirely unstructured and unconstrained, such as face-to-face situations in which the parent is merely told to amuse the child, or free play situations in which the two partners can do as they wish with whatever toys are available. Perhaps it is not surprising that under such circumstances mothers tend to carefully monitor the child's actions and sensitively attune their behavior accordingly, for they are under no pressure from external goals and can therefore let children take the initiative and merely follow their lead and adapt to their particular requirements. What is striking is that in more constrained situations, that is, in those where the adult does have some specific aim in mind that she must convey to the child and where she therefore sets out to direct the child's behavior in a particular direction, such adaptation also occurs. The interaction, that is, does not assume a unidirectional form in which the adult arbitrarily imposes her will on the child's. Instances of that no doubt do occur, but under most conditions adults go about the task of influencing their children in the same dyadic manner as described for unstructured situations, that is, by carefully monitoring the child's behavior in order to then intercalate their own appropriate responses at the appropriate moment of time.

This is illustrated in Schaffer and Crook's (1979, 1980) study of maternal control techniques applied to children in their second year. The sessions were conducted in a laboratory playroom and videotaped from behind a one-way mirror. To ensure that mothers took an active role in the interaction, they were instructed to make quite certain that the child played with all the toys available, not let him or her spend time with just one or two toys, and actively intervene in order to direct the child's play accordingly. As the results show, the mothers did indeed assume such a directive role: Approximately 45% of all their verbal utterances were found to have a control function, occurring at the average rate of one every 9 seconds. Yet the children were by no means overwhelmed by this seeming barrage, and a major reason for this is the way in which the mothers carefully timed their interventions. Controls, that is, rarely descended in bolt-out-of-the-blue fashion on the child but were emitted in such a manner as to ensure that the child's attention was appropriately focussed on a toy before some action on that toy was requested. Mothers tended to employ sequential strategies, whereby attention-directing devices (verbal and nonverbal) were used as a preliminary to action directives. The distinction between attention controls and action controls is thus a most useful one in any attempt to understand how mothers set about getting the child to perform some task. In many cases, however, the mother preferred to leave the first stage to the child's initiative, that is, she waited until the child's attention was spontaneously focused on a particular toy before issuing her action directive. In either case the mother did not leap in with such a directive without first establishing a mutual focus of attention. As shown by an analysis of the child's involvement state with the relevant object at the moment of time that the mother began to utter her action directive, in the great majority of cases the child was already visually attending to that object or even in physical contact with it. The success of this strategy is shown by the close association between the children's compliance rate and their involvement state: The probability of obtaining the required response was far greater when the child was already appropriately oriented to the toy. Again, the facilitative role of the mother's timing of her controls in relation to the child's ongoing behavior is highlighted.

A mother does not impinge on an inert child; the outcome of any attempt to influence behavior will depend (among other things) on his or her state and condition at that particular moment. By successfully manipulating this state the parent can avoid the clash of wills that the conflict model of socialization appears to regard as inevitable in any influence encounter (Stayton, Hogan, & Ainsworth, 1971), on the supposition that compliance is extracted from an invariably reluctant child. Parental regulation of child behavior can be accomplished relatively smoothly and without conflict under many conditions; a sensitive monitoring of the child's ongoing activity appears to be one of the more important prerequisites for doing so. Such monitoring means that the parent does not merely react to undesirable behavior after the event but can also anticipate such actions and use suitable diversionary tactics. As Holden (1983) found during observations carried out in supermarkets, mothers resorted to a great many such proactive controls by, for instance, engaging their children in conversation, providing them with some item of food, or diverting their attention with a toy or other object. The mothers who frequently employed this type of behavior had children who exhibited fewer undesirable actions. Proactive controls are not issued randomly; they reflect the mother's judgement that at a given moment of time it is necessary to employ such a tactic in order to attain a particular outcome with respect to the child's behavior. Again, the parent's action is seen to be influenced by the child's state.

Child's Developmental Level

That controls are adjusted to children's developmental level is hardly surprising. After all, as children get older their comprehensive abilities change, and as a result they become more competent in understanding a wide range of communicative messages. Thus, *how* an adult conveys directive requests can be expected to show progressive modification in the course of development, in the same way as adults' speech to children generally tends to undergo changes in the light of feedback information about the addressee's ability to comprehend that speech (the "motherese" phenomenon). There is also one further change, namely *what* adults convey to children. With increasing cognitive and motoric competence children will be expected to comply with increasingly more complex and demanding requests, and the content of controls will therefore change accordingly.

While conclusions are constrained by the rather limited age range covered by the various relevant studies, it does seem that the incidence of controls issued by parents to preschool children decreases over age (McLaughlin, 1983; Schaffer & Crook, 1979). However, though it may seem obvious at first sight that younger children require more guidance, there are several indications which suggest the need for caution in making such a generalisation. For one thing, Schaffer, Hepburn, and Collis (1983), in a study based on a number of set tasks which mothers had to convey to their children, found the mothers of 10-month-old infants giving out fewer verbal controls than the mothers of 18-month-old infants—presumably because the former did not yet have such serious expectations of success as the latter and also because they did not regard the verbal medium as particularly effective at this early age. For another, it appears that the nature of the task to be performed affects the adults' behavior. Power and Parke (1983) found that the incidence of socializing attempts changed between 11 and 17 months and especially so in the 14 to 17 months range; however, those aimed at self-care skills, household responsibilities, and participation in games increased whereas those concerned with independence and regulating attention decreased in incidence. Also relevant is a finding by Bridges (1979) who investigated mothers' behavior in an object retrieval game. When the object was familiar, 2-year-olds were provided with more directive clues than 2½-year-olds; when the object was unfamiliar there was no difference in the number of clues. Adjustment to the child's comprehension level presumably accounts for this pattern. And one further finding that affects conclusions about incidence refers to the distribution of attention controls and action controls over age: Schaffer and Crook (1979) noted that at 15 months attention-direction consumed more of the mothers' efforts; at 24 months, however, attention-direction had decreased and mothers then concentrated primarily on influencing the children's actions. Schaffer et al. (1983), though finding no significant change in the incidence of attention controls between 10 and 18 months, did find a doubling of action controls over this age range. Bearing in mind the sequential nature of attention-action strategies employed by parents, it appears that mothers of younger children felt it necessary to concentrate on the first stage of this sequence. At older ages, this aspect was more easily accomplished and the mothers were therefore able to focus their efforts on the children's actions.

Of particular interest are changes in the distribution of verbal and nonverbal communicative modes used by adults to convey directives to children of various ages, for the relationship between these two modes has implications for the understanding of early language development (Macnamara, 1972; Schaffer et al., 1983; Schnur & Shatz, 1984). Given children's initial linguistic incompetence, one might expect that adults would communicate to preverbal infants primarily by nonverbal means;

as children become more able to comprehend language verbal messages would then gradually increase and replace these nonverbal behaviors. The evidence (at least for the first 2 or 3 years) indicates a somewhat more complex picture. In the first place, linguistically conveyed controls are by no means absent in the preverbal period: As Rheingold and Adams (1980) showed, even neonates have spoken commands addressed to them. Similarly, Hepburn and Schaffer (1983) found mothers of 5-month-old infants using verbal controls during a bathing situation—generally in association with relevant nonverbal signals but sometimes without such support. Thus from the beginning adults appear to use language to influence their children's behavior; as we shall see below, however, it is necessary to examine the whole dyadic situation prevailing at the time to appreciate the spirit in which these remarks are made.

An additional consideration refers to the subsequent course of the relationship between verbal and nonverbal modes. According to Schaffer *et al.* (1983), no crossover effect could be observed between 10 and 18 months, whereby verbal controls gradually begin to take over from nonverbal controls. It is true that there was an increase in verbally conveyed requests, though this was largely due to the rise in action controls, and especially those that specified the precise action to be performed on the toy (e.g., "push," "draw") rather than containing such general action verbs as "do" or "try"—once again a reflection of the child's growing competence to which the mothers adapted their demands. However, nonverbal controls remained at the same level for both ages; for that matter, the major groupings of nonverbal categories employed (object handling, gestures, and demonstration) showed no change during this period. It is only when one examines the two modes over a wider age range that the expected trend becomes evident: McLaughlin (1983) found fewer nonverbal concomitants to verbal controls at 2½ and 3½ than at 1½ years of age; Schaffer and Crook (1979) noted a decrease in nonverbal controls from 15 to 24 months, particularly in two categories labelled "manipulating accessibility" and "eliciting or prohibiting action," and interpreted this as a response by the mothers to the children's growing motoric competence; and Bridges (1979) observed that mothers used more gestures to their 2-year-old than to their 2½-year-old children even when the object referred to was familiar. By 2½ years gestures occurred only when the child could not be expected to know the name of the object. As has been documented repeatedly, younger children need to have verbal utterances embedded in a nonverbal context to be meaningful. The nature of adult input when conveying requests shows that parents are aware of this requirement and also that, in line with the child's growing verbal sophistication, they are prepared gradually to loosen this association.

Another respect in which one might expect to find changes occur over age is in the explicitness of adults' verbal requests. A number of writers (e.g., Bellinger, 1979; Schneiderman, 1983) have reported such changes, pointing to a general tendency for explicitness to be greater when in speech to children with relatively poor linguistic comprehension. The most common criterion employed to measure explicitness is a syntactic one, which contrasts the use of imperatives with rather less direct request forms such as embedded directives (in interrogative form) or hints and suggestions (in declarative form). However, explicitness can be assessed by various standards which may show different developmental trends. Thus Schaffer et al. (1983) found the syntactic criterion not to show any change in the 10 to 18 months age range. On the other hand, when the mothers' speech was examined for the extent to which both the name of the toy on which they wanted the child to act and the action he or she was to perform on the toy were explicitly named, it was found that an *increase* in explicitness occurred, reflecting largely the above mentioned rise in the use of specific action verbs. And just to complicate the picture further, yet another index showed a *decrease* in explicitness over age: At the younger age the mothers' object references were almost entirely to the toys immediately confronting the child (e.g., "put the *brick* on" or "scribble with the *pencil*"); at the older age, on the other hand, the mothers also introduced the consequences of the child's action by referring to their products (e.g., "build a *tower*" or "draw a *picture*"). The older child is thus taken out of the immediate here-and-now situation and a less concrete and therefore less explicit set of references is introduced. Thus, three different criteria appear to indicate three different trends; the danger, however, lies in thinking of explicitness as a unitary entity when in fact the three indices tap different aspects, each related to age in its own specific way.

Child's Individuality

At any given age children differ in a variety of characteristics that have implications for the type of treatment they receive from others. One such characteristic is the child's sex (Maccoby & Jacklin, 1974); however, as far as recent studies of early control techniques are concerned, the literature on sex differences is ambiguous. Minton, Kagan, and Levine (1971) found 2-year-old boys to be more often reprimanded by their mothers than was the case for girls; the fact that boys had higher rates of violation of parental standards and were more likely to disobey adult injunctions could well be held responsible for this difference. On the other hand, neither Schaffer and Crook (1979, 1980) nor McLaughlin (1983) found any differences in either the incidence or the type of control used for boys and girls, nor were there any differences in the rates of compliance by these children according to sex. However, Power and Parke (1983) found some sex-linked differences in *what* adults attempted to influence, e.g., parents of girls were more likely to engage in attempts to encourage prosocial behavior and to discourage aggression than were parents of boys. Such differences are, of course, notoriously lacking in robustness; they reflect cultural stereotypes that, especially nowadays, are in course of rapid change and, where they are found, may well be a function of temperamental characteristics that have only a tenuous association with sex and would be better investigated in their own right.

One such temperamental factor is activity level. In so far as some children are from the very beginning more active than others and in so far as such children can pose greater problems of restraint and attention focussing for their caretakers than less active children, it seems likely that parental control techniques will differ accordingly if they are to have the desired effect. More work is badly needed on the relationship between such temperamental characteristics and socializing practices within the "normal" range; an examination of the pathological extreme is, however, often particularly instructive. Thus, Cunningham and Barkley (1979) compared the interactions of normal and hyperactive boys with their mothers, and found that in both free play and task situations the mothers of the hyperactive children issued twice as many controls (in the form of commands and command-questions) as the normal children's mothers. Hyperactive children on the whole were less compliant, and this together with their transient and disruptive behavior might well have accounted for their treatment. Cause-and-effect statements are obviously difficult to make on the basis of such findings, but the authors' observation that the control exerted by the mothers of the hyperactive children usually followed the child's disruptive behavior is suggestive. Simply keeping a distractible child on task requires special measures, and the fact that these mothers tended to impose more structure on the child's play and social interactions seems plausibly to be in response to the child's particular characteristics. Such characteristics are, however, often difficult to specify. Thus Cunningham, Reuter, Blackwell, and Deck (1981), in a report on retarded children's interactions with their mothers, found compliance rate to be no different compared with normal children. The controls to which the former were subjected by their mothers were, however, significantly greater than was found for the latter, and here, too, the difference held for both free play and task situations. In so far as the mothers of the retarded children responded less positively to instances of compliance and cooperation it is possible that their control behavior expressed their generally more negative affective evaluation of the child. This does not rule out the possibility, on the other hand, that it was the less responsive and more solitary nature of these children that elicited such parental behavior.

Another pathological group on whom some information about control problems is available are deaf children. The very fact that adults cannot resort to the usual communicative channel when conveying messages to their children may well place an extra strain on both partners in the interaction. An unresponsive child is likely to elicit attempts to provide additional stimulation—hence presumably the report by several authors that the mothers of deaf children are by and large more intrusive, controlling, and didactic (Goss, 1970; Schlesinger & Meadow, 1972; Wedell-Monnig & Lumley, 1980). In a comparison of the interactions of deaf and hearing children with their mothers Brinich (1980) found the mothers of the deaf children to provide more instructions and to engage in more attention-controlling behavior, but suggested that this pattern (similar to that found among the mentally retarded) was unrelated to either deafness or to retardation as such; instead it represents a reaction to the breakdown in reciprocal communication. Thus, "when a mother finds it difficult to establish reciprocal communication with her child (whether this be because of deafness, mental retardation, or other disorders interfering with communication) she may adapt to that situation by emphasizing control in the relationship. . . . This situation might be compressed into an aphorism like 'when communication breaks down, the powerful take control' " (p. 81). Just as with younger children there is by and large a need for more control than with older children, so in cases of pathology the adult will make up for the child's deficiencies by assuming greater direction. The communication process does not simply disintegrate; rather it takes a different form in which the parent adjusts to the child's particular characteristics by suitably modifying the nature of her contribution to the child-parent system. However, one must acknowledge that this may not take place spontaneously. Professional help is needed which in turn is subject to scientific enquiry and sometimes controversy, as seen in the debate about the respective merits of oral-only and total communication modes (Greenberg, 1980). Meadow, Greenberg, Erting, and Carmichael (1981) found that deaf children provided with oral-only communication spend less time in social interaction with their mothers, receive more parental behavior requests, and have the highest incidence of noncompliance when compared with deaf children receiving total communication, deaf children with deaf mothers, and hearing children with hearing mothers—a finding that must surely be one very persuasive argument against the use of the oral-only mode.

CONTROL DURING THE FIRST YEAR OF LIFE

At all stages of the life-span, from birth to death, human beings are subject to social influence processes. No developmental period is exempt; only the content of the influence and the manner of its impact are likely to vary over age.

This point needs to be stressed in relation to the very beginning of life, for an impression is frequently given that infancy is a period when children are shielded from the demands of their social partners. Thus a dichotomy is made between the first year on the one hand and post-infancy development on the other; the earlier period is seen as one of nurturance and indulgence during which the parent's role is confined to that of comforter, and only on reaching the second year are issues of control and socializing said to arise. For instance, Hoffman (1977) has asserted that at the end of infancy "the parent's role shifts dramatically from primarily that of caretaker to that of socialization agent. His actions change from being facilitative and nurturant to disciplinary." Similarly Maccoby and Martin (1983) refer to "a major change that occurs during the second year," namely "the onset of socialization pressure." And in the same vein Hetherington and Parke (1976), while agreeing that so-cialization is evident in the first year of life, do not consider it to begin in earnest until the second year when the child achieves mobility and starts to speak.

Such assertions arise from an artificially narrow definition of the socialization process which equates the process with *verbal* influences on the part of the parent and with *voluntary* compliance on the part of the child. When either or both these aspects are missing the nature of in-teractive forces are thought to be of a completely different kind, requir-ing different labels and different explanations. Whether there are indeed such differences from one developmental period to another is at present an open issue; what needs to be recognized is that social influences do function from the neonatal stage on and that caretakers not only attempt to steer their children's behavior into socially approved channels from the very beginning but clearly succeed in doing so. In so far as socializa-tion is a label used to designate the transformation of a biological orga-nism into a social one, the process may be said to start at birth.

Let us consider some of the very earliest influences exerted by adults over infants' behavior. These concern the regulation of such basic functions as waking-sleeping states and feeding patterns. How effec-tively and how rapidly adults are able to regulate infants' states and impose socially acceptable form on them has been described in detail by Sanders (summarized in Sanders, Stechler, Burns, & Lee, 1979). Infants begin life with an endogenously determined pattern of state fluctua-tions; thus a newborn tends to sleep for many short periods, randomly distributed throughout the day and interspersed with even shorter peri-ods of wakefulness. Such a pattern is inconvenient to caretakers; it does not fit into their own daily cycle and one of their earliest tasks therefore is to ensure that the infant's pattern conforms to their own timetable. As Sander has shown, the effects of this entrainment process are evident from the end of the first postnatal week on: more than half of the longest sleep periods of the 24 hours now occur during the night, whereas mobility and crying peaks have shifted to daytime periods. A coordination between infant state and caretaker activity is thus apparent. An *interpersonal* influence is clearly responsible for such changes in infants' behavior: As Sander was also able to show by means of "cross-fostering" experiments, different adults can produce different patterns in the same children. Individual specificity in the style of infant-caretaker adaptation is thus indicated, and the essentially social nature of the influences involved is further highlighted by cultural differences that occur in the development of waking-sleeping patterns (Super & Harkness, 1982). A similar picture emerges from studies of the feeding cycle during infancy: As the classical study by Marquis (1941) demonstrated, the adoption of either 3-hourly or 4-hourly schedules by caretakers will bring about correspondingly timed periods of restlessness in the infants. Once again, socially induced change has taken place; here too, as in the work by Sander, such change could be found to occur within the first 2 weeks of life. Whether the processes responsible for the change are basically different from those underlying change at subsequent developmental stages remains to be settled. Until this is done the use of socialization as an umbrella term to describe all adult-induced development is surely justified.

The manner whereby parents exert influence on such early functions as sleeping and feeding is, of course, very different from what one finds in later control episodes of the kind described in the previous section. In so far as verbal direction by the adult plays a major part in these controls it may be thought that such behavior would not become evident in the parental repertoire until the child is old enough to comprehend speech. That this is not so is seen in Hepburn and Schaffer's (1983) investigation of mothers' interactions with 5-month-old infants during a bathing session. A great many instances were found of mothers' attempts to change the infant's behavior, and a large proportion of these took verbal form. The mothers, that is, appeared to be requesting their infants to attend, to perform some action, or to refrain from some behavior in the same sort of way as has been described for older children. However, closer examination does reveal some differences. For one thing, a large proportion of verbal controls were accompanied by nonverbal actions, with the latter carrying the major communicative force. For another, mothers were often skilled in inserting their requests at points when the infant was about to perform the relevant action anyway; such anticipation is, of course, particularly easy in the context of a well-established routine such as bathing. And finally, many of the controls were in fact "pseudo-controls," in that they referred to an action that either the mother or the child was already carrying out at that moment. In addition, some requested an action that, given the child's developmental level, was totally unrealistic (e.g., "put on your socks," said laughingly to one of the 5-month-old infants) and therefore not expected to achieve a result.

That the compliance rate on the part of the infants approached 50% may at first sight seem surprising for so immature a being; given the fact that mothers tended to select those circumstances under which it would be easiest for the infant to comply, and that they did so by appropriately incorporating their requests into the sequence of the routine rather than have them impinge as isolated controls on an unprepared child, the *apparent* conformity of the child becomes rather more comprehensible. In any case, the highest compliance rates were found for nonverbal controls, the vast majority of which succeeded in their aim of eliciting some change in the child's behavior. Interestingly, the addition of verbal utterances to nonverbal controls seemed to detract from the effectiveness of the latter.

Why do adults indulge in such apparently unrealistic behavior as verbal requests addressed to preverbal infants? According to Rheingold and Adams (1980) even neonates are spoken to in this fashion—a tendency that seems to argue against the notion of parental adjustment to the child's competence level. Such apparent lack of realism is, however, by no means confined to the control function; it occurs, for instance, with respect to speech generally, which is found in almost all of adults' interactions with infants of any age. Why this is so can only be a matter of speculation. One consequence, however, is that infants have obtained a massive amount of experience of language input by the time they themselves reach the point of linguistic competence, and it is certainly conceivable that such experience in the previous phase will have played its part in enabling the infant to get to this point. The same applies to the control function: Being involved in such interactive formats right through the early months provides infants with plenty of opportunity to become acquainted with the demand characteristics of other people's requests, including the association of word and action, thus enabling infant, in due course, to enter such formats relatively rapidly and efficiently. And as far as the parent is concerned, it has the advantage that she can repeatedly test out the infant's ability to participate in control-compliance sequences and judge when the child is becoming capable of acting independently. At that point she can begin to hand over responsibility to the child. Up till then she herself may complete the sequence on his or her behalf.

Parental control of one kind or another is thus very much a feature of children's social experience during the first year of life. Indeed Power and Parke (1982), observing infants aged 8 to 10 months, found that the vast majority of interactions could be classified as parental attempts to influence the infants' behavior, either with regard to their attentive, their exploratory, or their social behavior—a conclusion that held for both laboratory and home settings and for both mothers and fathers. Power and Parke, moreover, make the valuable point that parents not only influence their children's behavior *directly* by means of the controls which they impose in play and other social interaction situations but also *indirectly* by the way in which they organise the child's physical environment. This latter, "managerial" function is exercised by setting limits to the number of home settings to which the child is given access ("floor freedom") and by determining the kinds of objects that the child can explore. In view of the fact that young children spend a greater part of their daily lives interacting with their inanimate environment than with other people (White, Kalsan, Shapiro, & Attanucci, 1977), such a managerial function is likely to play a most important role and deserves greater attention in any attempt to understand socialization processes than it has received so far.

Conclusions

Controls are thus a regular feature of parent-child interaction. They are not confined to any particular age range, nor are they reserved for such traditional areas of study as the socialization of toileting or of aggression. They are evident even in playful encounters, constituting an inevitable part of adult-child interaction under a wide range of circumstances. The greater the asymmetry of power between the two partners is, the more evident they are likely to be. This means that they are most prominent in the early years of childhood and gradually diminish as the child becomes more capable of regulating his or her own behavior. How eventually other-control comes to be replaced by self-control is one of the most important problems in developmental psychology that still needs solution. Work on this issue has begun (Kopp, 1982; Vaughn, Kopp, & Krakow, 1984; Wertsch, McNamee, McLane, & Budwig, 1980) and, once satisfactory definitions of self-control have been agreed on, the antecedent conditions which give rise to this development can then be determined. Do children whose parents are particularly skillful in adapting their controls to the individual child achieve self-control early? Are the conditions that foster compliance (an immediate reaction) identical to those that give rise to moral internalisation (a long-term product)?

Do different types of parental control strategies result in varying patterns of self-control? Answers to questions such as these will take one a considerable step further along the road to understanding how parents come to play a part in affecting the course of children's development.

The main thesis advanced here is that social influence cannot be understood unless conceived as a mutual, reciprocal process to which both partners contribute. This applies to all types of social situations and all types of individual—the mother and her newborn baby in a feeding situation, the teacher and student in a classroom, the captor and his prisoner in a "brainwashing" session, or any other interaction in which, at first sight, one partner appears to be more powerful than the other and can therefore exert pressure on him and control his behavior. Closer examination invariably shows that the nature of that pressure and control needs to be adapted to the characteristics of the less powerful individual if there is to be any chance of success. This applies equally to the content, the manner and the timing of the influence being applied: In each case the recipient affects the sender's behavior and in this way becomes a sender also.

REFERENCES

Ainsworth, M. D. S., Bell, S. M. V., & Stayton, D. J. (1971). Individual differences in strange-situation behavior of one-year-olds. In H. R. Schaffer (Ed.), *The origins of human social relations* (pp. 17–57). London: Academic Press.

Bellinger, D. (1979). Changes in the explicitness of mothers' directives as children age. *Journal of Child Language, 6,* 443–458.

Bijou, S. W. (1970). Reinforcement history and socialization. In R. A. Hoppe, G. A. Milton & E. C. Simmel (Eds.), *Early experiences and the processes of socialization* (pp. 43–58). New York: Academic Press.

Bijou, S. W., & Baer, D. M. (1962). *Child development.* New York: Appleton-Century-Crofts.

Bridges, A. (1979). Directing two-year-olds attention: Some clues to understanding. *Journal of Child Language, 6,* 211–226.

Brinich, P. H. (1980). Childhood deafness and maternal control. *Journal of Communication Disorders, 13,* 75–81.

Collis, G. M. (1977). Visual coorientation and maternal speech. In H. R. Schaffer (Ed.), *Studies in mother-infant interaction* (pp. 355–375). London: Academic Press.

Cunningham, C. E., & Barkley, R. A. (1979). The interactions of normal and hyperactive children with their mothers in free play and structured tasks. *Child Development, 50,* 217–224.

Cunningham, C. E., Reuter, E., Blackwell, J., & Deck, J. (1981). Behavioral and linguistic developments in the interactions of normal and retarded children with their mothers. *Child Development, 52,* 62–70.

Goss, R. N. (1970). Language used by mothers of deaf children and mothers of hearing children. *American Annals of the Deaf, 115,* 93–96.

Greenberg, M. T. (1980). Social interaction between deaf preschoolers and their mothers:

The effects of communication method & communication competence. *Developmental Psychology, 16,* 465–474.

Hepburn, A., & Schaffer, H. R. (1983). Les controles maternels dans la prima enfance (Maternal controls in early infancy). *Enfance, 1–2,* 117–127.

Hetherington, E. M., & Parke, R. D. (1976). *Child psychology: A contemporary viewpoint.* New York: McGraw-Hill.

Hoffman, M. L. (1977). Moral internalisation: Current theory and research. In L. Berkowitz (Ed.), *Advances in experimental social psychology,* (Vol. 10, pp. 85–133). New York: Academic Press.

Holden, G. W. (1983). Avoiding conflict: Mothers as tacticians in the supermarket. *Child Development, 54,* 233–240.

Jaffe, J., & Feldstein, S. (1970). *Rhythms of dialogue.* New York: Academic Press.

Kopp, C. B. (1982). Antecedents of self-regulation: A developmental perspective. *Developmental Psychology, 18,* 199–214.

Lamb, M. E., & Easterbrooks, M. A. (1981). Individual differences in parental sensitivity: Origins, components, and consequences. In M. E. Lamb & L. R. Sherrod (Eds.), *Infant social cognition: Empirical and theoretical considerations* (pp. 127–153). Hillsdale, N.J.: Erlbaum.

Maccoby, E. E., & Jacklin, C. N. (1974). *The psychology of sex differences.* Stanford, CA: Stanford University Press.

Maccoby, E. E., & Martin, J. A. (1983). Socialization in the context of the family: Parent-child interaction. In P. H. Mussen (Ed.), *Handbook of child psychology,* (4th ed.) Vol. IV: *Socialization, personality, and social development* (pp. 1–101). New York: Wiley.

McLaughlin, B. (1983). Child compliance to parental control techniques. *Developmental Psychology, 19,* 667–673.

Macnamara, J. (1972). Cognitive basis of language learning in infants. *Psychological Review, 79,* 1–13.

Marquis, D. P. (1941). Learning in the neonate: The modification of behavior under three feeding schedules. *Journal of Experimental Psychology, 29,* 263–282.

Meadow, K. P., Greenberg, M. T., Erting, C., & Carmichael, H. (1981). Interactions of deaf mothers and deaf preschool children: Comparisons with three other groups of deaf and hearing dyads. *American Annals of the Deaf, 126,* 454–468.

Messer, D. J. (1978). The integration of mothers' referential speech with joint play. *Child Development, 49,* 781–787.

Minton, C., Kagan, J., & Levine, J. A. (1971). Maternal control and obedience in the two-year-old. *Child Development, 42,* 1873–1894.

Murphy, C. M., & Meser, D. J. (1977). Mothers, infants and pointing: A study of a gesture. In Schaffer, H. R. (Ed.), *Studies in mother-infant interaction* (pp. 325–354). London: Academic Press.

Power, T. G., & Parke, R. D. (1982). Play as a context for early learning: Lab and home analyses. In I. E. Sigel & L. M. Laosa (Eds.), *The family as a learning environment.* New York: Plenum Press.

Power, T. G., & Parke, R. D. (1983). Patterns of mother and father play with their 8-month-old infant: A multiple analyses approach. *Infant Behavior and Development, 6,* 453–459.

Rheingold, H. L., & Adams, J. L. (1980). The significance of speech to newborns. *Developmental Psychology, 16,* 397–403.

Sanders, L. W., Stechler, G., Burns, P., & Lee, A. (1979). Change in infant- and caregiver variables over the first two months of life. In E. B. Thoman (Ed.), *Origins of the infant's social responsiveness* (pp. 349–407). Hillsdale, NJ: Erlbaum.

Schaffer, H. R. (1977). *Mothering.* London: Fontana; Cambridge, MA: Harvard University Press.

Schaffer, H. R. (1979). Acquiring the concept of the dialogue. In M. Bornstein & W. Kessen (Eds.), *Psychological development from infancy: Image and intention* (pp. 279–305). Hillsdale, NJ: Erlbaum.

Schaffer, H. R. (1984). *The child's entry into a social world.* London: Academic Press.

Schaffer, H. R., & Collis, G. M. (1986). Parental responsiveness and child behavior. In W. Sluckin & M. Herbert (Eds.), *Parental behaviour in animals and humans* (pp. 283–315). Oxford: Blackwell.

Schaffer, H. R., Collis, G. M., & Parsons, G. (1977). Vocal interchange and visual regard in verbal and preverbal children. In H. R. Schaffer (Ed.), *Studies in mother-infant interaction.* London: Academic Press.

Schaffer, H. R., & Crook, C. K. (1979). Maternal control techniques in a directed play situation. *Child Development, 50,* 989–998.

Schaffer, H. R., & Crook, C. K. (1980). Child compliance and maternal control techniques. *Developmental Psychology, 16,* 54–61.

Schaffer, H. R., Hepburn, A., & Collis, G. M. (1983). Verbal and nonverbal aspects of mothers' directives. *Journal of Child Language, 10,* 337–355.

Schlesinger, H. S., & Meadow, K. P. (1972). *Sound and sign: Childhood deafness and mental health.* Berkeley: University of California Press.

Schneiderman, M. H. (1983). "Do what I mean, not what I say!" Changes in mothers' action-directives to young children. *Journal of Child Language, 10,* 357–367.

Schnur, E., & Shatz, M. (1984). The role of maternal gesturing in conversations with one-year-olds. *Journal of Child Language, 11,* 29–41.

Stayton, D. J., Hogan, R., & Ainsworth, M. D. (1971). Infant obedience and maternal behavior: The origins of socialization reconsidered. *Child Development, 42,* 1057–1069.

Super, C. M., & Harkness, S. (1982). The infant's niche in rural Kenya and metropolitan America. In L. K. Adler (Ed.), *Cross-cultural research at issue* (pp. 47–55). New York: Academic Press.

Vaughn, B. E., Kopp, C. B., & Krakow, J. B. (1984). The emergence and consolidation of self-control from eighteen to thirty months of age: Normative trend and individual differences. *Child Development, 55,* 990–1004.

Watson, J. B. (1928). *Psychological care of infant and child.* New York: Norton.

Wedell-Monnig, J., & Lumley, J. M. (1980). Child deafness and mother-child interaction. *Child Development, 51,* 766–774.

Wertsch, J. V., McNamee, G. D., McLane, J. B., & Budwig, N. A. (1980). The adult-child dyad as a problem-solving system. *Child Development, 51,* 1215–1221.

White, B. L., Kalsan, B., Shapiro, B., & Attanucci, J. (1977). Competence and experience. In I. C. Uzguris & F. Weizmann (Eds.), *The structuring of experience* (pp. 115–152). New York: Plenum Press.

9

Attachment and Socialization
The Positive Side of Social Influence

John E. Richters and Everett Waters

> When one considers values in general and moral values in particular from a
> cognitive standpoint, one is faced with the same problem. Cognition does
> not offer the principle of determination, of preference, of value.
> (Loevinger, 1976, p. 43)

The belief that child-parent attachment plays an important role in social
development occupies center stage in most contemporary theories of
childhood socialization. The origins of this belief are easily traceable to
Freud's emphasis on the significance of infant-mother attachment for
virtually all aspects of subsequent personality development. Its en-
durance over the intervening decades has been sustained by a wealth of
empirical data linking attachment to a wide range of socialization outcomes in both childhood and adulthood (Waters, Hay, & Richters, 1986).

Included among these are patterns of social competence (Waters,
Wippman, & Sroufe, 1979), prosocial behavior (Lieberman, 1977), antisocial behavior (Sroufe, 1983), and behavior problems (Erickson, Sroufe,
& Egeland, 1985) in early childhood. In addition, the major longitudinal
studies of delinquent and criminal behavior have consistently documented links between family factors and subsequent antisocial behavior
(Glueck & Glueck, 1950; McCord & McCord, 1959; West & Farrington,
1977). Prominent among these have been parental characteristics such as
lack of warmth, poor supervision, inconsistency, and poor child-rearing
practices—factors that have been demonstrated in more recent studies

John E. Richters • Child and Adolescent Disorders Research Branch, National Institute
of Mental Health, Rockville, Maryland 20857.   Everett Waters • Department of
Psychology, SUNY at Stony Brook, Stony Brook, New York 11794-2500.

to be associated with anxious child-parent attachment (Ainsworth, Blehar, Waters, & Wall, 1978).

Ironically, the mechanisms of anaclitic and defensive identification proposed by Freud to explain the association between attachment and socialization have largely been invalidated by empirical research. Moreover, they have not been replaced in Bowlby's (1969, 1973, 1980) more recent ethological attachment theory by alternative explanatory constructs. Bowlby himself has long had an interest in the association between attachment and antisocial behavior, and his theory provides a rich source for speculation about attachment and socialization. Moreover, Bowlby accepts the basic premise that children unwittingly identify with—in the sense of modeling themselves after—their parents in the normal course of development. Nonetheless, ethological attachment theory posits no formal mechanism(s) through which child-parent attachment might *explain* the emergence of antisocial behavior; the link remains very much an association in search of an explanation.

The primary aim of this chapter is to rekindle among socialization researchers an interest in child-parent attachment as a powerful and perhaps decisive factor in the socialization process. In the first section we address ourselves in considerable detail to the role posited for attachment in both psychodynamic and more contemporary social learning/cognition views of socialization. Our emphasis is on the chief limitations of each in accounting for the emergence and stability of prosocial and antisocial behavior within individuals.[1]

In the second section we employ a social influence perspective to integrate the best features of each model into a single theoretical framework that emphasizes the role of child-parent attachment. Within the context of this framework we introduce and discuss a revised (i.e., non-Freudian) concept of child-parent identification as a mediating process to account for the attachment-socialization link.

In the final section we highlight features of this model that diverge from and complement existing models of socialization, with emphasis on its heuristic value for guiding and interpreting future socialization research.

TWO MODELS OF SOCIALIZATION

Among the most enduring of Freud's legacies to psychology have been his insights regarding the nature, significance, and interrelated-

---

[1]Although meaningful theoretical distinctions can be made among various forms of antisocial (Loeber, 1982; Loeber & Dishion, 1983) and prosocial (Radke-Yarrow, Zahn-Waxler, & Chapman, 1983) behavior, both terms are used in this chapter as broad references to characteristic patterns of behavior.

ness of early attachment relationships and socialization outcomes. Indeed, early child-parent attachment and the course of socialization are virtually inseparable within psychoanalytic theory. It is somewhat ironic, therefore, that the research traditions engendered by Freud's insights—namely, attachment and socialization—have proceeded by and large along separate trajectories. As a consequence of this separation, much of what we currently know about childhood socialization has accumulated outside of a unitary theoretical framework for interpreting its relevance to issues of attachment. We are left instead with two essentially different models of childhood socialization: Freud's psychoanalytic theory, and the more recent social learning and cognition perspectives. These perspectives represent not only different viewpoints on socialization, but distinct historical periods as well. Therefore, our review of existing models in the following section is organized both thematically and chronologically. Contemporary views have been shaped considerably by earlier failures of psychoanalytic theory in the empirical realm, and there is much to be gained through an understanding of how and why they arrived at the roles they posit for attachment.

Psychoanalytic Perspective

Attachment

The central importance of child-parent attachment in Freud's theory of personality is perhaps best captured in his characterization of the infant-mother relationship as "unique, without parallel, established unalterably for a lifetime as the first and strongest love object and as the prototype of all later love relationships" (Freud, 1940/ 1949, p. 188). This prototype not only forms the matrix on which subsequent personality development builds, according to Freud, but also provides the motivational core of a great deal of behavior throughout the lifespan. Moreover, the conflicts and defenses rooted in early attachment relationships continue to assert themselves throughout life in the form of various prosocial and antisocial behavior patterns.

Identification

Socialization was described by Freud as the process(es) through which a child's natural erotic and aggressive instincts are gradually brought under the control of the superego. Subsequently, socially unacceptable expressions of these instincts are prevented and/or punished by the superego. Moreover, Freud believed that the superego's characteristic patterns of influence on behavior are formed quite early in life, and remain substantially unchanged throughout the lifespan.

Identification within psychoanalytic theory means much more than a simple imitation of parental behaviors. The superego, in Freud's own term, represents the "precipitate" of parental influence (Freud, 1940/1949, p. 16). In particular, Freud believed that children identify with the superegos as well as the situational behaviors of their parents. As such, they are influenced not only by parental personalities, but also by familial, cultural, and societal values and standards reflected in those personalities. As Brown (1965) has noted, a major function of the superego for Freud was to account for the continuity of conscience and moral standards across generations. The attachment-relevant mechanisms through which the superego forms, and which constitute the core of the socialization process according to psychoanalytic theory, are *anaclitic* identification, which leads to formation of the ego ideal, and *defensive* identification, which leads to the formation of conscience. As principal components of the superego, the ego ideal and conscience are characterized as joint regulators of social conduct through their respective emphases on "thou shalt" and "thou shalt not."

As others have pointed out, Freud's views on identification are scattered across almost three decades of his theoretical writing (Bosso, 1985; Bronfenbrenner, 1960). Hence, it is difficult to summarize succinctly a unified portrait of his theory of identification. This difficulty derives in large measure from the fact that Freud often employed the same label to refer to fundamentally different concepts. In addition, his views on the dynamics of identification very much evolved over the years, leaving a difficult trail of theoretical loose ends. For present purposes, however, it is unnecessary to reconcile the ambiguities and discrepancies in Freud's theories of identification. Instead, we can summarize the central thesis of his attachment → identification → socialization model, which remained substantially intact throughout his writings.

Anaclitic Identification. This first phase of the identification process, according to Freud, is rooted in the child's initial total dependence on mother for basic biological and emotional needs. As the mother gradually and inevitably withdraws her constant attention, interaction, and affection, the child responds by acquiring the mother's characteristics in the service of becoming her/his own source of reinforcement and comfort. In Freud's terms, the child gives up the mother as a love object, and incorporates her into her/his superego (ego ideal). Thereafter, the superego takes over functions hitherto performed by the mother such as comforting, giving orders, judging actions, and threatening with punishment. A similar process is repeated with the father, and throughout life with various mother- and father-substitutes (e.g., teachers, admired public figures, employers, etc.). These subsequent non-parental identifications, however, are assumed to be substantially less powerful and more transient than prior parental identifications.

Defensive Identification. Although anaclitic or primary identification sets the foundation for socialization within Freud's model, he also posited a process of defensive identification to explain the development of conscience later in the preschool years. The dynamics of this process, subsequently labeled "identification with the aggressor" by Anna Freud (1946), were developed in detail for boys, with little attention to how and why the process emerges in girls. It is therefore necessary to present the dynamics of defensive identification separately for boys and girls.

Boys. As a result of the boy's strong attachment to his mother, he eventually sees himself in competition with his father for the mother's attention and affection (Oedipal complex). This perceived competition in turn results in an intolerable level of anxiety within the child. The chief causes of this anxiety are (1) fear of loss of the mother's love to the father, and (2) fear of loss of the father's love as well as fear of the father's retaliation through actual or threatened castration. Given the child's limited resources for dealing with this crisis, he opts to identify with—become more like—his father.

This so-called defensive maneuver accomplishes two goals. First, by becoming more like his father the boy enhances his potential for remaining the object of his mother's love and attention. Second, by so doing he protects himself against his father's retaliation. Not only does his father no longer have a reason to retaliate, but surely the father would never retaliate against someone who is so much like himself. Moreover, the father is more likely to continue loving a son who has developed in his image.

Girls. Freud himself pointed out that the dynamics of defensive identification in girls are "far more obscure and full of gaps" (Freud, 1924, p. 177). Obviously, his emphasis on castration anxiety makes no sense in the case of girls, who presumably believe they have already been castrated. Freud therefore supposed that girls hold their mothers—who have also been castrated—responsible for not having protected them from a castrating father. Thus, a love-hate relationship develops with the mother for allowing castration to take place, and similarly a love-hate relationship develops with the father for actually effecting the castration. The dynamics are further complicated by the girl's *increased* attraction to the father in an effort to recapture a penis (Electra complex).

Finally, in an effort to resolve her intolerable level of anxiety over her ambivalent (i.e., love/fear/hate) mother and father relationships, the girl adopts a defensive posture analogous to the defensive maneuver opted for by boys. That is, girls identify with—become more like—their mothers in an effort to ward off her competitive retaliation. At the same time, they assure themselves of their father's continuing love and attention because of their similarity to their mothers. Thus, whereas threat or perceived threat of castration marks the occasion for resolution of the

Oedipal complex in boys, the fact of castration marks the beginning of the Electra complex in girls. The details of exactly how and when the Electra complex is resolved in girls were never worked out in Freud's writing. He simply indicated that the Electra complex is abandoned much later in life, and then only incompletely.

Summary. It should be clear from this distilled presentation of anaclitic and defensive identification that they share in common a strong emphasis on the child's emotional ties to his/her parents. In both processes, the strength of the child's identification is directly related to her/his level of anxiety over the threat of loss of parental love and attention. Anxiety level, in turn, is directly related to the strength of child-parent attachment. Although this relation is perhaps more clear and straightforward in the anaclitic process, it is nonetheless also at the motivational core of the dynamics of defensive identification. Where normal emotional ties to the parents are missing, the child has no incentive or motivation to model her/himself after the parents or parent substitutes. Such a child "(fails) to build up the identifications which should become the core of a strong and efficient superego, act as a barrier against the instinctual forces, and guide his behavior in accord with social standards" (A. Freud, 1949, p. 193).

Weaknesses in Freud's Model(s) of Identification

Freud's theoretical writings on identification provided not only the impetus but also the rationale and direction for much of the early socialization research in psychology, anthropology, and eventually sociology (Wentworth, 1980). For psychologists in particular, the concept of identification was an understandably seductive one. As proposed by Freud, it seemed capable of explaining such diverse behaviors as self-control, self-recrimination, the development and expression of conscience, and sex-role development. Moreover, the processes of anaclitic and defensive identification seemed to lend themselves to fairly straightforward translations into falsifiable behavioral hypotheses (Fisher & Greenberg, 1978).

Psychoanalytic Language. Beginning in the 1940s and continuing through the late 1960s, researchers systematically subjected components of Freud's theories of attachment and identification to the chain and transit of empirical scrutiny. Unfortunately, most of these efforts were plagued by conceptual and methodological obstacles which ultimately conspired against a productive research enterprise. Perhaps the most notable of these derived from the very language of psychoanalytic theory (Baldwin, 1967/1980). Freud characteristically mixed explanatory metaphors with purely theoretical propositions in his writing, leaving researchers with little foothold for isolating predictions that would serve as decisive tests of his theory. Related to this is the fact that much of Freud's language defies a straightforward translation into operational definitions. Concepts such as penis envy, castration anxiety, defensive anxiety, and the like are essential components of psychoanalytic theory, yet they lack clear behavioral referents.

Operational Definitions. An inherent problem in psychoanalytic theory is that it is concerned primarily with the unconscious dynamics of thoughts and feelings. The links between these dynamics and overt behavior are explained only in generalities within Freud's writing. Moreover, they are explained at a level of abstraction that allows the same process to give rise to opposite behaviors, and opposing processes to give rise to identical behaviors. As a consequence, it was seldom clear whether experimental failures to find support for psychoanalytic concepts were due to structural weaknesses in Freud's theory, or instead were due to inadequate operationalizations of his concepts. Ironically, studies which appeared at face value to support Freudian concepts were often viewed with skepticism for the same reasons. The translation of Freudian concepts and processes into specific behavioral referents almost always required a creative leap outside the boundaries of psychoanalytic theory (Mowrer, 1950; Sanford, 1955; Sears, 1957; Stoke, 1954), and, in so doing, researchers often incurred the wrath of both critics and proponents of the theory. For proponents of psychoanalytic theory, resulting operational definitions were often viewed as superficial. For critics, such definitions seemed perhaps too close to the theory, and therefore lacked credibility and interpretability. Moreover, necessarily creative operational definitions often resulted in findings that were more parsimoniously interpreted from a non-Freudian perspective.

Let us consider, for example, an experimental study of castration anxiety reported by Sarnoff and Corvin (1959). The experimenters reasoned from Freud's writing that males with high levels of castration anxiety (1) would manifest a greater fear of death in general, and (2) would manifest even higher levels of fear of death when their castration anxiety levels were stirred by exposure to sexually arousing stimuli. Castration anxiety was operationalized in terms of the subjects' self-ratings of emotional arousal in response to viewing a cartoon of two dogs: one dog was depicted as blindfolded with a large knife suspended over its outstretched tail while the other dog observed. Placing aside other important issues of theory and method, one can well imagine a host of problems in defending responses to a dog cartoon as evidence for castration anxiety. The point here is not that the authors were obviously wrong or silly in their choice of an index, but rather that there are simply no external criteria available for evaluating the validity of their choice.

Psychoanalytic Resistance. Difficulties in operationalizing Freudian concepts were further compounded by the resistance of psychoanalysts themselves. Traditional psychoanalytic theorists have long held that psychoanalytic method provides the only legitimate basis for evaluating Freud's theory. As Freud himself argued, " . . . we now claim the right to reject unconditionally any such introduction of practical considerations under the field of scientific investigation" (Freud, 1916/1935, p. 24). This public stance, coupled with the difficult language of psychoanalytic theory, compelled many researchers to acknowledge that their studies were based on behavioral *reformulations* of the theory. Thus, positive findings were not necessarily interpretable as verification of Freud's theory, and failures were easily attributed to weaknesses in a particular reformulation rather than in the theory itself.

In perhaps the most ambitious study of anaclitic and defensive identification, for example, Sears and his colleagues (Sears, Rau, & Alpert, 1965) found it necessary to acknowledge the psychoanalytic parentage of their hypotheses, while at the same time emphasizing the independence of their study from—and in some instances its irrelevance to—psychoanalytic formulations of identification.

Freud's Model of Attachment. Finally, many of Freud's hypotheses about socialization and personality development were predicated on what is now widely accepted as his misunderstanding of the origins and nature of child-parent attachment. The central developmental mechanism in Freud's theory of attachment is drive reduction. In essence, the infant's first affective bond with the mother is posited by psychoanalytic theory to develop through repeated associations of the mother with pleasant feelings resulting from gratification of the infant's basic biological needs. In comparison with other aspects of Freud's overall theory, his model of attachment is quite explicit and therefore lends itself to more or less decisive empirical tests. As a result, his drive reduction hypothesis has been challenged repeatedly by studies that have failed to detect a consistent relation between gratification of biological needs by caretakers and the infant's subsequent attachment behavior toward them (Caldwell, 1964; Maccoby & Masters, 1970; Sears, Maccoby, & Levin, 1957).

Moreover, it has been demonstrated that infants frequently display a great deal of attachment behavior toward individuals who have not been associated with gratification of their basic needs (Ainsworth, 1963; Schaffer & Emerson, 1964). These lines of evidence are congruent with the findings from Harlow's earlier work with non-human primates, particularly his demonstration that infant monkeys prefer to seek comfort from and cling to cloth-covered surrogate mothers, rather than the wire-covered surrogates that feed them (Harlow, 1961). Given the central importance of attachment to Freud's model of socialization and personality development, there can be little doubt that this weak link in his theory also played a decisive role in the dissatisfaction of researchers with their own findings and, eventually, with Freud's theory.

Contemporary Perspectives

Failure in the search for empirical relations consistent with Freud's theories of identification had two discernible impacts on socialization research in psychology. The first was a gradual decline of interest in attachment, identification, and related motivational concepts among socialization researchers. The second was a redirection of socialization research away from individual differences constructs, toward a more general emphasis on basic processes of social learning (Bandura, 1986; Goslin, 1969). Thus, the post-Freudian period in psychology very much reflects a shift away from psychoanalytically *directed* thinking to research and theory that is more accurately characterized as psychoanalytically *inspired*; it also reflects a shift from the top-down to bottom-up approaches to understanding socialization.

As we shall see, the influence of Freud's basic insight concerning the importance of early experience is still evident in the focus of contemporary research on child-parent interaction and parental child-rearing practices. However, his emphasis on the child-parent attachment relationship as a special source of enduring influence has been largely lost.

Attachment

Although attachment and socialization are intimately linked within Freud's framework, post-Freudian research and theory concerning these constructs has proceeded along two separate trajectories.

Ethological Attachment Theory. Along one path, Bowlby's ethological attachment theory has totally replaced the mechanisms of attachment proposed by Freud, while at the same time preserving Freud's integrative perspective on attachment/love relationships across the lifespan (Bowlby, 1969, 1973, 1980). Bowlby's reformulation has also contributed greatly to our understanding of the relation between attachment and the closely related phenomena of grief and mourning in both childhood and adulthood. Moreover, the empirical research engendered by ethological attachment theory during the past two decades has demonstrated the model's ability to organize and bring coherence to much of what we currently know about the nature and correlates of child-parent attachment (Bretherton & Waters, 1985). As we pointed out earlier, however, Bowlby's theory is not, like Freud's, a grand theory of personality development; it makes no formal attempt to delineate the mechanisms through which child-parent attachment might influence the emergence of prosocial or antisocial behavior patterns.

Later in this chapter we will discuss in considerable detail an integrative model which reintroduces child-parent attachment as a cornerstone of socialization, and in so doing attempts to bridge the gap between Bowlby's attachment theory and contemporary models of socialization. Before turning to that model, we will consider the role posited for attachment in these contemporary models.

Social Learning Theory. Although post-Freudian socialization research developed in parallel with advancements in ethological attachment theory and research, it has nonetheless proceeded along a separate trajectory, by and large de-emphasizing the "prototype" model of attachment and its implications for socialization. In its place, attachment is typically characterized more narrowly as a source of leverage in parents' efforts to socialize their children.

It is somewhat misleading to speak of contemporary socialization research as a homogeneous enterprise. In fact, it represents quite a diverse body of theory and research, including emphases on parent-child interaction, child-rearing practices, children's peer relationships, children's attributions about themselves and others, and, of course, hybrids of each of these. Most of these areas are homogeneous, however, with respect to the role they assign to child-parent attachment in their working assumptions about socialization. Few theorists even discuss the nature of attachment in their formulations; most seem implicitly to endorse the behavioral or social learning model of attachment formalized by Gewirtz (1972). Elsewhere, we have discussed this model and its assumptions in detail (Waters *et al.*, 1986). In the present discussion we focus our attention more narrowly on its departures from the "prototype" model emphasized by Freud and Bowlby.

First, attachment is viewed within the social learning framework as descriptive shorthand for a learned behavior pattern originating in and maintained by parent-child interactions. Its chief defining characteristics are the manifest preference of parent and child for each other's company and the observable influence each has over the other's behavior. A relatively straightforward relation is therefore assumed between the amount of a child's attachment-relevant behavior (e.g., proximity seeking, separation distress) and the strength of his/her bond with the parent. Conversely, decreases in these behaviors—including normative age-related decreases—are assumed to reflect attenuations in the strength of attachment.

Consistent with this formulation, child-parent attachment is viewed as functionally similar to other relationships in childhood (e.g., peers) and adulthood (e.g., spouses). All such relationships, according to the social learning view, can be evaluated using the same behavioral criteria. Therefore, child-parent attachment is not afforded a unique status as the child's first attachment relationship, except to the extent that parents differ from others in terms of the frequency, duration and intensity of their contact with the child. Note that each of these parameters refers to the *quantity* or amount of parental influence, and not to a *qualitative* difference in the nature of that influence.

Finally, attachment is emphasized as a developmental *outcome* of early experience rather than as a source of influence on later development. Because of its emphasis on situational cues and contingencies, social learning theory neither predicts nor concerns itself particularly with phenomena such as the stability of attachment-relevant behavior across time. Behavioral stability is, in principle at least, explainable in terms of corresponding consistency in situational influences across time. If pressed, therefore, the model might attempt to accommodate behavioral stability by emphasizing the differential strength of behavior patterns (S-R connections) established through early and strong parental influence. This explanation really strains the model, however, because social learning theory contains no mechanism for predicting or explaining the causal priority of early over later experiences. Relations between early attachment and subsequent development are therefore assumed to be due primarily to consistency across time in parental child-rearing practices and other environmental contingencies. Not only is this assumption at odds with what we know about the stability of child-rearing practices, but the generalization of child-rearing effects beyond the time and space boundaries of family life is inconsistent with the basic postulates of the social learning model. When contingencies imposed by socialization agents for prosocial and antisocial behavior are removed, the model predicts a return to baseline patterns of behavior. In the absence of either an innate or internalized disposition for altruistic behavior, the social learning model provides no basis for expecting this baseline pattern to reflect other than a selfish desire for immediate gratification (Grusec, 1985).

Identification

Everyone familiar with the literature on childhood has been confronted with multiple uses of the term "identification," usually embedded in descriptions or explanations of socialization. Despite its popularity in usage, there is no single definition that is—or could be—consistent with all of the contexts in which the term identification is employed. It has been used variously as a synonym for internalization, modeling, imitation, and role-taking, to name a few. Not only do each of these phenomena differ semantically and conceptually from each other, but none refers to the theories or processes of identification introduced by Freud. These seemingly inconsistent uses of the term identification are easily reconciled, however, when one realizes that there are three senses in which it has been used in the literature on socialization: as a *process* of socialization, as a *disposition* or motive to behave like another, and more simply as a label for *behavioral similarity* with another person.

Only the latter two uses are evident in contemporary socialization research. Discussions of identification as a process that seemed to dominate research and theory through the 1960s (Goslin, 1969) are virtually non-existent in contemporary socialization literature. When such references are made, they are almost always in the form of historical footnotes (e.g., Bandura, 1986, p. 484), and refer specifically to difficulties with Freud's theories. Given the conceptual and methodological problems common to Freud's theories of attachment and identification, it is not surprising that they share similar fates in contemporary socialization research. We have already seen that the social learning reformulation of attachment reflects a more or less deliberate sacrifice of the prototype model and its implications in exchange for an operational definition with clear behavioral referents. Similarly, the inability of researchers to surmount the ambiguities and inconsistencies of Freud's theories of identification led ultimately to its abandonment for safer empirical ground. And, just as attachment without its motivational (i.e., prototype) core was reduced to and indexed by behavioral dependency, identification without attachment as its motivational core became "intermittently reinforced generalized imitation, indexed by behavioral similarity" (Gewirtz, 1969, p. 159).

Summary

In summary, the literature on early childhood reflects two fundamentally different views of the socialization process—each with its own strengths and weaknesses. The psychoanalytic perspective offers a theoretically rich account of socialization through its prototype model of child-parent attachment and the related processes of anaclitic and defensive identification. It highlights the unique nature of early attachment, and emphasizes its enduring significance for virtually all aspects of personality development. This prototype model held considerable appeal for early socialization researchers because of its promise for bringing coherence to much of what we know about continuities in social development. And it held particular promise for explaining why children characteristically internalize socially valued standards of behavior initially taught and modeled by their parents.

The success of Freud's model in the empirical arena, however, was extremely limited. Not only was child-parent attachment poorly understood at the time, but the mechanisms of identification proposed by Freud to explain its influence on development proved inherently resistant to empirical scrutiny. Following a lengthy post-Freudian period of unrequited theoretical and empirical interest in identification, socialization researchers found it necessary to free themselves from the constraints of Freudian theory, and from the ambiguities of motivational constructs in general. This freedom has allowed researchers to gain impressive empirical ground during the past two decades on a wide range of socialization phenomena. We have learned a tremendous amount about general processes of social learning and cognition, modeling, imitation, and the conditions under which children are likely to be influenced toward prosocial and antisocial behavior (Bandura, 1986).

Unfortunately, with the associated decline of interest in theoretical constructs, much of this evidence has accumulated outside the context of an integrative framework that views the course of socialization in a developmental context. Thus, although we have learned much about the *parameters* of situational influence, we know less about the *boundaries* of that influence, and less still about who is likely to be influenced under what circumstances and, perhaps most importantly, why. Yet it has long been clear that these are among the most important questions facing socialization researchers. And it has become increasingly evident that meaningful answers will require theoretical frameworks that can aid in the synthesis and interpretation of existing socialization data, while at the same time providing a guide for future research.

AN INTEGRATIVE MODEL

The early exclusion of attachment theory from research into basic processes of social learning and cognition was an understandable and perhaps necessary strategy. Although the resulting gains on these separate fronts have been impressive, neither focus *alone* can explain the emergence of a generalized disposition toward prosocial or antisocial behavior. Theories of social learning and cognition have been essential to our understanding of the mechanisms through which secure attachment relationships arise. And they have been equally successful in shedding light on important mechanisms of socialization. These mechanisms are not sufficient, however, to account for the generalized disposition toward prosocial behavior across time and situations that is the hallmark of an effective socialization process. Similarly, the prototype model of attachment holds considerable potential as a motivational cornerstone for socialization theory. Lest the realization of this potential once again founder on the shoals of empiricism, it will require a detailed specification of the processes through which attachment exerts its influence.

The Correlates of Secure Attachment

We know from existing research that characteristics of caregiver behavior that seem to engender secure child-parent attachment include availability, patience, consistency, contingent responsiveness, facilitation, cooperation rather than interference with the infant's ongoing behavior, and the maintenance of an affectively positive climate for interaction (Ainsworth et al., 1978; Grossman, Grossman, Spangler, Suess, & Unzner, 1985). We know also that when early parent-child interactions have been harmonious, the child will develop a secure attachment relationship and a wide range of socially valued concurrent and predictive correlates. Included among these are personal attributes such as self-esteem, social competence, self-control, empathy, ego-resilience, and positive affect. Securely attached children have also been found to be more reciprocal (e.g., sharing, successful verbal requests, social initiation, and shared laughter) in their interactions with peers, as well as more attentive, sociable, cooperative, and compliant with adults than are anxiously attached children. Thus, secure child-parent attachment is associated not only with multiple indices of personal competence, but also with behavior patterns that very much reflect a generalized prosocial orientation toward others (Waters et al., 1986).

Research and theory during the past decade have contributed greatly to our understanding of the knowledge, skills, and expectations that children acquire in the context of secure attachment relationships (Bowlby, 1969, 1973, 1980; Bretherton & Waters, 1985). It is not clear from such analyses, however, why these accomplishments are so characteristically associated with subsequent prosocial versus antisocial behavior outcomes. Or, perhaps more accurately, it has been deceptively easy to assume that these outcomes follow "naturally" from secure attachment relationships, without asking ourselves why. In fact, a little reflection will reveal that there is nothing at all obvious or self-evident about the link. It is well known, for example, that the most troublesome antisocial children, delinquents, and adult criminals are often among the most knowledgeable in terms of how to evaluate and behave in social situations, and how to anticipate accurately the likely responses of others (Cleckley, 1982; Wilson & Herrnstein, 1985). Yet these skills are employed in the service of antisocial rather than prosocial behaviors. Thus, although these characteristics are obviously necessary to acts of prosocial behavior, they are by no means sufficient to explain its emergence and continuity within individuals. Neither are we brought any closer to an understanding of prosocial motivation by knowing that a child is securely attached to his/her parent(s). There are certainly good reasons to expect prosocial behavior toward attachment figures from such a child, but how and why this should generalize across individuals, situations, and time, remain important questions.

Attachment and Identification

Elsewhere, we have outlined a rationale and framework for reintroducing the concepts of attachment and identification to mainstream research and theory on childhood socialization (Waters *et al.*, 1986). In brief, this developmental model holds that child-parent attachment and characteristics of parental modeling and child-rearing practices exert a major interactive influence on a wide range of socialization outcomes in early and middle childhood. In particular, it holds that stable patterns of secure attachment engender processes of child-parent identification in early childhood, and identification then becomes an important moderator of subsequent parental influence.

Identification, according to this model, is an age-appropriate response to the continuation of an interaction history that earlier gave rise to secure child-parent attachment. It begins to develop and is manifest during the preschool years through the child's patterns of (a) differential attentiveness to and preference for—rather than mere submissiveness to—parental approbation, values, and standards for behavior, and (b) responsiveness—rather than mere conformity—to parental socialization demands.

In a word, we are proposing that attachment contributes to socialization outcomes by rendering children more *socializable*. In so doing, we are highlighting a motivational dimension of the socialization process not easily addressed by more traditional models. This motivational core cuts across an array of socialization outcomes, and is reflected inter-alia in the child's *willingness* to obey, beyond mere obedience; *concern* about, beyond mere knowledge of, socially prescribed rules and roles; and *participation* in, beyond mere conformity to, the broader social community. In essence, the model proposes that this generalized prosocial disposition is acquired gradually through the child's history of participating in and benefiting from a prosocial system of reciprocal, cooperative interdependence with others. The socialization process, within this framework, is not portrayed—primarily at least—as a struggle between the child's selfish desires for immediate gratification and the demands of society. It is characterized instead as a process through which the child learns through her/his own experiences how personal gains can be maximized through participation in a prosocial system of commerce with others.

In the discussion that follows, we describe briefly the normative socialization process in terms of overlapping themes in the child's development: encapsulation during infancy, and commitment during early and middle childhood.

Encapsulation during Infancy

Ethological attachment theory and the research inspired by it converge to portray the secure attachment relationship as a prototype of prosocial commerce. It is a system in which the child has learned, through the cooperation and facilitation of attachment figures, to maximize the benefits available from and through their interactions. By virtue of the child's limited contact during the first few years with rule systems that differ dramatically from those of the family, he/she is virtually encapsulated within this system and its initially-implicit rules for engaging others, and through them, the environment.

Beginning in the first year of life, the quality of child-parent attachment develops and is maintained through mutual attentiveness to and cooperation with signals between partners. In early infancy, these signals are necessarily immediate, specific, situational, and non-verbal (although often vocal). As the child develops and acquires new abilities, however, there is a corresponding increase in the dimensions and demands of the relationship for both partners. Ultimately, the relationship evolves into what Bowlby has termed a "goal-corrected partnership" in which the child becomes increasingly aware of the attachment figure's goals, and his or her strategies for accomplishing them. This awareness is then reflected in the child's enhanced ability to organize and coordinate his own experience with the goals, expectations, and demands of attachment figures.

Maintaining cooperative interaction with an attachment figure gradually requires attentiveness to less immediate, more general, and increasingly verbal signals and cues. At the same time, it requires of attachment figures a sensitivity to the child's capabilities and needs for organization, a readiness and ability to adopt new strategies that will facilitate the child's assimilation of and/or accommodation to novel socialization demands, and the continued maintenance of a positive affective climate. Within the context of a secure relationship, attachment figures gradually and consistently escalate their expectations, monitoring carefully the child's ability to recognize, interpret, and respond to their demands. Thus, whatever stressors these changes in the relationship might otherwise bring are minimized by the facilitative attachment figure. As a consequence, the child continues to benefit maximally and suffer minimally from the relationship as its demands and dimensions expand.

It is within the context of this interaction history that the child also develops the powerful affective bond with attachment figures that Freud emphasized so strongly as the prototype of all future love relationships. Bowlby and others have preserved this prototype notion and its implications by discussing attachment in terms of "working models" (Bowlby, 1973, p. 203) and "assumptive worlds" (Parkes, 1982, p. 299). These metaphors refer to both the child's and parent's systems of expectations, beliefs, feelings, and attitudes about themselves, each other, and the world, based on their previous experiences.

The child, according to this view, constructs an initial working model of attachment figures consistent with her/his history of interactive experiences with those figures. For the securely attached child, this model will typically be characterized by positive feelings toward attachment figures, and the expectation that they will be reliable, sensitive, responsive, and available in times of need. Moreover, because this working model is the child's first well formulated model of human relationships in general, it will also influence her/his initial expectations about sibling, peer, and other adult relationships. In addition, because the child's working models of self and attachment figures are initially closely intertwined, a history of successful participation in a secure attachment relationship will also engender self perceptions of competence and self-esteem.

Similarly, when early child-parent interactions have been harmonious, parents will develop an equally positive working model of the child. And because this working model is also constructed from a particular interaction history, parents of a securely attached child will develop positive expectations about the future. Most notably, these expectations will reflect confidence about the abilities, cooperativeness, trustworthiness, and future socializability of the child. Conversely, if early child-parent interactions have not been harmonious, parents may be less likely to provide facilitating, cooperative, affectively positive, and age-appropriate rearing experiences for that child in the future.

It should be clear from this perspective that the period of encapsulation provides attachment figures with a set of more or less optimal socialization conditions. The child during this period is virtually insulated from exposure to dramatically different and/or potentially conflicting and inconsistent rule systems. Consequently, parents are in a powerful position to organize the child's experiences around a coherent and consistent set of rules and principles. They are therefore in a unique position to shape the child's initial models of him/herself, other people, and the world at large.

When these advantages of the encapsulation period have been exploited judiciously by sensitive and facilitating caretakers, a predictable outcome is the child's development of a secure attachment(s) and its concurrent correlates. We believe that the seeds of prosocial motivation are very much present within the context of secure relationships. It would doubtless be an overstatement to characterize the child as having made a conscious commitment to prosocial commerce at this point. Nevertheless, there is a limited though important sense in which the securely attached child is already *behaviorally* committed, by virtue of her/his active participation in the establishment and maintenance of an inherently prosocial child-parent attachment system. The child's prosocial motivation—or disposition to continue organizing her/his experience around prosocial themes—stems from and is maintained by the powerful reinforcing value of rules and principles which define the prosocial system through which he/she has benefited. It is through the system itself, beyond discrete events within that system, that the child has experienced the world and others in it as coherent, reliable, worthy of engaging, and secure. Equally important, it is the system itself that renders the child's world an orderly and predictable place through its guidelines and principles for future action.

Commitment during Early and Middle Childhood

During the first year(s) of life, the rudimentary parameters of prosocial commerce are already implicit in the immediate contingencies governing the securely attached child's interactions with and feedback from and through primary attachment figures. Gradually, as the child's cognitive and affective capacities develop, the rules and principles of this system are further elaborated and articulated by attachment figures through the complementary socialization processes of explicit instruction, reasoning, induction, and modeling. For the securely attached child, these processes are simply age-appropriate extensions of the rule system in which he/she has been participating, and from which he/she has been benefiting.

The boundaries of encapsulation are inevitably eroded as the child is gradually exposed to the alternative behaviors and potentially opposing rule/value systems of others. For some children this exposure begins quite early through television, and through interactions with and observations of older siblings and their friends, relatives, and family friends. For other children, particularly those from single child families and/or families that are otherwise relatively insulated from external influences, the period of encapsulation may be extended considerably. In either case, it is inevitable that parents lose their privileged status as exclusive gatekeepers of the child's experience. Whether and to what extent the child's exposure to non-parental influence also translates into an erosion of parental influence may provide one of the earliest indices of the child's socialization gains from the encapsulation period. That is, the introduction of relatively novel, competing systems of commerce, coupled with a decrease in direct parental supervision, represent the first serious challenges to a system of rules and standards which earlier defined and in some sense constrained the child's experience. These challenges confront children with their first opportunities to deviate, or to demonstrate commitment to parental standards of conduct. It is at this point that the concept of commitment may bear a more substantive and somewhat less tautological interpretation than our earlier reference to behavioral commitment during the encapsulation period.

Contrasting Views of Socialization

A consideration of the role of commitment in socialization requires a shift in levels of discourse. Our characterization of encapsulation is faithful to the available data on early parent-child relationships, and to what can be inferred reasonably from those data. With notable exceptions in the sociology literature, however, the concept of commitment has not received empirical attention in socialization research (Hirschi, 1969). As we discuss in more detail below, most existing models of socialization rely instead on anxiety reduction and avoidance of punishment as primary motivational forces. The present model, in contrast, emphasizes a more positive motivational core, and suggests that the concept of a child's commitment to prosocial commerce may provide a much needed heuristic for understanding individual differences in adherence to socially valued standards of conduct. The potential role of commitment is perhaps best understood by first examining the self-imposed limitations of alternative socialization models.

Anxiety and Negative Influence

Both psychoanalytic and contemporary models of socialization characterize the process primarily in negative terms, with particular emphasis on the struggle between the child's desires for immediate gratification and parental/societal demands. As we have already seen, the dynamics of this struggle are quite explicit in Freud's writings. And, although contemporary views make no such commitment to underlying dynamics, they nonetheless tacitly subscribe to the basic premise of socialization as fundamentally a process of taming. That is, they assume that the primary goal of socialization is to effect in children "a change from self-interest to interest in others" (Grusec, 1985, p. 263), and to "substitute societal demands for personal desires" (Grusec, 1985, p. 275). Unfortunately, this view also implies that the successful socialization process is one in which society prevails at the expense of the individual; as in all zero-sum systems, someone's gain necessarily implies someone else's loss.

This essentially negative view is also reflected in the cognitive and affective mechanisms emphasized in existing socialization models. Within psychoanalytic theory, the strength of identification is tied directly to the child's level of anxiety over the threat of loss of parental love. Anxiety level, in turn, is directly related to the strength of child-parent attachment. Contemporary social learning views also emphasize the primacy of love withdrawal as an anxiety-inducing source of parental socialization leverage. Children, according to this view, behave in accordance with parental standards primarily in the service of reducing their anxieties over possible loss of parental love. Note that the emphasis here is on the child's fear of not being loved rather than a desire to be loved, a fear of parental disapproval rather than a desire for parental approval, a fear of doing the wrong thing, rather than a desire to do what is considered right, and so forth.

Finally, this negative bias is evident in much of the contemporary emphasis on models of parental influence based on well known principles of insufficient and oversufficient justification, cognitive dissonance, and minimal sufficiency (Lepper, 1985). Particularly noteworthy in this regard are analyses of parental persuasion techniques and children's attributions about the causes of their own behavior. This model holds generally that if parents employ just enough subtle pressure to elicit compliance without also eliciting conscious awareness, children will attribute their behavior to internal rather than external causes. That is, children will be duped into thinking that they—and not their parents—are the cause of their own prosocial behavior. This self-attribution, in turn, presumably increases the future likelihood that the child will act in accordance with her/his prosocial self-image.

Commitment and Positive Influence

The present model, in contrast, emphasizes a more positive view of socialization. It does not assume that children either sacrifice their individuality or give up their self-interests in response to parental/societal demands. Nor does it assume that children adopt a prosocial orientation to others primarily out of fear and anxiety, or because they are tricked into believing that they are prosocial. Instead, it holds that children learn both how and why to define their interests, goals, and desires within the context of a broader social network. Only the *how* of this system (i.e., its rules and principles, and the skills needed to actively participate) can be accounted for by familiar processes of social learning and cognition (e.g., reinforcement and punishment, reasoning, induction, modeling). The *why* of a child's participation—that is, the child's level of commitment to prosocial commerce—derives in large measure ·from whether he or she has benefited consistently from this system in the past and can reasonably expect to continue benefiting in the future. The most effective socialization process, from this perspective, is one that consistently demonstrates to children through their successes and failures ways in which their desires can be aligned with and accomplished more reliably and satisfactorily through prosocial, rule-governed commerce with others.

There are, of course, significant elements of struggle throughout the socialization process. And there is abundant empirical evidence for the effectiveness of influence techniques based on anxiety, guilt arousal, and other forms of subtle, negative pressure (Aronson, 1981; Cialdini, 1984). It would therefore be a mistake for any theory to deny or ignore the role of such factors in the socialization process. Our point more simply is that these mechanisms *alone* do not provide the necessary foundation for an effective and efficient socialization process. They are no doubt necessary, highly effective, and desirable in gaining certain types of situational compliance. Alone, however, they are not sufficient to explain the normative developmental outcome of what appears to be a generalized prosocial disposition. In fact, a number of practical and theoretical considerations suggest that a socialization process based primarily on these negative mechanisms is unlikely to ensure compliance or conformity in the long run, let alone engender a positive orientation toward others.

Let us consider, for example, the problems inherent in relying on a child's anxiety over possible loss of parental love as a primary source of socialization leverage. If the child's primary motivation in the face of temptation is to avoid or reduce anxiety about the possibility of parental censure, compliance is only one of several available strategies. Obvious alternatives to compliance include not getting caught, or, once caught, to lie about the offending behavior. Each strategy holds potential for avoiding parental censure. When the child is under the direct surveillance of parents, of course, these latter options might not be considered viable— particularly among older children, who are more experienced at and capable of assessing risk. In more ambiguous circumstances, however, these latter options might be even more attractive than compliance to a child who is primarily interested in avoiding censure. Compliance ensures avoidance of parental censure at the expense of the desired behavior. On the other hand, not getting caught and lying when caught also circumvent parental censure, while at the same time allowing the child to engage in forbidden behavior. Why then, as in the normative case, do children more characteristically opt for compliance over its alternatives? Similar considerations render implausible the premise that children can be fooled—for very long, at least—into thinking that they are pro-socially motivated through the use of subtle parental pressure. As Maccoby (1985) has pointed out, "(children) develop uncanny skills at detecting the iron hand within the silken glove" (p. 366). Moreover, we know that the most troublesome misbehavior often occurs in the absence of parental and other supervision. Why, then, do such occasions not lead with equal force to self-attributions of internalized antisocial motivation?

Commitment and Cost-Benefit

The concept of cost-benefit offers a valuable heuristic for addressing such questions, because it focuses attention on multiple determinants of behavior. From a social learning perspective, a decision to engage in any particular behavior can be conceptualized broadly as a function of differential weights assigned by a child to the costs and benefits associated with compliance versus non-compliance. Thus, if parents are both vigilant about misbehavior and sensitive to subtle changes in behavior that might reflect attempts at deception, their children should learn to assign a higher weight to the risk of getting caught. If parents are also consistent in their punishment of misbehavior and/or deception, their children should also assign a higher weight to the cost of misbehavior. In short, if non-compliance under similar conditions in the past has not paid off, a child might reasonably be expected to comply under similar conditions in the future. Conversely, children who have more consistently benefited from non-compliance under similar circumstances in the past will be more likely to engage in non-compliance in the future.

On a superficial level, the cost-benefit model seems obviously true and perhaps therefore too simplistic. Upon closer scrutiny, however, the model becomes at once more elegant and complex as one considers individual differences in the relative weights a child might assign to (1) the costs and benefits associated with compliance, (2) the costs and benefits associated with non-compliance, (3) the risks associated with getting caught or discovered in a deception, and (4) the costs associated with getting caught. From the standpoint of the present model, commitment is a crucial variable in such analyses because of its potential for differentially weighting the benefits (both short and long term) of compliance and the costs of non-compliance. That is, commitment as we have conceptualized it implies something theoretically important about the benefit or value to the child of the expectations, opinions and continued cooperation of others, as well as the value to the child of future opportunities for continued participation.

Punishment versus Penalty

The importance of commitment to socialization is perhaps best captured in the seldom made distinction between *punishment* and *penalty* as potential costs of deviant behavior (Nadel, 1953). Whereas punishment refers to the relatively immediate, specific, and often short-term negative consequences of a deviant act, penalty refers to less immediate, more general, and longer-term consequences. For example, an act of deliberate disobedience may be punished variously by denying the child access to television for a restricted period, scolding, spanking, and/or other commonly used control techniques. The penalties for disobedience, on the other hand, may include parental disappointment, a loss of parental favor, and attenuation of the parents' trust of the child, a change in their expectations about future compliance, and a corresponding change in the freedoms and opportunities they make available to the child based on these expectations. Thus, in contrast to specific punishments invoked for a particular offense, these types of penalties may have wider ranging consequences. For the child who is committed to— who has learned to value—parental favor, trust, and approval, the penalties for deviant behavior may represent potential costs that far outweigh immediate, specific, and short-term punishments. For the child who has *not* benefited from prosocial commerce, on the other hand, these penalties will not constitute meaningful costs. The costs of deviant behavior for such a child may be assessed entirely in terms of relatively immediate punishments.

It follows from these considerations that the importance of commitment lies in the distinction between self-control and control by others. The child who is committed to a prosocial orientation is in a real sense self-motivated to preserve his/her status within a prosocial system. Violations of the rules and principles which define the system may threaten that status and all that it implies. Conversely, children who are not committed have nothing to lose by deviating from a prosocial orientation beyond the immediate consequences of their actions. They may be controllable in the short term by immediate contingencies administered by others, but cannot be counted on to self-govern their behavior along prosocial lines in the absence of these contingencies.

A child's commitment as we have conceptualized it may seem at first glance to provide parents with additional negative socialization leverage. That is, one might easily conclude that a child who is heavily committed to prosocial commerce should be that much more sensitive and responsive to explicit threats of love withdrawal and other symbols of disenfranchisement. From the standpoint of attachment theory, a heavy reliance by parents on negative withdrawal techniques is not only antithetical to, but is also likely to undermine the foundation of, a secure attachment relationship. After all, there is nothing very secure about a base that constantly threatens not to be there.

The available data suggest that parents of securely attached children are unlikely to rely heavily on such negative techniques. Moreover, it suggests that they have less need to resort to these techniques. One of the many risks inherent in relying on punishment and love withdrawal as primary control techniques is that a child might habituate to threats and/or stop caring about the penalties. If, however, as a result of a secure attachment relationship and all that it implies, the child is *self*-motivated to continue benefiting from parental/societal favor, etc., then threats of love withdrawal and its associated penalties (e.g., future uncertainty, loss of freedom, privilege), will be particularly potent because they are in a real sense *self*-generated. It is only in this sense that a child's actions can be meaningfully described as self-controlled.

Attachment to Deviant Parents

Our emphasis on attachment, commitment, and prosocial behavior tacitly addresses a question raised by Kagan (1982) about the implications of a child's secure attachment to deviant parents. If the child adopts parental standards and values that are not in accord with those of society, will such a child not be at a disadvantage at a later age? There are really two answers to this question. Certainly from the standpoint of traditional views of identification—particularly Freud's—one might be led easily to this conclusion. According to psychoanalytic theory, the child identifies with the parent's superego, which is the seat of conscience. Thus, if a child is raised by criminal or otherwise deviant parents, he/she is also expected to adopt deviant standards and values.

Within the present model, however, there is no basis for this expectation. That is, it matters not whether a parent is deviant per se in a particular domain of functioning such as a criminal career. What matters is whether the parent's deviance also translates into a non-prosocial system of commerce governing interactions with and/or modeled for the child. From the standpoint of attachment theory, the types of interactions and child-rearing practices that engender and maintain secure child-parent attachment are inherently prosocial. It is therefore unlikely that significant deviations from this type of system will lead to a secure attachment relationship.

In principle, of course, it is possible for a parent to interact with a child in ways that engender a secure child-parent relationship, yet still engage in deviant and/or criminal activities which are wittingly or unwittingly modeled for the child. The available data concerning child-rearing orientations of criminal parents, however, suggest that this may be an unlikely scenario. West and Farrington (1973), for example, reported that criminal fathers in their sample disapproved of criminality in their sons. More generally, West (1982) found in the same sample that "parental attitudes toward delinquency were almost always censorious, regardless of the parents' own delinquent history" (p. 49). In a related vein, Wheeler (1967) cited a substantial body of research documenting a high degree of intolerance for deviant behavior among those of lower educational and socioeconomic attainment. Even criminal parents are likely to express allegiance to the prevailing norms of society; they operate to "foster obedience to a system of norms to which (they themselves) may not conform" (Hirschi, 1969, p. 108). Finally, Hirschi found in his classic study of high-school students that those attached to a low-status parent were no more likely to become delinquent than those attached to a high-status parent. Although Hirschi defined attachment in much broader terms than those of ethological attachment theory, his findings are nonetheless consistent with the expectations of the present model.

CONCLUSION

More than two decades ago, Bronfenbrenner called for a moratorium on theoretical speculations about the origins and nature of identification, and redirected researchers to "the more modest and at once more challenging task of discovering what phenomena do in fact exist that require theoretical explanation" (1960, p. 39). The field of socialization research has come full circle during the intervening decades. We have learned much about the correlates and stability of prosocial and antisocial behavior, and we have succeeded considerably in documenting the basic processes of social learning and cognition that play a major role in social influence. At the same time, we still know relatively little about *who* is likely to be influenced toward prosocial or antisocial behavior, under *what* circumstances, and *why*. These questions have always been the *raison d'être* of socialization research and theory, and it is clear that meaningful answers will require theoretically rich models capable of mirroring complex motivational phenomena.

Freud's ambitious attempt to construct such a model has been criticized over the years on conceptual, theoretical, and empirical grounds. Nonetheless, his basic insights concerning the enduring significance of parent-child relationships, and his emphasis on the child's internalization of socially valued standards of conduct, continue to have a profound impact on our thinking about issues of socialization.

The model we have outlined preserves what we believe to be the chief strengths of both psychoanalytic and contemporary models of socialization. Namely, it reflects Freud's insights concerning the enduring significance of child-parent attachment, while at the same time drawing heavily from existing research on social learning and cognition for its specification of the mechanisms through which identification emerges. It nonetheless differs significantly from existing frameworks by emphasizing a much more positive view of the socialization process.

In abbreviated form, the attachment-identification model posits that a secure child-parent attachment relationship implies something important about the quality of the child's experiences to that point. Specifically, it indexes the extent to which the child has managed to participate in and benefit from an inherently prosocial system of commerce with others. In a very limited and perhaps tautological sense, the child is behaviorally committed to prosocial commerce at this point. As the child develops and the principles of this system are further elaborated and extended by sensitive and facilitating caregivers, this commitment intensifies and is manifest in her/his willingness to obey, concern about socially prescribed norms, and active participation in the broader community. In short, the child identifies with the particular form of commerce with and through others from whom he/she has learned to maximize benefits and minimize losses.

Although we have concentrated our attention on the seeds of socialization in infancy and childhood, this is *not* a claim that the quality of a child's early attachment(s) in any way ensures or determines or causes particular developmental outcomes. Rather, a secure attachment relationship is an interim developmental outcome which *inter alia* serves as a marker for a particular type of interaction history with caretakers. In the normative case we would expect such patterns to continue, ultimately giving rise to the child's commitment to prosocial commerce. Initial working models of self and others become the filters through which a child selects and interprets subsequent experience, resulting in a bias toward continuity. From an individual differences perspective, however, there are also numerous factors that might intervene to alter one's pattern of development. Obviously, parents may change their availability, sensitivity, and/or skills as parents, and children can learn new ways of orientations and insights. Thus, as Sroufe (1987) has pointed out, although there is a great deal of momentum toward continuity, there is ample opportunity for change as well.

At present, we have only limited knowledge of the conditions that influence continuity and discontinuity in socialization trajectories. And we have only begun to understand how particular individual characteristics and experiences of parents and children influence the emergence and maintenance of prosocial and antisocial behavior. As we learn more about these factors, they will no doubt play an important role in subsequent elaborations and refinements of the general model.

REFERENCES

Ainsworth, M. D. S. (1963). The development of infant-mother interaction among the Ganda. In B. M. Foss (Ed.), *Determinants of infant behavior* (Vol. 2, pp. 67–112). London: Methuen (New York: Wiley).

Ainsworth, M. D. S., Blehar, M., Waters, E., & Wall, S. (1978). *Patterns of attachment.* Hillsdale, NJ: Erlbaum.

Aronson, E. (Ed.). (1981). *The social animal.* San Francisco: W. H. Freeman and Company.

Baldwin, A. L. (1980). *Theories of child development* (2nd ed.). New York: John Wiley & Sons. (Original work published 1967)

Bandura, A. (1986). *Social foundations of thought and action: A social cognitive theory.* Englewood Cliffs, NJ: Prentice-Hall.

Bosso, O. R. (1985). *Attachment quality and sibling relations: Responses of anxiously attached/avoidant and securely attached 18 to 32 month old first-borns toward their second-born siblings.* Unpublished doctoral dissertation, University of Toronto, Toronto.

Bowlby, J. (1969). *Attachment and loss: Vol. 1. Attachment.* New York: Basic Books.

Bowlby, J. (1973). *Attachment and loss: Vol. 2. Separation: Anxiety and anger.* New York: Basic Books.

Bowlby, J. (1980). *Attachment and loss: Vol. 3. Loss: Sadness and depression.* New York: Basic Books.

Bretherton, I. & Waters, E. (Eds.). (1985). Growing points of attachment theory and research. *Monographs of the Society for Research in Child Development, 50* (1–2, Serial No. 209).

Bronfenbrenner, U. (1960). Freudian theories of identification and their derivatives. *Child Development, 31,* 15–40.

Brown, R. (1965). *Social psychology.* New York: The Free Press.

Caldwell, B. M. (1964). The effects of infant care. In M. L. Hoffman and L. W. Hoffman (Eds.), *Review of child development research* (Vol. 1, pp. 9–87). New York: Russell Sage Foundation.

Cialdini, R. B. (1984). *Influence: The new psychology of modern persuasion.* New York: Quill.

Cleckley, H. (1982). *The mask of sanity* (4th ed.). St. Louis, MO: C. Mosby Company.

Erickson, M. F., Sroufe, L., & Egeland, B. (1985). The relationship between quality of attachment and behavior problems in preschool in a high-risk sample. In I. Bretherton and E. Waters (Eds.), Growing points in attachment theory and research (pp. 147–166). *Monographs of the Society for Research in Child Development, 50* (1–2, Serial No. 209).

Fisher, S., & Greenberg, R. P. (1978). *The scientific evaluation of Freud's theories and therapy.* New York: Basic Books.

Freud, A. (1946). *The ego and the mechanisms of defense.* New York: International Universities Press.

Freud, A. (1949). Certain types and stages of social maladjustment. In K. R. Eissler (Ed.), *Searchlights on delinquency* (pp. 193–204). New York: International Universities Press.

Freud, S. (1935). *A general introduction to psycho-analysis.* New York: Liveright. (Original work published 1916)

Freud, S. (1949). *An outline of psychoanalysis.* New York: Norton. (Original work published 1940)

Freud, S. (1961). The dissolution of the oedipal complex. In *The complete works of Sigmund Freud* (Vol. XIX, pp. 173–179). London: Holgarth. (Original work published 1924)

Gewirtz, J. L. (1969). Mechanisms of social learning: Some roles of stimulation and behavior in early human development. In D. A. Goslin (Ed.), *Handbook of socialization theory and research* (pp. 57–212). Chicago: Rand McNally.

Gewirtz, J. L. (1972). On the selection and use of attachment and dependence indicators. In J. L. Gewirtz (Ed.), *Attachment and dependency* (pp. 179–215). Washington, DC: Winston.

Glueck, S., & Glueck, E. T. (1950). *Unraveling juvenile delinquency.* Cambridge, MA: Harvard University Press.

Goslin, D. A. (Ed.). (1969). *Handbook of socialization theory and research.* Chicago: Rand McNally.

Grossman, K., Grossman, K. E., Spangler, G., Suess, G., and Unzner, L. (1985). Maternal sensitivity and newborns' orientation responses as related to quality of attachment in Northern Germany. In I. Bretherton and E. Waters (Eds.), Growing points of attachment theory and research (pp. 233–256). *Monographs of the Society for Research in Child Development, 50* (1–2, Serial No. 209).

Grusec, J. E. (1985). The internalization of altruistic disposition: A cognitive analysis. In E. T. Higgins, D. N. Ruble, & W. W. Hartup (Eds.), *Social cognition and social development* (pp. 275–293). New York: Cambridge University Press.

Harlow, H. F. (1961). The development of affectional patterns in infant monkeys. In M. B. Foss (Ed.), *Determinants of infant behavior* (Vol. 1, pp. 75–97). New York: Wiley.

Hirschi, T. (1969). *Causes of delinquency.* Berkeley, CA: University of California Press.

Kagan, J. (1982). *Psychological research on the human infant: An evaluative summary.* New York: W. T. Grant Foundation.

Lepper, M. R. (1985). Social-control processes and the internalization of social values: An attributional perspective. In E. T. Higgins, D. N. Ruble, & W. W. Hartup (Eds.), *Social cognition and social development* (pp. 294–330). New York: Cambridge University Press.

Lieberman, A. F. (1977). Preschoolers' competence with a peer: Influence of attachment and social experience. *Child Development, 48,* 1277–1287.

Loeber, R. (1982). The stability of antisocial and delinquent child behavior: A review. *Child Development, 53,* 1431–1446.

Loeber, R., & Dishion, T. (1983). Early predictors of male delinquency: A review. *Psychological Bulletin, 94,* 68–99.

Loevinger, J. (1976). *Ego development: Conceptions and theories.* San Francisco: Jossey-Bass.

Maccoby, E. E. (1985). Let's not overattribute to the attribution process: Comments on social cognition and behavior. In E. T. Higgins, D. F. Ruble, & W. W. Hartup (Eds.), *Social cognition and social development* (pp. 356–370). New York: Cambridge University Press.

Maccoby, E. E., & Masters, J. (1970). Attachment and dependency. In P. Mussen (Ed.), *Carmichael's manual of child psychology* (3rd ed., Vol. 2, pp. 73–157). New York: Wiley.

McCord, W., & McCord, J. (1959). *Origins of crime: A new evaluation of the Cambridge-Sommerville study.* New York: Columbia University Press.

Mowrer, O. H. (1950). Identification: A link between learning theory and psychotherapy. In O. H. Mowrer (Ed.), *Learning theory and personality dynamics* (pp. 573–615). New York: Ronald Press.

Nadel, S. F. (1953). Social control and self-regulation. *Social Forces, 31,* 265–273.

Parkes, C. M. (1982). Attachment and the prevention of mental disorders. In C. M. Parkes and J. Stevenson-Hinde (Eds.), *The place of attachment in human behavior* (pp. 295–309). London: Tavistock Publications.

Radke-Yarrow, M., Zahn-Waxler, C., & Chapman, M. (1983). Children's prosocial dispositions and behavior. In E. M. Hetherington (Ed.), *Socialization, personality, and social development*, Vol. 4 of P. H. Mussen (Ed.), *Handbook of child psychology* (4th ed., pp. 469–545). New York: Wiley.

Sanford, N. (1955). The dynamics of identification. *Psychological Review, 62,* 106–117.

Sarnoff, I. & Corvin, S. M. (1959). Castration anxiety and fear of death. *Journal of Personality, 27,* 374–385.

Schaffer, H. R. & Emerson, P. E. (1964). Patterns of response to physical contact in early development. *Journal of Child Psychology and Psychiatry, 5,* 1–13.

Sears, R. R. (1957). Identification as a form of behavior development. In D. B. Harris (Ed.), *The concept of development* (pp. 149–161). Minneapolis: University of Minnesota Press.

Sears, R. R., Maccoby, E. E., & Lewin, H. (1957). *Patterns of child-rearing*. Evanston, IL: Row Peterson.

Sears, R. R., Rau, L., & Alpert, R. (1965). *Identification and child-rearing*. Stanford, CA: Stanford University Press.

Sroufe, L. A. (1983). Infant-caregiver attachment and patterns of adaptation in preschool: The roots of maladaptation and competence. In M. Perlmutter (Ed.), *Minnesota Symposium in Child Psychology*, (Vol. 16, pp. 41–81). Hillsdale, NJ: Erlbaum.

Sroufe, L. A. (1987). *The role of infant-caregiver attachment in development*. Unpublished manuscript, University of Minnesota, Institute of Child Development, Minneapolis.

Stoke, S. M. (1954). An inquiry into the concept of identification. In W. E. Martin and C. B. Stendler (Eds.), *Readings in child development* (pp. 227–239). New York: Harcourt, Brace.

Waters, E., Hay, D., & Richters, J. (1986). Infant-parent attachment and the origins of prosocial and antisocial behavior. In D. Olweus, J. Block, and M. Radke-Yarrow (Eds.), *Development of antisocial and prosocial behavior: Research, theories, and issues* (pp. 97–125). New York: Academic Press.

Waters, E., Wippman, J., & Sroufe, L. A. (1979). Attachment, positive affect, and competence in the peer group: Two studies in construct validation. *Child Development, 50,* 821–829.

Wentworth, W. M. (1980). *Context and understanding: An inquiry into socialization theory.* New York: Elsevier.

West, D. J. (1982). *Delinquency: Its roots, careers, and prospects.* Cambridge, MA: Harvard University Press.

West, D. J. & Farrington, D. P. (1973). *Who becomes delinquent?* London: Heinemann Educational Books.

West, D. J. & Farrington, D. P. (1977). *The delinquent way of life.* London: Heinemann Educational Books.

Wheeler, S. A. (1967). Sex offenses: A sociological critique. In J. Gagnon and W. Simon (Eds.), *Social deviance* (pp. 77–102). New York: Harper & Row.

Wilson, J. Q. & Herrnstein, R. J. (1985). *Crime and human nature.* New York: Simon and Schuster.

10

The Social Context of Infant Imitation

Ina Č. Užgiris

The diversity in the panorama of human cultural modes of existence across geography and history is impressive; no less impressive is the ability of children born into the different regions of this panorama to acquire appropriate value orientations, modes of action, and social skills. In the literature on socialization and personality development, concepts such as imitation have been given an important place in accounting for the facility with which children's enculturation seems to take place (e.g., Bandura & Walters, 1963; Goslin, 1969). However, there has been relatively little concern in this literature with the origin or the developmental course of the ability to learn from observing and imitating others.

In contrast, in research on infancy, the phenomenon of imitation has been studied from a developmental perspective, but there has been relatively little interest in linking imitative ability with social development and socialization. The questions being asked have been of a different sort: When do infants begin to imitate? What are they able to imitate at different developmental periods? What do their imitation abilities reveal about their cognitive capacities? The focus has been on determining what infants are able to do, not on when or how they employ these abilities in interactions on either the interpersonal or societal level.

This state of affairs is somewhat ironic because imitation in infancy almost invariably takes place in the context of a social encounter. However, there is some basis for the present disjunction. In the socialization literature, imitation has been approached largely from the perspective of

Ina Č. Užgiris • Department of Psychology, Clark University, Worcester, Massachusetts 01610.

the social group, with emphasis on the modeling situation and not on the personal or developmental characteristics of the observer exposed to the modeling (Yando, Seitz, & Zigler, 1978). In contrast, studies with a developmental orientation have emphasized the dependence of imitation on the observer's cognitive abilities and skills (Kuhn, 1973). Imitation has been treated as a reflection of the observer's understanding of the modeled act. In the most recent edition of the *Handbook of Child Psychology*, changes in infant imitation are still discussed only in relation to the characteristics of the observer, that is, in relation to the ability to translate information from one modality into another and to execute sequences of actions (Harris, 1983) or to represent and remember (Olson & Sherman, 1983). But there is a growing recognition that imitation must be studied as an interactive phenomenon to which the model and the observer both contribute (Clementson-Mohr, 1982; Kaye, 1982; Užgiris, 1981b, 1984).

When imitation is considered from an interactive perspective, it appears to have a role in social development at several levels. First, as a mode of social interchange, imitation can help bring the infant into engagement with others. It can contribute to the expansion and elaboration of social encounters during infancy and early childhood. Second, in the course of interpersonal interactions, imitation can facilitate the construction of socially effective forms of action. It can also facilitate the acquisition of a broad range of competencies that are utilized in social interaction. Third, imitation can contribute to the acquisition of cultural knowledge and cultural views. Because infants largely interact with older individuals who are members of a cultural group, they experience interactions influenced by these individuals' understandings and beliefs. Through imitation, infants partake of the culturally toned ways for carrying out social tasks. Moreover, even infants' experience of imitative exchanges within different types of activities may be influenced by cultural factors. At all these levels, the role of imitation may be better appreciated if imitation is viewed not only as a way for learning and acquiring information, but also as a way of relating to others.

The aim of this chapter is to present an interactive view of imitation and to discuss the recent literature on infant imitation from this perspective. One assumption underlying this view is that, for humans, imitation is basically an interpersonal event; although a comparative-developmental approach to imitation is important (Mitchell, 1987), it is auxiliary to understanding human imitation. Another assumption is that imitation is a social exchange and, therefore, bidirectional; that is, the model is influenced by the observer's actions as the observer is influenced by the model's actions. Thus, the study of imitation's role in socialization requires an examination of interactions, not only of the nature of available models and the observer's responses to specific models.

A final assumption is that imitation serves an affiliative function as well as a learning function. This dual role of imitation has a long history in the traditional link between imitation and identification (Goslin, 1969) and in the relation of imitation to the acquisition of new patterns of behavior (Bandura, 1971; Piaget, 1945/1962). Current finer-grained studies of parent-child activities during play, problem-solving, and everyday interactions make it possible to discuss imitation from an interactive point of view.

In this chapter, research on imitation during infancy is reviewed with the aim of highlighting the two main ways in which imitation facilitates "the integration of a child into a social world" (Richards, 1974). That is, imitation contributes to *the implementation of interpersonal exchanges* between the infant and others, and it facilitates *the appropriation of understandings, valuations, and skills* that are a part of social activities. To illustrate these two functions, research on imitation in play, language acquisition, affect expression, and early peer interactions is examined. These research literatures are somewhat distinct and provide different windows on the role of imitation in infant social development. They also suggest a number of questions pertaining to infant imitation that require more focused examination if the place of imitation in early socialization is to be better understood.

Current research indicates that even young infants are capable of imitating others in certain contexts. With development, the variety and complexity of actions that can be imitated increases. On this basis alone, imitation could be expected to have some role in early social development. It is argued, however, that it is necessary to view imitation as part of ongoing interactions, taking place in the context of specific social activities, in order to grasp the manner in which imitation is involved in getting the child to become a full-fledged participant of social groups. Although the cultural dimension of interactions is mentioned, the emphasis in this chapter is placed on the level of interpersonal exchanges, because it is at this level that developing individual competencies and cultural influences meet.

SOCIAL INTERACTION AND DEVELOPMENT

Several lines of thinking are currently converging to make the pervasive role of culture in human development a prominent topic of discussion. Researchers interested in such diverse aspects of development as cognition, language, emotional expressivity, and self-concept are turning to cross-cultural evidence for a grip on the processes shaping the developmental course in these domains. It almost seems that the more capable the human infant is shown to be and the more constrained by inherent tendencies to progress along particular developmental paths, the more critical it becomes to determine how the existing cultural and social diversity around the world is created and maintained. More detailed information about development in other cultures casts a new light on observations of childhood in our own. Hence, there has emerged a new interest in theoretical positions that explicitly consider the cultural framework for human development (Rogoff, 1990).

A number of authors have remarked on the human form of life's dependence on cultural transmission. The relevant environment for humans is increasingly seen as one that has been created or shaped by human endeavors. Adaptation proceeds by "technical innovation rather than [by] morphological or behavioral change" (Bruner, 1972, p. 688). The role played by observational learning in the evolution of this new type of adaptation and in the transmission of culture from one generation to the next has been discussed by Bruner (1972) in his analysis of the characteristics of human infancy. He posited a tie between the playful and instructional interactions during infancy within which both instrumental and symbolization skills emerge and the subsequent ability of the young to successfully enter the cultural mode of life.

Interest in the social world of the infant was strengthened by a new appreciation of the infant's social interests and abilities (Richards, 1974). In contrast to an earlier view prevalent in the socialization literature, in which the first task for caregivers was seen to be the creation of a social orientation in the infant, the newer view posits the infant to have both interests and abilities for social interaction practically from birth (Newson, 1974; Schaffer, 1977; Trevarthen, 1977, 1979; Trevarthen & Hubley, 1978). Rheingold (1969) presented an early statement against the one-way conception of socialization in her eloquent essay on "the social and socializing infant." In subsequent years, a number of empirical studies have documented the infant's considerable skills for eliciting, maintaining, and regulating social interaction (e.g., Bullowa, 1979; Tronick, 1982; Užgiris, 1979). These studies point to the need to consider socialization as an interplay between the inclinations and skills brought by the human infant and the expectations and values held by the caregiving adults during which new modes of understanding and acting are jointly constructed.

These emphases direct attention to the interactive framework in which imitation and observational learning occur, and suggest a need to examine them as social phenomena. Several theoretical positions provide direction to such an examination and, in fact, imply that a better term for both modeling and imitation might be "tutoring" or "apprenticeship interactions."

A model of the steps in the joint construction of various culturally significant achievements is contained in the work of Bruner and his colleagues (Bruner, 1975, 1977; Ninio & Bruner, 1978; Ratner & Bruner, 1978; Wood, Bruner, & Ross, 1976). In this model, the adult's instructional role includes elements of demonstration, pacing, and cueing; it also requires interpretation of the infant's contributions as relevant, adjustment to the infant's skills, and flexibility in following the inclinations of the infant. From demonstrations, the infant learns not only how to carry out specific acts, but also the structure of the whole activity, becoming able to introduce and test variations within it. Modeling of the whole activity serves to create a goal and to arouse interest, whereas demonstration of specific constituents of the activity has a more direct tutorial function. The notion of scaffolding is important for this model. It refers to the tuning of the adult's actions so as to enable the infant to successfully participate in an activity. This is accomplished by steering the infant's efforts and eliminating other options until each constituent part of the activity can be taken over by the infant (Wood, 1980). In the process of such joint activity, there is both demonstration and imitation, but they are embedded in and regulated by the larger framework of social interaction.

A similar emphasis on activity as the appropriate unit of analysis is evident in Soviet psychology. Leont'ev (1981b) has explicitly written about the subordination of actions and operations to goal-defined activities. An interesting aspect of Leont'ev's formulation is the suggestion that participation in an activity can instill new motives. For example, a child's initial motive for participating in a play activity of going to the store might be "to shop," but, through engaging in this activity, the motives "to buy what has been requested" and "to remember what has been requested" can appear (Istomina, 1977). Although Leont'ev does not specifically address activities during infancy, he makes it clear that joint activities with others have been tremendously important for the emergence of culture during human evolution and have a similarly important role in socialization during ontogenesis (Leont'ev, 1981a). In ontogenesis, as in the evolution of human culture, shared understanding and collaborative actions are said to develop in the course of engaging in common activities with others.

The process of adult-child interaction has been discussed in greater detail by Vygotsky (1962, 1978), whose views are attracting increasing attention among U.S. psychologists (e.g., Rogoff & Wertsch, 1984; Wertsch, 1985). Vygotsky's statement concerning the social construction of human knowledge has become quite familiar:

> Every function in the child's cultural development appears twice: first, on the social level, and later on the individual level; first, between people (interpsychological) and then inside the child (intrapsychological). (Vygotsky, 1978, p. 57)

Although his notion of internalization admits to various interpretations, it is clear that he viewed the guidance from a more competent member of the culture during joint activity and the symbolic reconstruction of this activity (usually through language) as indispensable factors for the acquisition of higher forms of human mentation. He saw a role for demonstration and for imitation during such guided interactions:

> In the child's development, . . . imitation and instruction play a major role. They bring out the specifically human qualities of the mind and lead the child to new developmental levels. In learning to speak, as in learning school subjects, imitation is indispensable. What the child can do in cooperation today he can do alone tomorrow. Therefore the only good kind of instruction is that which marches ahead of development and leads it; it must be aimed not so much at the ripe as at the ripening functions. (Vygotsky, 1962, p. 104)

The above statement alludes to Vygotsky's notion of a zone of proximal development, the contention that children can act more competently under the guidance of a more experienced member of the culture and then internalize significant aspects of such joint activities. The details of instructional interaction in the zone of proximal development are beginning to be examined, largely with preschool children (e.g., Rogoff & Gardner, 1984; Wertsch, McNamee, McLane, & Budwig, 1980), but similar principles can be extended to interactions during infancy (e.g., Rogoff, Malkin, & Gilbride, 1984). These interactions share several significant features. Before the child is able to carry out the activity, there are frequent demonstrations by the adult, the child's actions are interpreted as being relevant to the joint activity, the accomplishment of the activity is highlighted through verbal commentary, and the child is guided to actively participate in the final phases of accomplishment.

A comprehensive discussion of the role of social interaction in infant development has been presented by Kaye (1982). His account is allied with Bruner's and Vygotsky's ideas in the emphasis placed on joint activity, but he is particularly concerned with showing how infant actions and adult interpretations of those actions mesh at different developmental phases to lead up to the achievement of symbolization by the infant. In this process, imitation plays a role, but a role that changes as the infant's capacities and understandings of social relations develop. Kaye's consideration of imitation in the context of infant-adult interaction and his recognition that the behavioral phenomenon of imitation may be the outcome of different processes represents a position close to my own (Užgiris, 1981b, 1984). It is important to be concerned, however, not only with the processes that underlie different instances of imitation, but also with the consequences of participating in imitative interactions for the developing child. These consequences may include the direct acquisition of an understanding or skill as well as more indirect effects on problem-solving and social competence through the appropriation of the cultural structuring of tasks and interpersonal relations (Užgiris, 1989).

Imitation in the Context of Interaction

The perspective on imitation presented in this chapter highlights three characteristics of human imitation which have not been emphasized in the experimental literature. First, imitation involves a social encounter; there has to be a model for there to be imitation. In most instances, the model is present to observe the imitation. Even in cases of delayed imitation, the imitation often takes place when the model is present during a subsequent encounter. At least for infants, the prototypic imitation situation involves an interpersonal exchange. Delayed imitation in the absence of the model, imitation of idealized models, and imitation of aspects of the non-human environment represent interesting derivative cases.

Second, from this perspective, imitation appears as an event extending over time. The model has the opportunity to monitor whether the observer does imitate. Moreover, the model can react to the imitation in a variety of ways, both positive and negative, among which is the option of imitating the observer in turn. Thus, sequences of modeling and imitation may take place with the roles of model and observer alternating between the participants. In instructional situations, the sequence of modeling and imitation may not involve an exchange of roles, but a modification of the modeling to keep pace with the actions of the observer.

Third, in the context of an interpersonal encounter, the model's actions are related to the ongoing interaction. The acts performed by the model are not arbitrary, but are related to the acts of the observer and to a mutual goal; at times, they may be imitations of the previous acts of the observer. In adult-child interaction, the modeling by the adult is selective; it builds on those actions of the child that are somewhat related to the goal action. It may be even said that the model provides new meaning for the child's actions by presenting them to the child in a new relation within the ongoing interaction.

Considered in this framework, the modeling-imitation sequences can be seen to be akin to the tutoring or instructional interactions between children and more competent individuals that are deemed important for the transmission of culture. In the descriptions of such interactions, the role of imitation is rarely highlighted (e.g., Greenfield & Lave, 1982), for imitation still tends to be conceived as an immediate replication in the fashion of a semi-automatic response to an instigation by a model. But when understood more broadly, modeling and imitation can be seen to be central to such tutorial interactions. Once an activity is mastered, the child will have learned to carry out a number of specific acts that have been modeled during the process of instruction. More importantly, the child may also have learned something more general: a discourse routine, a way of problem-solving, a method of planning, or some other culture-based mode of action that was concomitantly modeled in the course of the interaction.

In the recent literature on imitation, the learning of new patterns of action through imitation has been accentuated. However, when imitation is viewed within the framework of social interaction, its link to forces affecting group cohesion becomes evident. In social encounters, imitation can reflect empathy and may function to enhance a sense of togetherness and affiliation. It can also relate to conformity or compliance with cultural standards. These relations are mentioned not to suggest that these various phenomena be subsumed under imitation, but to indicate that imitation takes place in many contexts and that the role of imitation in different kinds of social encounters merits examination.

Research on Imitation during Infancy

The study of imitation in the context of social interaction requires naturalistic or semi-naturalistic approaches. In contrast, however, the great majority of recent work on imitation in infancy has been carried out under controlled laboratory conditions. It has been guided mainly by two questions necessitating strict experimental procedures: When are infants first able to imitate? and, What are the limitations on the ability to imitate at different ages? The question of neonatal imitation has been extensively discussed by Meltzoff and Moore (1983, 1985) and age-related changes in infant imitation have been described by Kaye (1982) and Užgiris (1981a); these questions need not be taken up here. Studies pertaining to these questions indicate the constraints that may operate on the use of imitation during social interactions, but do not inform about its actual use.

The controlled laboratory studies that have been conducted during the past decade fill in one of the gaps pointed out by Hartup and Coates (1970) in their influential review of this topic by providing data on the beginnings and the course of imitation during infancy. The second gap that they pointed out remains largely unfilled; still "little is known about the factors influencing imitation in the everyday socialization of the child" (p. 110). There are convincing demonstrations that infants are able to imitate some acts modeled by a strange experimenter in a constrained situation from birth on, but there is very little information on how often infants do actually imitate others, what motivates their imitations, what kinds of acts they prefer to imitate, and what they gain from imitating others. Some inferences along these lines can be drawn from the available studies, but specific information is still lacking (Poulson, Nunes, & Warren, 1989).

Even the description of change in imitation with development depends to a considerable extent on the definition of imitation. Imitation is not a theory-free notion; different aspects of the imitative exchange have been stressed by different theoretical positions. However, attempts to introduce specific terms for different types of imitative exchanges have not been widely adopted. In the writings from cultural anthropology, social psychology, and animal behavior, the term imitation denotes the generic concept. In keeping with this usage, Yando *et al.* (1978) urged the adoption of a descriptive definition of imitation as "the motoric or verbal performance of specific acts or sounds that are like those previously performed by a model" (p. 4). In this definition, the aspect of similarity is made central. Many other broad definitions of imitation include the additional requirement that observation of the model be a determinant for the observer's acts (Parton, 1976). Adoption of this latter requirement predisposes research toward experimental studies, because its satisfaction is more problematic in observations of ongoing social interactions.

In the present overview of imitation research, the term imitation is used in the generic sense. Although the exchanges classified as imitation in the more naturalistic studies do not always meet the criteria for imitation invoked in experimental research, they do entail an increase in similarity between two individuals involved in the same situation. This chapter presents studies in order to indicate the wide range of social interactions in which imitation has been noted to occur and to point out areas for further research. For this reason, the review of studies is organized in terms of domains of activity rather than in terms of developmental periods. It is organized around the topics of *imitation during infant-adult play,* in *language acquisition,* in *affective exchanges,* and during *peer interactions.* The first two topics reflect more strongly the instructional and cognitive functions of imitation, whereas the latter illustrate the social function of imitation, its role in establishing and maintaining contact with other individuals. The studies discussed do not exhaust the literature relevant to infant imitation, but are illustrative.

Imitation during Infant-Adult Play Interactions

Imitation during play can be both a means for indicating a common interest and a way for acquiring conceptions or skills that increase the common ground between the participants. Play is an important activity within which to study imitation, but few investigations of infant play interactions have focused specifically on imitation. A greater number of studies on infant play have included imitation as a coding category, but with other issues as their main concern. Additional information on imitation can be gleaned from studies of play in which modeling is used as a technique for increasing the probability of particular types of play. Also, laboratory studies on imitation of specific actions can be included in this category, because a semi-playful atmosphere is usually maintained in such studies.

This research indicates that imitation does occur during ongoing play interactions, although the frequency of imitative exchanges is not very high. Moreover, it indicates that infants can and do imitate a variety of actions on objects when such actions are specifically presented for imitation. On the basis of available data, very little can be said either about delayed effects of modeling or about the persistence of imitation effects.

There are relatively few systematic data on imitation during play in the first six months of life. Studies on mother-infant face-to-face interaction mention the occurrence of imitation during the first few months of life, but call it "magnetic" (Trevarthen, 1979) to stress its fleeting character. Most authors mention the more frequent incidence of maternal imitation than of infant imitation (e.g., Papoušek & Papoušek, 1977; Trevarthen, 1977). In our research on mother-infant interaction (Užgiris, Benson, Kruper, & Vasek, 1989), we specifically examined matching of the partner's acts by both infant and mother during face-to-face interaction in the laboratory. We found few instances of matching among 2–3 month old infants and only slightly more instances among 5–6 month olds; significantly more matching by infants was found in the 8–9 month old group. However, the frequency of matching by the mothers exceeded infant matching in all age groups. These results suggest that mothers use imitation for social engagement with their infants, but young infants are constrained by limitations on their imitation skills.

In a longitudinal study of 17 mother-infant pairs, we obtained similar results (Užgiris, Vasek, & Benson, 1984). These mothers were videotaped for 11 min. of face-to-face interaction with their infants when the infants were around 2½, 5½, 8½, and 11½ months of age. No toys were available during this interaction. The observed increase in the frequency of matching episodes initiated by mothers and by infants is shown in Table 1. Moreover, we found not only an increase in the frequency of matching, but also a lengthening of the matching episodes due to a greater number of reciprocal turns taken by the two partners. As matching by infants increased, mothers reciprocated and also were

TABLE 1.   Mean Number of Matching Episodes in the Longitudinal Sample
(N = 17)

Age (months)	Mother matches infant's act	Infant matches mother's act	Total episodes
2–3	5.6[a]	0.8[a]	6.4[a]
5–6	5.9[b]	1.5[b]	7.4[b]
8–9	11.2[a,b]	2.4[a]	13.9[a,b]
11–12	15.6[a,b]	5.7[a,b]	21.6[a,b]

Note: All means sharing a superscript differ significantly from each other at least at $p < .05$, using the Wilcoxon T test.

more often the first to match an act of the infant. Toward the end of the first year of life, infants regularly reciprocated the matching acts of their mothers. These results demonstrate that imitative exchanges are not confined to intense face-to-face encounters of early infancy, but become an increasing constituent of interpersonal interactions during the first year of life.

Comparable results have been obtained by Pawlby (1977) in Britain. She observed eight mother-infant pairs in relatively unstructured interaction at weekly intervals, starting when the infants were 4 months old and continuing until they were about 10 months old. The sessions took place in a laboratory room equipped with toys, but the mothers were allowed to determine the use of the toys and the course of the interaction. She found both consistencies and changes in imitation during this age period.

At all ages, mothers imitated their infants more frequently than infants imitated them. Overall, an average of 8.6 imitations was observed during each session, which took up about 16% of the interaction time. Almost half of the imitations were made up of more than a single exchange, illustrating the reciprocal nature of imitation and modeling during social interaction. Across age, the imitation of facial expressions declined, while the imitation of object-related acts and speech-related vocalizations increased. Whether these changes were due to changes in modeling by the mothers or to changes in infant interests is not answered by Pawlby's study. Nevertheless, her data support the claim that modeling-imitation exchanges are a regular part of play interactions in the first year of life and that they focus on actions that are in the process of being developed by the infant (i.e., object-related actions after about 6 months of age).

Imitation by both mothers and infants during interaction in the home was reported by Masur (1987). She found that the types of acts imitated and imitation frequency varied with setting (bathtime or playtime) and with the age of the infant (10 months or 14 months). Mothers were particularly likely to imitate infants' vocalizations and words, which is consistent with the trend reported by Pawlby (1977). Correlational analyses showed that infants who imitated more of their mothers' acts had mothers who imitated more of their infants' acts, demonstrating the reciprocity inherent in early imitations.

Another study of imitation during play interaction was conducted by Waxler and Yarrow (1975) with 19 month-old children and their mothers. Since the study had a different theoretical orientation, all manipulation of toy materials by the mother was considered modeling, whereas imitation was coded only for the child. Imitation made up a small proportion of the interaction time, but it was not rare. The frequency of maternal demonstrations and their variety were correlated with imitation in the child. Although those children whose mothers reinforced imitation were generally more imitative, there was considerable individual variation in both maternal reinforcement and in the children's responses to reinforcement. The authors pointed out that maternal modeling was most effective when it was accompanied by some communication directing the child's attention to the modeling. They suggested that modeling not only presents information about how to manipulate specific toys, but also conveys the mother's engagement and interest to the infant.

Given that modeling-imitation exchanges take place during infant-adult interactions, what is their importance for the infant? The more controlled experimental studies show that modeling by adults can get infants to perform a variety of specific acts, but the long-term effects of such modeling-imitation experiences are not addressed by these studies. To claim that modeling and imitation are involved in the modification of infant behavior toward socially meaningful and effective forms, it would be important to demonstrate that such experiences have persistent effects. However, current studies only demonstrate that infants become increasingly able to imitate socially meaningful acts in controlled settings.

With the exception of studies of imitation by neonates, there are relatively few controlled investigations of imitations by infants under 12 months of age. The existing ones show that infants become more likely to imitate a greater variety of specific acts modeled by an experimenter between about 4 and 12 months of age (Abravanel, Levan-Goldschmidt, & Stevenson, 1976; Killen & Užgiris, 1981; Rodgon & Kurdek, 1977; Užgiris, 1972). Simple arm and hand movements, vocal sounds, and highly practiced acts with objects are most readily imitated. Only toward the end of the first year do infants begin to imitate conventional, socially meaningful actions such as waving "bye" or "driving" a toy car

(Killen & Užgiris, 1981). However, these actions rarely seem to be learned during the interaction in the laboratory; rather, their performance seems to be instigated by the model's actions. It can only be inferred that infants learn such conventional actions from modeling-imitation exchanges embedded in interactions at home, but direct evidence for this is lacking.

Our longitudinal observations of mother-infant interaction over a set of toys showed that mothers demonstrate the kinds of play actions that have been called conventional throughout the infant's first year of life (Užgiris, 1983). Following a period of face-to-face interaction, the 17 mother-infant pairs in this study were videotaped while playing with the same three toys at each of the visits to the laboratory. The toys were a string puppet representing a doll, a squeak toy shaped like a clothespin, and a wooden dog on wheels. The mothers were asked to introduce the toys one by one and to spend 2 minutes playing with each. The order of the toys was varied across infants. We noted the kinds of acts that were used to Initiate interaction with the partner (Initiations) and the kinds of acts that were exchanged during a bout of interaction (Interactive acts). For these toys, moving the puppet by pulling on the string, squeaking the clothespin, and rolling the dog were considered conventional actions. The frequency of initiations and of interactive acts changed with infants' age; therefore, the prevalence of conventional acts is shown in Table 2 as a percentage of total acts.

As would be expected, all initiations at the youngest age were by the mothers. Even at this age, over half of the initiations by the mothers involved conventional acts. At older ages, the frequency of initiations by mothers and infants became more nearly equal. As can be seen in Table

TABLE 2.   Percentage of Conventional Initiations and
Conventional Interactive Acts During Toy Play

Observation age (months)	Initiations (%)	Interactive acts (%)
	Mothers	
2–3	57	30
5–6	74	45
8–9	61	44
11–12	60	45
	Infants	
2–3	0	0
5–6	0	6
8–9	2	4
11–12	6	18

2, the majority of initiations by mothers continued to be of conventional acts. We also examined the proportion of conventional acts during interaction bouts. For the mothers, these constituted slightly less than half of their interactive acts at all four observations. The infants engaged in very few conventional acts until the last observation session. At that time, they constituted 18% of their interactive acts. At the same session, infants also responded to some of their mothers' conventional acts by imitating them. These observations indicate that infants are shown various socially meaningful actions repeatedly, even before they have the motor skill to carry them out. Once infants become able to carry out more complex actions, such actions begin to include conventional items, which can facilitate shared activity with others. However, it can only be inferred that these conventional actions are acquired through the process of modeling-imitation exchanges occurring in the course of everyday play activities.

That modeling can be an effective instructional strategy even with 6-month-old infants has been demonstrated in a study by Kaye (1977). Over a series of trials, infants were taught to reach around a Plexiglass barrier to obtain a toy. The principal instructional strategy used by the mothers was to demonstrate the reaching action and then to allow their infants a turn at the task. An important feature of this strategy was the coordination of the demonstrations with infants' gaze direction. It can be extrapolated that instructional use of modeling requires sensitivity to cues from the learner. A similar point regarding the importance of embedding demonstrations within jointly regulated exchanges can be drawn from studies by Kaye and Marcus (1978, 1981).

During the second year of life, infants imitate various actions that have conventional meaning; they also begin to imitate unconventional actions and more complex combinations of actions (Killen & Užgiris, 1981; Masur & Ritz, 1984; McCabe & Užgiris, 1983; McCall, Parke, & Kavanaugh, 1977). Although it seems likely that a number of the actions shown in response to modeling are already familiar to the infant, the imitation of unconventional actions demonstrates that, at this age, infants become able to incorporate novel acts into their own activities with greater ease. This implies that acquisition of socially important behavior through imitation becomes more likely in the second year of life.

The increasing efficacy of modeling in getting infants to perform various actions and sequences of actions during the second year is also evident in studies of pretend play, in which modeling is often used to instigate the occurrence of such play (e.g., Bretherton, O'Connell, Shore, & Bates, 1984; Corrigan, 1982; Fenson & Ramsay, 1981; Ungerer, Zelazo, Kearsley, & O'Leary, 1981; Watson & Fischer, 1977). Because in these studies several activities are typically modeled before the child begins to play, they demonstrate that modeling is effective even with some delay, but they do not provide information about the long-term effects of modeling. Recent experimental studies, however, demonstrate that infants may be able to imitate specific models even after considerable delay (Meltzoff, 1985, 1988).

The studies mentioned above indicate that (1) infants are exposed to modeling of conventionally meaningful actions during interactions with adults from the earliest months, and (2) toward the end of the first year of life, infants begin to engage in conventionally meaningful actions themselves. During the second year, they become increasingly responsive to modeling by adults. That the appearance of conventionally meaningful actions in infants' activities is influenced by modeling is not established by these studies, but longitudinal studies of mother-child play suggest that modeling does have a role in their acquisition and interpersonal use.

Already in the first year of life, infants begin to participate in games having a conventional structure such as pat-a-cake, peek-a-boo, give-and-take, build-and-knock-down (Crawley, Rogers, Friedman, Iacobbo, Criticos, Richardson, & Thompson, 1978; Gustafson, Green, & West, 1979). Repeated observations on individual dyads show that initially mothers enact most of the game, but with age, infants begin to participate more actively and to take over certain parts in the game. Bruner and his associates have described this progression for peek-a-boo (Bruner & Sherwood, 1976), other appearance-and-disappearance games (Ratner & Bruner, 1978), give-and-take (Bruner, 1978), and labeling during book "reading" (Ninio & Bruner, 1978). While there is ample modeling of different parts of such games by the mother, these descriptions make it clear that the modeling does not produce immediate imitation by the child, but has an effect only as a constituent within the larger structure of the game activity.

In summary, it can be stated that laboratory studies indicate that infants can imitate when presented with demonstrations of various acts during the first year of life, and even more so during the second. Observational studies show that mothers and infants engage in modeling-imitation exchanges during play and that these exchanges tend to be reciprocal; that is, both mothers and infants imitate the other's actions. There is also evidence that modeling embedded within an instructional interaction can be effective, but there is little data on how frequently infants participate in such instructional interactions during everyday life. Although infants seem to be exposed to considerable modeling of culturally meaningful activities in relation to toys, games, and everyday routines (e.g., Valsiner, 1984), the modeling is clearly embedded within larger cooperative interaction structures. This suggests that the learning function of imitation may be embedded within the social interaction function, particularly during early infancy.

Imitation in Language Acquisition

In the past decade, interest in the role of imitation during language acquisition has been growing. It is obviously true that children learn the specific language to which they are exposed. The questions of interest are whether children's linguistic progress is related to the type of language they hear and whether imitation of such language is an effective language learning strategy. A number of studies have documented that the language of a child's conversational partner changes in keeping with the child's linguistic competence (for reviews, see Snow, 1984; Snow & Ferguson, 1977). Furthermore, there is increasing evidence that imitation by the child may be a productive strategy in language acquisition, at least for some children.

As has been pointed out by Snow (1981), some of the diversity of opinion regarding the productiveness of an imitation strategy may have arisen because of different definitions of imitation. Some studies have focused on spontaneous imitations, whereas others have obtained elicited imitations through instructions to imitate. Studies have also differed with respect to criteria of exactness and timing in classifying utterances as imitations. Kuczaj II (1982) has suggested a further distinction between imitative utterances (where the child duplicates an utterance made by the conversational partner) and repetitive utterances (where the child repeats her or his own utterance) because these two types of replication may serve different functions for the child. He posits that imitation may provide practice in linguistic forms new to the child, whereas repetition may help consolidate forms that are beginning to be used spontaneously.

In an analysis of replicated utterances in the language corpus of one child, Kuczaj II (1982) found that between 2 and 3½ years of age, exact imitations declined more rapidly than reduced imitations. In contrast, both expanded and modified imitations increased during the same age period. The pattern for repetitions was similar, although the increment for expanded and modified repetitions was less marked. Snow (1981) has also reported a decline in exact imitations and an increase in expanded imitations for one child between 2 and 3 years of age. For 14 children studied at a younger age (between about 1½ and 2½ years), Kuczaj II (1983) reported that exact and reduced imitations were the most frequent types of replications of model utterances, although there was some variation among individual children. We found also that exact and reduced imitations were the most frequent in the speech of a sample of 14 children whom we observed at 18 and 24 months of age, but there was a slight increment in modified imitations at the older age (Užgiris, Broome, & Kruper, 1989). These data demonstrate that children actively use others' utterances during language acquisition and deal with them differently as their own linguistic competence changes.

An important aspect of the data on linguistic imitation is the recognition of individual differences in the use of imitation. Bloom, Hood, and Lightbown (1974) drew attention to this difference and suggested that imitation may be a productive strategy for children who use it, but it should not be considered a universal aspect of language acquisition. Marked differences in the prevalence of imitation among children's utterances have been observed in other studies as well (e.g., Corrigan, 1980; Ramer, 1976; Ryan, 1973). What is the source of this difference in the use of imitation?

The literature suggests that it may be related to maternal imitation of children's utterances. Folger and Chapman (1978) reported a high correlation ($r_s = .77$) between the frequency of maternal imitations and the frequency of child imitations for six children in the second half of the second year of life. A similar correlation was obtained by Seitz and Stewart (1975) for a sample of somewhat older children. We have obtained significant correlations between different subtypes of maternal and child imitation at different ages during the second year (Užgiris, Broome, & Kruper, 1989). Moreover, the incidence of maternal imitation has been found to be related to the level of children's language competence, leading Snow (1984) to generalize that the "most striking and reproducible finding about social interaction and language acquisition is the finding that semantically contingent speech facilitates children's learning of language" (p. 86).

The most interesting aspect of these findings is the suggestion that participation in modeling-imitation exchanges influences the child in two ways. There seems to be sufficient evidence to say that imitation plays a role in children's learning of language, the symbol system most important for cultural transmission as well as for productive participation in the life of the culture. But, in addition, the evidence suggests that in the course of social interactions during which the act of imitation is experienced as a means of social exchange—a means that achieves or increases understanding—children adopt imitation as a strategy. The significant correlations between maternal and child imitation frequencies during specific age periods imply that those children who have partners inclined toward imitative exchanges adopt imitation as a strategy for learning (Speidel & Nelson, 1989). The acquisition of this strategy demonstrates another level of socialization in addition to the learning of specific acts. Imitation as a form of activity is first engaged in jointly with another, but then becomes a strategy in the child's self-directed activities.

Affective Imitation

Consideration of the role of imitation in infants' social relationships is quite recent. There have been almost no studies specifically addressed to the question of the function of imitation in the development of social ties, although it has been suggested that the behavioral similarity resulting from imitation may promote social interest and involvement. Some relevant empirical studies come from work on affect expression and discrimination during early infancy and from work on peer interactions among older infants. Although the basic facial expressions for different emotions seem to be biologically prescribed and present in neonates, they constitute only the starting point for emotional socialization (Campos, Barrett, Lamb, Goldsmith, & Stenberg, 1983). Interaction with others serves to maintain and modify these expressions as well as to teach about the appropriate occasions for their display (Malatesta & Izard, 1984). Intensive analyses of mother-infant interaction indicate that mothers are highly responsive to the emotional expressions of their infants (e.g., Malatesta & Haviland, 1982). Moreover, even young infants appear able to discriminate different facial expressions in others and to respond to them (Field, Woodson, Cohen, Greenberg, Garcia, & Collins, 1983; also see Kaitz, Meschulach-Sarfaty, Auerbach, & Eidelman, 1988). Matching of facial expressions and emotional states seems to play an important role in initial emotional socialization.

Most descriptions of early face-to-face interaction mention the tendency of mothers to "echo" or "mirror" the emotional states of their infants (e.g., Kaye, 1979; Papoušek & Papoušek, 1977; Trevarthen, 1977). This tendency appears to be embedded within a general pattern of interaction with young infants which includes repetitiveness, higher vocal pitch, and variation in the intensity of engagement, leading Papoušek and Papoušek (1981) to consider it part of intuitive parenting. The achievement of congruence in emotional state and in action is important for the sense of "attunement" (Stern, Hofer, Haft, & Dore, 1985) or affiliation between the infant and caregiver and seems to be achieved, in part, through the mother's imitation of her infant. As has been fervently argued by Newson (1974), it is the treatment of the human infant as an intending, communicating being that leads the infant to become one.

However, the adult imitations of the infant are selective in several ways. First, only those expressions and actions of the infant that make sense to the adult are matched or interpreted. These behavioral reflections and interpretations by the adult are available for observation by the infant and this selectivity on the part of adults highlights the socially meaningful acts for the infant. In addition, adults attribute a rich meaning to infant gestures and vocalizations (Stern, 1977; Trevarthen, 1979). We have found that both mothers and fathers (Kruper & Užgiris, 1987) make frequent comments about the feeling states of their 2½-month-old infants during face-to-face interaction and accompany these comments with appropriate expressive and vocal displays. They make fewer such interpretive comments when interacting with infants in the second half of the first year of life, when infants' feelings and goals are clearer.

Moreover, adults selectively respond to only some of the interpretable expressions and actions shown by infants. Malatesta and Haviland (1982) reported that mothers more often reflect back or respond contingently to positive emotional expressions in younger infants and to negative expressions in older infants. In addition, they noted that mothers tend to respond much more often to categorical emotional expressions than to poorly formed expressions, possibly highlighting clear affective signals. Finally, adult responses are selective in the sense that they attempt to modify infant expressions in a direction that they consider appropriate. Kaye (1979) has described how modifying imitations are used by mothers to gradually shift the infant's state toward the desired state. It is quite conceivable that cultural beliefs about infants influence what and how is selectively responded to by adults during face-to-face interactions. In turn, such selective responding may influence infant affective expressions toward socially appropriate forms.

For their part, infants seem able to respond to adult facial expressions with imitation. Studies by Meltzoff and Moore (1983) show that under certain conditions even neonates may be able to imitate the facial movements of adults and facial emotional expressions (Field, Woodson, Greenberg, & Cohen, 1982). The ability of young infants to respond to emotional expressions in more complex ways is also attested to by their reactions to posed maternal unresponsiveness or depression (Cohn & Tronick, 1983; Tronick, Als, Adamson, Wise, & Brazelton, 1978). Clear evidence of emotional responsiveness to the facial expressions of emotion by others is present in the second half of the first year of life (Campos, Barrett, Lamb, Goldsmith, & Stenberg, 1983). Infants' ability to use the facial expressions of others to guide their own actions has been observed toward the end of the first year in studies of social referencing (Feinman, 1982).

These findings indicate that with respect to emotional expressivity as well, adult modeling and infant imitation must be viewed as components of a larger system of interaction. Adult modeling is responsive to infant states and occurs in relation to them. Infant imitation of adult expressions can result in a modification of infant state, but this shift by the infant must be understood not only as a response, but also as a communication to the adult. The small amount of research on older infants suggests that modeling and imitation contribute to the learning of facial display rules, emblematic expressions, and combinations of expressions (e.g., Demos, 1982). Moreover, the verbal labeling of emotional states by parents continues the socialization of affective expressions begun in early infancy (Lewis & Michalson, 1983). Nevertheless, the prime function of affective imitation during infancy seems to be affiliative and communicative rather than instructional for both adults and infants. Imitative exchanges seem to foster involvement and mutuality rather than being occasions for the learning of new forms of emotional expression.

Imitation during Peer Interactions

A growing number of studies show that imitation occurs frequently in the interactions among young children. Performance of the same action on an object seems to be a way of starting social interaction among toddlers (Mueller & Lucas, 1975). Imitations constitute an important category of play among infant peers (Goldman & Ross, 1978; Eckerman, Davis, & Didow, 1989; Hvastja-Stefani & Camaioni, 1983) as well as among siblings (Abramovitch, Corter, & Lando, 1979; Dunn & Kendrick, 1979). It does not seem that the prime function of these imitations is to understand or learn the actions of the peer; rather, imitation seems to communicate social interest and similarity, which are noticed by the peer being imitated.

Although not involving peer interaction, the findings from a recent study of autistic children are also of interest (Tiegerman & Primavera, 1984). A comparison of adult imitative and non-imitative contingent responding to object manipulations by autistic children showed that imitation was significantly more successful in increasing the frequency and duration of their eye gaze to the experimenter. For these children, imitation of their actions appeared to exert a strong pull toward a social exchange with the imitating adult. It seems plausible that imitation has a similar role in the peer encounters of normal infants.

The contention that mutual imitation is a form of dialogue in action for infants and young children receives support from several studies. In a study of children in their third year of life, Nadel-Brulfert and Baudonniere (1982) observed groups of three children interacting in a playroom equipped with identical toys for each of them. Considerable time was spent by the children in pursuit of similarity, in the sense of simultaneously holding identical objects and of engaging in similar activities with the objects. Both verbalizations and toy offers were used to achieve this similarity. The authors reported that children who were imitated by others also engaged in a great deal of imitation themselves ($r = .60$).

In a subsequent study (Nadel-Brulfert, Baudonniere, & Fontaine, 1983; Nadel, 1986), these authors compared the interactions of dyads under two conditions: when duplicates of toys were available and when all objects in the playroom were different. They found that solitary activity was significantly more frequent in the absence of duplicate toys. Verbal interaction and exploratory play did not differ between the two conditions, but positive emotional expressions were more frequent in the duplicate toy condition. These findings show that imitation of the ongoing activities of peers is an important means of social interaction for young children. Imitative exchanges may foster continued interaction by communicating shared understanding of ongoing activities and by facilitating the elaboration of games (Eckerman & Didow, 1988). Imitation also seems to be a strategy used by older preschool children to initiate and sustain interactions (Grusec & Abramovitch, 1982; Lubin & Field, 1981). Those who imitate their peers tend to be more often imitated by others (Abramovitch & Grusec, 1978), suggesting that imitation expresses reciprocity during interactions throughout early childhood.

At older ages, imitation may become a more conscious strategy and the imitations of others may be judged in more complex ways (Thelen, Dollinger, & Roberts, 1975). There are indications that even at the preschool age, children begin to distinguish between genuine attempts at social interaction and "teasing" imitations or ingratiating imitations (Lubin & Field, 1981). Thus, the specific meanings of imitation during social interaction rapidly diversify, but imitation remains a form of social exchange available throughout the lifetime.

Issues with Respect to Imitation in the Social Context

The preceding overview of studies indicates that modeling and imitation are features of many types of infant experiences. Infants attend to and are able to learn from demonstrations by adults in the course of interacting with them. At the same time, adults are inclined to view infant imitations as communications and to adjust their own actions to correspond better with those of the infant. In sequences of interaction, modeling and imitation intertwine to form a reciprocally patterned activity. In the context of these modeling-imitation exchanges, infants encounter the socially meaningful and culturally appropriate forms of various actions. However, the extent to which participation in these exchanges contributes to early socialization relative to other kinds of infant-adult interactions and means of influence remains undetermined. This state of affairs may be expected to change as infant imitation begins to be studied as an interpersonal phenomenon.

It is clear that even during infancy, imitative exchanges are not the products of a single stamp. Their features vary with the individual characteristics of the participants (including the developmental level of the infant), the relation between the participants, the mode of interaction, the type of setting, and the goal of the activity. In order to better understand the functions of imitation for social development, it will be necessary to study how the various determinants of interpersonal interaction affect imitative exchanges and their short-term or longer-term consequences. Several issues that require investigation in order to clarify the role of imitative interactions in infant development are discussed in the next section of the chapter.

The Concept of Imitation

In the literature dealing with older children, the terms "imitation" and "observational learning" are often used interchangeably. However, there is an important shade of difference in the meaning of the two terms. Observational learning more clearly suggests that the model is not interacting with the observer during the modeling; in fact, the observer may be a witness to an interaction taking place between the model and another individual. It may be important, therefore, to note that the observational learning situation almost never occurs in studies of infant imitation.

Studies with infants typically establish some relation between the model and the infant; minimally, the model elicits the infant's attention prior to beginning each demonstration and often shares any materials used in modeling with the infant. The model's activity is a demonstration for the infant rather than an action for the self that the infant happens to witness. The studies of toddler play in which modeling is used to increase the incidence of pretend activities come closest to an observational learning design. It may be that the distance between infant activities and normal adult activities is too great for the observational learning design to work. Or, the infant's attentional capacities may not be sufficient to allow the infant to be in the position of observer for any length of time. However, by not recognizing this difference in procedure, we might be overlooking an important difference in the functions of imitation during infancy and later childhood.

The ability to take in information from events in which one is not actively participating may be a later developmental achievement. A recent study pertinent to this issue found that at 18 months of age, children are able to imitate acts directed by a model to another person (Hay, Murray, Cecire, & Nash, 1985). Moreover, when another person was the recipient of the model's actions, these children more often directed their imitative actions to this other person than when they themselves were the recipients of the model's actions. However, the imitation of actions directed to another person was not frequent even at this age. It seems plausible to assume that infants become able to imitate actions in which they do not directly participate only when they become capable of forming relations between two independent events.

A related issue has to do with the dyadic or triadic nature of the modeling situation. When the modeling involves a personal action directed to the observer, the situation can be considered dyadic. In contrast, when the model performs an action directed to another person or object, the situation can be considered triadic. In studies on infants under 6 months of age, the modeling-imitation situations are normally dyadic in character. The modeling consists of facial movements, emotional expressions, body gestures, or vocalizations directed to the infant; no other object is involved. This is as would be expected, because infants become able to actively share a focus of attention with another only in the second half of the first year of life (e.g., Collis & Schaffer, 1975; Scaife & Bruner, 1975). The achievement of play around an object (Trevarthen, 1977) and of cooperative play (Hubley & Trevarthen, 1979) reflects the ability to incorporate an additional element into a dyadic interaction. Consistent with this, imitation of actions on objects has been reported during the second 6 months of life. At what age infants become able to imitate actions which they observe directed to another person has not been established.

In the literature on older children, the distinction is sometimes made between instances where the actions of others serve to inform the observer about the appropriateness of a known type of behavior and instances where the actions of another serve as a model for constructing a novel action. The criterion of novelty is unquestionably difficult to apply, but the distinction between disinhibition and acquisition has been made mostly in relation to actions that are socially disapproved in at least some situations. In relation to infant imitation, the above distinction points up two noteworthy aspects of existing studies. The activities that are modeled for infants during the first year of life generally consist of actions that infants also perform on their own. Only the demonstrations of complex actions, requiring the coordination of several distinct acts (McCall, Parke, & Kavanaugh, 1977), or of counterconventional actions (Killen & Užgiris, 1981), might qualify as novel. These kinds of acts are not imitated with any frequency until the middle of the second year of life. In addition, it is noteworthy that infants are usually presented with socially acceptable acts for imitation; they are shown hugging and feeding, not hitting or destroying. Knowledge of when infants begin to respond differentially to socially acceptable and unacceptable models might be an interesting way to investigate socialization.

When imitation is viewed in the context of interaction, it becomes important to consider the interpersonal situation within which modeling and imitation take place. The dyadic or triadic nature of the situation, the direct or indirect involvement of the infant, and the social evaluation of the acts being modeled are important variables to consider in order to understand development in infant imitation. Knowledge of the impact of these variables would further understanding of the place of imitation in early social development.

The Functions of Imitation

The review of research on infant imitation strongly suggests that imitative actions can serve more than one function. Studies of mother-infant interaction during the early months of life and of peer interaction during the second and third years of life imply that imitation is a means of initiating and maintaining social interactions. That modeling and imitation constitute a mode of social exchange and a way of establishing symmetry in an interpersonal relationship has been suggested by Wallon (1949), but his proposition has received little attention. The well-supported observation that mothers imitate various actions of their infants (Malatesta & Haviland, 1982; Pawlby, 1977; Užgiris, Benson, Kruper, & Vasek, 1989) can be interpreted in this light; it seems to be a way for constructing a social exchange with the infant and of introducing some symmetry into the relationship. The link between empathy and these early imitative exchanges remains to be explored.

Imitation can also serve to increase the infant's understanding of observed actions and to promote the learning of new forms of action. This is the function of imitation that Piaget (1945/1962) stressed. The studies on infant play and on language acquisition provide the best illustrations of how models become objectives that initially may be only partially reproduced, but eventually are incorporated into the infant's own repertoire. These kinds of imitations also take place in the context of social interaction, although this fact was not emphasized by Piaget. During interaction, the model is presented repeatedly; moreover, each presentation of the model takes into account the replication produced by the child. The new understanding may be achieved as much through the adult's contingently provided guidance as through repeated attempts on the part of the child. Location of the accommodative function of imitation within an interactive framework highlights the link between imitation and the sociocultural world in addition to the link between imitation and the developmental level of the child that was rightly emphasized by Piaget.

At times, imitation can also serve an instrumental function. It is difficult to find examples of such instances during the first 2 years of life, but preschoolers already seem to use imitation as a means to distinct goals. Teasing or charming through imitation indicate an awareness of the instrumental value of imitation. The positive or negative valuation of particular instrumental uses of imitation is likely to differ between cultures, but an instrumental use of imitation in line with the cultural view attests to the socialization of imitation itself.

Acceptance of the idea that imitation can have several functions suggests that it is important to study it in its functional context. It may be as important to know how the different functions of imitation differentiate and intertwine during the early years of life as to know which specific actions are imitated with what frequency by children of different ages.

The Model's Relation to the Infant

Very few studies have directly compared the imitation of different models by infants. The theoretical link of imitation with affiliation as well as findings of greater imitation of nurturant models by preschool children suggest that infants should imitate parents more readily than strangers. However, existing evidence does not support this expectation.

In most of the laboratory studies of imitation, the models have been relative strangers to the infants. In their work with newborns, Meltzoff and Moore (1983) make a point of not letting the infant have any contact with the model prior to modeling. They imply that interest in the novelty of the model is related to imitation. We have directly compared the infant's mother and a female stranger as models of a variety of actions on objects for 12, 17, and 22 month old infants and found no significant difference between them in terms of imitation (McCabe & Užgiris, 1983). There was some difference in terms of attention in favor of the experimenter. We have also compared the imitation of mothers and strangers by 10-month and 12-month-old infants during play interaction in the laboratory (Užgiris, 1983). Again, there were no differences in the imitation of actions on objects or gestures modeled by mothers or experimenters. Kaye (1982) also reported that an experimenter was as successful in teaching 6-month-old infants to reach around a barrier by using a demonstration strategy as had been mothers who used the same technique. Finally, modeling of social acts for 18-month-old infants was found to be equally successful whether carried out by mothers or by strangers (Hay *et al.*, 1985).

Although not abundant, the evidence is consistent in giving no advantage to the child's mother as a model. It is conceivable that modeling of a greater range of acts or in more varied contexts would yield a different result. However, it is possible that if the modeling-imitation process is of great importance for the social development of a young child, it would not be very closely tied to an existing relation between the child and the model. In fact, the studies on early interaction argue that participation in modeling-imitation exchanges builds an affiliative relationship between the partners. This suggests that the identity of the model may begin to have an effect when the child's cognitive understanding of interpersonal relations and statuses develops during the preschool years. Clearly, more studies comparing infants' imitations of different models are needed.

Individual Differences in Imitation

Most studies of imitation in infancy comment on the great individual variation in the frequency with which infants imitate modeled actions. Examination of reported data reveals that invariably some infants do not imitate at all, whereas others imitate a variety of actions and readily repeat their imitations. This individual difference in the propensity to imitate has received explicit attention in the language acquisition literature. Although it was first suggested that imitation may be a style of language learning used only by some children (Bloom, Hood, & Lightbown, 1974), later studies showed that children fall along a continuum of imitativeness (e.g., Ramer, 1976). The finding of a correlation between maternal and child imitativeness suggests an explanation for individual differences in the interactive patterns of different dyads.

In our research on imitation during mother-infant interaction, we found considerable variation in both maternal and infant imitation (Benson, Vasek, & Užgiris, 1983). The range of variability was as great when the infants were 2½ months of age as when the infants were 11-12 months. In our longitudinal sample, the ranks of mother-infant pairs in terms of amount of imitation were quite unstable in the course of the first year of life. The variability in the use of imitation by both mothers and infants from one session to the next suggests that imitativeness is not an individual trait, but a mode of exchange that can be flexibly engaged in by both adults and children in accord with their current needs or with situational demands.

Clearly, more research is needed to understand what factors contribute to the wide individual differences in imitation that are usually obtained. However, because of the marked cross-situational variability in imitation, it appears that the answer will more likely come from examining features of the interaction within which the modeling-imitation is taking place than from thinking about the traits of the participants.

Cultural Differences in Imitation

It is a commonplace observation that much of children's learning in traditional societies takes place through imitation of adults' activities. There is no reason to assume that the modeling-imitation form of interaction would not be found in all human groups. However, societies may differ in the degree to which this form of interaction is used in various contexts as well as with children at different developmental levels. There is so little systematic information on cross-cultural variation in the prevalence of imitative interactions that the lack of evidence must be pointed out in order to avoid generalizing a picture drawn primarily from U.S. and West European data.

This issue has been raised recently with respect to the form of adult-child interactions during language acquisition (Ochs & Schieffelin, 1984; Schieffelin & Ochs, 1983). Although the pattern of maternal speech to young infants so typical of our society had been observed in some non-Western societies (e.g., Mundy-Castle, 1980), it was found to be practically nonexistent in two other cultures. Among the Kaluli, other children (but not the mother) engage in "conversations" with the infant during which the mother speaks for the infant. Although infants can observe and listen to these conversations, their own actions do not seem to regulate the course of them. At a later period, however, a very specific instruction to imitate the adult's utterance is used.

Direct instruction to imitate appropriate expressions is also used with children learning language in Samoa. As is clearly pointed out by the authors, once the modeling-imitation instruction is adopted, it serves not so much to teach the child specific linguistic forms as to convey to the child the society's view of social relations that are also embedded in aspects of linguistic discourse. The use of the explicit instruction "say" followed by modeling is similarly employed by U.S. parents to teach politeness routines to preschoolers (Greif & Gleason, 1980). Routines that incorporate imitations also serve to make interactions with young children more predictable (Watson-Gegeo & Gegeo, 1986).

Cultural differences in young children's play have been discussed as well (e.g., Feitelson, 1977). Imitation of adult activities in children's play is widely noted, but societies differ in the extent to which adults participate in children's play by providing specific objects for play or by contributing to the creation of play scenarios. This difference in adult participation may reflect a difference in viewing children's play as an appropriate context for affiliative or instructional interactions.

It is also likely that adults having different roles with respect to the child may interact differently even within the same domain of activity. An instructional goal may give a different structure to modeling-imitation exchanges than a goal of social participation. It has been demonstrated that mothers and teachers adopt different goals even when engaged in the same task with the child (Wertsch, Minick, & Arns, 1984). It seems likely that adults and siblings also adopt different goals when engaging in similar activities. Their goals are themselves a reflection of the social life within which they participate. Thus, to gain a better grasp of how modeling and imitation influence infants' enculturation, it is important to examine the variation across cultures in the types of activities during which infants are engaged in imitative interactions as well as activities during which they remain nonparticipating observers.

CONCLUDING SUMMARY

It was pointed out at the beginning of this chapter that socialization relies on the social interests and inclinations of the human infant. These interests provide the foundation for interpersonal interactions to which both adults and infants actively contribute. Cultural modes of interpretation, communication, and action permeate these interactions from their inception. The importance of imitation for socialization is best understood when it is viewed in the context of infant-adult interaction.

Typically, imitation is not an isolated event, but occurs during a social encounter. Both modeling and imitation form parts of an exchange within the larger framework of a joint activity. To study the exchange, the effect of the observer's imitation on the model as well as the effect of the model's demonstration on the observer need to be considered. In the course of an encounter, adjustments in both modeling and imitation take place in accord with earlier exchanges. Moreover, the modeling-imitation exchange can serve different functions during different activities and at different developmental periods.

Studies providing evidence on the occurrence of imitation in four realms of activity were reviewed. The modeling-imitation type of exchange was observed during play, linguistic, affective, and peer interactions. In all these realms, the modeling-imitation exchange seems to be a constituent of larger activities and to be influenced by the structure of those activities. Within instructional activities, modeling by the adult can serve to define the goal of the activity and to demonstrate specific acts, but it is continuously adjusted to the performance of the infant. Participation by the infant results not only in the learning of specific acts, but in the attainment of new motives for action and an appreciation of the larger structure of activities. Within social activities, imitation can communicate involvement and show specific interests, but it takes off from the interest expressed by the partner and adjusts to the flow of the interaction. Thus, the role of modeling-imitation exchanges in various activities needs to be considered over time.

Because most studies of imitation in infancy have not been concerned with imitation during ongoing activities, many aspects of the modeling-imitation exchange require further study. Little is known about differences in effectiveness of modeling directed to the infant and modeling directed to another person observed by the infant. Very little is known about infants' sensitivity to the social evaluation of modeled actions. Participation in imitative exchanges varies greatly between infants, but little is known about the origins and effects of such differences. Little is known, too, about cultural influences on the prevalence of modeling-imitation exchanges in different realms of activity.

How does participation in modeling-imitation relate to socialization? Examination of the literature suggests relations at several different levels. First, imitative exchanges seem to promote social contact. Imitations form a part of early affective exchanges between infants and adults and contribute to maintaining their engagement with each other. They seem to serve a similar function during early peer interactions. By contributing to affiliation among participants, imitative exchanges link the infant with others and thereby facilitate various types of social influences.

At another level, modeling-imitation exchanges contribute to the infants' acquisition of numerous socially meaningful acts. They learn games and routines, ways to handle toys, and ways to address people. In the context of interactions with adults or older children, they acquire the culturally-specific features of human modes of action. Central among these acquisitions are symbolic systems that unlock the cultural heritage and make the child its guardian.

During instructional interactions, infants also learn the structures of various activities and, as a result, learn to monitor actions, make plans, order ideas, and evaluate alternatives. Joint instructional activities create external forms of these functions which children can observe and internalize. And, in the course of gaining from instructional interactions, children may acquire the format of a modeling-imitation exchange, which relates to socialization at still another level. Although derived from social interaction, the externalizing-internalizing format is a very general way for advancing understanding. The creation of external models for intellectual puzzles in the form of analog-objects or for personal experiences in the form of artistic works makes social interchange around them possible. They become cultural objects which, when confronted by another generation, contribute to the continuity of cultural experience. But, as in the interpersonal modeling-imitation exchanges, the relation is bidirectional, since innovative variation is added to the imitations and the models are continuously reinterpreted in the course of interaction with them.

The current research on imitation during infancy shows that imitation functions to engage infants in social interaction as well as to facilitate learning of specific types of actions. In the first year of life, these two functions may be less distinct than in later childhood. With development in children's abilities, the nature, effects, and prime uses of imitative interactions do change. To better understand the nature of modeling-imitation exchanges, it is important to study them as part of ongoing interactions, to note the mutual adjustments and reciprocal learning on the part of both participants. To better understand the effects of participation in modeling-imitation exchanges, it is important to study the course of such exchanges with the same and with new partners over time. Moreover, to better understand the role of modeling-imitation interactions in the socialization of children, it is important to consider the larger activities within which such interactions occur and the cultural significance attributed to those activities.

ACKNOWLEDGMENTS

The writing of this paper and some of the research results reported in it have been made possible by support from the Spencer Foundation. The sharing of ideas with Janette B. Benson, Susan Broome, Jan C. Kruper, Marie Vasek, and other students is gratefully acknowledged.

REFERENCES

Abramovitch, R., Corter, C., & Lando, B. (1979). Sibling interaction in the home. *Child Development, 50,* 997–1003.

Abramovitch, R., & Grusec, J. E. (1978). Peer imitation in a natural setting. *Child Development, 49,* 60–65.

Abravanel, E., Levan-Goldschmidt, E., & Stevenson, M. B. (1976). Action imitation: The early phase of infancy. *Child Development, 47,* 1032–1044.

Bandura, A. (Ed.). (1971). *Psychological modeling: Conflicting theories.* Chicago: Aldine-Atherton.

Bandura, A., & Walters, R. H. (1963). *Social learning and personality development.* New York: Holt, Rinehart & Winston.

Benson, J. B., Vasek, M., & Užgiris, I. Č. (1983, April). *Individual variation in mother-infant interaction.* Paper presented at the meeting of the Society for Research in Child Development, Detroit, MI.

Bloom, L., Hood, L., & Lightbown, P. (1974). Imitation in language development: If, when, and why. *Cognitive Psychology, 6,* 380–420.

Bretherton, I., O'Connell, B., Shore, C., & Bates, E. (1984). The effect of contextual variation on symbolic play development from 20 to 28 months. In I. Bretherton (Ed.), *Symbolic play* (pp. 271–298). New York: Academic Press.

Bruner, J. S. (1972). Nature and uses of immaturity. *American Psychologist, 27,* 687–708.

Bruner, J. S. (1975). The ontogenesis of speech acts. *Journal of Child Language, 2,* 1–19.

Bruner, J. S. (1977). Early social interaction and language acquisition. In H. R. Schaffer (Ed.), *Studies in mother-infant interaction* (pp. 271–289). New York: Academic Press.

Bruner, J. S. (1978). Learning how to do things with words. In J. S. Bruner & A. Garton (Eds.), *Human growth and development* (pp. 62–84). Oxford: Clarendon Press.

Bruner, J. S., & Sherwood, V. (1976). Peek-a-boo and the learning of rule structures. In J. Bruner, A. Jolly, & K. Sylva (Eds.), *Play—Its role in development and evolution* (pp. 277–285). New York: Basic Books.

Bullowa, M. (Ed.). (1979). *Before speech.* New York: Cambridge University Press.

Campos, J. J., Barrett, K. C., Lamb, M. E., Goldsmith, H. H., & Stenberg, C. (1983). Socioemotional development. In M. M. Haith and J. J. Campos (Eds.), *Handbook of child psychology: Vol. 2. Infancy and developmental psychobiology* (pp. 783–915). New York: Wiley.

Clementson-Mohr, D. (1982). Towards a social-cognitive explanation of imitation development. In G. Butterworth & P. Light (Eds.), *Social cognition* (pp. 53–74). Chicago: University of Chicago Press.

Cohn, J. F., & Tronick, E. R. (1983). Three-month-old infants' reaction to simulated maternal depression. *Child Development, 54,* 185–193.

Collis, G., & Schaffer, H. R. (1975). Synchronization of visual attention in mother-infant pairs. *Journal of Child Psychology and Psychiatry, 16,* 315–320.

Corrigan, R. (1980). Use of repetition to facilitate spontaneous language acquisition. *Journal of Psycholinguistic Research, 9,* 231–241.

Corrigan, R. (1982). The control of animate and inanimate components in pretend play and language. *Child Development, 53,* 1343–1353.

Crawley, S. B., Rogers, P. P., Friedman, S., Iacobbo, M., Criticos, A., Richardson, L., & Thompson, M. A. (1978). Developmental changes in the structure of mother-infant play. *Developmental Psychology, 14,* 30–36.

Demos, E. V. (1982). Facial expressions of infants and toddlers: A descriptive analysis. In T. Field & A. Fogel (Eds.), *Emotions and early interaction* (pp. 127–160). Hillsdale, NJ: Erlbaum.

Dunn, J., & Kendrick, C. (1979). Interaction between young siblings in the context of family relationships. In M. Lewis & L. A. Rosenblum (Eds.), *The child and its family* (pp. 143–168). New York: Plenum Press.

Eckerman, C. O., Davis, C. C., & Didow, S. M. (1989). Toddlers' emerging ways of achieving coordinations with a peer. *Child Development, 60,* 440–453.

Eckerman, C. O., & Didow, S. M. (1988). Lessons drawn from observing young peers together. *Acta Paediatrica Scandinavica, 77,* 55–70.

Feinman, S. (1982). Social referencing in infancy. *Merrill-Palmer Quarterly, 28,* 445–470.

Feitelson, D. (1977). Cross-cultural studies of representational play. In B. Tizard & D. Harvey (Eds.), *Biology of play* (pp. 6–14). Philadelphia: J. B. Lippincott.

Fenson, L., & Ramsay, D. S. (1981). Effects of modeling action sequences on the play of twelve-, fifteen-, and nineteen-month old children. *Child Development, 52,* 1028–1036.

Field, T. M., Woodson, R., Cohen, D., Greenberg, R., Garcia, R., & Collins, K. (1983). Discrimination and imitation of facial expressions by term and preterm neonates. *Infant Behavior and Development, 6,* 485–489.

Field, T. M., Woodson, R., Greenberg, R., & Cohen, D. (1982). Discrimination and imitation of facial expressions by neonates. *Science, 218,* 179–181.

Folger, J. P., & Chapman, R. S. (1978). A pragmatic analysis of spontaneous imitations. *Journal of Child Language, 5,* 25–38.

Goldman, B. D., & Ross, H. S. (1978). Social skills in action: An analysis of early peer games. In J. Glick & K. A. Clarke-Stewart (Eds.), *The development of social understanding* (pp. 177–212). New York: Gardner.

Goslin, D. A. (Ed.). (1969). *Handbook of socialization theory and research.* Chicago: Rand McNally.

Greenfield, P., & Lave, J. (1982). Cognitive aspects of informal education. In D. A. Wagner & H. W. Stevenson (Eds.), *Cultural perspectives on child development* (pp. 181–207). San Francisco: Freeman.

Greif, E. B., & Gleason, J. B. (1980). Hi, thanks, and goodbye: More routine information. *Language in Society, 9,* 159–166.

Grusec, J. E., & Abramovitch, R. (1982). Imitation of peers and adults in a natural setting: A functional analysis. *Child Development, 53,* 636–642.

Gustafson, G. E., Green, J. A., & West, M. J. (1979). The infant's changing role in mother-infant games: The growth of social skills. *Infant Behavior and Development, 2,* 301–308.

Harris, P. L. (1983). Infant cognition. In M. M. Haith and J. J. Campos (Eds.), *Handbook of child psychology: Vol. 2. Infancy and developmental psychobiology* (pp. 689–782). New York: Wiley.

Hartup, W. W., & Coates, B. (1970). The role of imitation in childhood socialization. In R. A. Hoppe, G. A. Milton, & E. C. Simmel (Eds.), *Early experiences and the processes of socialization* (pp. 109–142). New York: Academic Press.

Hay, D. F., Murray, P., Cecire, S., & Nash, A. (1985). Social learning of social behavior in early life. *Child Development, 56,* 43–57.

Hubley, P., & Trevarthen, C. (1979). Sharing a task in infancy. In I. Č. Užgiris (Ed.), *New Directions for Child Development: Vol. 4. Social interaction and communication during infancy* (pp. 57–80). San Francisco: Jossey-Bass.

Hvastja-Stefani, L., & Camaioni, L. (1983). Effects of familiarity on peer interaction in the first year of life. *Early Child Development and Care, 11,* 45–54.

Istomina, Z. M. (1977). The development of voluntary memory in preschool-age children. In M. Cole (Ed.), *Soviet developmental psychology* (pp. 100–159). White Plains, NY: Sharpe.

Kaitz, M., Meschulach-Sarfaty, O., Auerbach, J., & Eidelman, A. (1988). A reexamination of newborn's ability to imitate facial expression. *Developmental Psychology, 24,* 3–7.

Kaye, K. (1977). Infants' effects upon their mothers' teaching strategies. In J. Glidewell (Ed.), *The social context of learning and development* (pp. 173–206). New York: Gardner Press.

Kaye, K. (1979). Thickening thin data: The maternal role in developing communication and language. In M. Bullowa (Ed.), *Before speech* (pp. 191–206). New York: Cambridge University Press.

Kaye, K. (1982). *The mental and social life of babies.* Chicago: University of Chicago Press.

Kaye, K., & Marcus, J. (1978). Imitation over a series of trials with feedback: Age six months. *Infant Behavior and Development, 1,* 141–155.

Kaye, K., & Marcus, J. (1981). Infant imitation: The sensorimotor agenda. *Developmental Psychology, 17,* 258–265.

Killen, M., & Užgiris, I. Č. (1981). Imitation of actions with objects: The role of social meaning. *Journal of Genetic Psychology, 138,* 219–229.

Kruper, J. C., & Užgiris, I. Č. (1987). Fathers' and mothers' speech to young infants. *Journal of Psycholinguistic Research, 16,* 597–614.

Kuczaj II, S. A. (1982). Language play and language acquisition. In H. W. Reese (Ed.), *Advances in child development and behavior* (Vol. 17, pp. 197–232). New York: Academic Press.

Kuczaj, II, S. A. (1983). *Crib speech and language play.* New York: Springer-Verlag.

Kuhn, D. (1973). Imitation theory and research from a cognitive perspective. *Human Development, 16,* 157–180.

Lelwica, M., & Haviland, J. M. (1983, April). *Response or imitation: Ten-week-old infants' reactions to three emotion expressions.* Paper presented at the meeting of the Society for Research in Child Development, Detroit, MI.

Leont'ev, A. N. (1981a). *Problems in the development of mind.* Moscow: Progress Publishers.

Leont'ev, A. N. (1981b). The problem of activity in psychology. In J. V. Wertsch (Ed.), *The concept of activity in Soviet psychology* (pp. 37–71). Armonk, NY: Sharpe.

Lewis, M., & Michalson, L. (1983). *Children's emotions and moods: Developmental theory and measurement.* New York: Plenum Press.

Lubin, L. & Field, T. (1981). Imitation during preschool peer interaction. *International Journal of Behavioral Development, 4,* 443–453.

Malatesta, C. Z., & Haviland, J. M. (1982). Learning display rules: The socialization of emotion expression in infancy. *Child Development, 53,* 991–1003.

Malatesta, C. Z., & Izard, C. E. (1984). The ontogenesis of human social signals: From biological imperative to symbol utilization. In N. A. Fox & R. J. Davidson (Eds.), *The psychobiology of affective development* (pp. 161–206). Hillsdale, NJ: Erlbaum.

Masur, E. F. (1987). Imitative interchanges in a social context: Mother–infant matching behavior at the beginning of the second year. *Merrill-Palmer Quarterly, 33,* 453–472.

Masur, E. F., & Ritz, E. G. (1984). Patterns of gestural, vocal, and verbal imitation performance in infancy. *Merrill-Palmer Quarterly, 30,* 369–392.

McCabe, M., & Užgiris, I. Č. (1983). Effects of model and action on imitation in infancy. *Merrill-Palmer Quarterly, 29,* 69–82.

McCall, R. B., Parke, R. D., & Kavanaugh, R. D. (1977). Imitation of live and televised models by children 1–3 years of age. *Monographs of the Society for Research in Child Development, 42*(5, Serial No. 173).

Meltzoff, A. N. (1985). Immediate and deferred imitation in fourteen- and twenty-four-month-old infants. *Child Development, 56,* 62–72.

Meltzoff, A. N. (1988). Infant imitation after a 1-week delay: Long-term memory for novel acts and multiple stimuli. *Developmental Psychology, 24,* 470–476.

Meltzoff, A. N., & Moore, M. K. (1983). The origins of imitation in infancy: Paradigm, phenomena, and theories. In L. P. Lipsitt (Ed.), *Advances in infancy research* (Vol. 2, pp. 263–300). Norwood, NJ: Ablex.

Meltzoff, A. N., & Moore, M. K. (1985). Cognitive foundations and social functions of imitation and intermodal representation in infancy. In J. Mehler & R. Fox (Eds.), *Neonate cognition* (pp. 139–156). Hillsdale, NJ: Erlbaum.

Mitchell, R. W. (1987). A comparative-developmental approach to understanding imitation. In P. P. G. Bateson & P. H. Klopfer (Eds.), *Perspectives in ethology, Vol. 7: Alternatives* (pp. 183–215). New York: Plenum Press.

Mueller, E., & Lucas, T. (1975). A developmental analysis of peer interaction among toddlers. In M. Lewis & L. Rosenblum (Eds.), *Friendship and peer relations* (pp. 223–257). New York: Wiley.

Mundy-Castle, A. (1980). Perception and communication in infancy: A cross-cultural study. In D. R. Olson (Ed.), *The social foundations of language and thought* (pp. 231–253). New York: Norton.

Nadel, J. (1986). *Imitation et communication entre jeunes enfants* [Imitation and communication between young children]. Paris: Presses Universitaires de France.

Nadel-Brulfert, J., & Baudonniere, P. M. (1982). The social function of reciprocal imitation in 2-year-old peers. *International Journal of Behavioral Development, 5,* 95–109.

Nadel-Brulfert, J., Baudonniere, P. M., & Fontaine, A. M. (1983, August). *The social function of synchronic imitation as a basis for emotional exchange in two-year-olds.* Paper presented at the meeting of the International Society for the Study of Behavioral Development, Munich, Germany.

Newson, J. (1974). Towards a theory of infant understanding. *Bulletin of the British Psychological Society, 27,* 251–257.

Ninio. A., & Bruner, J. S. (1978). The achievement and antecedents of labelling. *Journal of Child Language, 5,* 1–15.

Ochs, E., & Schieffelin, B. B. (1984). Language acquisition and socialization. In R. A. Shweder & R. A. LeVine (Eds.), *Culture theory: Essays on mind, self, and emotion* (pp. 276–320). New York: Cambridge University Press.

Olson, G. M., & Sherman, T. (1983). Attention, learning, and memory in infants. In M. M. Haith and J. J. Campos (Eds.), *Handbook of child psychology: Vol. 2. Infancy and developmental psychobiology* (pp. 1001–1080). New York: Wiley.

Papoušek, H., & Papoušek, M. (1977). Mothering and the cognitive head-start: Psychobiological considerations. In H. R. Schaffer (Ed.), *Studies in mother-infant interaction* (pp. 63–85). New York: Academic Press.

Papoušek, H., & Papoušek, M. (1981). How human is the human newborn, and what else is to be done? In K. Bloom (Ed.), *Prospective issues in infancy research* (pp. 137–155). Hillsdale, NJ: Erlbaum.

Parton, D. A. (1976). Learning to imitate in infancy. *Child Development, 47,* 14–31.

Pawlby, S. J. (1977). Imitative interaction. In H. R. Schaffer (Ed.), *Studies in mother-infant interaction* (pp. 203–224). New York: Academic Press.

Piaget, J. (1962). *Play, dreams and imitation in childhood* (C. Gattegno & F. M. Hodgson, Trans.). New York: Norton. (Original work published 1945)

Poulson, C. L., Nunes, L. R. P., & Warren, S. F. (1989). Imitation in infancy: A critical review. In H. W. Reese (Ed.), *Advances in child development and behavior, Vol. 22* (pp. 271–298). San Diego: CA: Academic Press.

Ramer, A. L. H. (1976). The function of imitation in child language. *Journal of Speech and Hearing Research, 19,* 700–717.

Ratner, N., & Bruner, J. S. (1978). Games, social exchange, and the acquisition of language. *Journal of Child Language, 5,* 391–401.

Rheingold, H. L. (1969). The social and socializing infant. In D. A. Goslin (Ed.), *Handbook of socialization theory and research* (pp. 779–790). Chicago: Rand McNally.

Richards, M. P. M. (Ed.). (1974). *The integration of a child into a social world.* Cambridge, England: Cambridge University Press.

Rodgon, M. M., & Kurdek, L. A. (1977). Vocal and gestural imitation in 8-, 14-, and 20-month-old children. *Journal of Genetic Psychology, 131,* 115–123.

Rogoff, B. (1990). *Apprenticeship in thinking: Cognitive development in social context.* New York: Oxford University Press.

Rogoff, B., & Gardner, W. (1984). Adult guidance of cognitive development. In B. Rogoff & J. Lave (Eds.), *Everyday cognition: Its development in social context* (pp. 95–116). Cambridge, MA: Harvard University Press.

Rogoff, B., Malkin, C., & Gilbride, K. (1984). Interactions with babies as guidance in development. In B. Rogoff & J. V. Wertsch (Eds.). *New Directions for Child Development:*

Vol. 23. Children's learning in the "zone of proximal development" (pp. 31–44). San Francisco: Jossey-Bass.

Rogoff, B., & Wertsch, J. V. (Eds.). (1984). *New Directions for Child Development: Vol. 23. Children's learning in the "zone of proximal development."* Cambridge, MA: Harvard University Press.

Ryan, J. (1973). Interpretation and imitation in early language development. In R. Hinde & J. Stevenson-Hinde (Eds.), *Constraints on learning* (pp. 427–443). New York: Academic Press.

Scaife, M., & Bruner, J. S. (1975). The capacity for joint visual attention in the infant. *Nature, 253,* 265–266.

Schaffer, H. R. (1977). *Mothering.* Cambridge, MA: Harvard University Press.

Schieffelin, B. B., & Ochs, E. (1983). A cultural perspective on the transition from prelinguistic to linguistic communication. In R. M. Golinkoff (Ed.), *The transition from prelinguistic to linguistic communication* (pp. 115–131). Hillsdale, NJ: Erlbaum.

Seitz, S., & Stewart, C. (1975). Imitations and expansions: Some developmental aspects of mother-child communications. *Developmental Psychology, 11,* 763–768.

Snow, C. E. (1981). The uses of imitation. *Journal of Child Language, 8,* 205–212.

Snow, C. E. (1984). Parent-child interaction and the development of communicative ability. In R. L. Schiefelbusch & J. Pickar (Eds.), *The acquisition of communicative competence* (pp. 69–107). Baltimore: University Park Press.

Snow, C. E., & Ferguson, C. A. (Eds.). (1977). *Talking to children: Language input and acquisition.* New York: Cambridge University Press.

Speidel, G. E., & Nelson, K. E. (Eds.). (1989). *The many faces of imitation in language learning.* New York: Springer-Verlag.

Stern, D. N. (1977). *The first relationship.* Cambridge, MA: Harvard University Press.

Stern, D. N., Hofer, L., Haft, W., & Dore, J. (1985). Affect attunement: The sharing of feeling states between mother and infant by means of inter-modal fluency. In T. Field & N. Fox (Eds.), *Social perception in infants* (pp. 249–268). Norwood, NJ: Ablex.

Thelen, M. H., Dollinger, S. J., & Roberts, M. C. (1975). On being imitated: Its effect on attraction and reciprocal imitation. *Journal of Personality and Social Psychology, 31,* 467–472.

Tiegerman, E., & Primavera, L. H. (1984). Imitating the autistic child: Facilitating communicative gaze behavior. *Journal of Autism and Developmental Disorders, 14,* 27–38.

Trevarthen, C. (1977). Descriptive analyses of infant communicative behaviour. In H. R. Schaffer (Ed.), *Studies in mother-infant interaction* (pp. 227–289). New York: Academic Press.

Trevarthen, C. (1979). Communication and cooperation in early infancy: A description of primary intersubjectivity. In M. Bullowa (Ed.), *Before speech* (pp. 321–347). New York: Cambridge University Press.

Trevarthen, C., & Hubley, P. (1978). Secondary intersubjectivity: Confidence, confiding, and acts of meaning in the first year. In A. Lock (Ed.), *Action, gesture and symbol* (pp. 183–229). New York: Academic Press.

Tronick, E. Z. (Ed.). (1982). *Social interchange in infancy,* Baltimore: University Park Press.

Tronick, E., Als, H., Adamson, L., Wise, S., & Brazelton, T. B. (1978). The infant's response to entrapment between contradictory messages in face-to-face interaction. *Journal of the American Academy of Child Psychiatry, 17,* 1–13.

Ungerer, J. A., Zelazo, P. R., Kearsley, R. B., & O'Leary, K. (1981). Developmental changes in the representation of objects in symbolic play from 18 to 34 months of age. *Child Development, 52,* 186–195.

Užgiris, I. Č. (1972). Patterns of vocal and gestural imitation in infants. In F. J. Mönks, W. W.

Hartup, & J. de Witt (Eds.), *Determinants of behavioral development* (pp. 467–471). New York: Academic Press.

Užgiris, I. Č. (Ed.). (1979). *New directions for child development: Vol. 4. Social interaction and communication during infancy.* San Francisco: Jossey-Bass.

Užgiris, I. Č. (1981a). Experience in the social context: Imitation and play. In R. L. Schiefelbusch & D. D. Bricker (Eds.), *Early language: Acquisition and intervention* (pp. 139–168). Baltimore: University Park Press.

Užgiris, I. Č. (1981b). Two functions of imitation during infancy. *International Journal of Behavioral Development, 4,* 1–12.

Užgiris, I. Č. (1983). *The role of imitation in pre-verbal communication.* Final report to the Spencer Foundation (7-1-1981–7-31-1983).

Užgiris, I. Č. (1984). Imitation in infancy: Its interpersonal aspects. In M. Perlmutter (Ed.), *The Minnesota Symposia on Child Psychology: Vol. 17. Parent-child interactions and parent-child relations in child development* (pp. 1–32). Hillsdale, NJ: Erlbaum.

Užgiris, I. Č. (1989). Infants in relation: Performers, pupils, and partners. In W. Damon (Ed.), *Child development today and tomorrow.* San Francisco: Jossey-Bass.

Užgiris I. Č., Vasek, M. E., & Benson, J. B. (1984). *A longitudinal study of matching activity in mother-infant interaction.* Poster presented at the meeting of the International Conference on Infant Studies, New York, NY.

Užgiris, I. Č., Benson, J. B., Kruper, J. C., & Vasek, M. E. (1989). Contextual influences on imitative interactions between mothers and infants. In J. J. Lockman & N. L. Hazen (Eds.), *Action in social context: Perspectives on early development* (pp. 103–127). New York: Plenum Press.

Užgiris, I. Č., Broome, S., & Kruper, J. C. (1989). Imitation in mother-child conversations: A focus on the mother. In G. E. Speidel & K. E. Nelson (Eds.), *The many faces of imitation in language learning* (pp. 91–120). New York: Springer-Verlag.

Valsiner, J. (1984). Construction of the zone of proximal development in adult-child joint action: The socialization of meals. In B. Rogoff & J. V. Wertsch (Eds.), *New directions for child development: Vol. 23. Children's learning in the "zone of proximal development"* (pp. 65–76). San Francisco: Jossey-Bass.

Vygotsky, L. S. (1962). *Thought and language.* Cambridge, MA: MIT Press.

Vygotsky, L. S. (1978). *Mind in society.* Cambridge, MA: Harvard University Press.

Wallon, H. (1949). *Les origines du caractere chez l'enfant* [The origins of personality in the child]. Paris: Presses Universitaires de France.

Watson, M. W., & Fischer, K. W. (1977). A developmental sequence of agent use in late infancy. *Child Development, 48,* 828–836.

Watson-Gegeo, K. A., & Gegeo, D. W. (1986). Calling-out and repeating routines in Kwara'ae children's language socialization. In B. B. Schieffelin & E. Ochs (Eds.), *Language socialization across cultures* (pp. 17–50). New York: Cambridge University Press.

Waxler, C. Z., & Yarrow, M. R. (1975). An observational study of maternal models. *Developmental Psychology, 11,* 485–494.

Wertsch, J. V. (1985). *Vygotsky and the social formation of mind.* Cambridge, MA: Harvard University Press.

Wertsch, J. V., McNamee, G. D., McLane, J. B., & Budwig, N. A. (1980). The adult-child dyad as a problem-solving system. *Child Development, 51,* 1215–1221.

Wertsch, J. V., Minick, N., & Arns, F. J. (1984). The creation of context in joint problem-solving. In B. Rogoff & J. Lave (Eds.), *Everyday cognition: Its development in social context* (pp. 151–171). Cambridge, MA: Harvard University Press.

Wood, D. J. (1980). Teaching the young child: Some relationships between social interaction, language, and thought. In D. R. Olson (Ed.), *The social foundations of language and thought* (pp. 280–296). New York: Norton.

Wood, D. J., Bruner, J. S., & Ross, G. (1976). The role of tutoring in problem solving. *Journal of Child Psychology and Psychiatry, 17,* 89–100.

Yando, R., Seitz, V., & Zigler, E. (1978). *Imitation: A developmental perspective.* Hillsdale, NJ: Erlbaum.

11

The Joint Socialization of Development by Young Children and Adults

Barbara Rogoff

> The young child is often thought of as a little scientist exploring the world and discovering the principles of its operation. We often forget that while the scientist is working on the border of human knowledge and is finding out things that nobody yet knows, the child is finding out precisely what everybody already knows.
>
> (Newman, 1982, p. 26)

This chapter focuses on how young children and adults together manage children's socialization through children's participation in cultural activities with the guidance of adults. Interactions and arrangements between caregivers and infants or toddlers are the basis for the discussion.

First, the chapter considers how such joint involvement can be conceptualized. The main part of the chapter then describes features of adult-child interactions, as well as noninteractive arrangements made between adults and children, in order to examine differing aspects of the joint socialization of children's development. Finally, the chapter ad-

This chapter has been reprinted in Gellatly, A., Rogers, D., & Sloboda, J. A. (Eds.). (1989). *Cognition and social worlds*. Oxford: Clarendon Press. The text *Apprenticeship in thinking: Cognitive development in social context* (Rogoff, B., 1990, New York: Oxford University Press) has expanded on this chapter.

Barbara Rogoff • Department of Psychology, University of Utah, Salt Lake City, Utah 84112.

dresses cultural variations and universals in the goals and means used by young children and adults that may bring about the child's entry into skilled participation in the culture.

The chapter builds on Vygotsky's concept of the *zone of proximal development*, in which child development is viewed as a social activity with children participating in activities beyond their competence through the assistance of adults or more experienced peers. In social interaction in the zone of proximal development, children are able to participate in activities that are beyond their capabilities when working independently. Through such social guidance, children are presumed to gradually internalize the skills that were practiced with adult support so that they can be performed independently (Vygotsky, 1978; Wertsch, 1979). Thus, the zone of proximal development is a dynamic region of sensitivity to learning experiences in which children develop, guided by social interaction.

In Vygotskian theory, children's interaction within the zone of proximal development is part of a larger sociocultural theory that places human skills and achievements in the context of the technologies, practices, and values available through cultural history. These sociocultural technologies and skills include inventions such as literacy, mathematics, mnemonic skills, and approaches to problem-solving and reasoning. In effect, cultural inventions channel the skills of each generation, with individual development mediated by the guidance of people who are more skilled in their use. Children are introduced to the culture through the guidance of its more experienced members (Laboratory of Comparative Human Cognition, 1983; Rogoff, 1982; Rogoff, Gauvain, & Ellis, 1984; Vygotsky, 1978).

Cole (1981) suggests that the zone of proximal development is where culture and cognition meet. It is in this sensitive zone that variations in social interaction may be expected to yield adaptations of individuals to their specific cultural surroundings. Their adaptations will simultaneously show similarities across many cultural contexts, based on cross-cultural commonalities in the processes of communication and of child development, and variations according to the specific goals and means available for appropriate development in each culture.

This chapter extends the concept of zone of proximal development by stressing the *interrelatedness* of children's and adults' roles, in a process of *guided participation*. The thesis is that the rapid development of young children into socialized participants in society is accomplished through a finely tuned combination of children's skills and the guidance of adults (or older children). The elaboration presented in this chapter, while consistent with the Vygotskian approach, emphasizes the role of children as active participants in their own socialization. They do not simply receive the guidance of adults; rather, they seek, structure, and even demand the assistance of those around them in learning how to solve problems of all kinds. The aim of this chapter is to stress the complementary roles of children and adults in fostering children's development.

Young children appear to come equipped with ways of ensuring proximity and involvement with more experienced members of society, and of becoming involved with their physical and cultural surroundings. The infant's strategies (if one ignores connotations of intentionality) appear similar to those appropriate for anyone learning in an unfamiliar culture: Stay near a trusted guide, watch the guide's activities and get involved when possible, and attend to any instruction provided.

Infants' strategies are complemented by features of adult-child interaction that are well adapted to the gradual immersion of children in the skills and beliefs of the society. Adults arrange the occurrence of children's activities and facilitate learning by regulating the difficulty of the tasks and by modeling mature performance during joint participation in activities. While adults may rarely regard themselves as explicitly teaching infants or young children, they routinely adjust their interaction and structure children's environments and activities in ways consistent with providing support for their learning.

In elaborating the concept of the zone of proximal development, Rogoff and Gardner (1984) emphasized that although more experienced people play an important role in socialization, this role is meshed with the efforts of children to learn and develop. Rogoff (1986) proposed that guided participation with schoolchildren involves adults leading children through the process of solving a problem, and children participating at a comfortable but slightly challenging level:

> Adults provide guidance in cognitive development through the arrangement of appropriate materials and tasks for children, as well as through tacit and explicit instruction occurring as adults and children participate together in activities. Adults' greater knowledge and skill allow them to assist children in translating familiar information to apply to a new problem, and to structure the problem so that the child can work on manageable subgoals. The effectiveness of adults in structuring situations for children's learning is matched by children's eagerness and involvement in managing their own learning experiences. Children put themselves in a position to observe what is going on; they involve themselves in the ongoing activity; they influence the activities in which they participate; and they demand some involvement with the adults who serve as their guides for socialization into the culture that they are learning. Together, children and adults choose learning situations and calibrate the child's level of participation so that the child is comfortably challenged. (p. 38)

This chapter extends these ideas by focusing on processes of guided participation with *younger children*. The themes include how adults facilitate the development of infants and toddlers, how children themselves channel their own development and the assistance they receive, and similarities and variations in the processes of social guidance that may occur in varying cultures. First, however, it is necessary to examine the notion of the interrelatedness of the individual child's role and that of the social context—including the adults and older children who provide guidance.

MUTUALITY OF INDIVIDUAL EFFORT AND SOCIAL FACILITATION

This section examines alternative conceptualizations of how mutual involvement of adults and children may contribute to development. It has been common in developmental psychology to focus attention alternatively on the contribution of each partner, by examining either how adults teach children, or how children develop independently. This chapter argues for the necessity of considering the *mutual involvement* of children and the social world in understanding child development. But such mutual involvement could be understood in different ways. In order to explore ways of conceptualizing the mutual roles of adults and children in fostering children's development, it is useful to draw a relationship with the parallel question of nature and nurture that has long interested psychologists. By analogy, we may regard the role of the child as "nature" and the role of social partners as "nurture."

The history of psychology has long pitted nature against nurture, with questions of how much of development should be credited to nature and how much to nurture. This traditional view places the two in opposition. Most developmentalists, as one reads in early chapters of introductory texts, are no longer trying to figure out if development is "more nature" or "more nurture." Instead, they view nature and nurture as interacting to produce development: Development does not occur solely through individual effort or preprogramming, nor does it occur entirely under the direction of the environment.

However, the notion of interaction often involves an assumption that the interacting entities are separable (see Rogoff, 1982). In other words, in an interactional view, nature and nurture are often regarded as independent influences—each definable in terms not involving the other—that happen to co-occur.

In contrast with the idea that the two are separate but interacting influences on development, the present chapter is built on the premise that nature and nurture (i.e., the child and the social world) are not separable. They are mutually involved to an extent that precludes regarding them as independently definable. In this view, development is made up of both individual effort or tendencies and the larger sociocultural context in which the individual is embedded and has been since before conception. Thus, biology and culture are not viewed as alternative influences but aspects of a system in which individuals develop.

This stance is reflected in Vygotsky's efforts (Wertsch, 1985) to study development at four *interrelated* levels. The level with which developmental psychologists traditionally deal is termed ontogenetic development—changes in thinking and behavior associated with age. But this level is merely a grain of analysis differing from the other three: Phylogenetic development is the slowly changing species history that leaves a legacy for the individual in the form of genes. Sociocultural development is the changing cultural history that leaves a legacy for the individual in the form of technologies such as literacy, number systems, and computers, as well as value systems and scripts and norms for the handling of situations met by the individual. Microgenetic development is the moment-to-moment learning by individuals in particular problem contexts, built upon the individual's genetic and sociocultural background. In this system, the roles of the individual and the social world are seen as interrelated in the levels of analysis reflecting learning, ontogenetic development, phylogenetic development, and sociohistorical development.

A similar concept of embeddedness of nature and nurture is found in Piaget's work. As Furth (1974) explains, contrary to popular belief, Piaget's theory does not focus on the importance of nature. Rather, the individual's development in Piagetian theory is based on the species-typical genetic background *and* the species-typical environment, which together form the basis of the individual's effort to construct an understanding of reality.

It should be noted that, despite the theoretical adherence of both Vygotsky and Piaget to the idea that nature and nurture are inseparable supports for individual development, both theorists chose to emphasize one or the other aspect for further elaboration in their theories. Thus, although Piaget noted the role of social arrangements of the environment—and variations in the species environment—he elaborated upon the individual's independent construction of a notion of the world. Vygotsky, on the other hand, allowed an important role for the individual's active efforts in becoming socialized, but stressed the sociocultural arrangements that facilitate the individual's socialization.

Vygotsky (1962, 1978) suggested that, rather than deriving explanations of psychological activity from the individual's characteristics plus secondary social influences, psychologists should focus on the social unit of the activity and regard individual functioning as derived from that.

The present chapter attempts to keep the roles of both the individual and the social environment in focus, to acknowledge that they build integrally on each other. This perspective is consistent with other work on socialization in the early years (Brazelton, 1982; Papousek, Papousek, & Bornstein, 1984; Schaffer, 1984). Wartofsky (1984) argues for the importance of keeping both angles in view at once—that children are embedded in a social world and that children are active participants in their own development.

> The child is *not* a self-contained homunculus, radiating outward in development from some fixed configuration of traits, dispositions, or preformed potencies; and . . . the world, in turn, is not some eternal and objective network of causal factors converging on the neonate to shape an unresisting, passive blob to its external, pregiven structures. To put this positively: the child is an agent in its own *and* the world's construction, but one whose agency develops in the context of an ineluctably social and historical praxis, which includes both the constraints and potentialities of nature and the actions of other agents. Nurture, in short, is both given *and* taken; and so is Nature. (Wartofsky, 1984, p. 188)

SOCIAL FACILITATION OF INDIVIDUAL DEVELOPMENT

Working from observations of adults instructing children aged 6 to 9 years, Rogoff and Gardner (1984) proposed that guided participation involves the following activities:

1. Providing a bridge between familiar skills or information and those needed to solve a new problem,
2. Arranging and structuring problem-solving, and
3. Gradually transferring the responsibility for managing problem-solving to the child.

These activities seem relevant for the guidance of younger children as well. This section elaborates on these three features of adults' and young children's arrangements for socialization and development. It stresses the entwinement of adults' and children's activities, the active role of both participants, and the possibility that teaching and learning can occur tacitly (as well as explicitly) in the arrangements and interaction between adults and young children.

Until we arrive at the section which addresses cross-cultural universals and variations, the terms "adult" and "child" refer to the adults and children who have been observed in North American and Western European research—largely middle class and English speaking.

Providing Bridges between Familiar Skills or Information and Those Needed in Novel Situations

Adults help young children find the connections between what they already know and what is necessary to handle a new situation (D'Andrade, 1981; Erickson, 1982). For older children this may involve specifying exactly how the new situation resembles the old. For example, in a classification task (Rogoff & Gardner, 1984), some mothers made comments such as "You need to put the things together that go together, just like on Sesame Street when they say 'three of these things belong together.'"

For very young children, the bridging role of adults involves assisting children in understanding how to act in new situations by provision of emotional cues regarding the nature of the situation, nonverbal models of how to behave, verbal and nonverbal interpretations of behavior and events, and verbal labels to classify objects and events. All of these adult activities are coupled with young children's efforts (intentional or not) to pick up information about the nature of situations and their caregivers' interpretations.

Emotional and Nonverbal Communication

From the first year of life, children look to adults to interpret situations that are ambiguous from the child's point of view, in a process termed *social referencing* (Feinman, 1982; Gunnar & Stone, 1984). Interpretations offered by adults inform infants about the appropriate approach to take to a new situation. For example, if a child is crawling toward its mother and reaches what appears to be a dropoff, the child searches the mother's face for cues regarding the safety of the situation. If the mother's emotional expression indicates fear the child does not proceed, but if the mother has an encouraging expression the child carefully crawls across clear glass suspended a foot above what appears to be the floor (Sorce, Emde, Campos, & Klinnert, 1985).

Young children are so skilled in obtaining information from glances, winces, and mood that one of the greatest challenges of testing preschoolers is to avoid nonverbal actions that may be construed as cues. Children press for and use such cues even when given standardized intelligence tests (Mehan, 1976). Such skill and interest are indicative of the salience of social referencing for very young children.

Such referencing is facilitated by the ability that appears by 8 to 12 months of age to obtain information through observation of the direction in which caregivers point and gaze (Bruner, 1983; Butterworth & Cochran, 1980). The development of such skill is supported by the efforts of mothers to regulate joint attention during the first year. If an infant appears not to understand a pointing gesture, mothers facilitate the baby's comprehension by touching the indicated object (Lempers, 1979). With babies as young as 3 months, mothers attempt to achieve joint reference by introducing an object between themselves and the infant as a target for joint attention, using a characteristic intonation and shaking the object (Bruner, 1983). From ages 6 to 18 months, infants are more than four times as likely to engage in joint attention when interacting with their mothers as when interacting with a peer (Bakeman & Adamson, 1984). Bakeman and Adamson attribute this pattern to the mother's socialization of reference, "embedding it within the interpersonal sphere well before infants can structure this integration by themselves" (p. 1288). Thus the infant's use of social referencing builds on earlier skills and social guidance, providing more advanced means to gather information regarding their mothers' (and others') interpretation of new situations.

Mothers and other adults may at times intentionally attempt to communicate a particular understanding of a new situation through managing their emotional and nonverbal communication. For example, at a doctor's office a mother may try to mask her apprehension when her baby is receiving a shot, in order to minimize the baby's reaction to the situation. Or parental management of cues may enter into instruction in potentially frightening situations, as suggested in the following advice to parents on teaching 3-week-old babies to swim in the bathtub:

> Your attitude toward water is important. An infant who sees her mother wince in terror every time she floats in deep water is not going to have a very confident picture of the strange situation. Since panic is the single most deadly factor in water, parents should be acutely aware of their responsibility in teaching their child a healthy respect for water. . . . If you show enjoyment of the water, she will imitate your excitement and pleasure. . . . Lift your baby into the water, and rest her on your bent knees, facing you. Dip your hands into the water, and pat your baby's body to help her adjust to the water temperature. Talk and smile constantly throughout the entire session. Gradually lower your knees until the baby is completely submerged in water, head resting comfortably on your knees, body on your thighs. Take this part slowly, allowing enough time for your baby to become acquainted with the water. (Poe, 1982, pp. 12, 20)

Such intentional communication of how to interpret a situation may be rare. But in a less self-conscious fashion, middle-class adults seem almost inevitably to provide interpretation for the baby's actions, their own actions, and events in the environment (Shotter & Newson, 1982). For example, mothers may respond to the baby's attempts to push an approaching spoon away with a running commentary such as, "You getting full? Try another bite, Mama wants you to grow up big and strong." For babies learning to eat from a spoon, adults frequently provide supplementary cues regarding the appropriate action for the child—they can be observed to open their own mouths wide at the time the baby is to do the same (Valsiner, 1984). To ensure a happy response to a potentially startling event, adults make an exaggerated face of surprise and enjoyment, for example, commenting, "Isn't that funny?" when concerned that a jack-in-the-box might startle a baby (Rogoff, Malkin, & Gilbride, 1984).

Words as a Cultural System for Bridging

In addition to such interpretive comments and actions, the provision of a language system teaches children the meanings and distinctions important in their culture. Labels categorize objects and events in ways specific to the language of the child's culture. Roger Brown pointed out this function of language learning in his comments about the Original Word Game:

> The Original Word Game is the operation of linguistic reference in first language learning. At least two people are required: one who knows the language (the tutor) and one who is learning (the player). In outline form the movements of the game are very simple. The tutor names things in accordance with the semantic custom of his community. The player forms hypotheses about the categorial nature of the things named. He tests his hypotheses by trying to name new things correctly. The tutor compares the player's utterances with his own anticipations of such utterances and, in this way, checks the accuracy of fit between his own categories and those of the player. He improves the fit by correction. In concrete terms the tutor says "dog" whenever a dog appears. The player notes the phonemic equivalence of these utterances, forms a hypothesis about the non-linguistic category that elicits this kind of utterance and then tries naming a few dogs himself. . . . In learning referents and names the player of the Original Word Game prepares himself to receive the science, the rules of thumb, the prejudices, the total expectancies of his society. (Brown, 1958, pp. 194 & 228)

Clearly, the Original Word Game requires two active partners. Language development is facilitated by social involvement as well as by the child's natural propensity to learn language. In this view, Chomsky's Language Acquisition Device cooperates with Bruner's Language Acquisition Support System, which "frames or structures the input of language and interaction to the child's Language Acquisition Device in a manner to 'make the system function'" (Bruner, 1983, p. 19).

Consistent with this emphasis on the social supports for language acquisition are Moerk's (1983) careful analyses of maternal language input to Roger Brown's subject Eve. Eve's mother provided sufficiently rich and frequent input, with semantic and linguistic redundancy, and contingent instructional relationships between mother's and child's ut- terances, for her framing of Eve's language development to be consid- ered an important contribution to the child's efforts to learn language.

The process of communication, itself a social activity, can be re- garded as the bridge between one understanding of a situation and another. For an adult and child to communicate successfully, the adult must search for common reference points, translating the adult's under- standing of the situation into a form that is within the child's grasp (Rogoff, 1986; Wertsch, 1984). Adults insert their interaction into the ongoing activity of an infant, waiting for the infant to be in the appropri- ate state and providing verbal and nonverbal commentary on the object or event to which the baby is already attending (Kaye, 1982; Schaffer, 1984).

Adjustment of the adult's perspective in the service of communica- tion is also apparent in the way adults occasionally misclassify an atypical exemplar of a category in order to avoid confusing toddlers about the basic nature of the category. For example, adults may agree that a whale is a fish, or that an electric outlet is "hot." Bruner (1983, based on Deutsch & Pechmann) suggests that the fact that a physicist mother is unlikely to share an identical concept of "electricity" with her 4-year-old does not matter as long as their shared meaning is sufficient to allow their conversation about shocks to continue. This effort to com- municate draws the child into a more mature understanding that is linked to what the child already knows. In the process of communicat- ing, adults tie new situations to more familiar ones, drawing connec- tions from the familiar to the novel through the adult's verbal and non- verbal interpretation.

Structuring Situations for Child Involvement

Choice and Structuring of Situations

Adults frequently make arrangements for children, selecting ac- tivities and materials they consider appropriate for children at that age or interest level (Laboratory of Comparative Human Cognition, 1983; Valsiner, 1984). Such choices may frequently be made without the inten- tion of providing a specific learning experience, but may also be de- signed explicitly for the socialization or education of the child. Whiting

(1980) cogently states the responsibility of parents and other caregivers for arranging children's learning environments:

> The power of parents and other agents of socialization is in their assignment of children to specific settings. Whether it is caring for an infant sibling, working around the house in the company of adult females, working on the farm with adults and siblings, playing outside with neighborhood children, hunting with adult males, or attending school with age mates, the daily assignment of a child to one or another of these settings has important consequences on the development of habits of interpersonal behavior, consequences that may not be recognized by the socializers who make the assignments. (p. 111)

By making such choices and adjusting tasks and materials to children's competence and needs, adults tacitly guide children's development. Parents designate some objects as appropriate for children, following the recommendations of toy manufacturers and cultural lore. For example, children of different ages are presented with books adjusted to their interests and skills: cardboard or plastic picture books, paper picture books with a few words, books with pictures and text, books with pure text. Adults determine the activities in which children's participation is allowed or discouraged, such as chores, parental work and recreational activities, television shows, the birth of a sibling, or the death of a grandparent. Adults arrange the social environment to promote or avoid certain relationships, by assigning child care to a sibling or grandparent or baby sitter, or encouraging or discouraging particular playmates.

It would be misleading to consider the choice of activities to be the sole responsibility of adults. Children are very active in directing adults towards desirable or away from undesirable activities. Children's preferences are clear in their refusal to enter some activities, and their insistence on others. Their attempts to communicate desire for involvement in specific activities begins during the last half of the first year of life. Rogoff et al. (1984b) cite an example of a 9-month-old attempting to get an adult to work a jack-in-a-box: The baby began by pushing the box across the floor towards the adult, and patted the top of the box when the adult asked "What?" The adult responded to the baby's actions as a request, and asked "Should we make Jack come out?" The adult tried to get the baby to turn the handle (an action too difficult for this 9-month-old), and the baby responded with a series of frustrated yet determined moves—whining and fumbling with the box—that expressed his desire to have the box opened. Finally the adult began to turn the handle and the baby immediately relaxed. The adult asked sympathetically, "Is that what you wanted?" and the baby stared at the handle and let out a big sigh of relief.

Structuring Situations through Division of Responsibility

In addition to arranging and structuring learning activities by providing access and regulating the difficulty of tasks, adults structure children's involvement in learning situations by handling more difficult aspects of the task themselves and organizing the child's involvement with the more manageable aspects of the activity. In engaging the child in an appropriate handling of the situation, the adult creates a "scaffolded" or supported situation in which the child can extend current skills and knowledge to a higher level of competence (Wertsch, 1979; Wood, Bruner, & Ross, 1976). Although the term scaffold could imply a rigid structure or one that does not involve the child, most users of the term include notions of continual revisions of scaffolding responding to children's advancements. Bruner (1983) characterizes scaffolding in language development as the adult acting on a motto of "where before there was a spectator, let there now be a participant" (p. 60).

An example of adult support is provided by the way adults structure children's developing narration skills by asking appropriate questions to organize children's stories or accounts (McNamee, 1980). If the child stops short or leaves out crucial information, the adult prompts, "What happened next?" or "Who else was there?" Such questions implicitly provide children with the cues they need to internalize as they develop narration skills. Adults' questions fill in the outline of what narratives involve. Building on Bruner's perspective, McNamee suggests that "if story schemas exist for young children, they hover in the air between adults and children as they converse" (p. 6).

Adults interacting with children may structure tasks by determining the problem to be solved, the goal, and how the goal can be segmented into manageable subgoals. For example, the joint cleanup of a toddler's room may require the adult, even with a cooperative toddler, to define the goal (cleaning up the room), to segment the task into subgoals (picking up dirty clothes and putting toys in their proper places), and to determine the specifics of each subgoal (e.g., can you find all the blocks and put them in the box?). The adult's structuring of the problem may be tailored to the child's level of skill. With a novice, the adult may take responsibility for managing the subgoals as well as making sure the overall goal is met. A more experienced child may take responsibility for the subgoals, and eventually for the whole task. Such changes in the division of responsibility are an important feature of guided participation, in which the child becomes increasingly responsible for managing the situation as skills increase.

Transfer of Responsibility for Managing Situations

Children take on increasing responsibility for managing situations over the course of years as well as through the process of becoming familiar with a particular task. Effective transfer of responsibility for managing a situation requires adults to be sensitive to children's competence in particular tasks so that responsibility is given when the child is able to handle it. Similarly, such decisions require knowledge (again, it may be tacit) of what skills and knowledge are needed in order to be able to independently handle that situation, and are facilitated by knowledge of the course of development of skill in handling that particular situation. In addition to adults' adjustment of support according to children's skills, children are active in arranging for participation at an appropriate level.

Adults' Adjustment of Support

Scaffolding requires revision as the child gains in understanding. One form of scaffolding involves providing sufficient redundancy in messages so that if a child does not understand one aspect of the communication, other forms are available to make the meaning clear. As children develop greater understanding, adults and older children adjust the level of scaffolding necessary to support the young child's learning and performance by reducing the level of redundancy.

For example, mothers assisting preschoolers in a counting task adjusted the level of their assistance to children's correctness (Saxe, Gearhart, & Guberman, 1984). When children made accurate counts, mothers shifted their directives to a more superordinate level in the task structure so that children had more responsibility for determining the subgoals regarding how to obtain one-to-one correspondence, and when children counted inaccurately, mothers shifted to a subordinate level in the task structure, taking over management of the subgoals themselves.

In early parent-child communication, adults facilitate infants' language acquisition by supporting verbal messages with enough redundant nonverbal information to ensure understanding (Greenfield, 1984). As infants become able to comprehend verbal messages, adults decrease the nonverbal information. Messer (1980) observed that maternal discourse was organized in episodes referring to specific objects, and within the episodes the mothers provided great redundancy regarding the identity of the object of reference. This organization of maternal speech was greatest for younger children, again suggesting that the structure of maternal communication provides a continually modified scaffold for learning.

Researchers in prelinguistic development have noted that adults carry on conversations with infants in which the adult's role as conversational partner is adjusted to the baby's repertoire:

> The mothers work to maintain a conversation despite the inadequacies of their conversational partners. At first they accept burps, yawns, and coughs as well as laughs and coos—but not arm-waving or head movements—as the baby's turn. They fill in for the babies by asking and answering their own questions, and by phrasing questions so that a minimal response can be treated as a reply. Then by seven months the babies become considerably more active partners, and the mothers no longer accept all the baby's vocalizations, only vocalic or consonantal babbles. As the mother raises the ante, the child's development proceeds. (Cazden, 1979, p. 11)

Caregivers simplify their own language, they repeat and expand upon infants' contributions, and they provide visual supports and redundant information to assist an infant's understanding (Bruner, 1981, 1983; Hoff-Ginsberg & Shatz, 1982; Messer, 1980; Moerk, 1983; Snow, 1977; Zukow, Reilly, & Greenfield, 1982). Mothers report that their conversations with 2-year-olds help the children learn to talk (Miller, 1979).

The modification of discourse by adults speaking to infants and young children may provide support for children's conversation and language learning. In the earliest months, the restriction of parental baby talk to a small number of melodic contours may enable infants to abstract vocal prototypes (Papousek et al., 1984).

Caregivers make the context of statements explicit by clarifying their own and the child's intentions and specifying the referents of a statement (Ochs, 1979). Such provision of background knowledge is reduced as children gain language facility. The structure of mother-child discourse allows children to participate in conversations that are beyond their competence in discourse, and may help children advance their skills (Bernstein, 1981). Some evidence regarding the impact of adult language input on children's language development is discussed in a later section on the influence of guided participation.

Children's Role in Arranging Participation

While it is certainly true that adults carry great responsibility in socialization—they are more knowledgeable and have authority—children are also very active in gaining skill through social interaction. Children participate by indicating their readiness for greater responsibility and even by managing the transfer of information. Adults do not simply solve problems and report their solutions, nor do children passively observe adults and extract the relevant information spontaneously. An adult assesses a child's current understanding of the material and adjusts the scaffolding to support the child's developing skill, and the child simultaneously adjusts the pace of instructions and guides the adult in constructing the scaffold.

An example of an infant seeking a more active role is found in Rogoff *et al.*'s (1984b) description of an adult and a 12-month-old working a jack-in-a-box together. Initially, the adult performed all aspects of manipulating the toy (turning the handle to get the bunny out of the box, and pushing the bunny back into the box), while the baby concentrated solemnly on the actions. In the second episode of play with the jack-in-a-box, the baby attempted to push the bunny back in the box, and the adult encouraged, "Close it up," while helping the baby push the lid down. In the third episode, the baby began to participate in cranking the handle, and in the fourth episode the baby seemed to demand some independence in managing the handle while the adult encouraged this involvement:

> The baby grabbed the box on its sides and shoved it back and forth on the tray, and the adult paused in cranking. The baby looked at the crank and slowly reached for it, confirming the adult's interpretation that he had been demanding a turn. Putting the baby's hand on the crank and turning the crank, the adult said, "Okay now, you do it." (Rogoff *et al.*, 1984b, pp. 40–41)

Over the course of this interaction, the baby eventually participated in winding the handle, pushing the bunny back in the box, and closing the box, while the adult supported the baby's involvement by winding the handle to near the end of the cycle and assisting the baby in holding the lid down on the springy bunny.

Negotiations regarding level of participation and the nature of the activity can be managed by babies through eye contact, joint attention, smiles or cries, and posture changes. They can indicate interest by looking eagerly toward an object or event, leaning forward and gesturing toward the object or event with their arms, and making enthused grunts. In a negative situation, or if the adult seems not to understand the baby's cues, the baby's activity may change from joint attention to listlessness, then gaze aversion, and finally to turning away entirely. Kaye (1977) found that 6-month-old infants' actions, especially gaze aversion, controlled their mothers' efforts to teach them to reach around a barrier.

In addition to their contribution to managing joint interaction, young children influence their participation in adults' ongoing activities that may not have interaction with the child as a focus. Children's attempts to learn from adult activities may go unnoticed by parents, who are likely to view children's attempts to "help" or be involved in adult activities as just an inevitable aspect of childhood. During the first year, babies seem to be automatically interested in whatever object an adult is handling, and try to grasp it themselves. An adult's manipulation of a toy facilitates contact by 11- to 13-month-olds with the same toy, with markedly similar actions performed on the toy (Eckerman, Whatley, & McGhee, 1979). Toddlers follow their parents around the house, trying to be involved in ongoing activities. Rheingold (1982) found that children aged 18 to 30 months spontaneously and energetically helped their parents or a stranger in the majority of the household chores that the adults performed in a laboratory or home setting. Many of the parents reported that they commonly circumvented their child's efforts to participate at home by trying to do chores while the child was napping, to avoid the child's "interference."

The propensity to seek proximity to and involvement with adults assists infants and toddlers in acquiring information about the environment and about the activities of the person who is followed (Hay, 1980). Their eagerness to be involved may force a busy parent to give them some role in activities, allowing them to stir the batter, put tape on the present, carry the napkins to the table, help turn the screwdriver, and so on.

In such activities, the adult's and child's roles are likely to fit the characteristics of guided participation. For pragmatic reasons, the adult may try to keep the child from getting involved in an aspect of the activity that is too far beyond the child's skill, for example, to avoid broken eggs, torn wrapping paper, or damage to the child or to objects. On the other hand, the child is likely not to be satisfied with an aspect of the job that is too simple and will insist on greater involvement if given an obvious make-work role. Thus, even in interaction with a reluctant adult, the adult and child together may contribute to the child's learning through guided participation.

An example of how a child's insistence on involvement may be instrumental is provided by my daughter, who at age 3½ was interested in sewing. I was getting ready to leave the house and noticed that a run had started in the foot of my stocking. My daughter volunteered to help sew the run, but I was in a hurry and tried to avoid her involvement by explaining that I didn't want the needle to jab my foot. I began to sew, but could hardly see where I was sewing because my daughter's head was in the way, peering at the sewing. Soon she suggested that I could put the needle into the stocking and she would pull it through, thus avoiding sticking my foot. I agreed and we followed this division of labor for a number of stitches. When I absentmindedly handed my daughter the needle rather than starting a stitch, she gently pressed my hand back toward my foot, and grinned when I glanced at her, realizing the error. The same child at 4 years of age asked me, as we worked in the kitchen, "Can I help you with the can opener by holding onto your hand while you do it? . . . That's how I learn." These incidents illustrate the eagerness with which children approach the possibility of learning through involvement with adult activities, as well as their active role in the "instruction." The child arranges for participation in the activity, and the adult tacitly (sometimes unwillingly) provides access and information.

Does Guided Participation Influence Learning and Development?

Thus far, I have suggested that the integrated role of children seeking involvement and structuring their participation, and of adults providing information and arranging for children's activities, may in part be responsible on a day-to-day basis for the rapid progress of children in becoming socialized participants in the intellectual and social aspects of their society. But the existence of such interaction and arrangements between adults and children does not prove that they are influential in children's learning and development.

I would argue, however, that guided participation does play a role in children's learning and development. So much of what children are able to do requires being embedded in their culture. They would certainly not learn English without exposure to that language, nor would they develop scripts for restaurants, peek-a-boo, or book-reading without involvement in those activities, as observers or participants. Many of the skills that developmental psychologists study are tied closely to the technology (e.g., books, number systems, language, logic, television) of the culture in which children develop and which children learn to master, with the assistance of people who already participate skillfully in culturally important activities.

A variety of studies finds an association between children's experiences and their independent skills. In Rogoff et al.'s (1984b) observations of adults and infants playing with a jack-in-a-box, the infant's understanding of the game script and skill in manipulating the toy improved over the course of repeated episodes in single sessions. Similarly, babies who participated in monthly games of roll-the-ball with their mothers were able to return the ball almost two months earlier than they returned any items in a standard test of infant development (Hodapp, Goldfield, & Boyatzis, 1984). The extent to which mothers expand on infants' pointing gestures by labeling objects is associated with the number of object names in the child's vocabulary (Masur, 1982), and the pattern of joint adult-child construction of propositions from one-word utterances appears to form the foundation of children's combinations of words (Scollon, 1976).

Several studies provide evidence that an important function of social interaction with adults may be the direction of young children's attention. Attention may be an important individual activity that can be channeled by the highlighting of events by social partners. Mothers who more frequently encourage their 4-month-olds' attention to objects, events, and environmental properties have babies with greater speaking vocabularies and Bayley scores at age 12 months, even when the effect of 4-month infant vocalization and the effect of 12-month maternal stimulation are partialed out (Papousek et al., 1984). In an experiment in which the level of maternal focusing of attention was increased (by having an encouraging observer comment on the effectiveness of the mother's naturally occurring efforts to stimulate her infant), infants showed greater exploratory competence as much as two months after the intervention (Belsky, Goode, & Most, 1980). Active involvement of a supportive parent or experimenter in children's exploration of novel objects, compared with these adults' more passive presence, led to more active object exploration by 3- to 7-year-olds (Henderson, 1984a, 1984b).

It is hardly surprising that children learn what they are taught; it is but a short extension to argue that on a day-to-day basis what children learn and are taught contributes to the development of what they know. In this perspective, development is built upon learning, and at the same time, learning is based on development. Children contribute to their own development through their eagerness and management of learning experiences as well as through their employment of the knowledge they already have at hand. At the earliest ages this "knowledge" includes their reflexes and aspects of behavior necessary for eating and protection, as well as primordial schemas for social interaction and learning systems such as language (Slobin, 1973). Soon, however, their inborn behavioral repertoire is modified with experience to reflect their history of learning experiences in the knowledge they bring to each new situation.

CULTURAL UNIVERSALS AND VARIATIONS IN GUIDED PARTICIPATION

Most research on the zone of proximal development, guided participation, scaffolding, and adult-child interaction has involved middle-class parents and children in North America and Britain. How then do the processes observed in such samples relate to the broader spectrum of child-rearing practices around the world? How do observations made in nonindustrial societies relate to and extend our perspective? In this final section, some speculations are offered regarding cultural universals and variations in the processes of guided participation.

Universality of Guided Participation

The general outline of guided participation appears in diverse cultural groups. Caregivers around the world are likely to play an instrumental role in helping children extend their existing knowledge to encompass new situations. Caregivers and children around the world are likely to devote attention to the arrangements of activities for children, and to revise children's roles in activities as their skill and knowledge develop. They are likely to participate in joint activities that serve the function of socializing children to more mature roles in their culture.

Ethnographic accounts of teaching and learning in different cultures suggest that adults structure children's activities and provide well-placed instruction in the context of joint activities, and that children are active participants in their own socialization (Fortes, 1938; Greenfield, 1984; Rogoff, 1986; Ruddle & Chesterfield, 1978). Children participate in the cultural activities of their elders, with adjustment of their responsibilities according to their own initiative and skill. Adults may provide guidance in specific skills in the context of their use. For example, toddlers in India learn at an early age to distinguish the use of their right and left hands, as the former is the clean hand used for eating, and the latter the "dirty" hand used for cleaning oneself after defecation.

> If a child did not learn to eat with the right hand by participation and observation, a mother or older sister would manipulate the right hand and restrain the left until the child understood and did what was required. One of the earliest lessons taught a child of one-and-a-half to two years of age was to distinguish between the right and left hand and their distinctly separate usages. . . . Although we judged that the Indian style of eating required considerable manipulative skill, we observed a girl, not quite two, tear her chapati solely with her right hand and pick up her vegetable with the piece of chapati held in the right hand. (Freed & Freed, 1981, p. 60)

It is notable that the caregivers relied on children's participation as well as structuring the situation, and the children achieved an impressive understanding of the difficult concept required to differentiate right and left. Joint participation and learning through social activity may be especially available to young children, who spend so much of their time in intimate contact with the activities and interpretations of more skilled members of their culture.

Cultural Variations in What Is Learned
and the Means of Transmission

Though the process of guided participation may have widespread use in socialization of children around the world, there are also striking cultural differences in such adult-child interaction. Different cultural groups vary in the skills and values that are fostered, as well as the means used to transmit these culturally appropriate skills and values.

Differences in Skills and Values Promoted

The most important differences across cultures in the social guidance of development involve variation in the skills and values that are promoted. Relevant skills (e.g., reading, weaving, sorcery, healing, eating with the right hand) vary from culture to culture, as do the objects and situations available for the practice of skills and the transmission of values.

Cross-cultural psychologists and sociocultural theorists have argued that basic to the differences in behavior across cultural (or historical) groups are the tools developed for the solution of problems (Cole & Griffin, 1980; Rogoff *et al.*, 1984a; Vygotsky, 1962, 1978). For example, there is speculation that modes of remembering and classifying information vary as a function of the possibility of making lists (Goody, 1977), and that the presence of literacy and Western schooling influence the specific cognitive skills that are practiced and learned (Rogoff, 1981b; Scribner & Cole, 1981). Mathematics skills vary as a function of the technology available—notches on sticks, paper and pencil long division, or hand calculators. Currently, speculations abound regarding the effect computers have on the thinking of children who learn to use them (Papert, 1980). Television's effects on children's thinking and social skills has long been a matter of discussion. Such technologies have been termed "cultural amplifiers," and their function is an integral part of the practice of the skills developed in each culture (Cole & Griffin, 1980).

Skills for the use of cultural amplifiers such as literacy are socialized by parents of very young children even before children have contact with the technology itself. Middle-class U.S. parents teach their children "literate" forms of narrative in preschool discourse, as they embed their children in a way of life in which reading and writing are an integral part of communication, recreation, and livelihood (Cazden, 1979; Taylor, 1983). Picture books made of durable materials are offered to babies and bedtime stories become a part of the baby's daily routine.

A fascinating comparison of middle-class school-oriented practices for inculcating literacy with those of families from two communities whose children have difficulty in reading is available in Heath (1982). Parents in a white Appalachian milltown taught their preschool children a respect for the written word but did not involve book characters or information in the children's everyday lives; their children did well in the first years of learning to read but had difficulty with required to *use* literate skills to express themselves or interpret text. Preschool children of rural origin in a black milltown learned a respect for skillful and creative use of language but were not taught about books or the style of analytic discourse used in school; the difficulty they had in learning to read kept them from making use of their creative skills with language in the school setting. Early childhood in these communities did not include reading and writing in the texture of daily life, and the children experienced difficulties in the use of literacy in school.

Differences in the Means by Which Adults and Children Communicate

Research indicates that adult-child communication strategies vary across cultures (Field, Sostek, Vietze, & Leiderman, 1981; Leiderman, Tulkin, & Rosenfeld, 1977). Such cultural variations in communication strategies would deeply influence the ways in which parents and children collaborate in the child's socialization. If such differences are not recognized, it may be easy for Western researchers to overlook the structuring and joint participation that occurs in other cultures, because it may be at variance with child-rearing practices familiar in middle class Western settings.

The most striking cultural differences may involve the explicitness and intensity of verbal and nonverbal communication, the interactional status roles of children versus adults, and the extent of reliance on face-to-face interaction.

The extent of reliance on explicit, declarative statements compared with tacit, procedural and subtle forms of verbal and nonverbal instruction appears to vary across cultures (Jordan, 1977; Rogoff, 1982; Scribner & Cole, 1973), with an emphasis on explicit verbal statements in cultures that emphasize Western schooling (Rogoff, 1981b; Scribner, 1974). Differences in use of explicit statements may also relate to cultural values regarding the appropriate use of language, subtlety, and silence, as well as to the adequacy of other forms of communication for most purposes. For example, among the Navajo, who have frequently been characterized as teaching quietly by demonstration and guided participation (e.g., Cazden & John, 1971), talk is regarded as a sacred gift not to be used unnecessarily.

Though researchers have focused on talking as the appropriate means of adult-child interaction, this emphasis may reflect a cultural bias in overlooking the information provided by gaze, postural changes, and touch. U.S. infants have been characterized as "packaged" babies who do not have direct skin contact with their caretaker (Whiting, 1981), and often spend more than a third of their time in a room separate from any other people. This may necessitate the use of distal forms of communication such as noise. In contrast, children who are constantly in the company of their caregivers may rely more on nonverbal cues such as direction of gaze or facial expression. And infants who are in almost constant skin-to-skin contact with their mothers may manage effective communication through tactile contact in squirming and postural changes. Consistent with this suggestion that vocalization may be less necessary when there is close contact between adults and infants, Freed and Freed (1981) report work by Lewis in 1977 showing that U.S. infants and small children are less likely to vocalize when held on the lap, and more likely to vocalize when out of the mother's arms and lap.

Another important cultural difference in adult-child communication involves the interactional status of children. In some societies, young children are not expected to serve as conversational peers with adults, initiating interactions and being treated as equals in the conversation (Blount, 1972; Harkness & Super, 1977). Instead, they may speak when spoken to, replying to informational questions, or simply carrying out commands.

Ochs and Schieffelin (1984) suggest that there may be two cultural patterns of speech between children and their caregivers. In cultures that adapt situations to children (as in middle-class U.S. families), caregivers simplify their talk, negotiate meaning with children, cooperate with children in building propositions, and respond to verbal and nonverbal initiations by the child. In cultures that adapt the child to the normal situations of the culture (as in Kaluli, New Guinea and Samoan families), caregivers model unsimplified utterances for the child to repeat to a third party, direct the child to notice others, and build interaction on situational circumstances to which the caregiver wishes the child to respond.

In both patterns, the child participates in activities of the society, but the patterns vary in terms of the child's versus the caregiver's responsibility to adapt in the process of learning or teaching the more mature forms of speech and action. It seems likely that the adaptation of caregivers to children may be more important in societies that segregate children from adult activities, thus requiring them to practice skills or learn information outside of the mature context of use (Rogoff, 1981a). In societies in which children are integrated in adult activities, the child is assured a role in the action (at least as an observer), and socialization may proceed with less explicit child-centered interaction to integrate the child in the activities of society.

Efforts to instruct children may thus vary in terms of the children's responsibility to observe and analyze the task, versus the caregivers' responsibility to decompose the task and motivate the child. Dixon, Levine, Richman, and Brazelton (1984) noted that Gusii (Kenyan) mothers taught their 6- to 36-month-old infants using clear "advance organizers" in instruction, often modeling the expected performance in its entirety, appearing to expect the task to be completed exactly as specified if the child attended to it, giving the children the responsibility for learning. This contrasted with the efforts of American mothers, who concentrated on arousing the child's interest and shaping the child's behavior step by step, providing constant encouragement and refocusing, and taking the responsibility for teaching.

Related to the cultural variations suggested here in the interactional role of children are differences that have been observed in the use of face-to-face interaction. Face-to-face interaction may be a prototype in U.S. research on mother-child communication because of the didactic role assumed by middle-class U.S. mothers, who rely on their own efforts to motivate children to learn, in contrast with communities in which the responsibility for learning belongs to the children. There appears to be cultural variation in the extent to which mothers rely on this position for communication. In many cultures, mothers commonly hold infants facing away from them (Martini & Kirkpatrick, 1981; Sostek, Vietze, Zaslow, Kreiss, van der Waals, & Rubinstein, 1981).

Variation in infant positioning from facing the mother to facing the same way as the mother may reflect cultural values regarding the social world in which the child is to be embedded, as well as the means by which children are socialized. Martini and Kirkpatrick (1981) note that Marquesan mothers (in the South Pacific) appeared strained and awkward when asked to interact with their babies in a face to face orientation. In everyday activities, babies were usually held facing outward and encouraged to interact with and attend to others (especially slightly older siblings) instead of with the mother. The authors report that this is consistent with a general cultural value of embeddedness in a complex social world. Marquesan infants learn a different lesson in their socialization than do U.S. infants engaged in face-to-face interaction, but their mothers appear to provide similarly rich guidance in developing culturally appropriate skills and values. Marquesan mothers actively arrange infants' social interactions with others. If babies appear to get self-absorbed, mothers interrupt and urge attention to the broader social environment:

> [Mothers] consistently provided the infant with an interactively stimulating world, first by interacting, next by encouraging and making effective his attempts to make contact, and finally by directing others to interact with the infant. Caregivers . . . shaped the infants' attention towards others and ob-

jects, and shaped their movements towards effective contact and locomotion. By the end of the first year, infants were becoming interactants able to accompany and learn from older children in an environment supervised by adults. (Martini & Kirkpatrick, 1981, p. 209)

SUMMARY

This chapter proposes that middle-class Western children, as well as children in other cultures, learn and develop in situations of joint involvement with more experienced people in culturally important activities. Adults and children collaborate in children's socialization as they negotiate the nature of children's activities and their responsibilities in participation. They work together to adapt children's knowledge to new situations, to structure problem-solving attempts, and to regulate children's assumption of responsibility for managing the process. This guidance of development includes tacit forms of communication and distal arrangements of children's learning environments, as well as explicit verbal interaction. The mutual roles played by adults and children in children's development rely both on the adults' interest in fostering mature skills and on children's own eagerness to participate in adult activities and push their own development.

These joint socialization roles may be universal, although cultures vary in the goals of socialization and the means used to implement them. Cultures vary in the explicitness or subtlety of verbal and nonverbal communication, the orientation of the infant towards parents versus siblings or other caregivers, the adaptation of children to the adult world or vice versa, and the accessibility of caregivers to infants through proximal and distal forms of communication. The variations as well as the similarities across cultures in how adults and infants interact may be instrumental in the rapid socialization of infants to be participating members of their cultures.

REFERENCES

Bakeman, R., & Adamson, L. B. (1984). Coordinating attention to people and objects in mother-infant and peer-infant interaction. *Child Development, 55*, 1278–1289.

Belsky, J., Goode, M. K., & Most, R. K. (1980). Maternal stimulation and infant exploratory competence: Cross-sectional, correlational, and experimental analyses. *Child Development, 51*, 1163–1178.

Bernstein, L. E. (1981). Language as a product of dialogue. *Discourse Processes, 4*, 117–147.

Blount, B. G. (1972). Parental speech and language acquisition: Some Luo and Samoan examples. *Anthropological Linguistics, 14*, 119–130.

Brazelton, T. B. (1982). Joint regulation of neonate-parent behavior. In E. Z. Tronick (Ed.), *Social interchange in infancy* (pp. 7–22). Baltimore: University Park Press.

Brown, R. (1958). *Words and things*. New York: Free Press.

Bruner, J. S. (1981). Intention in the structure of action and interaction. In L. P. Lipsitt (Ed.), *Advances in infancy research* (Vol. 1, pp. 41–56). Norwood, NJ: Ablex.

Bruner, J. S. (1983). *Child's talk: Learning to use language*. New York: Norton.

Butterworth, G., & Cochran, G. (1980). Towards a mechanism of joint visual attention in human infancy. *International Journal of Behavioral Development, 3*, 253–272.

Cazden, C. (1979). Peekaboo as an instructional model: Discourse development at home and at school. In *Papers and reports on child language development*, No. 17. Stanford University, Department of Linguistics.

Cazden, C. B. & John, V. P. (1971). Learning in American Indian children. In M. L. Wax, S. Diamond, & F. O. Gearing (Eds.), *Anthropological perspectives in education* (pp. 252–272). New York: Basic Books.

Cole, M. (1981, September). *The zone of proximal development: Where culture and cognition create each other* (Report #106). San Diego: University of California, Center for Human Information Processing.

Cole, M., & Griffin, P. (1980). Cultural amplifiers reconsidered. In D. R. Olson (Ed.), *The social foundations of language and thought* (pp. 343–364). New York: Norton & Company.

D'Andrade, R. G. (1981). The cultural part of cognition. *Cognitive Science, 5*, 179–195.

Dixon, S. D., Levine, R. A., Richman, A., & Brazelton, T. B. (1984). Mother-child interaction around a teaching task: An African-American comparison. *Child Development, 55*, 1252–1264.

Eckerman, C. O., Whatley, J. L., & McGhee, L. J. (1979). Approaching and contacting the object another manipulates: A social skill of the one-year-old. *Developmental Psychology, 15*, 585–593.

Erickson, F. (1982). Taught cognitive learning in its immediate environments: A neglected topic in the anthropology of education. *Anthropology and Education Quarterly, 13*, 149–180.

Feinman, S. (1982). Social referencing in infancy. *Merrill-Palmer Quarterly, 28*, 445–470.

Field, T. M., Sostek, A. M., Vietze, P., & Leiderman, P. H. (Eds.). (1981). *Culture and early interactions*. Hillsdale, NJ: Erlbaum.

Fortes, M. (1938). *Social and psychological aspects of education in Taleland*. Oxford: Oxford University Press.

Freed, R. S. & Freed, S. A. (1981). *Enculturation and education in Shanti Nagar: Vol. 57, Part 2. Anthropological Papers of the American Museum of Natural History*. New York.

Furth, H. G. (1974). Two aspects of experience in ontogeny: Development and learning. In H. Reese (Ed.), *Advances in Child Development and Behavior* (Vol. 9, pp. 47–66). New York: Academic Press.

Goody, J. (1977). *The domestication of the savage mind*. Cambridge, MA: Cambridge University Press.

Greenfield, P. M. (1984). A theory of the teacher in the learning activities of everyday life. In B. Rogoff & J. Lave (Eds.), *Everyday cognition: Its development in social context* (pp. 117–138). Cambridge, MA: Harvard University Press.

Gunnar, M. R., & Stone, C. (1984). The effects of positive maternal affect on infant responses to pleasant, ambiguous, and fear-provoking toys. *Child Development, 55*, 1231–1236.

Harkness, S. & Super, C. M. (1977). Why African children are so hard to test. In L. L. Adler (Ed.), *Issues in Cross-Cultural Research. Annals of the New York Academy of Sciences, 285*, 326–331.

Hay, D. F. (1980). Multiple functions of proximity seeking in infancy. *Child Development, 51*, 636–645.

Heath, S. B. (1982). What no bedtime story means: Narrative skills at home and school. *Language in society, 11*, 49–76.

Henderson, B. B. (1984a). Parents and exploration: The effects of context on individual differences in exploratory behavior. *Child Development, 55,* 1237–1245.

Henderson, B. B. (1984b). Social support and exploration. *Child Development, 55,* 1246–1251.

Hodapp, R. M., Goldfield, E. C., & Boyatzis, C. J. (1984). The use and effectiveness of maternal scaffolding in mother-infant games. *Child Development, 55,* 772–781.

Hoff-Ginsberg, E., & Shatz, M. (1982). Linguistic input and the child's acquisition of language. *Psychological Bulletin, 92,* 3–26.

Jordan, C. (1977, February). *Maternal teaching, peer teaching, and school adaptation in an urban Hawaiian population.* Paper presented at the meeting of the Society for Cross-Cultural Research, East Lansing, Michigan.

Kaye, K. (1977). Infants' effects upon their mothers' teaching strategies. In J. D. Glidewell (Ed.), *The social context of learning and development* (pp. 173–206). New York: Gardner Press.

Kaye, K. (1982). Organism, apprentice, and person. In E. Z. Tronick (Ed.), *Social interchange in infancy* (pp. 183–196). Baltimore: University Park Press.

Laboratory of Comparative Human Cognition. (1983). Culture and cognitive development. In W. Kessen (Ed.), *History, theory, and methods.* In P. H. Mussen (Ed.), *Handbook of child psychology* (Vol. I, pp. 294–356). New York: Wiley.

Leiderman, P. H., Tulkin, S. R., & Rosenfeld, A. (Eds.). (1977). *Culture and infancy.* New York: Academic Press.

Lempers, J. D. (1979). Young children's production and comprehension of nonverbal deictic behaviors. *Journal of Genetic Psychology, 135,* 93–102.

Martini, M., & Kirkpatrick, J. (1981). Early interactions in the Marquesas Islands. In T. M. Field, A. M. Sostek, P. Vietze, & P. H. Leiderman (Eds.), *Culture and early interactions* (pp. 189–213). Hillsdale, NJ: Erlbaum.

Masur, E. F. (1982). Mothers' responses to infants' object-related gestures: Influences on lexical development. *Journal of Child Language, 9,* 23–30.

McNamee, G. D. (1980). *The social origins of narrative skills.* Unpublished dissertation, Northwestern University, Evanston, IL.

Mehan, H. (1976). Assessing children's school performance. In J. Beck, C. Jenks, N. Keddie, & M. F. D. Young (Eds.), *Worlds apart* (pp. 161–180). London: Collier McMilian.

Messer, D. J. (1980). The episodic structure of maternal speech to young children. *Journal of Child Language, 7,* 29–40.

Miller, P. J. (1979). *Amy, Wendy, and Beth: Learning language in South Baltimore.* Austin: University of Texas Press.

Moerk, E. L. (1983). *The mother of Eve—as a first language teacher.* Norwood, NJ: Ablex.

Newman, D. (1982, April). Perspective-taking versus content in understanding lies. *Quarterly Newsletter of the Laboratory of Comparative Human Cognition, 4,* 26–29.

Ochs, E. (1979). Introduction: What child language can contribute to pragmatics. In E. Ochs & B. Schieffelin (Eds.), *Developmental pragmatics* (pp. 1–17). New York: Academic Press.

Ochs, E., & Schieffelin, B. B. (1984). Language acquisition and socialization: Three developmental stories and their implications. In R. Schweder & R. LeVine (Eds.), *Culture and its acquisition* (pp. 276–320). Chicago: University of Chicago Press.

Papert, S. (1980). *Mindstorms: Children, computers, and powerful ideas.* New York: Basic Books.

Papousek, M., Papousek, H., & Bornstein, M. H. (1984). The naturalistic vocal environment of young infants. In T. M. Field & N. Fox (Eds.), *Social perception in infants* (pp. 269–297). Norwood, NJ: Ablex.

Poe, P. (1982). Beginning in the bathtub. *American Baby, 44,* (19), 12–20.

Rheingold, H. L. (1982). Little children's participation in the work of adults, a nascent prosocial behavior. *Child Development, 53,* 114–125.

Rogoff, B. (1981a). Adults and peers as agents of socialization: A Highland Guatemalan profile. *Ethos, 9,* 18–36.

Rogoff, B. (1981b). Schooling and the development of cognitive skills. In H. C. Triandis & A. Heron (Eds.), *Handbook of cross-cultural psychology* (Vol. 4, pp. 233–294). Rockleigh, NJ: Allyn & Bacon.

Rogoff, B. (1982). Mode of instruction and memory test performance. *International Journal of Behavioral Development, 5,* 33–48.

Rogoff, B. (1986). Adult assistance of children's learning. In T. E. Raphael (Ed.), *The contexts of school based literacy* (pp. 27–40). New York: Random House.

Rogoff, B., & Gardner, W. P. (1984). Guidance in cognitive development: An examination of mother-child instruction. In B. Rogoff & J. Lave (Eds.), *Everyday cognition: Its development in social context* (pp. 95–116). Cambridge, MA: Harvard University Press.

Rogoff, B., Gauvain, M., & Ellis, S. (1984a). Development viewed in its cultural context. In M. H. Bornstein & M. E. Lamb (Eds.), *Developmental psychology* (pp. 533–571). Hillsdale: NJ: Erlbaum.

Rogoff, B., Malkin, C., & Gilbride, K. (1984b). Interaction with babies as guidance in development. In B. Rogoff & J. V. Wertsch (Eds.), *Children's learning in the "zone of proximal development"* (pp. 31–44). San Francisco: Jossey-Bass.

Ruddle, K., & Chesterfield, R. (1978). Traditional skill training and labor in rural societies. *The Journal of Developing Areas, 12,* 389–398.

Saxe, G. B., Gearhart, M., & Guberman, S. B. (1984). The social organization of early number development. In B. Rogoff & J. V. Wertsch (Eds.), *Children's learning in the "zone of proximal development"* (pp. 19–30). San Francisco: Jossey-Bass.

Schaffer, H. R. (1984). *The child's entry into a social world.* London: Academic Press.

Scollon, R. (1976). *Conversations with a one-year-old.* Honolulu: University Press of Hawaii.

Scribner, S. (1974). Developmental aspects of categorized recall in a West African society. *Cognitive Psychology, 6,* 475–494.

Scribner, S., & Cole, M. (1973). Cognitive consequences of formal and informal education. *Science, 182,* 553–559.

Scribner, S., & Cole, M. (1981). *The psychology of literacy.* Cambridge, MA: Harvard University Press.

Shotter, J., & Newson, J. (1982). An ecological approach to cognitive development: implicate orders, joint action, and intentionality. In G. Butterworth & P. Light (Eds.), *Social cognition: Studies in the development of understanding* (pp. 32–52). Brighton, Sussex: Harvester.

Slobin, D. I. (1973). Cognitive prerequisites for the development of grammar. In C. A. Ferguson & D. I. Slobin (Eds.), *Studies of child language development* (pp. 175–208). New York: Holt, Rinehart, & Winston.

Snow, C. (1977). Mother's speech research: From input to interaction. In C. Snow & C. Ferguson, *Talking to children* (pp. 31–49). New York: Cambridge University Press.

Sorce, J. F., Emde, R. N., Campos, J. J., & Klinnert, M. D. (1985). Maternal emotional signaling: Its effect on the visual cliff behavior of 1-year-olds. *Developmental Psychology, 21,* 195–200.

Sostek, A. M., Vietze, P., Zaslow, M., Kreiss, L., van der Waals, F., & Rubinstein, D. (1981). Social context in caregiver-infant interaction: A film study of Fais and the United States. In T. M. Field, A. M. Sostek, P. Vietze, & P. H. Leiderman (Eds.), *Culture and early interactions* (pp. 21–37). Hillsdale, NJ: Erlbaum.

Taylor, D. (1983). *Family literacy.* Exeter, NH: Heinemann Educational Books.

Valsiner, J. (1984). Construction of the zone of proximal development in adult-child joint action: The socialization of meals. In B. Rogoff & J. V. Wertsch (Eds.), *Children's learning in the "zone of proximal development"* (pp. 65–76). San Francisco: Jossey-Bass.

Vygotsky, L. S. (1962). *Thought and language.* Cambridge, MA: M.I.T. Press.

Vygotsky, L. S. (1978). *Mind in society: The development of higher psychological processes.* Cambridge, MA: Harvard University Press.

Wartofsky, M. (1984). The child's construction of the world and the world's construction of the child. In F. S. Kessel & A. W. Siegel (Eds.), *The child and other cultural inventions* (pp. 188–215). New York: Praeger.

Wertsch, J. V. (1979). From social interaction to higher psychological processes. *Human Development, 22,* 1–22.

Wertsch, J. V. (1984). The zone of proximal development: Some conceptual issues. In B. Rogoff & J. V. Wertsch (Eds.), *Children's learning in the "zone of proximal development"* (pp. 7–18). San Francisco: Jossey-Bass.

Wertsch, J. V. (1985). *Vygotsky and the social formation of mind.* Cambridge, MA: Harvard University Press.

Whiting, B. B. (1980). Culture and social behavior: A model for the development of social behavior. *Ethos, 8,* 95–116.

Whiting, J. W. M. (1981). Environmental constraints on infant care practices. In R. H. Munroe, R. L. Munroe, & B. B. Whiting (Eds.), *Handbook of cross-cultural human development* (pp. 155–179). New York: Garland.

Wood, D., Bruner, J. S., & Ross, G. (1976). The role of tutoring in problem solving. *Journal of Child Psychology and Psychiatry, 17,* 89–100.

Zukow, P. G., Reilly, J., & Greenfield, P. M. (1982). Making the absent present: Facilitating the transition from sensorimotor to linguistic communication. In K. Nelson (Ed.), *Children's language* (Vol. 3, pp. 1–90). New York: Gardner Press.

12

Bringing Babies Back into the Social World

Saul Feinman

'Well! I've often seen a cat without a grin,' thought Alice; 'but a grin without a cat! It's the most curious thing I ever saw in all my life!'
(Dodgson, 1865/1940, p. 94).

Almost everything that Alice encountered in her *Adventures in Wonderland* was somewhat other than it should have been. A baby turned out to be a pig, white roses were painted red by playing-card gardeners, and a cat disappeared into its own grin. Even the author's name, Lewis Carroll, was not real but the pseudonym of Charles Lutwidge Dodgson.

Alice's astonishment as the Cheshire Cat vanished into its own grin might also be an appropriate reaction when we enter the world of developmental research and encounter a plethora of studies that focus on infants' unassisted, asocial individual responses. There can be little question but that *homo sapien* is one of the most social of species and that its young are the quintessential altricial offspring. Furthermore, just as it can be assumed that a white rabbit *will not* have "a waistcoat-pocket or a watch to take out of it" (Dodgson, 1865/1940, p. 2), it is equally reasonable to expect that the altricial young of a highly social species *will* spend much of their time interacting with conspecifics, *will* be dependent upon more mature individuals, and *will* often respond to situations in concert with others rather than as solitary individuals. Consequently, we may feel that, along with Alice, we have gone "down the rabbit hole" when

Saul Feinman • Child and Family Studies, Department of Home Economics, University of Wyoming, Laramie, Wyoming 82071.

we find that developmental research seems to be most interested in how human infants function as solitaires, how they respond to situations without assistance from others, and even perhaps how they develop as individual systems that are closed to social influences.

DOWN THE RABBIT HOLE: SELF-SUFFICIENCY IN INFANCY

Although infants, especially in traditional human societies, are enmeshed in a rich and intricate social web, developmental researchers have conducted literally thousands of studies designed to examine the ways that infants solve problems and respond to stimuli and tasks by themselves. In such investigations—which make up the lion's share of our understanding of cognitive development in infancy—significant others are either physically excluded or, if present, asked not to assist the infant. With the potential influence of other people thus restricted, observation focuses upon how the infant, as an isolated individual entity, reacts to a stimulus, solves a problem, or constructs reality. This removal of social influence from the study of infants' cognitive functioning may be likened to the Mad Hatter's tea party where, although the table is laid for many guests, only the Hatter, the March Hare, and the Dormouse are in attendance.

Developmental research on infancy seems, at least to a considerable degree, to have embraced a paradigm that can be termed the *self-sufficiency perspective*. Despite the undeniable fact that human infants are the altricial, dependent offspring of a highly social species, the self-sufficiency approach downplays the role of the social nexus in influencing infant behavior and development. Furthermore, it directs our attention almost exclusively to the examination of individual behavior, ignoring what the infant can produce in concert with others. As Alice might have said, "Curious and curiouser!"

The Self-Sufficiency Trinity

The self-sufficiency perspective can be seen as a trinity, having three major constituent components, all of which focus on the infant as a separate and solitary entity and stress the philosophical values of achievement through self-reliance and solitude. First of all, the infant is seen as often *responding alone* to stimuli in the environment, without benefit of assistance from others. Second, the infant is seen as facilitating her own development through direct, experiential interaction with the world, and not through reliance upon other people, that is, the infant is seen as *developing alone*. Third, the infant is seen as spending a significant amount of time by herself and as having or acquiring the ability to cope with *being alone*. Thus, the self-sufficiency perspective views human infants as responding alone, developing alone, and being alone.

Responding Alone

Probably the request most commonly made of parents by infant researchers is to refrain from influencing the child, so that her "own" response to the situation can be observed. Be it an encounter with visual stimuli in the habituation paradigm, an unfamiliar adult, or a new physical environment, hundreds of researchers have asked thousands of mothers to let us see how the baby reacts "by herself." If, for example, the baby is seated on the mother's lap during an emotion-discrimination study, the mother is asked to attempt to control her own tactile, tension, and vocal reactions to the stimuli (LaBarbera, Izard, Vietze, & Parisi, 1976). Similarly, in stranger-response studies, researchers have spent about 30 years asking primary caregivers to respond neutrally or in a controlled mildly positive manner when the infant looks to them after the stranger comes into view (Brooks & Lewis, 1976). An even more extreme approach is to try to arrange for the child to be alone when encountering the experimental stimulus (Morgan & Ricciuti, 1969).

Yet, the very methodological efforts that we have to make in order to observe individual response testify to infants' social nature. If infants were not so strongly driven to be influenced by others' reactions, we would not need to control or restrict these reactions. Indeed, the finding that infants were irresistibly drawn to look towards their caregivers when confronted with a novel stimulus was one of the major hints that led to the postulation and investigation of the process of social referencing in which infants' reactions to situations were found to be influenced by their mothers' emotional cues (Feinman, 1982). That it is often difficult, if not impossible, to get infants to focus on a novel stimulus when their mothers have just left the room indicates their disinclination to respond individually. Rather, they would prefer to retrieve the attachment figure first and check out the new environment later, while in the company of that significant other. Not a bad strategy for an altricial, social being, however inconvenient it may be for researchers!

The potency of this infant strategy has been noted by numerous researchers who have suffered subject loss when attempting to study infants in the absence of a significant caregiver. Thus, for instance, when Zarbatany and Lamb (1985) wanted to see how 12-month-olds would be influenced by a familiarized stranger in the absence of the mother, maternal separation made a significant number of infants so distressed that they could not continue to participate in the experiment. But when the influence of the mother was examined (and, therefore, she was present), there was no subject loss due to distress. Furthermore, although it was virtually impossible to get rhesus macaque babies to explore unfamiliar physical objects when their mothers were physically absent, exploration was quite evident when mothers were present (Harlow & Harlow, 1969). Babies—whether human or macaque—seem to take a "first-things-first" approach—and the presence and emotional availability of an attachment figure takes precedence over making sense of novel stimuli.

Developing Alone

While theories of infant development do recognize the existence of social influences in the first years of life, the depth and strength of this cognizance is somewhat limited. Perhaps the strongest indication that infant development is viewed primarily as an asocial matter is found in the Piagetian perspective. Although some of Piaget's earliest writings did acknowledge the impact of peer social influences upon cognitive growth (Forman & Kraker, 1985; Piaget, 1926, 1928), the overall thrust of his work generated a theory of development in which social factors played, at best, a minor role (Piaget & Inhelder, 1966/1969). In the Piagetian view, it is direct experiential contact (motor activity, especially) with the world rather than what is learned from other people that is the primary force that drives the infant's cognitive development. Piaget does not explicitly deny the presence of other people in the developing child's immediate environment. They are there, and the child exists in their social context, but cognitive growth derives mainly from direct experiential learning rather than from social learning.

An analogy can be appropriately drawn between the historical relationship of Switzerland to Europe and that of Piaget's vision of the child's relationship with her social environment. (The fact that Piaget was Swiss makes this analogy especially intriguing.) Although Switzerland is located in Europe, it has been politically, militarily (at least since the 16th century), and somewhat geographically (due to mountainous borders) isolated from other European states. Much of Swiss history appears to be a concerted effort in self-determined isolationism. Analogously, the Piagetian infant lives within a family and community, but develops through what is functionally a socially isolated process. Although there are other people around, the child is primarily interested in exploring the world by herself. As Bruner (1983b, p. 138) has noted, "The world is a quiet place for Piaget's growing child. He is virtually alone in it, a world of objects that he must array in space, time and causal relationships . . . [in which] others give him little help."

Being Alone

Even relatively solitary species with altricial young, e.g., cheetahs, exhibit an affiliative tendency on a more focused scale, that is, the offspring show a notable desire to be in proximity to their primary caregiver. In social species, this pronounced preference for being with a primary caregiver coexists with a broader, less discriminating affiliative tendency (Schachter, 1958) to be in the company of pack, troop, pride, or herd members. As a result, the young altricial offspring of species that do not cache their young are almost always in the company of conspecifics. Being alone when one is altricial and young, and especially if one is a member of a socially organized group of conspecifics, is a rarity indeed.

Of course, altricial young often wander off to investigate the environment. But they return at relatively frequent intervals to touch base (i.e., the secure base phenomenon) and are usually within the visual and/or auditory range of an older conspecific. Anderson's (1972) account of toddlers and their mothers in London parks illustrates this point quite well. The children go off to explore while their mothers stay seated on a bench (the locus of the secure base). They stay within a relatively close radius of this base, are rarely out of their mothers' visual or auditory range, and return to her at frequent intervals for no apparent reason other than to "touch base." On the rare occasion that they stay away for too long, wander too far, or get in over their depth, they are usually retrieved.

Early research studied isolated infants in order to demonstrate the critical role that the familiar social context plays in development. Harlow's investigations of the deleterious effects of social privation upon macaque babies (Harlow & Harlow, 1969; Seay, Hansen, & Harlow, 1962), and the work beginning in the 1950s concerning the impact of separation upon human infants (Bowlby, 1972; Heinicke, 1956; Heinicke & Westheimer, 1966) are salient examples of this theme. More recent work focuses on less dramatic loss of social contact. In the Strange Situation that is commonly utilized to measure attachment (Ainsworth, Blehar, Waters, & Wall, 1978), two of the eight standardized 3-minute-episodes involve the infant's separation from the mother. Although the contemporary state of the art of the Strange Situation indicates that attachment is classified most validly from observations made at the reunion with mother after the separation, some investigators have noted that response at and during separation is significant (Schaffer & Emerson, 1964). And, even with the emphasis on reunion behavior for attachment classification, there is nevertheless a strong interest in how infants behave during brief separations (Adams & Passman, 1981; Weinraub & Lewis, 1977). Most recently, there has been interest in how infants react when mothers are "emotionally unavailable" (Sorce & Emde, 1981), that is, when the infant is in the presence of a significant other but is functionally isolated because of the other's unresponsiveness.

"Being alone" appears to be an accepted part of the everyday routine for infants in modern industrial societies. Although the altricial young of most species rarely sleep alone, American parents are encouraged to have the infant sleep in a separate room and to refrain from responding to all of the infant's noises while asleep. Thus, a contemporary text on pediatric nursing (Scipien, Barnard, Chard, Howe, & Phillips, 1986) notes that "The anxious new parent who puts baby to bed and then returns in one or two minutes to 'see why the baby is crying' needs to be reassured that most babies do cry for a short time when put to bed (p. 594). . . . Encourage parents to put baby in separate room" (p. 598). Benjamin Spock's *Baby and Child Care* devotes five pages to advising parents how to prepare infants and toddlers for separation at bedtime and parental absence from home (Spock, 1968, pp. 351–356). The implication is that infants should be able to (or be socialized to be able to) tolerate "being alone."

This cultural expectation appears to be echoed at least tacitly in infancy research. Earlier work on extreme social isolation appeared to reflect the implicit belief that long-term separation was not healthy for the infant and was difficult if not impossible to cope with. More recent work on less extreme social privation seems to suggest that the infant is capable of coping with brief separation. Although investigators have emphatically stated that attachment classifications are not rank-order judgments, securely attached infants turn out to be those who, upon reunion with the caregiver, approach and make contact with her, but then, after a respectable period of secure-base-touching, return to their play activity (Ainsworth *et al.*, 1978; Lamb, Thompson, Gardner, Charnov, & Estes, 1984; Lamb, Thompson, Gardner, & Charnov, 1985). Thus, "security" of attachment is reflected, in part, by the infant's ability to be alone for at least brief periods of time and then to continue functioning independently after the caregiver has returned.

Generally, developmental research appears to imply that it is important to see how infants function while alone, and that it is reasonable to expect infants to be able to cope with brief periods of solitude. Being alone can perhaps be considered to be the crux of the self-sufficiency trinity, inasmuch as infants who spend time alone, either functionally or physically, will need to be able to respond and develop alone as well.

The Ecological Validity of the Self-Sufficiency Perspective

Although it does seem odd to view altricial, social organisms as responding, developing and being alone, the ecological validity of this self-sufficiency perspective may be a matter of cultural variation as to the extent to which human infants do indeed spend time alone and need to function without assistance. If they are left alone either literally or functionally (i.e., if other people are present but unavailable) for significant periods of time, then they will need to be able to cope with being, responding, and developing alone.

In hunting and gathering groups—the quintessential human society that Bowlby (1969) refers to as our environment of evolutionary adaptiveness—infants are rarely if ever alone. "In many cultures, especially in Africa, South America, and parts of Asia, mothers and infants are almost inseparable, with babies carried around all day in slings on their mothers' backs or sides" (Lamb & Bornstein, 1987, p. 48). Konner's (1972, 1977) description of infancy in the Zhun/Twa hunter-gatherers of southern Africa is representative of infants' social experiences among many traditional peoples. For the first few weeks after birth, infants are carried around virtually all the time by their mothers. This pattern of contact forms the template for a high-frequency, on-demand continual feeding schedule, and for a high level of maternal responsiveness. Konner notes that Zhun/Twa mothers virtually never ignore rhythmical crying; not only are infants fed when they cry, but their close proximity to mothers sometimes allows the mother to anticipate the cry and feed the infant before crying occurs. This pattern is typical of that found in most carrying species (Blurton Jones, 1972).

As infants mature, they spend less time in proximity to their mothers but the overall frequency of maternal contact still remains very high. Separation from mother, when it occurs, does not leave the infant alone, but, rather, in the company of other familiar people—a pattern noted by Ainsworth (1967) for the Ganda as well.

From the beginning, infants also spend a lot of time in the company of other people. When carried about by the mother, the infant attracts much attention, especially from prepubescent girls. Later on as a toddler, the child joins in the company of a mixed-age play group, following the group as much as possible, and often being carried by the older children when she tires. Rather than being excluded from adult gatherings, infants are held, kissed, touched, talked to, and passed from person to person as adults sit together around the fire. Furthermore, the physical locus of children's play and adults' work areas often overlap, and infants have relatively easy access to adults' work objects. Thus, infants are integrated into, rather than segregated from, the broad social world of the adult community. In this ecological setting, in which infants are virtually never alone and often participate in the active, multifaceted social world of adults and older children, the self-sufficiency perspective would not appear to possess much validity.

In contemporary, western, industrial societies, although infants do spend a considerable amount of time in the company of responsive primary caregivers and other people (Feinman & Roberts, 1986), and often receive social assistance in making sense of the world (Whiten, 1977), the levels of contact, responsiveness, and assistance are considerably lower than in traditional societies (Konner, 1977). The physical separation of children's living and sleeping space from that of the adults was noted by Smith (1983, p. 17) in her description of childhood in Edwardian England: "The nursery was generally at the very top of the house, as remote as possible from adult life below." A more recent account echoes this arrangement: "If babies are as far from parents as possible during sleeping hours, parents and infants both sleep better" (Scipien et al., 1986, p. 594). It would appear that babies do spend a fair amount of time "beyond the pale" of the modern adult settlement.

Because infants in industrial societies are more likely to be physically separated and socially isolated (e.g., taking a nap in a crib in a separate bedroom), and because of greater concern about "spoiling" the child (which achieved its most extreme expression in the rather Draconian child-rearing philosophy of Truby King [Newson & Newson, 1974]), adults tend to be less responsive to infant crying. Thus, Wolff (1969) noted that American mothers sometimes ignored infants' rhythmical cries, a finding that Konner (1972) attributes to the greater ease of blocking out the irritation of infant crying when separated from it by one or more solid walls. Child-rearing practices such as these would seem to be reasonably compatible with the self-sufficiency *zeitgeist.*

In contrast, one explanation of the very high stress experienced by Japanese babies separated from mother in the Strange Situation (Lamb *et al.*, 1985) is that they had rarely, if ever, experienced separation before, even when asleep (Caudill & Weinstein, 1969; Lebra, 1976). The Japanese pattern appears to fall somewhere in between the polar extremes represented by the Zhun/Twa and the United States. Perhaps the greater the deviation of the infant's social arrangements from the highly integrated pattern noted in hunter-gatherer groups, the greater the validity of the self-sufficiency perspective for understanding infants.

From a less relativistic vantage point, the appropriateness of the self-sufficiency approach to raising and studying infants may be more questionable. Bowlby (1969) and others (e.g., Feinman, 1980; Tiger, 1987) have suggested that the ethos and environment of hunting and gathering is the ecological setting for which all humans, not just hunter-gatherers, are best suited. In this light, cultural perspectives which deviate radically from this basic template will not be especially adaptive, or will at least cause considerable difficulty. For example, although it is possible for humans, as a diurnally-oriented species, to accommodate to a nocturnal existence, the adjustment is not an easy one (Melbin, 1987).

Similarly, deviation in modern societies from the basic carrying and continuous feeding strategy utilized by human hunter-gatherers (Blurton Jones, 1972) appears to be associated with increased crying and digestive upset.

If human infants are best adapted to social arrangements in which they are rarely, if ever, alone, and in which they receive assistance in making sense of the environment, then modern practices that deviate significantly from this pattern are likely to result in negative outcomes and considerable upset. Similarly, scientific perspectives that emphasize the infant's aloneness—even if it is encouraged and facilitated by the culture and by parental practices—are likely to be off target. Thus, even in modern societies, the self-sufficiency approach may be somewhat flawed.

The Origins of the Self-Sufficiency Perspective on Infancy

Three central values that are prescribed for adults in modern societies appear to form the ideological nucleus of childrearing and scientific beliefs about self-sufficiency: (1) individual achievement, (2) solitude, and (3) self-reliance. Among traditional peoples, these characteristics are not especially desired for adults, let alone for infants. In most traditional societies, valued activities, for example, hunting, yield group products rather than, or at least in addition to, individual accomplishments (Service, 1979; Turnbull, 1961). Instead of self-reliance and solitude, many preliterate societies emphasize social participation and dependency, as illustrated in Dorothy Lee's (1959) account of Margaret Mead's perspective on food distribution among the Arapesh:

> The ideal distribution of food is for each person to eat food grown by another, eat game killed by another, eat pork from pigs that have been fed by people at a distance. . . It is insured that every mouthful the Arapesh consumes has been the medium of social participation. (p. 155)

The values of individual achievement, solitude, and self-reliance do, however, occupy a place of distinction and honor in modern western societies. Anticipatory socialization prepares even very young children to behave in accordance with these standards; thus, such values come to form the core of child-rearing goals. Researchers, as enculturated societal members, probably pick up these values through their own direct participation in the culture as well as by noting that parents and children are influenced by them.

Achievement

Modern western societies value achievement and hard work, not just for the goods and services that they yield, but as ends in themselves. Achievement motivation, the work ethic, and upward mobility can be recognized as moral as well as practical values in modern industrialism and in the forerunners of that way of life (McClelland, 1961; Weber, 1920/1958). Furthermore, the individualistic emphasis in industrial nation states, that is, the belief that accomplishments by individuals are more important than those by groups, leads to a stress upon individual achievement and individual performance (see recent work on individualism and competition in education, Johnson & Johnson, 1987; Kohn, 1986).

The values of achievement, hard work, upward mobility, and individualism appear to have become associated with our conceptualization of development. At least implicitly, we have come to view development as achievement, and to regard developmental milestones in infancy as accomplishments. In industrial society, development is the realm in which the infant is encouraged to achieve. Parents in modern western societies seem to expect that particular stages will be "achieved" or reached by certain ages, and they engage in socialization to ensure that these timetables are met. Although parents in traditional societies may be as pleased as we are about such developments, they are not as likely to match the intensity of our future-oriented concern about the timeline of developmental achievement (Bruner, 1983b, p. 131).

Although achievement may be psychologically satisfying, it also is task-oriented, often a struggle, and not necessarily enjoyable. Analogously, the language that we use to describe development, even in infancy, makes the process sound like hard, task-oriented work rather than pleasure or fun. After all, we do refer to developmental achievements as developmental *tasks*! It is in this view of development-as-work (in contrast to development-as-fun) that Bruner describes Piaget (and by implication his view of children's development) as "Swiss, Protestant, logical, obsessed, driven into his eighties" (Bruner, 1983b, p. 138).

Just as achievement is seen as the means to upward mobility, development is usually conceptualized as an upward progression of ordinally-ranked stages, that is, "development-as-upward-mobility." Nonetheless, development within the lifespan is no more inherently a series of ordinally-ranked steps than sociocultural evolution represents movement from lower to higher social forms (the spectre of Herbert Spencer!) or than species evolution is a sequentially ordered progression towards superior life forms. Thus, in commenting upon her observation of human-like patterns of hunting among baboons, Strum (1987, p. 132) notes, "I had thought I had witnessed an evolutionary step forward—if 'forward' means 'more like human.'" Analogously, Bruner (1983b, p. 131) suggests that "Human beings, whatever their age, are completed forms of what they are. Growing is becoming different, not better or faster." In this light, individual development can be viewed as change, plain and simple, as a nominal array rather than an ordinal sequence, without any implications of improvement or of forward or upward movement.

An even more radical view is that development constitutes downward rather than upward progression. The finding that physiological responsivity to caloric load (i.e., knowing when one has had enough to eat) is more sensitive in young children than adults (Birch & Deysher, 1986) is consistent with the conceptualization of development as a downward progression. That children become capable of more rather than less deceptive behavior as they mature (Bretherton, 1984) also fits with this view of "development as growing down." Perhaps the most eloquent statement of this view is that offered by the naturalist Aldo Leopold in *A Sand County Almanac* (1949):

> When I call to mind my earliest impressions, I wonder whether the process ordinarily referred to as growing up is not actually a process of growing down; whether experience, so much touted among adults as the thing children lack, is not actually a progressive dilution of the essentials by the trivialities of living (p. 120).

The perception of development as an upward progression—and not as nonordered or downward—implies that just as the career development of a young adult is seen as the application of hard work in the pursuit of higher levels of accomplishment, development is seen as the way that the infant reaches more advanced stages of motor, cognitive and social activity (i.e., "cradle careers"). And, just as we place a premium upon individual accomplishments at school or work, development in infancy is thought of as individual achievement. Indeed, the accounting of accomplishment in infancy centers even more exclusively upon what each individual does. For adults, we recognize the importance not only of each person's performance (e.g., the batting average of a single baseball player), but of group products as well (e.g., how many games a baseball team wins). In contrast, studying the development of the infants in a child care center would focus exclusively upon what each individual infant had accomplished, with any consideration of "group achievement" being merely an average of individual scores.

The conceptualization of development as individual achievement in which hard work is expended in the service of an upwardly mobile progression of skill attainment is the philosophical cornerstone of the self-sufficiency edifice. It is in the context and service of achievement that solitude and self-reliance function; the infant is expected not only to subsist but to achieve higher levels of development as well. Survival and maintenance through solitude and self-reliance is difficult enough for altricial young. To be expected to grow and achieve new heights under such asocial circumstances further dramatizes the scale of what is expected from the infant.

Solitude

The valuing of individual achievement does not, of necessity or by definition, mean that the individual cannot be assisted by others. Thus, although the accomplishment per se is considered a product of the individual, it need not be achieved in solitude or without guidance from others. Solitude and self-reliance in development are espoused not because they are logically implied by individual achievement but, rather, because they are socially valued.

"I find it wholesome to be alone the greater part of the time . . . I love to be alone. I never found the companion that was so companionable as solitude." So said Henry David Thoreau (1854/1866, p. 147) in his essay Solitude in Walden. Thoreau's apostolic preaching of the virtues of solitude goes so far as to equate the needs of people with those of asocial life forms or inanimate objects—"I am no more lonely . . . than Walden Pond itself. What company has that lonely lake, I pray?" (Thoreau, 1854/1866, p. 148). Perhaps the valuation of solitude is greatest in societies with a widely dispersed distribution of small settlements scattered over a large land mass (e.g., USA or Canada) or which have geographically isolated pockets that are remote from other population centers (e.g., the high mountain pastures and valleys of the Appenzell in northwestern Switzerland). Or possibly it is associated with the belief that solitude shields the individual from evil, and that being alone is a nobler religious state: "God is alone, —but the devil, he is far from being alone; he sees a great deal of company; he is legion" (Thoreau, 1854/1866, p. 149).

Being alone and somewhat socially isolated is the culturally prescribed condition for the nuclear family in many industrial societies. In combination with the tendency to keep young children in the home until age 5 or 6, this belief has functioned to isolate the mother-infant dyad—a trend that has weakened recently, primarily because of the reentry of women into the labor force (Feinman & Lewis, 1984). When mother and infant stay home together for much of the day, infants spend a good deal of their time either by themselves or in a relatively limited social context, that is, with one person. Indeed, the isolated dyadic arrangement of American and English children during the last several generations may have led not only to less contact with other people but with the mother as well. Thus, Konner (1977) has noted that babies in hunter-gatherer and other traditional societies (e.g., !Kung, Guatemala) spend more time than American or English middle-class babies not only with other people but with their mothers as well. The finding of greater maternal avoidance of infants in isolated than in group living mother-infant pairs among several monkey species (Hinde & Spencer-Booth, 1967; Kaplan, 1972; Wolfheim, Jensen, & Bobbitt, 1970) may be analogous to this difference between traditional and modern societies.

Furthermore, within the home, modern child-rearing advice advocates the desirability of separate rooms for each child. With its possible origins in the individual cells of the anchoritic monastery and the middle-class Victorian inclination to place children's living quarters at some distance from the adult household (Smith, 1983), the provision of separate rooms for children, even in infancy, would seem to result in more time alone for the infant.

Solitude is also the culturally prescribed circumstance in which learning, thinking, and working are supposed to occur. "A man thinking or working is always alone, let him be where he will. The really diligent student in one of the crowded hives of Cambridge College is as solitary as a dervis in the desert" (Thoreau, 1854/1866, p. 147). Whether one is aiming to learn about one's self or about the physical environs, solitary study and isolation come highly recommended to us in our homes, schools, and workplaces. The value of being alone is advocated even for babies, as in the suggestion that parents be advised to allow "the baby some time to be alone to begin learning about the environment" (Scipien et al., 1986, p. 594). Piaget's quiet, solitary childhood world of cognitive development, with its detachment "from the hurly-burly of the human condition" (Bruner, 1983b, p. 138) reflects this belief in the virtue of solitude.

The value of quiet solitude seems to be reflected in the closed system models (von Bertalanffy, 1981) that are the underpinnings of much of the modern developmental psychology of infancy. Unlike the noisy, hectic and incredibly unpredictable open system world of the child in earlier theories of infant development (e.g., Freud, 1920/1952), more recent work, with its experimental and methodological bent, produces "quieter" data by forcing the child into a closed system paradigm. As Valsiner (1984) has suggested, developmental psychology's embracement of an asocial closed model of child development may be the product of its emulation of the hard science models of classical mechanics (physics envy?) in which the richness of environmental factors was sacrificed in favor of a cleaner but simplified experimental method. Whatever the ecological validity of this simplification for the physical sciences, its acceptance in the study of infant development leads to a closed system solitudinous model of child development in which social forces do not play a significant role.

Self-Reliance

In his poignant description of the value system of Appalachia, which he termed "The Mountain Ethos," Kai Erikson notes that the core values of all human societies are contrasting tendencies, of which the most far-reaching and influential is the tension between "a sense of independence . . . and a need for dependence" (Erikson, 1976, p. 88). The Piagetian metatheory of the self-reliant child, and the focusing of research upon the infant's own response to stimuli reflect one particular resolution of the independence versus dependence question, specifically an answer that, although recognizing the importance of dependency, finds greater salience and desirability in independence. The stronger emphasis of independence over dependence in developmental theory probably reflects the resolution of this issue within the society at large.

Among traditional peoples, excessive self-reliance is likely to be frowned upon. Although the group as an entity would probably be economically self-sufficient, no one individual or nuclear family is likely to be so. If such societies produced a developmental theorist, she would probably view the developing child as being greatly influenced by other people, as often responding in concert with other people, and as inextricably enmeshed in the intimacy of the social nexus.

Occidental agrarian and industrial societies, while not denying the importance of cooperative effort and social facilitation, place special importance upon the fruits of self-reliant labor. In America, self-reliance is glorified in the image of the self-sufficient farm family of the colonial and federal period. With fairly simple agrarian tools and much hard work, each family produced all that it needed and was self-sufficient, especially over the mountains on the western frontier. The division of labor in the family, which sent solitary individuals off to perform specific tasks during much of the day, called for each person to rely upon his or her own labor and wits (Larkin, 1988, Ch. 1). The westward migration across the Great Plains during the later part of the 19th century further emphasized and reified the values of self-reliance on the frontier.

The ethos of self-reliance found its most fervent advocate in the person of the 19th century American philosopher, Ralph Waldo Emerson. In his essay *Self-Reliance*, Emerson argued, "It is only as a man puts off all foreign support and stands alone that I see him to be strong and to prevail. . . Is not a man better than a town" (1865/1883, p. 87). In 19th century American fiction, the cause of self-reliance was championed by none more strenuously than Horatio Alger in his many stories for prepubescent children (for boys, really). Through determination, hard work, honesty, and some good fortune, Alger's young heroes rise from a childhood of poverty to an adulthood of wealth and esteem (Alger,

1866/1962). In contrast, Alger's villains (also young) start out with all of the advantages of privilege but, despite (or, indeed, perhaps because of) such assistance, fall from grace.

It is interesting to note that the good fortune that befell the prototypical boy hero of Alger's stories usually took the form of a small but significant "foot up" provided by a benefactor. Thus, the extreme philosophy of individualism found in the writings of Emerson and others, for example, Adam Smith (1784/1937), is tempered by Alger's advocacy of the doctrine of stewardship in which a benefactor provides a small financial start and some continued guidance to the ambitious but honest boy. Similarly, Elinore Pruitt Stewart's account of early 20th century life in Wyoming, *Letters of a Woman Homesteader* (1914; portrayed in the movie *Heartland*), juxtaposes the snowbound isolation of a solitary canyon cabin with the gathering of neighbors from a 30-mile radius for a wedding or funeral.

This individualistic philosophy of self-reliance appears to be equally germane to the lives of contemporary industrial peoples. The proliferation of popular publications in the self-help genre tells readers to be their own best friends, to try to solve problems on their own, to become full people in their own right before entering into relationships with others, and to look out for Number 1. This "ugly individualism," as Kohn (1986) calls it in his critique of competition in modern society, may be an even more extreme statement of the self-sufficiency ethic than that expressed in previous centuries. So strong is the desire of many people in modern society to perceive themselves as independent actors and free-thinkers that, even when it is abundantly clear that they have been swayed by others, they deny the impact of this influence (Hood & Sherif, 1962; Webster, 1975).

The self-reliance theme that runs through contemporary developmental research on infancy parallels that found in the broader society at large. Just as economic success in western, capitalistic society is viewed as resting primarily upon what the individual can do for himself or herself, development is regarded as a lone venture for the child. Indeed, it has been suggested (Bruner, 1984) that Piaget is the developmental theorist of capitalism. In much the same way as the theory of dependence (the notion that workers' lives were or should be regulated for them) was rejected by the rising middle class in the 18th century, Bowlby (1969) avoided the term "dependency" in describing the relationship of the child with her caregiver, choosing to use the term "attachment" instead. In the development of children as in the development of capitalism, dependency would appear to be a dirty word. Thus, the social desirability of self-reliant rugged individualism that pervades western society is reflected in theory about infant development as well.

RETURNING TO SOCIAL REALITY THROUGH SOCIAL GUIDANCE

Meanwhile in Moscow and Chicago

As a boy growing up in the Belorussian town of Gomel, Lev Vygot-sky (1896–1934) resided in an intimate environment of warmth, in-quisitiveness, and interaction. At home with his parents and his many brothers and sisters, Vygotsky was enveloped in a rich social context that facilitated learning through conversation: "The dining room was . . . a place for communication as there was invariably lively and interesting conversation during the obligatory evening tea at a large table. Talks over the samovar were one of the family traditions which played an important role in the formation of the mentality of all the children" (Levitin, 1982, quoted in Wertsch, 1985, p. 4). As an adult, his work took him to Moscow in the 1920s, a time of Marxist ideological fervor during which the leitmotif of societal influence upon the indi-vidual was in the air.

From this background emerged the hypothesis that the acquisition and performance of any new skill occurs twice—first socially with the guidance of other people, and later solitarily by the individual without assistance. Linked to this conceptualization of development was Vygot-sky's interest in what children could accomplish with the *zone of proximal development*, "the distance between the actual developmental level as determined by independent problem solving and the level of potential development as determined through problem solving under adult guid-ance or in collaboration with more capable peers" (Vygotsky, 1978, p. 86). (Actually, Vygotsky seems also to have included peers of equal ability as legitimate collaborators in the zone [Vygotsky, 1978, pp. 87–88]). Rather than viewing development as a lone venture for the young child, Vygotsky envisioned it as an inherently and necessarily social process.

At about the time that Lev Semenovich Vygotsky, in Moscow, was formulating his ideas about the zone of proximal development (and for a good many years before), George Herbert Mead (1868–1931) was lectur-ing to flocks of students at the University of Chicago about (among many other ideas) the notion that the origins of thought were to be found in social life. "It is absurd to look at the mind simply from the standpoint of the individual human organism; for, although it has its focus there, it is essentially a social phenomenon; even its biological functions are primarily social" (Mead, 1934, p. 133). For Mead, not in-clined to let himself become an insulated, detached observer amidst the hustle and bustle of early 20th century life in the raw and open city of Chicago, social reality was an undeniable, external and objective fact of life that had a powerful impact upon individual thought and action (Coser, 1971, p. 353).

The availability through release and English translation of Vygotsky's work (1934/1962, 1978) to western developmental psychologists helped to stimulate the formulation of a revised, more socially-oriented conceptualization of development. Mead's impact upon developmental research was delayed primarily by disciplinary barriers and intellectual insularity. Because Mead's students were sociologists, social psychologists and philosophers, his ideas did not find their way into developmental psychology. During the last decade or so, however, Mead's views about the social formation of mind have become more closely associated with developmental theory, resulting in contemporary research which is more clearly cognizant of the importance of social influences in development.

Social Guidance in Infant Development

Inspired by Vygotsky's concept of the zone of proximal development and Mead's sociological emphasis upon the social formation of mind, a social guidance zeitgeist has made its presence felt in recent years. In this guidance-in-development view, an adult (or older child) guides the infant's learning by "arranging appropriate sequences of materials and tasks and by transmitting information and strategies to her as they participate together in an activity" (Rogoff, Malkin, & Gilbride, 1984, p. 33). The influence of this method is hypothesized to be most powerfully expressed in the realm of Vygotsky's zone of proximal development, where effective solutions emanate within the socially facilitative context of joint activity. Nonetheless, social guidance can also occur outside of the zone, inasmuch as infants are inclined to be receptive to adult input even in situations where they are developmentally ready to formulate an independent response.

Due to such receptivity, the infant's development is guided by the adult's provision of both *structure* and *meaning*. Through organizing, arranging, and simplifying tasks, sequencing and ordering activities, offering opportunities, limiting access, managing focus, and gradually transferring responsibility to the child, the adult structures the infant's participation. By conveying information, strategies and definitions, the adult endows the situation with meaning. For example, when adults were asked to encourage a baby to talk and to play with toys, including a jack-in-the-box (Rogoff *et al.*, 1984), they structured the joint activity for the infant (managed focus and involvement with the toys), and offered meaning (showed the baby that they interpreted as funny the popping out of the jack-in-the-box—actually a bunny-in-the-box).

The guiding of infant behavior and development through structure and meaning occurs naturally, and usually in the absence of adult self-awareness that teaching is occurring (Rogoff *et al.*, 1984). It is found in many commonplace activities that occur when adults and infants "work" together, for example, during meal-time (Valsiner, 1984), and when they play together (Rogoff *et al.*, 1984). Social guidance of development has been observed in traditional as well as modern societies, as exemplified by Bruner's (1976) description of how !Kung adults induct the young into unfamiliar situations through playing, dancing, singing, sitting and storytelling.

The social guidance theme also can be detected in recent interest in the role of mentoring in the development of young adults (Bronfenbrenner, 1988) and, in particular, the question of whether there are western counterparts to the Japanese *sensei* (*xiansheng* in Chinese)—the teacher or master who guides development of character as well as skill. It is interesting to note that the character of *sensei* or master was highlighted in popular American cinema (the *Star Wars* trilogy and *The Karate Kid*) at about the same time that the social guidance theme began to emerge in developmental research. In *The Karate Kid*, Daniel learns karate and acquires character and courage through the definitions conveyed to him by his *sensei*, for example, when Mr. Miyage tells him that karate is to be used for defense only. But he also is influenced by the environmental structure created for him by the *sensei*: the car-washing, deck-sanding, and fence-painting activities that Mr. Miyage arranges for him are, in actuality, experiences in which he learns the basic defensive maneuvers of karate. As with a parent guiding development in infancy, the *sensei's* mentoring provides both structure and meaning to facilitate the pupil's development.

Guidance through Structure: Scaffolding

The initial movement away from the self-sufficiency perspective involved the component of social guidance that is least antagonistic to the virtue of self-sufficiency, namely, the provision of structure but not of meaning. Creating facilitative structures that make it easier for the child to construct the meaning of the situation is more ideologically in tune with the ethos of self-help than is the furnishing of meaning itself. Following an untempered self-sufficiency approach, a baby who encounters a new toy would be left to her own devices in figuring out what to do with it. In a modest move away from total self-sufficiency, the adult structures or "scaffolds" the environment so as to increase the infant's chances of responding adaptively, and then lets the infant do the rest by herself.

In the guidance-through-structure approach, which first surfaced in developmental research during the mid-1970s (e.g., Wood, Bruner, & Ross, 1976) and best known by the term "scaffolding," the adult guides by supporting, tutoring, structuring, and constructing a framework–a scaffold–which facilitates the infant's development. Within scaffolding, the adult very rarely, if ever, provides exact demonstrations of the specific desired actions. Indeed, one salient theme that runs through the scaffolding literature is the concern that "too much" assistance not be offered to the child. Development is to be guided more through facilitation than direct tuition, that is, through structure rather than meaning. The adult helps the infant along by supporting her activities with a scaffold, but it is ultimately up to the infant to define the situation and complete the task.

As is implied by the term "scaffolding" itself, there is a spatial, topographical and physical metaphor implicit in the guidance-through-structuring process. An associated theme is that of management and, in particular, the managing of physical variables—actual as well as metaphorical. Thus, Wood et al. (1976) note that scaffolding includes adult activities such as recruitment, reduction in degrees of freedom, direction maintenance, marking critical features, and frustration control. Each of these techniques involves spatial metaphor (e.g., marking critical features), management (e.g., frustration control), or both (e.g., direction maintenance). Such methods were used by an adult tutor (experimenter) to assist preschool children in constructing a model with interlocking wooden blocks. The tutor structured and managed the child's block activities but allowed "him to do as much as possible for himself" and "where possible . . . she left the child to his own devices" (Wood et al., 1976, p. 92).

The theme of "help, but not too much of it" also emerges in Bruner's discussion of how his Language Acquisition Support System (LASS) supports Chomsky's (1965) Language Acquisition Device (LAD; Bruner, 1983a, in an essay written in the 1970s). Bruner argues that the adult facilitates the child's language development by introducing new procedures within a scaffold that ensures "that the child's ineptitudes can be rescued or rectified by appropriate intervention" (Bruner, 1983a, p. 60), and then gradually removing this support structure while handing over the procedure to the child (the "handover principle," as Bruner calls it).

Guidance through environmental structure and opportunity management is emphasized in Valsiner's (1984, 1985) concepts of the zone of free movement (ZFM) and the zone of promoted actions (ZPA), and in a related study of meal socialization during infancy. Valsiner defines the zone of free movement as "the area of environment, or subset of objects in an area, and a set of allowed actions with these objects which the child has unlimited access to in his/her individual exploratory actions" (Valsiner, 1985, p. 136). The zone of promoted actions is a "sub-part (subset) of the ZFM that the adult and sibling caregivers try to promote for the developing child" (Valsiner, 1985, p. 136), that is, those actions which are encouraged. While meanings and definitions delineate the boundaries of the ZFM and ZPA, it is the structure afforded to the child by the promotion or restriction of access to opportunities that constitutes the primary social influence of these zones upon development.

The scaffolding view of guidance-in-development, with its emphasis upon organization and management, its utilization of structure to facilitate the infant's discovery of meaning, and its concern that "too much" assistance not be offered, has come to provide theoretical direction for a significant, although still relatively small, number of recent investigations of infant development. Jumping off from Bruner's earlier work (Bruner & Sherwood, 1976; Ratner & Bruner, 1978) on scaffolding within the context of mother-infant games, Hodapp, Goldfield and Boyatzis (1984) examined maternal scaffolding in the games of roll-the-ball and peek-a-boo between 8 and 16 months. Structuring behaviors such as attention-getting and physical stage-setting were often performed by the mother and served to raise the infant's level of participation in the game. Indeed, the infants were usually able to perform game-related actions, for example, returning or uncovering, within the game context before they exhibited such behavior in cognitive testing. Similarly, Ross and Lollis (1987) found that when structure was temporarily withdrawn, that is, when the adult failed to initiate turn-taking, 9- to 18-month-old infants emphatically communicated their need for it to be restored. Vandell and Wilson (1987) noted that siblings as well as mothers provide scaffolding for 6- to 9-month-olds. Infant peers do not seem to offer such structural guidance for each other; rather, competence in peer relations during infancy may be enhanced through scaffolded experiences with more sophisticated interaction partners.

Although the guidance-through-structure perspective upon which scaffolding is founded does allow the infant to rely upon others to some degree, it still tacitly maintains a high expectation for self-sufficiency. In what could be termed its "minimalist" approach to assistance, such guidance aims to have the infant contribute as much as she possibly can, inasmuch as the adult provides a scaffold but insists that the infant determine the meaning of the situation by herself. Structural guidance appears to implicitly say to the infant "we will put you in the right place, organize the environment for you, give you a few hints . . . but then it's up to you," an approach that is very much in line ideologically with

Horatio Alger's doctrine of stewardship in which a benefactor provides a step up to the hero.

Guidance through Meaning: Social Referencing

A more "generous" approach to social guidance is found in social referencing—"a process characterized by the use of one's perception of other persons' interpretations of the situation to form one's own interpretation of that situation" (Feinman, 1982, p. 445). In social referencing, meaning per se about how to feel and perhaps also what to do with regard to an object or event is provided. Thus, the adult strays even further from the expectation for infant self-sufficiency by offering an answer rather than scaffolding the environment so that an answer can be discovered by the infant. In the referencing paradigm, an infant who encounters a new toy and looks quizzically towards her father will get an answer—rather than merely a hint or facilitative structuring—to her tacit questioning. The father's smile or joyous tone of voice indicates a positive interpretation of the toy, while a frown tells his daughter that he did not like it. Through facial, vocal, or tactile expression of emotion, adults can influence the infant's interpretation of whether the stimulus is something to be liked or disliked, something to feel happy or sad about. Being influenced about "how to feel" does not necessarily provide direct behavioral models to imitate. Consequently, the integrity of infant self-sufficiency in the translation of emotional reaction into specific behavior is preserved pretty much intact.

Referencing messages can take on a more instrumental, action-oriented form which influences "what to do" in addition to "how to feel." For example, in responding pleasurably to the new toy, the father may end up showing his infant daughter how to hold and manipulate it. The provision of guidance about behavior as well as feelings reduces self-sufficiency somewhat more. Thus, emotional referencing is a more self-sufficient process than instrumental referencing inasmuch as the latter shapes specific behaviors as well as attitudes while the former directly influences attitudes only.

The typical emotional referencing study utilizes an experimental paradigm in which the adult employs facially or vocally expressed emotional cues to provide a message that is linked to the referent object or event. Such investigations have found that infants respond more favorably to the referent after receiving a positive message than after receiving a neutral or negative message. Children between 9 and 18 months respond less reluctantly and more enthusiastically (e.g., smile more, approach more readily) to a reduced visual cliff (Sorce, Emde, Campos,

& Klinnert, 1985), new toys or toy-like objects (Feinman & Roberts, 1988; Hornik, Risenhoover, & Gunnar, 1987; Klinnert, 1984; Svejda & Campos, 1982; Zarbatany & Lamb, 1985) and adult strangers (Boccia & Campos, 1983; Feinman & Lewis, 1983; Feinman, Roberts & Morissette, 1986) after seeing or hearing a positive message. Instrumental communication was found to modify infants' contact with a large black rabbit (e.g., techniques for touching the rabbit) in the one study that has aimed to distinguish empirically between emotional and instrumental referencing (Hornik & Gunnar, 1988).

There is also evidence that a selectivity postulate, that is, the prediction that infants will be more influenced by some people than by others (Campos & Stenberg, 1981; Feinman, 1982), influences referencing outcomes. Zarbatany and Lamb (1985) found that, despite similar rates of infant looking to mother and stranger, only the mother influenced infant behavior to the toy. Klinnert, Emde, Butterfield and Campos (1986) reported that a stranger's response to a toy robot affected infant behavior when the mother appeared puzzled, suggesting that a knowledgeable stranger may be a better referee than an apparently confused mother. Although referencing implies an overall reduction in self-sufficiency, the selectivity findings indicate that infants may be more self-reliant when the adult appears to be less trustworthy or knowledgeable.

Similarly, the ambiguity postulate proposes that social referencing is more likely to occur in equivocal situations (Campos & Stenberg, 1981; Feinman, 1982, 1985; Klinnert, Campos, Sorce, Emde, & Svejda, 1983). Sorce et al. (1985; J. J. Campos, personal communication, April, 1981) noted a major impact of mother's message upon infant's crossing behavior of a reduced visual cliff (an ambiguous event), but no influence upon crossing behavior for the clearcut stimuli of either a surface with no depth cues or a full visual cliff. Zarbatany and Lamb (1985) found that initially uncertain infants were more influenced than were initially fearful infants. Gunnar and Stone (1984) noted a stronger referencing effect with an ambiguous toy than with pleasant or aversive toys. Thus, the increased reliance upon others' influence appears to be especially salient when the situation is ambiguous. In contrast, clearcut situations seem to encourage infants to rely more upon their own interpretations.

The basic prediction of social referencing theory, that is, that interpretive meaning about how to feel and what to do influences the infant, contrasts markedly with the self-sufficiency perspective on development. It suggests that the social guidance provided through the influence of others' interpretative meaning plays a significant role in how the infant comes to make sense of the world. The two major postulates of referencing theory, however—selectivity and ambiguity—temper that claim by noting that there are circumstances in which the infant becomes reluctant to depend upon other people and is more self-reliant in defining situations. To quote the title of an earlier work: "Mother knows best but sometimes I know better" (Feinman, 1985).

The definition of social referencing noted above envisions a broad conceptualization of this process, allowing for a wide range of variations which differ as to the levels of infant self-sufficiency they imply. Adults could wait until the infant has initially appraised the situation before providing their own interpretation. In this case, referencing performs a reappraisal function, influencing the infant only after she has formulated an initial understanding of the event. Studies in which the adult provides a referencing message only after the infant appears to have reacted to the stimulus fit within the referencing-as-reappraisal mold. For example, Sorce et al. (1985) asked the mother to display facially expressed emotion only after the child had looked at the reduced visual cliff and then glanced at her. In contrast, referencing can influence initial appraisal if the adults convey their opinions before the baby has constructed a preliminary definition of the situation. In studies that my colleagues and I have done on referencing-as-initial-appraisal, interpretative emotional meaning is provided by the mother as soon as the referent stimulus—an adult female stranger (Feinman & Lewis, 1983; Feinman et al., 1986) or a toy robot (Feinman & Roberts, 1988)—appears.

Referencing-as-reappraisal affords the infant a greater degree of self-sufficiency, allowing her to figure things out for herself before any adults provide assistance. Only after she has tried by herself to understand it does anyone attempt to influence her. Social influence prior to initial appraisal implies a lower expectation for infant self-reliance, reflecting a more socially enmeshed, proactive and intrusive image of social referencing's role in development.

Referencing may also vary with regard to whether the infant has to elicit adult provision of interpretative meaning (solicited referencing) or if it is volunteered (offered referencing). In some studies the adult provides a message only if the baby requests it, for example, by first looking at the object and then to the adult. For example, in Klinnert's (1984) investigation of the impact of mother's emotional communication upon infants' reactions to unusual toys, approximately 40% of the original sample was eliminated from consideration because they did not appear to be soliciting referencing from the mother. In contrast, in Svejda and Campos's (1982) study on the impact of vocally expressed emotion upon infants' encounters with toys, the mother offered the referencing message when the infant began to move towards the toy—regardless of whether she seemed to be requesting such information. In solicited referencing, meaning is provided only if requested; offered referencing, in contrast, calls for the adult to "catch the gaze" of the infant (Langhorst, 1983) or otherwise engage her attention in order to provide interpretative meaning.

Clearly, offered social referencing deviates further than solicited referencing from the self-sufficiency paradigm. The solicited form of referencing implies a higher level of self-reliance because the assistance that the infant receives is triggered by her own actions. In contrast, by providing assistance before it is requested, the adult may be seen as removing a degree of freedom from the infant's cognitive processing of the stimulus and, thus, reducing the infant's independence in offered referencing.

The definition of social referencing followed in this chapter (Feinman, 1982, 1983) has been termed the "broad" conceptualization of referencing (Bretherton, 1984; Uzgiris & Kruper, in press). Within what is, by comparison, called the "narrow" conceptualization, referencing would be a label restricted to affective, solicited and reappraisal situations, thus removing instrumental, offered and initial appraisal referencing from the realm of the phenomenon (Campos, 1983; Klinnert *et al.*, 1983). It is probably not coincidental that the forms of referencing excluded when the conceptualization is constricted are those that are most alien to the self-sufficiency perspective. Interestingly, the narrow conceptualization is accepted by those researchers whose interest in referencing derives from their earlier work on emotional development (Klinnert *et al.*, 1983), a phenomenon that has been influenced more by traditions in individual psychology than social psychology. In contrast, the broad conceptualization which I proposed (Feinman, 1982) is reflective of my own interest in referencing as social influence and as a social construction of reality process. This sociological focus appears to lend itself to a more radical departure from the self-sufficiency paradigm.

How Social Guidance Brings Babies Only Part of the Way Back

In the social guidance perspective, help from others is viewed as important because it assists the infant in developing to the point where she can function self-sufficiently. Thus, the "raison d'être" for social guidance is not that it enables infants and adults to solve problems together in the here and now but, rather, that it endows the infant with the capacity to function alone later on. What the infant accomplishes with assistance is viewed, at least tacitly, as an intermediate, transitional product of a developmental process in which the ultimate end-product is individual accomplishment. The social-product outcomes of scaffolding and referencing that result from dyadic or group action appear not to be valued in themselves but, rather, as a means of facilitating the infant's self-sufficient performance.

Although Vygotsky did criticize the practice of testing children only for what they can accomplish by themselves, he still referred to self-reliant performance as the "*actual* developmental level" while calling that which occurs in conjunction with others the "*potential* developmental level" (Vygotsky, 1978, p. 85). Similarly, the title of Griffin and Cole's (1984) article on learning within the zone of proximal development—"Current activity for the future"—reflects the forward-looking orientation of the social guidance perspective and its implicit relegation of the social products of such guidance to the category of means rather than valued goals. Probably the clearest exposition of this view of socially shared accomplishment as a discounted transitional state is found in the three-stage model of development (Bruner, 1983a; Campione, Brown, Ferrara, & Bryant, 1984) in which first the adult does all for the child, next the adult and child share in the product, and finally the child does it all by herself. In this model, the ultimate intention is to advance the infant's individual development rather than to produce collective social solutions within infant-adult dyads or larger groups.

Within some situations, for example, socialization of eating, the goal of self-sufficiency seems to be naturalistically appropriate. "The adult begins with full control over the spoon and uses it to get food to the child's mouth. The end goal for the adult is for the child to use the spoon efficiently without any dependence on the adult. Gradually, control over the actions involving the spoon is transferred from the adult to the child" (Valsiner, 1984, p. 71). In other realms of activity, however, socially produced outcomes may be appropriate not only as transitional states on the road to self-sufficiency but also as legitimate end products in themselves. Thus, even if a child is capable of building a tower of blocks by herself, she may wish to engage in this activity with her parent—not necessarily because she needs assistance but because social products are often superior ("None of us is as smart as all of us"[Kohn, 1987, p. 54]), and because the company and conversation of social activity is enjoyable in itself.

By viewing socially assisted outcomes as intermediate states on the path to individually independent action, the social guidance perspective downplays the importance of social products as end-goals in themselves. Furthermore, this view also ignores the importance of social guidance in socialization of the infant for learning to "play in the sand box" (without kicking sand in others' faces!). When working and playing with others is seen as a means for enabling the individual infant to be able to function independently, social interaction comes to be viewed as an activity that the infant engages in because she needs to obtain assistance rather than as something that she does because she enjoys it. This view devalues the intrinsic salience of social products in themselves, and paints an overly individualistic portrait of life in human groups.

Furthermore, even the joint products that do occur within the context of social guidance often are not allowed to express their full social nature. Because of the caveat that the adult provide no more than the minimum assistance needed in scaffolding, the observed performance is not really what the infant and adult could produce together, but, rather, what the infant can accomplish with some assistance from the adult. Similarly, research in the social referencing paradigm does not call for the adult and infant to create, through truly dyadic interaction, a collective understanding of the situation. Rather, the adult communicates a definitional message about the situation to the infant and then usually restricts any further interaction with the infant so that the impact of this message upon the infant's individual response to the situation can be observed.

In a social world, the infant develops as an individual with assistance from other people. The social guidance perspective's acknowledgement of this component of the social nature of the infant's *umwelt* is reflected in its focus upon investigating how the structure and meaning that others provide facilitates individual performance. But the social nature of the infant's environment also includes cooperative action that results in the creation of joint, socially shared products. It is this shared-response aspect of sociality that the social guidance perspective has not incorporated into its view of infant development. Thus, although social guidance brings babies part of the way back into the social world by recognizing the influence of others upon individual infant response, it still maintains the self-sufficiency perspective's blindness to infant participation in the generation of joint, social response.

THE REST OF THE WAY BACK THROUGH SOCIAL PRODUCTION

A Full Social Psychology of Infancy

A comprehensive social psychological account of human social life calls for answers to two conceptually distinct questions. The first focuses upon how individuals socially influence each other, and how they are affected by interacting in groups. The relevant dependent outcomes here are individual perceptions, thoughts, actions, and development. Clearly, the social guidance perspective falls under the rubric of this approach inasmuch as it investigates the influence of others upon individual performance and development. Through scaffolding and social referencing, infants are exposed to and influenced by structure and meaning provided by other people.

The second component of a full social psychological view is more distinctly sociological in that it focuses upon dependent outcomes that are the characteristics of social entities per se rather than of individuals. Here the emphasis is placed upon how groups process information, respond to situations, solve problems, and maintain social integrity. The generation of group outcomes, that is, social production, and the development of the group as a superorganic integrated system are the issues of concern in this approach. Thus, research is directed to studying the manner in which individuals work together in a group to produce collectively formulated outcomes.

Research on the social entities to which infants belong, for example, infant-parent dyads, families, peer dyads, has focused either upon the ways in which infants are socially guided or upon how the individuals interact and get along with each other (e.g., attachment, infant-sibling relationships). But the ways in which infants in concert with others generate social products has been virtually ignored. Although research on infants' social relationships and their social guidance has greatly enhanced our knowledge of the infant's social world, a *full* social psychological understanding of infancy requires the consideration of social production within the social entities to which infants belong.

The Significance of Social Entities and their Properties

Socially produced outcomes, that is, accomplishments that result when two or more people work together cooperatively, are a part of the life of any group-living individual. While a self-sufficiency orientation might view such collective solutions as "second best"—what you have to settle for when you can't do it by yourself—group accomplishments are sometimes more highly valued expressly because of, rather than despite, their social character.

Once we recognize the existence of social products, we also must acknowledge the social entities that produce them. The existential reality of social entities is a concept that goes at least as far back as the French sociological theorist, Emile Durkheim's notion of "social facts," properties of group life that have their own characteristics, existence, and reality independent of specific individuals (Durkheim, 1895/1938). Contemporary small groups research has paid much attention to social products and processes that are associated with groups per se, such as goals, valued activities, status structure, judgment, problems solving, and learning—superorganic phenomena that transcend the individual group members (Ridgeway, 1983; Shaw, 1981). Similarly, the concept of family developmental tasks (Duvall & Miller, 1985, Ch. 3) suggests that families as well as individuals are faced with problems to solve and goals to reach. Thus, groups as well as individuals process information, formulate responses, and engage in action.

Just as individuals change, evolve, grow and develop, so do families and friendships. That social entities can evolve and develop is indicated in Bales' (1970) work on how small groups of apparently equal-status individuals develop so that inequality emerges out of the initial equality. Similarly, the concept of family life cycle (Duvall & Miller, 1985, Ch. 3) suggests that families change and develop. From a sociological perspective, the concepts of existence, production and development are as applicable to dyads, families, small groups, communities, and societies as to individuals.

Although infants do participate in dyads, families and other social entities, their involvement in group processes and group products has been ignored. Sociologists —who study group activities and outcomes—have pretty much ignored infancy. Developmental psychologists—who study infancy—have failed "to deal adequately with dyadic [let alone group] interactions" (Feldman, 1985, p. 104). Nevertheless, Feldman did note that "rapprochement between social and developmental psychology is viable" (p. 104), a theme that underlies Feinman and Lewis's (1984) effort to illustrate how social psychological principles concerning small group dynamics could be applied to those groups which included infants and toddlers.

Recognition of the existential reality of the mother-infant dyad and of characteristics that are attributed to that dyad as a social entity per se (rather than to either individual person in it) is implicit in research on the synchronization of tempo and content in mother-infant interaction (Fogel, 1977; Stern, 1977). Clearly, by its very nature and definition, synchrony is a feature of the dyad rather than of either individual. The existence, characteristics and products of social entities to which infants belong has been explicitly noted in discussions of social guidance. For example, Saxe, Gearhart, and Guberman (1984) characterize the goals that are established when mothers teach their children about numbers as being "located neither in the head of the mother nor in that of the child" (p. 29). Similarly, Vygotsky has been interpreted as implying that processes such as thinking and memory can be attributed to groups as well as to individuals (Rogoff & Wertsch, 1984; Wertsch, 1985, pp. 60–61): ". . . mental functions, such as thinking, reasoning, problem solving, or logical memory can be carried out in collaboration by several people . . . as well as by an individual. That is, dyads or groups as well as individuals can be agents that think and remember" (Rogoff & Wertsch, 1984, p. 2).

Social Products as Well as Social Assistance

Self-sufficiency calls for the infant to solve problems within an atmosphere of self-reliant solitude—either actual physical solitude or functional solitude in which other people, although physically present, do not provide assistance. Social guidance removes the requirement for self-reliance and solitude from learning. The infant does not have to figure out the answer all by herself; others can help in this process. Nonetheless, although others can assist the infant in formulating her response to the situation, she is expected to produce the response per se by herself.

Social guidance seems to follow a traditional educational model in which the adult is the teacher and the infant is the pupil. Indeed, the very titles of some articles testify to the recognition of this metaphor for infants, for example, "Parents as teachers" (Brachfeld-Child, 1986), "The role of the older child as teacher for the younger" (Stewart, 1983), as well as for more verbal children, for example, "Maternal teaching strategies" (Laosa, 1978, 1980). In this pedagogical model, the teacher helps the pupil to understand, but the pupil is required to perform on her own. Although the teacher may be present when the pupil performs (i.e., is tested), she will not collaborate with the pupil then in producing a joint response. In the social guidance of infants, the adult functions much like a traditional teacher. She helps the child figure out a solution to the problem but then withdraws as much as possible to allow for the emergence of the individually based response that derives from such learning. Thus, while learning is social, response is not. If indeed the adult does assist the infant in producing a jointly created outcome, it is with the expectation that the near future will witness self-sufficient performance by the child.

Social guidance releases the infant from the necessity of learning alone. Releasing her from the necessity of acting alone is accomplished by expanding our conceptualization of the meaning of adult-infant interaction, so as to view it as an opportunity to generate social products. Just as small groups research in social psychology examines how the group as a whole responds to a problem or task, so we can ask how adult-infant dyads formulate collective solutions.

It is interesting to note that education research has begun recently to ask how children formulate and produce social responses in cooperation with their peers (Johnson & Johnson, 1987; Kohn, 1986). Inasmuch as the social guidance model of adult-infant interaction is founded upon the template of a traditional view of student learning and performance, the emergence of interest in social products within educational psychology suggests that a similar interest would be appropriate in developmental psychology as well.

Viewing interaction not only as facilitating infant development, but also as generating social products that are salient in and of themselves, changes the way in which we investigate social interaction in infancy. In this more sociological view, play between the infant and her parent could be studied not only to consider how each individual influences the other but also with an eye to examining socially produced outcomes. Similarly, an adult might engage the child in activity that is not directed as much towards facilitating infant development as it is towards finding a common plane on which they can interact in the present. Such outcomes occur in joint or negotiated social referencing, in which mutual influence between adult and infant as to the definition of the situation results in a collectively agreed-upon understanding—an understanding which is a dyadic product (Emde, in press). Similarly, although social games are usually conceptualized as indices or facilitators of the infant's cognitive and social development (Gustafson, Green, & West, 1979; Ross, 1982; Ross & Goldman, 1977), they can also be thought of as being the socially produced outcomes of infant-adult or infant-peer dyadic interaction.

Social guidance research has focused almost exclusively upon adult-infant interaction probably because older siblings are less effective guides than adults, and infant peers provide virtually no guidance (Vandell & Wilson, 1987). From a social product perspective, however, sibling and even peer interaction becomes more interesting. Even if the participants cannot guide each other's development, their interaction may very well yield some socially produced outcomes. Although previous sibling and peer research in infancy (e.g., Dunn & Kendrick, 1982; Mueller & Brenner, 1977) has tacitly embraced a social influence model by examining how each individual affects the other, it has not considered the nature of the collective outcomes that can be produced in sibling and peer dyads. A social product orientation would sensitize us to the importance of examining such outcomes in infants' interactions with peers and siblings as well as with adults.

Developmental research on infancy has examined how the behavior of one individual impacts upon that of another. For example, attachment research has investigated the influence of maternal sensitivity upon the security of infant attachment (Ainsworth *et al.*, 1978). Conversely, investigators have looked at how the infant's characteristics or behavior affect the adult, for example, the effect of infant crying on adults (Boukydis, 1985). Furthermore, there is a virtual cornucopia of studies that examine how infants interact, get along, and form relationships with mothers, fathers, siblings, grandparents, substitute caregivers, and peers (e.g., DeStefano & Mueller, 1982; Dunn & Kendrick, 1982; Lamb, 1978; Myers, Jarvis, & Creasey, 1987; Ragozin, 1980).

But infant research has neglected to examine the collective products, reactions and problem-solving that result from infants' social interaction with others. Even in the rare instances when what could be considered social products are studied (e.g., social games, joint play), research usually focuses upon how these products aid future infant development or reflect the concurrent developmental status of the infant. A social production approach to examining infant development would emphasize the importance of studying cognition and problem solving within the context of collective outcomes that infants generate not by themselves but, rather, in concert with others.

The Nature of Social Production during Infancy

The social product view of interaction is cognizant of the existence and significance of self-reliant information processing and action, and of socially enabled individual outcomes. But it also recognizes that these activities do not constitute the be-all-and-end-all of the infant's world. Because infants in their natural environments do participate in social as well as individual outcomes, the ecological and content validity of a perspective that neglects to acknowledge this social involvement is bound to be compromised. Widening the angle of the lens through which we see infancy produces a richer and more natural image of infant activity and development.

Naturalness and Ease of Interaction

When the infant is expected to appraise and act self-sufficiently, the adult is asked to follow the rule of being physically present but informationally-unavailable. Within the social guidance paradigm, the adult is expected to abide by the rule of providing "help, but not too much of it." These modalities of interacting with infants are similar to many formal educational encounters, not only in the intended goal, but in style as well. Such interchanges between adult and infant, as between teacher and pupil, cannot be characterized as free-flowing, relaxed, or spontaneous. Rather, the adult or teacher functions within the context of a role which defines, shapes, and restricts her behavior with the child.

That such modes of behavior when interacting with infants occur in everyday settings cannot be denied; self-sufficiency and social guidance are not the hypothetical inventions of infant researchers. Parents and teachers *do* utilize these approaches in attempting to facilitate learning and development. Self-sufficiency and social guidance in child-rearing and school-based education involve rule-based interaction in structured circumstances, characterized by a noticeable degree of restrictiveness, self-restraint, and loss of spontaneity.

The self-restraint that is required by the rules of self-sufficiency and social guidance seems to rub against the natural inclination to be nurturant with young children. Often, the desire to interact with infants in a freer and more generous manner breaks through the barriers of self-restraint. Thus, Wood *et al.* (1976) reported that the adult experimenter in their study often strayed from the path carved out by the rules that limited the amount of assistance she was to provide. They noted that many of these "transgressions" or "violations" derived from the "tendency to offer more help than allowed by the rules" (Wood *et al.*, 1976, p. 96).

Similarly, although mothers in a social referencing study were asked to restrict the duration of communication to their infants about a stranger, they talked considerably longer, especially when providing a positive message (Feinman & Lewis, 1983). Being more vigorous in restraining the length of the communication seemed to make everyone— mothers and experimenters alike—uncomfortable, and it interfered with the natural interactional flow. Rather than try to stem the tide of more free-flowing interaction of mother with infant, we relaxed the rules somewhat and then statistically controlled for message length in analyzing the data. It seemed to be easier and more appropriate to control data analysis than to control mothers!

Similar results occur when child-rearing advice encourages parents to curb "excessive" responsivity to their children, as illustrated dramatically in the Newsons' discussion of the Truby King Mothercraft doctrine that influenced infant care in England during the 1930s. "One's baby screamed and tears splashed down one's cheeks while milk gushed through one's jersey. But one must never pick the baby up—it was practically incestuous to enjoy one's baby" (Newson & Newson, 1974, p. 62). Although mothers did attempt to suppress the natural urge to respond to their babies' hunger and distress, the sense of angst that emerges from the first-hand accounts narrated by the Newsons is emotionally exhausting. Many mothers did finally rise up in revolt against such restrictiveness, returning to a more nurturant and comfortable style of infant care. As one mother put it, "My daughter was born during the Truby King period, and it took a month of untold agony for myself and the child before I threw every book I had out of the house and all my well-meaning and Truby King-obsessed relatives with them.

From then on, mother and child progressed happily" (Newson & Newson, 1974, p. 62).

Perhaps what is seen when adults "break the rules" that restrict free interaction in self-sufficiency and social guidance situations is an emergence of the way in which they would prefer to behave with infants. That this more free-flowing and amicable interaction is characterized by the indulgence that has been described for adult-child interaction in traditional peoples (Konner, 1977) is not especially surprising. Indeed, the restrictions imposed by some research paradigms and child rearing methods seem to go against the grain of what adults would prefer (*ceteris paribus*) to be doing with infants.

The joint production of an outcome seems to require fewer rules that restrict what the adult can or cannot do for/with the child. And when rules do not dominate, interaction can be more relaxed and spontaneous, free of anxiety about going beyond the delineated boundaries. Interacting with the infant to generate a jointly produced outcome, with little concern for a strict accounting of who contributes how much to the effort, allows the adult's behavior to be less stylized and self-conscious.

There is a certain quality of "uptightness" to self-sufficiency, social guidance, and formal educational interactions with children that is relieved considerably when the focus shifts to a socially generated joint outcome. Working together with a child to produce a joint outcome loosens up the stiffness and relieves tension in the interaction for two functionally interwoven yet conceptually distinct reasons. There is less need for rules and role-playing, inasmuch as the adult can relax and just interact naturally with the infant. Furthermore, generating a social product through cooperative interaction calls for a greater level of adult involvement and help—behavior that occurs naturally in many "violations" within the self-sufficiency and social guidance paradigms. Social-production-driven interaction seems to function through more nurturant and helping modes of adult behavior that are very natural and comfortable for adults when they interact with babies.

Intersubjectivity

In social guidance, with its emphasis upon progress and development, assistance is oriented towards altering the child's subjective understanding of the situation to bring it into comformity with the adult view. Thus, the achievement of a common perspective on the world, that is, intersubjectivity, proceeds by getting the infant to see the world through older eyes. There is an implicit standard of correctness in this arrangement: The adult perspective is viewed as the more valid one.

Adult accommodation to the child's perspective is merely an intermediate step taken to establish the rapport needed to get the child ultimately to understand the situation as the adult does. Similarly, there is also an implicit inequality in social guidance: The adult, as the representative of the desirable viewpoint, clearly is the higher status actor.

In contrast, creating a socially formulated product with a young child makes the adult more of an equal partner—a collaborator rather than a tutor. Intersubjectivity is achieved by finding common ground rather than by adult insistence that her own grown-up view is the one to be followed. Not only will the adult modify the infant's understanding of the situation, but the infant will influence the adult as well; thus social influence will be bidirectional and mutual. Instead of playing Pygmalion by molding and shaping the infant's behavior, the adult more readily accepts the child in her present state as a fully formed (although smaller) collaborator. Although the infant will, in all likelihood, learn and develop through this collaboration, the upward-and-onward goal that drives guidance-in-development interchanges is much less in evidence within adult-infant dyad social production. As a result, intersubjectivity does not derive from adult manipulation, however gentle, of the infant's understanding but, rather, represents the common meeting ground of the perspectives of the two actors.

Where does self-sufficiency fit in this scheme of things? At first glance, it would seem that leaving an infant to figure out a situation on her own implies an acceptance of the infant's contemporaneous perspective. But having the infant figure out the situation by herself is only half of the story. We expect the infant not only to be self-sufficient in formulating a response, but to arrive at the correct, adult-approved response as well. If an infant, on her own, comes up with an answer that does not indicate progress along the developmental path towards eventual adult maturity and sophistication, her self-sufficient trajectory is intercepted by well-meaning adults who guide her in the "right" direction. Despite what looks like a hands-off, laissez-faire attitude, the self-sufficiency perspective sees the infant's viewpoint as something to be managed, shaped, and modified.

Social guidance aims to reorient the infant so that eventually she comes to see the world through adult-tinted glasses. The self-sufficiency view envisions the infant as needing less guidance in correcting her vision of the world, but still expects that such change will nevertheless occur. Both of these perspectives emphasize the salience of development as an upward progression in which the child matures and/or is socialized into the adult mold. In either of these frameworks, the infant's present view of the world is seen as an intermediate stage in the process of growing up and, therefore, as being in need of developmental change. In contrast, a social product orientation is more accepting of the infant's current understanding, and lacks the missionary zeal of the "gospel according to adulthood."

Temporal and Task Orientation

With their valuation of the developmental achievement, self-sufficiency and social guidance look to the future. Interaction with infants today is oriented towards what the child will be able to do tomorrow on her own. The adult's pleasure derives from knowing that she has helped the child to achieve and progress. Within this perspective, the relevant end-products of what goes on today are to be observed in the future.

In contrast, social production focuses on the here and now, on joint outcomes that can be appreciated for what they offer contemporaneously and not just for what they contribute to the future development of the infant. By focusing on the present, on what the infant and adult together can do today, the social product paradigm implicitly espouses a certain degree of what perhaps can be termed "developmental relativism." The importance of growth and maturation are by no means denied when an adult interacts with an infant to produce a meaningful joint outcome in the present. Nonetheless, the social product approach encourages a more relativistic view by emphasizing the salience of what can be accomplished in the here and now. By so doing, it implicitly suggests that although achievement for the future is important, accomplishment in the present is just as significant. Furthermore, it seems to be telling us that in the rush to help the infant develop for the future, we should not forget to "enjoy the moment."

A forward-looking concern for achievement and progress seems to go hand-in-hand with a developmental task orientation. The word "task" in everyday language conjures up the image of something—especially something tedious or difficult—that is done because it needs to be done or out of a sense of duty. There is a distinct absence of expectation for pleasure or fun in the word "task," other than perhaps for the sense of accomplishment and/or relief that derives from its completion. Perhaps becoming habituated to the phrase "developmental task" has desensitized us to its semantic implications of difficulty, tediousness, duty, and necessity. These connotative meanings seem to become more evident when we substitute the fair synonym of "chore" for "task." Performing "developmental chores" doesn't sound particularly enjoyable or exciting, does it!

Task orientation also characterizes formal educational models which emphasize individual achievement, although in this setting tasks are typically referred to as "assignments"—another term that does not exactly inspire visions of revelry. Analogously, the image of development that is portrayed by both the self-sufficiency and social guidance perspectives emphasizes the importance of progress and achievement through the mastery of developmental tasks. A task-oriented approach to development, socialization and education would seem to engender a sense of "development as a task," a chore that, while not especially fun to engage in, must nonetheless be done.

The social product approach seems to have a more pleasure-oriented quality to it. Although such interchanges are productive, the emphasis upon task completion is less relentless because the adult may be willing to reshape the task goal so that it is enjoyable. It may be that adult-infant dyadic task aims are redefined more readily because the orientation towards task completion is modulated by a present-oriented, genial, *gemutlich,* "pleasure-of-your-company" quality in their interaction. This feature of social production seems to imbue adult-infant interaction with a greater sense of fun, and perhaps reflects a somewhat more tempered achievement orientation. In contrast, social guidance interactions are less likely to be thusly diverted, given the educational orientation of the adult-infant interchange. Similarly, adult surveillance of self-sufficient action by the infant is likely to draw it back on task if it strays.

Social Orientation for Task Performance

The nonpleasurable connotations of task-orientation seem to be less evident in a social setting than in individual achievement. While in no way denying the stresses and strains of group processes, working together with others in a group to complete a task seems to be more fun than doing it alone. Thus, educational activity in which achievement is measured at the group level rather than individually appears to be especially pleasurable as well as productive (Johnson & Johnson, 1987). Similarly, members of small groups that are assigned a goal to accomplish together seem to enjoy working with others on a task, even if the task is not an inherently interesting or pleasant one (Webster, 1975).

Perhaps it is the sheer act of sociality—of discussing possible solutions with fellow group members, of conversing and interacting—that makes task performance more pleasurable in the company of others. The positive impact of sociality upon task-oriented work probably resides not in the mere presence of others but, rather, in the processes that are involved in generating a communal product—in conversation, give and take, sharing, and working together towards a common goal. Although social guidance is characterized by the involvement of an adult in infant activity, a sense of shared goals does not seem to be as strongly expressed. It is in the service of the infant's development rather than of a commonly shared dyadic goal that the adult helps the infant. The social production modality, even when its drive to task completion and achievement proceeds unabatedly, seems to engender more enjoyable interaction.

In social production, although the group strives to accomplish the defined task, its activity cannot focus exclusively upon task-oriented behavior per se. Part of the work of a group—even one as small and simple as a dyad—is the maintenance of social relations and group cohesion. In this light, social psychologists have noted that in task groups there usually is an individual who plays the role of emotional leader, complementing the efforts of the more goal-oriented instrumental leader (Bales, 1970; Webster, 1975). While an individual working by herself can focus all of her time and energy upon task completion, a group effort must devote some resources to social maintenance. As a result, task orientation is more tempered when a group outcome is generated than within the context of individual effort.

Clearly, social guidance interaction does require that some time and effort be devoted to social relationship concerns. But because this type of interaction is more clearly structured—founded as it is upon the teacher-pupil model of formal education—social maintenance may divert less time from task-related activities per se. Furthermore, the fact that the adult is present for the express purpose of guiding the child in task completion maintains the intensity of goal orientation at a high level. Indeed, goal orientation has the potential to be even more relentless and unyielding in social guidance than in self-sufficiency. Just as the teacher may encourage the pupil to keep trying to achieve when she becomes fatigued, distracted, or confused, so that adult guide gently prods the baby to be persistent and to stay on task.

Furthermore, task performance by a group may be more pleasurable and comfortable because the social setting is the natural, evolutionarily adapted context in which important tasks are appropriately tackled. If, as Bowlby (1969) has suggested, humans are best suited to their hunting-and-gathering environment of evolutionary adaptiveness, then they should be most comfortable doing things in a manner that fits within that environment. Given the social product orientation of most traditional societies, it makes sense to expect that, when faced with the need to accomplish a task of any considerable significance, we would be most comfortable doing so socially. Although social guidance often comforts us when we have to engage in individual task performance, it may be towards the social production approach to task performance that humans are biased.

This bias appears to be especially strong during infancy. In traditional societies, adults and older children may spend a modicum of time alone and therefore need to be able to perform some activities in a solitary manner. But infants are virtually never alone. If a hunter-gatherer baby is involved in activity that generates an outcome, it is most probably a socially produced outcome. In this light, it would make sense for infants to find the social production mode particularly appealing.

A More Social Existence

Given the social nature of the human species, infants need to be socialized not only in performance of individual developmental tasks but for social relations as well. As a consequence, social guidance must facilitate the development of social as well as cognitive skills. Furthermore, a social existence implies that relationships and groups are as important as individuals. Therefore, concern with the development of these social entities would seem to be appropriate. Thus, how infants function within a particular social entity, such as an infant-adult dyad, is significant not only because of its consequences for the infant's own development, but also for its impact upon the development of that dyadic relationship.

The self-sufficiency perspective operates within a markedly narrower scope of sociality, focusing primarily upon cognitive development, and pretty much ignoring the infant's need to acquire social capability. Experiential interaction with the physical environment may facilitate the baby's understanding of the world of objects but it is rather unlikely to teach her much about how to get along and interact with other people. Learning to live in a social world seems not to be a topic on the agenda of the self-sufficiency approach to development, other than in the sense that, because the infant encounters social as well as physical objects in exploring the world, she may learn about people through this process. Furthermore, its exclusive focus upon individual development leads to the virtually total lack of concern for how superorganic, social entities grow and develop.

Although the guidance-in-development approach is more evidently social—in that the infant receives assistance from others—it too has a rather narrowly constricted focus on social existence. Guidance can be provided to facilitate social as well as cognitive development, but the extant research focuses primarily upon how adults help infants learn about the physical world. Exceptions can be found in social referencing studies that have examined how the mother's provision of definitional meaning can affect the infant's understanding of people (e.g., strangers). Furthermore, the social guidance paradigm expends virtually no effort on examining the growth and development of social entities. Although guidance may be provided within the context of dyadic interaction, the maturation and future of that dyad seems to be of little interest. The social products of the dyad are viewed as significant because of their impact upon the future development of the infant, not for what they imply for the development of the dyad.

The social product perspective not only retrieves the infant from the unnatural and uncomfortable realm of untempered self-sufficiency, but it brings her back into the heart of the social group as well. By interacting with others to generate a joint outcome, the infant is socialized to become a functioning and functional member of the group. Because the process of social production is inherently a collaborative one, the infant learns how to work and play with others, a considerably more socially intricate skill than learning how to be a pupil who is tutored and guided.

Furthermore, a focus upon the significance of socially produced outcomes necessitates the examination of how dyads, relationships, families, and other social entities grow and change. If social outcomes are salient, then so is the future development of the entities that produce them. Indeed, it is the social product orientation that envisions a fully social existence for the developing infant, a stimulating yet softer world in which she functions and grows within a rich and intricate network of relationships and groups.

Epilogue

Because developmental theory has been cast in the mold of self-sufficiency for so long, and in that of social guidance for the last decade or so, extant infant research has flowed from the questions and assumptions of these perspectives. As a consequence, studies that examine the infant within a social product viewpoint are rare. Some social guidance studies have focused upon the social production of joint outcomes, for example, joint referencing. Investigations of free play within the context of parent-infant, sibling-infant, and peer interaction have generated data that may lend themselves to secondary analysis in examining issues that are relevant within the context of a social product approach. Nevertheless, the comparative dearth of studies that look at the infant through the lens of the social product viewpoint is blatantly evident. What infants accomplish not only through assistance *from* others but also through collaboration *with* others will need to be investigated directly. The full social psychological study of infancy must consider not only how infants develop as individuals and are socially influenced in that development by others, but also how they fit into social groups and collaborate in social production, and how the groups to which they belong develop as social entities.

The self-sufficiency and social guidance models have their origins in the ideology, social structure, and historical origins of modern industrial societies. As industrial, western belief systems have championed the moral supremacy of rugged individualism, so has developmental theory espoused the virtues of the infant who heroically facilitates her own development through experiential exploration of the world around her. Analogously, the cultural origins of the social guidance perspective can be found within the formal educational models of industrial societies. To the extent that the "natural" state of humanity is located in its hunter-gatherer origins, in societies that emphasize interdependency and social production, then the implications of the social product perspective for developmental research on infancy may be paralleled by implications for the broader arena of child-rearing and societal values.

REFERENCES

Adams, R. E., Jr., & Passman, R. H. (1981). The effects of preparing two-year-olds for brief separations from their mothers. *Child Development, 52,* 1068–1070.

Ainsworth, M. D. S. (1967). *Infancy in Uganda: Infant care and the growth of love.* Baltimore: The Johns Hopkins Press.

Ainsworth, M. D. S., Blehar, M. C., Waters, E., & Wall. S. (1978). *Patterns of attachment: A psychological study of the strange situation.* Hillsdale, NJ: Erlbaum.

Alger, H. (1962). *Ragged Dick and Mark, the Match Boy.* New York: Macmillan. (Original work published 1866)

Anderson, J. W. (1972). Attachment behaviour out of doors. In N. Blurton Jones (Ed.), *Ethological studies of child behaviour* (pp. 199–215). London and New York: Cambridge University Press.

Bales, R. F. (1970). *Personality and interpersonal behavior.* New York: Holt, Rinehart and Winston.

Bertalanffy, L. von (1981) *A systems view of man.* Boulder, CO: Westview Press.

Birch, L. L., & Deysher, M. (1986). Caloric compensation and sensory specific satiety: Evidence for self regulation of food intake by young children, *Appetite,* 323–331.

Blurton Jones, N. (1972). Comparative aspects of mother-child contact. In N. Blurton Jones (Ed.), *Ethological studies of child behaviour* (pp. 305–328). London and New York: Cambridge University Press.

Boccia, M. L., & Campos, J. J. (1983, April). *Maternal emotional signals and infants' reactions to strangers.* Paper presented at the Biennial Meeting of the Society for Research in Child Development, Detroit, MI.

Boukydis, C. F. Z. (1985). Perception of infant crying as an interpersonal event. In B. M. Lester & C. F. Z. Boukydis (Eds.), *Infant crying: Theoretical and research perspectives* (pp. 187–215). New York: Plenum Press.

Bowlby, J. (1969). *Attachment and loss: Vol 1. Attachment.* New York: Basic Books.

Bowlby, J. (1972) *Attachment and loss: Vol. 2: Separation.* New York: Basic Books.

Brachfeld-Child, S. (1986). Parents as teachers: Comparisons of mothers' and fathers' instructional interactions with infants. *Infant Behavior and Development, 9*, 127–131.

Bretherton, I. (1984). Social referencing and the interfacing of minds: A commentary on the views of Feinman and Campos. *Merrill-Palmer Quarterly, 30*, 419–427.

Bronfenbrenner, U. (1988, August). *Division 7 (Developmental Psychology) Presidential address.* Presented at the Annual Meeting of the American Psychological Association, New York.

Brooks, J., & Lewis, M. (1976). Infants' responses to strangers: Midget, adult, and child. *Child Development, 47*, 323–332.

Bruner, J. (1976). Nature and uses of immaturity. In J. Bruner, A. Jolly, & K. Silva (Eds.), *Play: Its role in evolution and development* (pp. 28–64). New York: Basic Books.

Bruner, J. (1983a). *Child's talk: Learning to use language.* New York: Norton.

Bruner, J. (1983b). *In search of mind.* New York: Harper & Row.

Bruner, J. (1984). Vygotsky's zone of proximal development: The hidden agenda. In B. Rogoff & J. V. Wertsch (Eds.), *Children's learning in the "zone of proximal development"* (pp. 93–97). San Francisco: Jossey-Bass.

Bruner, J., & Sherwood, V. (1976). Peek-a-boo and the learning of rule structures. In J. Bruner, A. Jolly, & K. Silva (Eds.), *Play: Its role in evolution and development* (pp. 277–285). New York: Basic Books.

Campione, J. C., Brown, A. L., Ferrara, R. A., & Bryant, N. R. (1984). The zone of proximal development: Implications for individual differences and learning. In B. Rogoff & J. V. Wertsch (Eds.), *Children's learning in the "zone of proximal development"* (pp. 77–91). San Francisco: Jossey-Bass.

Campos, J. J. (1983). The importance of affective communication in social referencing: A commentary on Feinman. *Merrill-Palmer Quarterly, 29*, 83–87.

Campos, J. J., & Stenberg, C. R. (1981). Perception, appraisal, and emotion: The onset of social referencing. In M. Lamb & L. Sherrod (Eds.), *Infant social cognition* (pp. 273–314). Hillsdale, NJ: Erlbaum.

Caudill, W., & Weinstein, H. (1969). Maternal care and infant behavior in Japan and America. *Psychiatry, 32*, 12–43.

Chomsky, N. (1965). *Aspects of the theory of syntax.* Cambridge, MA: M.I.T. Press.

Coser, L. A. (1971). *Masters of sociological thought: Ideas in historical and social context.* New York: Harcourt, Brace, Jovanovich.

DeStefano, C. T., & Mueller, E. (1982). Environmental determinants of peer social activity in 18-month-old males. *Infant Behavior and Development, 5*, 175–183.

Dodgson, C. L. (1940). *Alice's adventures in wonderland.* New York: Macmillan. (Original work published 1865)

Dunn, J., & Kendrick, C. (1982). *Siblings: Love, envy, & understanding.* Cambridge, MA: Harvard University Press.

Durkheim, E. (1938). *The rules of sociological method.* New York: The Free Press. (Original work published 1895)

Duvall, E. M., & Miller, B. C. (1985). *Marriage and family development* (6th ed.). New York: Harper & Row.

Emde, R. N. (in press). Social referencing research: Uncertainty, self and the search for meaning. In S. Feinman (Ed.), *Social referencing and the social construction of reality in infancy.* New York: Plenum Press.

Emerson, R. W. (1883). *Essays: First and second series.* Boston: Houghton Mifflin. (Original work published 1865)

Erikson, K. T. (1976). *Everything in its path: Destruction of community in the Buffalo Creek flood.* New York: Simon and Schuster.

Feinman, S. (1980). The utility of evolutionary theory for the social sciences. In S. G.

McNall & G. Howe (Eds.), *Current perspectives in social theory* (Vol. 1, pp. 127–159). Greenwich, CT: JAI Press.

Feinman, S. (1982). Social referencing in infancy. *Merrill-Palmer Quarterly, 28*, 445–470.

Feinman, S. (1983). How does baby socially refer? Two views of social referencing: A reply to Campos. *Merrill-Palmer Quarterly, 29*, 467–471.

Feinman, S. (1985). Emotional expression, social referencing and preparedness for learning in infancy: Mother knows best, but sometimes I know better. In G. Zivin (Ed.), *The development of expressive behavior: Biology-environment interactions* (pp. 291–318). Orlando, FL: Academic.

Feinman, S., & Lewis, M. (1983). Social referencing at ten months: A second order effect on infants' responses to strangers. *Child Development, 54*, 878–887.

Feinman, S. & Lewis, M. (1984). Is there social life beyond the dyad? A social psychological view of social connections in infancy. In M. Lewis (Ed.), *Beyond the dyad* (pp. 13–41). New York: Plenum Press.

Feinman, S. & Roberts, D. (1986, April). *Frequency and duration of social contact during the first year.* Paper presented at the Fifth International Conference on Infant Studies, Los Angeles.

Feinman, S., & Roberts, D. (1988, April). *Social referencing within the context of the infant-sibling-mother triad.* Paper presented at the Sixth International Conference on Infant Studies, Washington, D.C.

Feinman, S. Roberts, D., & Morissette, P. L. (1986, April). *The effect of social referencing on 12-month-olds' responses to a stranger's attempts to "make friends."* Paper presented at the Fifth International Conference on Infant Studies, Los Angeles.

Feldman, S. S. (1985). Development reconsidered [Review of *Beyond the dyad*]. *Contemporary Psychology, 30*, 104–105.

Fogel, A. (1977). Temporal organization in mother-infant face-to-face interaction. In H. R. Schaffer (Ed.), *Studies in mother-infant interaction* (pp. 119–151). London: Academic.

Forman, E. A., & Kraker, M. J. (1985). The social origins of logic: The contributions of Piaget and Vygotsky. In M. W. Berkowitz (Ed.), *Peer conflict and psychological growth* (pp. 23–39). San Francisco: Jossey-Bass.

Freud, S. (1952). *A general introduction to psychoanalysis.* New York: Washington Square Press. (Original work published 1920)

Griffin, P., & Cole, M. (1984). Current activity for the future: The zo-ped. In B. Rogoff & J. V. Wertsch (Eds.), *Children's learning in the "zone of proximal development"* (pp. 45–64). San Francisco: Jossey-Bass.

Gustafson, G. E., Green, J. A., & West, M. J. (1979). The infant's changing role in mother-infant games: The growth of social skills. *Infant Behavior and Development, 2,* 301–308.

Harlow, H. F., & Harlow, M. K. (1969). Effects of various mother-infant relationships on Rhesus monkey behaviors. In B. M. Foss (Ed.), *Determinants of infant behavior IV* (pp. 15–36). London: Methuen.

Heinicke, C. (1956). Some effects of separating two-year-children from their parents: A comparative study. *Human Relations, 9,* 105–176

Heinicke, C., & Westheimer, I. (1966). *Brief separations.* New York: International Universities Press.

Hinde, R. A., & Spencer-Booth, Y. (1967). The effect of social companions on mother-infant relations in rhesus monkeys. In D. Morris (Ed.), *Primate ethology* (pp. 343–364). New York: Doubleday.

Hodapp, R. M., Goldfield, E. C., & Boyatzis, C. J. (1984). The use and effectiveness of maternal scaffolding in mother-infant games. *Child Development, 55,* 772–781.

Hood, W. R., & Sherif, M. (1962). Verbal report and judgment of an unstructured stimulus. *Journal of Psychology, 54,* 121–130.

Hornik, R., & Gunnar, M. R. (1988). A descriptive analysis of infant social referencing. *Child Development, 59,* 626–634.

Hornik, R., Risenhoover, N., & Gunnar, M. (1987). The effects of maternal positive, neutral, and negative affective communications on infant responses to new toys. *Child Development, 58,* 937–944.

Johnson, D. W., & Johnson, R. T. (1987). *Learning together and alone: Cooperative, competitive and individualistic learning.* Englewood Cliffs, NJ: Prentice-Hall.

Kaplan, J. (1972). Differences in the mother-infant relations of squirrel monkeys housed in social and restricted environments. *Developmental Psychology, 5,* 43–52.

Klinnert, M. D. (1984). The regulation of infant behavior by maternal facial expression. *Infant Behavior and Development, 7,* 447–465.

Klinnert, M. D., Campos, J. J., Sorce, J. F., Emde, R. N., & Svejda, M. (1983). Emotions as behavior regulators: Social referencing in infancy. In R. Plutchik & H. Kellerman (Eds.), *The emotions* (Vol. 2, pp. 57–86). New York: Academic Press.

Klinnert, M. D., Emde, R. N., Butterfield, P., & Campos, J. J. (1986). Social referencing: The infant's use of emotional signals from a friendly adult with mother present. *Developmental Psychology, 22,* 427–432.

Kohn, A. (1986). *No contest: The case against competition.* Boston: Houghton Mifflin.

Kohn, A. (1987, October). It's hard to get left out of a pair. *Psychology Today,* pp. 53–57.

Konner, M. J. (1972). Aspects of the developmental ethology of a foraging people. In N. Blurton Jones (Ed.), *Ethological studies of child behaviour* (pp. 285–304). London and New York: Cambridge University Press.

Konner, M. J. (1977). Infancy among the Kalahari Desert San. In P. H. Leiderman, S. R. Tulkin & A. Rosenfeld (Eds.), *Culture and infancy: Variations in the human experience* (pp. 287–328). New York: Academic Press.

LaBarbera, J. D., Izard, C. E., Vietze, P., & Parisi, S. A. (1976). Four- and six-month-old infants' visual responses to joy, anger, and neutral expressions. *Child Development, 47,* 535–538.

Lamb, M. E. (1978). Infant social cognition and "second-order" effects. *Infant Behavior and Development, 1,* 1–10.

Lamb, M. E., & Bornstein, M. H. (1987). *Development in infancy: An introduction* (2nd ed.). New York: Random House.

Lamb, M. E., Thompson, R. A., Gardner, W. P., Charnov, E. L., & Estes, D. (1984). Security of attachment as assessed in the Strange Situation: Its study and biological interpretation. *Behavioral and Brain Sciences, 7,* 127–147.

Lamb, M. E., Thompson, R. A., Gardner, W., & Charnov, E. L. (1985). *Infant-mother attachment: The origins and developmental significance of individual differences in Strange Situation behavior.* Hillsdale, NJ: Erlbaum.

Langhorst, B. H. (1983, April). *Early antecedents of affect referencing.* Paper presented at the Biennial Meeting of the Society for Research in Child Development, Detroit.

Laosa, L. M. (1978). Maternal teaching strategies in Chicano families of varied educational and socioeconomic levels. *Child Development, 49,* 1129–1135.

Laosa, L. M. (1980). Maternal teaching strategies in Chicano and Anglo-American families: The influence of culture and education on maternal behavior. *Child Development, 51,* 759–765.

Larkin, J. (1988). *The reshaping of everyday life.* New York: Harper & Row.

Lebra, T. S. (1976). *Japanese patterns of behavior.* Honolulu: University of Hawaii Press

Lee, D. (1959). *Freedom and culture.* Englewood Cliffs, NJ: Prentice-Hall.

Leopold, A. (1949). *A Sand County Almanac.* New York: Oxford University Press.

McClelland, D. C. (1961). *The achieving society.* Princeton, NJ: Van Nostrand Reinhold.

Mead, G. H. (1934). *Mind, self and society.* Chicago: University of Chicago Press.

Melbin, M. (1987). *Night as frontier: Colonizing the world after dark.* New York: The Free Press.

Morgan, G. A., & Ricciuti, H. N. (1969). Infants' responses to strangers during the first year. In B. M. Foss (Ed.), *Determinants of infant behavior IV* (pp. 253–272). London: Methuen.

Mueller, E., & Brenner, J. (1977). The origins of social skills and interaction among play-group toddlers. *Child Development, 48,* 854–861.

Myers, B. J., Jarvis, P. A., & Creasey, G. L. (1987). Infants' behavior with their mothers and grandmothers. *Infant Behavior and Development, 10,* 245–259.

Newson, J., & Newson, E. (1974). Cultural aspects of childrearing in the English-speaking world. In M. P. M. Richards (Ed.), *The integration of a child into a social world* (pp. 53–82). London and New York: Cambridge University Press.

Piaget, J. (1926). *The language and thought of the child.* London: Routledge & Kegan Paul.

Piaget, J. (1928). *Judgment and reasoning in the child.* London: Routledge & Kegan Paul.

Piaget, J., & Inhelder, B. (1969). *The psychology of the child.* New York: Basic Books. (Original work published 1966)

Ragozin, A. S. (1980). Attachment behavior of day-care children: Naturalistic and laboratory observations. *Child Development, 51,* 409–415.

Ratner, N., & Bruner, J. S. (1978). Games, social exchange and the acquisition of language. *Journal of Child Language, 5,* 391–401.

Ridgeway, C. L. (1983). *The dynamics of small groups.* New York: St. Martin's.

Rogoff, B., Malkin, C., & Gilbride, K. (1984). Interaction with babies as guidance in development. In B. Rogoff & J. V. Wertsch (Eds.), *Children's learning in the "zone of proximal development"* (pp. 31–44). San Francisco: Jossey-Bass.

Rogoff, B., & Wertsch, J. V. (1984). Editors' notes. In B. Rogoff & J. V. Wertsch (Eds.), *Children's learning in the "zone of proximal development"* (pp. 1–6). San Francisco: Jossey-Bass.

Ross, H. S. (1982). Establishment of social games among toddlers. *Developmental Psychology, 18,* 509–518.

Ross, H. S., & Goldman, B. D. (1977). Establishing new social relations in infancy. In T. Alloway, P. Pliner, & L. Krames (Eds.), *Attachment behavior* (pp. 61–79). New York: Plenum Press.

Ross, H. S., & Lollis, S. P. (1987). Communication within infant social games. *Developmental Psychology, 23,* 241–248.

Saxe, G. B., Gearhart, M., & Guberman, S. R. (1984). The social organization of early number development. In B. Rogoff & J. V. Wertsch (Eds.), *Children's learning in the "zone of proximal development"* (pp. 19–30). San Francisco: Jossey-Bass.

Schachter, S. (1958). *The psychology of affiliation: Experimental studies of the sources of gregariousness.* Stanford, CA: Stanford University Press.

Schaffer, H. R., & Emerson, P. E. (1964). The development of social attachments in infancy. *Monographs of the Society for Research in Child Development, 29* (3, Serial No. 94).

Scipien, G. M., Barnard, M. U., Chard, M. A., Howe, J., & Phillips, P. J. (1986). *Comprehensive pediatric nursing* (3rd ed.). New York: McGraw-Hill.

Seay, B., Hansen, E., & Harlow, H. F. (1962). Mother-infant separation in monkeys. *Journal of Child Psychology and Psychiatry, 3,* 123–132.

Service, E. R. (1979). *The hunters* (2nd ed.). Englewood Cliffs, NJ: Prentice-Hall.

Shaw, M. E. (1981). *Group dynamics: The psychology of small group behavior* (3rd ed.). New York: McGraw-Hill.

Smith, A. (1937). *An inquiry into the nature and causes of the wealth of nations.* New York: Random House. (Original work published 1784)

Smith, J. (1983). *Edwardian children.* London: Hutchinson.

Sorce, J. F., & Emde, R. N. (1981). Mother's presence is not enough: Effect of emotional availability on infant exploration. *Developmental Psychology, 17,* 737–745.

Sorce, J. F., Emde, R. N., Campos, J. J., & Klinnert, M. D. (1985). Maternal emotional signaling: Its effect on the visual cliff behavior of 1-year-olds. *Developmental Psychology, 21*, 195–200.

Spock, B. (1968). *Baby and child care* (rev. ed.). New York: Simon and Schuster.

Stern, D. (1977). *The first relationship: Infant and mother*. Cambridge, MA: Harvard University Press.

Stewart, E. P. (1914). *Letters of a woman homesteader*. Boston: Houghton Mifflin.

Stewart, R. B., Jr. (1983). Sibling interaction: The role of the older child as teacher for the younger. *Merrill-Palmer Quarterly, 29*, 47–68.

Strum, S. C. (1987). *Almost human: A journey into the world of baboons*. New York: Random House.

Svejda, M. J., & Campos, J. J. (1982, March). *Mother's vocal expression of emotion as a behavior regulator*. Paper presented at the Third International Conference on Infant Studies, Austin, TX.

Thoreau, H. D. (1866). *Walden*. Boston: Ticknor & Fields. (Original work published 1854)

Tiger, L. (1987). *The manufacture of evil: Ethics, evolution and the industrial system*. New York: Harper & Row.

Turnbull, C. M. (1961). *The forest people: A study of the Pygmies of the Congo*. New York: Simon and Schuster.

Užgiris, I. Č., & Kruper, J. C. (in press). The links between imitation and social referencing. In S. Feinman (Ed.), *Social referencing and the social construction of reality in infancy*. New York: Plenum Press.

Valsiner, J. (1984). Construction of the zone of proximal development in adult-child joint action: The socialization of meals. In B. Rogoff & J. V. Wertsch (Eds.), *Children's learning in the "zone of proximal development"* (pp. 65–76). San Francisco: Jossey-Bass.

Valsiner, J. (1985). Parental organization of children's cognitive development within home environment. *Psychologia, 28*, 131–143.

Vandell, D. L., & Wilson, K. S. (1987). Infants' interactions with mother, sibling, and peer: Contrasts and relations between interaction systems. *Child Development, 58* 176–186.

Vygotsky, L. S. (1962). *Thought and language*. Cambridge, MA: M.I.T. Press. (Original work published 1934)

Vygotsky, L. S. (1978). *Mind in society: The development of higher psychological processes*. Cambridge, MA: Harvard University Press.

Weber, M. (1958). *The Protestant ethic and the spirit of capitalism*. New York: Charles Scribner's Sons. (Original work published 1920)

Webster, M., Jr. (1975). *Actions and actors: Principles of social psychology*. Cambridge, MA: Winthrop.

Weinraub, M., & Lewis, M. (1977). The determinants of children's responses to separation. *Monographs of the Society for Research in Child Development, 42* (4, Serial No. 172).

Wertsch, J. V. (1985). *Vygotsky and the social formation of mind*. Cambridge, MA: Harvard University Press.

Whiten, A. (1977). Assessing the effects of perinatal events on the success of the mother-infant relationship. In H. R. Schaffer (Ed.), *Studies in mother-infant interaction* (pp. 403–425). London: Academic Press.

Wolff, P. H. (1969). The natural history of crying and other vocalizations in early infancy. In B. M. Foss (Ed.), *Determinants of infant behavior IV* (pp. 81–109). Methuen: London.

Wolfheim, J. H., Jensen, G. D., & Bobbitt, R. A. (1970). Effects of group environment on the mother-infant relationship in pigtailed monkeys (Macaca Nemestrina). *Primates, 11*, 119–124.

Wood, D., Bruner, J. S., & Ross, G. (1976). The role of tutoring in problem solving. *Journal of Child Psychology and Psychiatry, 17*, 89–100.

Zarbatany, L., & Lamb, M. E. (1985). Social referencing as a function of information source: Mothers versus strangers. *Infant Behavior and Development, 8*, 25–33.

Author Index

Abelson, R., 74, 93r
Abramovitch, R., 100,
    107r, 234–235, 244r, 246r
Abravanel, E., 226, 244r
Ackerman-Ross, S., 46, 58r
Adams, J.L., 179, 182r
Adams Jr., R.E., 285, 320r
Adamson, L.B., 233, 249r,
    260, 276r
Adler, A., 97, 107r
Ainsworth, M.D., 150,
    152, 159r, 170, 172, 182r,
    184r, 186, 192, 198, 211r,
    285, 287, 310, 320r
Alexander, T., 50, 58r
Alger, H., 294, 301, 320r
Alpert, R., 192, 213r
Alpert, S., 28, 36, 38r
Als, H., 233, 249r
Altman, I., 57, 61r
Amsterdam, B.K., 124,
    131r
Anderson, J.W., 285, 320r
Andersson, B.E., 42, 47,
    53, 58r
Andrews, J., 51, 59r
Angst, J., 99, 108r
Apfel, N., 52, 58r
Arsenian, J., 123, 132r
Arms, F.J., 242, 250r
Aronson, E., 11, 17r, 205,
    211r
Attanucci, J., 181, 184r
Auerbach, J., 232, 246r

Baer, D.M., 167, 182r
Bakemann, R., 260, 276r
Baker-Ward, L., 46–47, 54–
    55, 60r

Bakwin, H., 143, 159r
Baldwin, A.L., 190, 211r
Baldwin, J.M., 158, 159r
Baldwin, L.M., 65, 93r
Bales, R.F., 308, 317, 320r
Bandura, A., 115, 131r,
    157, 159r, 193, 196, 197,
    211r, 215, 217, 244r
Bank, S., 100, 107r
Barkley, R.A., 176, 182r
Barnard, M.U., 285, 288,
    293, 324r
Barrett, K.C., 232–233,
    245r
Barry, H., 100, 107r
Bates, E., 228, 245r
Bateson, G., 64, 93r
Bateson, P.P.G., 150, 159r
Baudonniere, P.M., 234–
    235, 248r
Baumrind, D., 6, 10, 17r,
    65, 90, 93r, 114, 131r
Beavers, W.R., 65, 93r
Becker, W., 90, 93r
Bell, C., 51, 59r
Bell, R.Q., 7, 10, 14, 17r,
    155, 159r
Bell, S.M., 170, 182r
Bellinger, D., 175, 182r
Belsky, J., 64, 93r, 270,
    276r
Benson, J.B., 224, 238,
    240, 250r
Berardo, F.M., 65, 95r
Bergman, A., 120–121,
    123, 127, 133r
Berndt, T.J., 98, 107r
Bernstein, L.E., 258, 266,
    270, 272, 276r

Bevan, W., 144, 160r
Bijou, S.W., 167, 182r
Birch, H.G., 6, 18r
Birch, L.L., 291, 320r
Bishop, D.S., 64–65, 94r
Blackwell, J., 176, 182r
Blehar, M.C., 150, 159r,
    186, 198, 211r, 285, 310,
    320r
Blicharski, T., 47, 60r
Bloom, L., 231, 240, 245r
Blount, B.G., 274, 276r
Blurton Jones, N., 287,
    289, 320r
Bobbitt, R.A., 293, 325r
Boccia, M.L., 302, 320r
Bookstein, F.L., 46, 53, 59r
Borke, H., 127, 131r
Bornstein, M.H., 266,
    278r, 287, 323r
Boslett, M., 99, 109r
Bosso, O.R., 188, 211r
Boukydis, C.F., 310, 320r
Bower, T.G., 5–6, 17r
Bowlby, J., 127–128, 132r,
    143, 150, 160r, 186, 193,
    198, 201, 211r, 285, 287–
    288, 295, 317, 320r
Boyatzis, C.J., 269, 278r,
    300, 322r
Boyd, E.F., 155, 161r
Boyle, P., 46–47, 54, 60r
Brachfeld-Child, S., 309,
    321r
Brackbill, Y., 138, 141, 160r
Brazelton, T.B., 12, 17r,
    233, 249r, 258, 274, 276r,
    277r
Brenner, J., 310, 324r

Bretherton, I., 127, 132r, 193, 198, 211r, 228, 245r, 291, 304, 321r
Bridges, A., 173–174, 182r
Brinich, P.H., 177, 182r
Broberg, A., 46, 53, 59r
Brody, G.H., 64, 93r, 97n, 107r
Bromley, L., 26, 38r
Bronfenbrenner, U., 57, 58r, 64, 93r, 188, 209, 211r, 298, 321r
Brooks, J., 283, 321r
Brooks-Gunn, J., 47, 59r, 115–116, 122n, 123–124, 128, 132r, 133r
Broome, S., 231, 250r
Brotherson, M.J., 64, 96r
Brown, A.L., 305, 321r
Brown, R., 188, 211r, 261–262, 277r
Brownell, A., 77, 93r
Brownlee, E.M., 46, 48, 59r
Bruner, J.S., 5, 17r, 46, 58r, 218–219, 228, 237, 245r, 248r, 249r, 251r, 260–262, 264, 266, 277r, 280r, 284, 289, 293, 295, 298–300, 305, 312, 321r, 324r, 325r
Brush, L.R., 52, 58r
Bryant, B.K., 52, 58r, 105, 107r
Bryant, N.R., 305, 321r
Buber, M., 126, 132r
Buchanan, A., 48, 59r
Buck, R., 79, 93r
Budwig, N.A., 181, 184r, 220, 250r
Buhrmester, D., 105, 108r
Bullowa, M., 218, 245r
Burchinal, M., 44, 58r
Burke, M., 97n, 107r
Burns, P., 178, 182r
Burr, W.R., 65, 94r
Burton, R.V., 4, 6, 11, 17r
Busse, T.V., 50, 58r
Butterfield, P., 302, 323r
Butterworth, G., 260, 277r

Cairns, R.B., 150, 160r
Caldwell, B.M., 4, 7, 10, 17r, 192, 211r
Camaioni, L., 234, 246r
Campbell, J.D., 4, 6, 11, 17r
Campione, J.C., 305, 321r
Campos, J.J., 142, 160r, 162r, 232–233, 245r, 279r, 301–304, 320r, 321r, 323r, 324r, 325r
Carew, J., 48, 58r
Carey, W.B., 6, 17r
Carmichael, H., 48, 61r, 177, 182r
Caron, R.F., 138, 160r
Carroll, L: see Dodgson, C.L.
Cassidy, J., 127, 133r
Catania, A.C., 139, 160r
Cattell, R., 78, 93r
Caudill, W., 288, 321r
Cazden, C., 266, 272–273, 277r
Cecire, S., 237, 240, 246r
Chapman, M., 155, 160r
Chapman, R.S., 231, 246r
Chard, M.A., 288, 293, 324r
Charnov, E.L., 285, 288, 323r
Chess, S., 6, 17r
Chesterfield, R., 271, 279r
Choi, W., 87, 94r
Chomsky, N., 299, 321r
Cialdini, R.B., 205, 211r
Clarke-Stewart, K.A., 42, 44, 48–49, 51–52, 54, 58r, 64, 93r
Cleckley, H., 198, 211r
Clementson-Mohr, D., 216, 245r
Coates, B., 222, 246r
Cochran, G., 260, 277r
Cochran, M.M., 46–48, 50–52, 58r
Coe, C.L., 26, 34, 38r
Coelen, C., 48–50, 52, 60r
Cohen, D., 232–233, 246r
Cohn, J.F., 233, 245r
Cole, M., 50, 58r, 254,

Cole, M. (cont.) 272–273, 277r, 279r, 305, 322r
Collis, G.M., 170, 173–175, 182r, 184r, 232, 237, 245r
Connolly, J., 48, 58r
Connolly, K.J., 48–50, 61r
Conroy, M., 52, 54, 59r
Cook, K.V., 113, 134r
Cooley, C.H., 117, 132r
Corley, R., 44, 46, 60r
Cornielson, F.S., 123, 132r
Corrigan, R., 228, 231, 245r
Corter, C., 100, 107r, 234, 244r
Corvin, S.M., 191, 213r
Coser, L.A., 297, 321r
Crawley, S.B., 228, 245r
Creasey, G.L., 311, 324r
Criticos, A., 228, 245r
Crockenberg, S.B., 105, 107r
Crook, C.K., 171, 173–175, 184r
Cunningham, C.E., 176, 182r

Dale, N., 100, 104, 108r
Daly, E., 79, 93r
D'Andrade, R.G., 259, 277r
Daniels, D., 100, 106, 107r
David, J., 48, 59r
Davis, C.C., 234, 245r
Deck, J., 176, 182r
DeFries, J.C., 106–107, 108r
Demos, E.V., 234, 245r
DePaulo, P., 150, 162r
DeStefano, C.T., 311, 321r
Deysher, M., 291, 320r
DiBiase, R., 130, 132r
Dickson, W.P., 52, 54, 59r
Didow, S.M., 234, 235, 245r
Dishion, T., 186n, 212r
Dittman, L., 48, 51–52, 61r
Dixon, S.D., 274, 277r
Dodgson, C.L., 281, 321r

Dollinger, S.J., 235, 249r
Dore, J., 232, 249r
Dorval, B., 46–47, 54–55, 60r
Doyle, A., 48, 58r
Dunn, J., 64, 93r, 94r, 97n, 98–100, 102–104, 106, 107r, 108r, 109r, 234, 245r, 309, 311, 321r
Dunn, L., 49, 58r
Durkheim, E., 307, 321r
Duval, S., 115, 132r
Duvall, E.M., 308, 321r
Dweck, C.S., 130, 132r
Dyer, J.L., 49, 51, 60r

Easterbrooks, M.A., 170, 182r
Eckerman, C.O., 234–235, 245r, 268, 277r
Edwards, C.P., 54, 58r, 121, 132r
Egeland, B., 185, 211r
Eidelman, A., 232, 246r
Elder, G.H., 65, 94r
Ellis, S., 254, 279r
Emde, R.N., 117, 132r, 142, 162r, 259, 279r, 285, 301–304, 309, 321r, 323r, 324r
Emerson, P.E., 6, 18r, 153, 163r, 192, 213r, 285, 324r
Emerson, R.M., 3, 17r
Emerson, R.W., 1, 17r, 294, 321r
Epple, G., 29, 38r
Epstein, N.B., 64–65, 94r
Erickson, F., 259, 277r
Erickson, M.F., 185, 211r
Erikson, E.H., 119, 128, 132r
Erikson, K.T., 294, 321r
Ernst, L., 99, 108r
Ershler, J., 51, 59r
Erting, C., 177, 182r
Estes, D., 286, 288, 323r
Etzel, B.C., 138, 152, 160r
Eysenck, H.J., 79, 94r
Eysenck, S., 78, 79, 95r

Fahrenbach, C.E., 27, 39r
Falbo, T., 98–99, 108r
Farrington, D.P., 185, 209, 213r
Fein, G.G., 42, 58r
Feinman, S., 17, 17r, 64–65, 94r, 142, 160r, 233, 245r, 259, 277r, 283, 288, 292, 301–304, 312, 321r, 322r
Feiring, C., 64, 94r, 99, 108r, 113, 133r
Feitelson, D., 241, 245r
Feldman, S.S., 308, 322r
Felstein, S., 170, 182r
Fenson, L., 228, 245r
Ferguson, C.A., 228, 249r
Ferrara, R.A., 305, 321r
Ferri, E., 51, 58r
Field, T.M., 144, 155, 160r, 232–233, 235, 246r, 247r, 273, 277r
Fiene, R.J., 52, 58r
Fischer, K.W., 228, 250r
Fisher, S., 190, 211r
Fitzgerald, H.E., 141, 160r
Fogel, A., 308, 322r
Folger, J.P., 231, 246r
Fontaine, A.M., 235, 248r
Forman, E.A., 284, 322r
Fortes, M., 271, 277r
Fosburg, S., 52, 58r
Foss, B.M., 9, 18r
Fowler, W., 46–47, 51, 53–55, 58r, 59r
Freed, R.S., 271, 274, 277r
Freed, S.A., 271, 274, 277r
Freeman, H., 46, 48, 59r
Frenkel, R.E., 123, 132r
Freud, A., 189–190, 211r
Freud, S., 2, 18r, 114, 118–119, 130, 132r, 150, 157, 160r, 187–189, 192, 211r, 293, 322r
Friedman, S., 228, 245r
Fuchs, W.L., 46–47, 51, 61r
Fulker, D.W., 106, 108r
Furman, W., 105, 108r
Furth, H.G., 257, 277r

Gallimore, R., 100, 109r
Garber, H., 47, 54–55, 59r
Garcia, H., 232, 246r
Gardner, H., 79, 94r
Gardner, W.P., 220, 248r, 255, 258, 259, 279r, 286, 288, 323r
Gatride, M., 50, 58r
Gauvain, M., 254, 279r
Gay, J., 50, 58r
Gearhart, M., 265, 279r, 308, 324r
Gegeo, D.W., 241, 250r
Gepphart, U., 130, 132r
Gewirtz, J.L., 4, 7, 18r, 138–139, 141, 143, 148, 149, 150–154, 155–158, 160r–161r, 162r, 194, 196, 212r
Gilbride, K., 220, 248r, 261, 263, 267, 269, 279r, 297, 297–298, 324r
Glantz, F., 48–50, 52, 60r
Gleason, J.B., 241, 246r
Glick, J.A., 50, 58r
Glueck, E.T., 185, 212r
Glueck, S., 185, 212r
Goelman, H., 52–53, 59r
Goldberg, S., 6, 18r, 37, 38r, 130, 133r
Golden, M., 46, 48, 59r
Goldfarb, W., 143, 162r
Goldfield, E.C., 269, 278r, 300, 322r
Goldfoot, D.A., 27, 38r
Goldman, B.D., 234, 246r, 309, 324r
Goldsmith, H.H., 232–233, 245r
Goode, M.K., 270, 276r
Goodman, N., 51, 59r
Goodson, B.D., 52, 58r
Goody, J., 272, 277r
Goslin, D.A., 193, 196, 212r, 215, 217, 246r
Goss, R.N., 177, 182r
Gottlieb, B., 77, 94r
Gottman, J.M., 64, 79, 94r, 95r
Goy, R.W., 27, 38r
Graham, P., 103, 105, 109r

Grajek, S., 98–99, 109r
Green, J.A., 228, 246r, 309, 322r
Greenacre, P., 121, 132r
Greenberg, M.T., 177, 182r, 183r
Greenberg, R.P., 190, 211r, 232–233, 246r
Greenfield, P.M., 220, 246r, 265–266, 271, 277r, 280r
Greif, E.B., 241, 246r
Griffin, P., 272, 277r, 305, 322r
Grossi, M.T., 46, 48, 59r
Grossman, K.E., 198, 212r
Grotevant, H.D., 88, 94r
Gruber, C.P., 42, 58r
Gruen, C.E., 57, 61r
Grusec, J.E., 194, 203–204, 212r, 235, 244r, 246r
Guberman, S.B., 265, 279r, 308, 324r
Gunnar, M.R., 259, 277r, 302, 323r
Gunnarsson, L., 51, 59r
Gurman, A.S., 64, 94r
Gustafson, G.E., 228, 246r, 309, 322r

Haft, W., 232, 249r
Hager, J.L., 141, 163r
Haley, J., 64, 93r
Hamilton, E., 79, 94r
Handin, K.H., 81, 95r
Hansen, E., 285, 324r
Harkness, S., 179, 184r, 274, 277r
Harlow, H.F., 192, 212r, 284–285, 322r, 324r
Harlow, M.K., 284–285, 322r
Harris, M., 52, 58r
Harris, P.L., 216, 246r
Hartup, W.W., 98, 108r, 222, 246r
Haskins, R., 47, 59r
Haviland, J.M., 128, 133r, 232–233, 238, 247r
Hawkins, P.D., 52, 58r

Hay, D.F., 185, 194, 198–199, 213r, 237, 240, 246r, 268, 277r
Hayes, W.A., 48, 59r
Heath, S.B., 273, 277r
Heber, R., 47, 54–55, 59r
Heckhausen, H., 129, 132r
Heinicke, C., 285, 322r
Henderson, B.B., 270, 278r
Hepburn, A., 173–175, 179, 182r, 184r
Herrnstein, R.J., 198, 213r
Hess, E.H., 149, 150, 162r
Hess, R.D., 52, 54, 59r
Hetherington, E.M., 97n, 108r, 178, 182r
Hinde, R.A., 125, 132r, 141, 149, 162r, 293, 322r
Hirschi, T., 203, 209, 212r
Hodapp, R.M., 269, 278r, 300, 322r
Hofer, L., 232, 249r
Hoff-Ginsberg, E., 266, 278r
Hoffman, M.L., 167, 178, 182r
Hoffman, H.S., 150, 162r
Hogan, R., 172, 184r
Holden, G.W., 172, 182r
Holm, R.A., 37, 39r
Holman, T.B., 65, 94r
Honig, A.S., 46, 52, 54, 59r, 61r
Hood, L., 231, 240, 245r
Hood, W.R., 295, 322r
Hornik, R., 302, 323r
Howe, J., 285, 288, 293, 324r
Howes, C., 46–50, 52, 54, 59r, 60r
Hubbell, R., 47, 51–52, 59r
Hubley, P., 218, 237, 249r
Hughes, M., 48, 61r
Hulsebus, R.C., 138, 152, 162r
Hvastja-Stefani, L., 234, 246r
Hwang, C.P., 46, 53, 59r

Iacobbo, M., 228, 245r
Inhelder, B., 5, 18r, 284, 324r
Istomina, Z.M., 219, 246r
Izard, C.E., 232, 247r, 283, 323r

Jaccard, J., 74, 87–88, 94r
Jacklin, C.N., 175, 182r
Jackson, D.D., 64, 78, 93r, 94r
Jaffe, J., 170, 182r
James, W., 114, 118, 132r
Jarvis, P.A., 311, 324r
Jaskir, J., 122n, 133r
Jay, P., 26, 38r
Jensen, G.D., 293, 325r
John, V.P., 273, 277r
Johnson, D.W., 289, 309, 313, 323r
Johnson, J.E., 51, 59r
Johnson, R.T., 289, 309, 313, 323r
Jordan, C., 273, 278r

Kagan, J., 46–47, 59r, 125, 175, 182r, 208, 212r
Kahn, M.D., 100, 107r
Kaitz, M., 232, 246r
Kalsan, B., 181, 184r
Kaplan, J., 293, 323r
Kaplan, K., 127, 133r
Kaufman, I.C., 31, 39r
Kavanaugh, R.D., 228, 237, 247r
Kaye, H., 138, 162r, 216, 220, 222, 228, 232–233, 239, 246r, 262, 267, 278r
Kearsley, R.B., 46–47, 59r, 228, 249r
Kendrick, C., 64, 93r, 99–100, 108r, 234, 245r, 310–311, 321r
Kennell, J., 99, 109r
Khan, N., 46, 53, 59r
Khana, P., 46, 58r
Killem, N., 226–229, 237, 247r
Kinney, P.F., 52, 59r

Kirkpatrick, J., 274, 276, 278r
Klaus, M., 99, 109r
Klinnert, M.D., 142, 162r, 259, 279r, 301–304, 323r, 324r
Kniskern, D.P., 64, 94r
Koch, H., 100, 108r
Kogan, K.L., 99, 109r
Kohlberg, L., 158, 162r
Kohn, A., 289, 295, 305, 309, 323r
Konner, M.J., 287–288, 292, 313, 323r
Kontos, S., 49, 58r
Kopp, C.B., 181, 182r, 184r
Korner, A.F., 6, 18r
Koslowski, B., 12, 17r
Kraker, M.J., 284, 322r
Krakow, J.B., 181, 184r
Kreiss, L., 274, 279r
Krolick, G., 46, 61r
Krug, R., 90, 93r
Kruper, J.C., 224, 231, 233, 238, 247r, 250r, 304, 325r
Kuczaj II, S.A., 228, 247r
Kuhn, D., 216, 247r
Kurdek, L.A., 226, 248r
KVOD Guide, 4, 18r

Laboratory of Comparative Human Cognition, 254, 262r
LaBarbera, J.D., 283, 323r
Ladd, G.W., 98, 107r
Lally, J.R., 46, 54, 59r
Lamb, M.E., 46, 53, 59r, 100, 103, 108r, 170, 182r, 232–233, 245r, 283, 285, 287–288, 302, 311, 323r, 325r
Lancee, W., 79, 93r
Lande, J., 46–47, 53, 61r
Landesman, S., 66, 94r
Lando, B., 234, 244r
Langhorst, B.H., 304, 323r
Laosa, L.M., 81, 96r, 309, 323r
Larkin, J., 294, 323r
Larsen, J.M., 47, 59r

Larson, R., 97n, 108r
Lave, J., 220, 246r
Lazar, I., 47, 51–52, 59r
Lebra, T.S., 288, 323r
Lee, A., 178, 182r
Lee, D., 289, 323r
Lee, V.E., 44, 47, 58r, 59r
Leggett, E.L., 130, 132r
Leiderman, P.H., 273, 277r, 278r
Lempers, J.D., 260, 278r
Leont'ev, A.N., 219, 247r
Leopold, A., 291, 323r
Lepper, M.R., 204, 212r
Levan-Goldschmidt, E., 226, 244r
Levi, S., 74, 93r
Levin, H., 4, 6, 18r
Levine, J.A., 175, 182r, 274, 277r
Levine, S., 37, 38r
Levinson, R.W., 79, 94r
Levy, D.M., 97, 108r, 143, 162r
Lewin, H., 192, 213r
Lewis, M., 6–7, 14, 17, 17r, 18r, 33, 37, 38r, 64, 64–65, 79, 94r, 95r, 99, 108r, 111, 113–117, 121–129, 122n, 130, 133r, 234, 247r, 283, 285, 292, 308, 312, 321r, 322r, 325r
Liaw, F.R., 47, 59r
Lieberman, A.F., 48, 59r, 185, 212r
Lightbown, P., 231, 240, 245r
Lipsitt, L.P., 138, 162r, 163r
Loeber, R., 186n, 212r
Loehlin, J.C., 107, 108r
Loehr, S., 54, 58r
Loevinger, J., 185, 212r
Logue, M.E., 54, 58r
Lollis, S.P., 300, 324r
Lorenz, K., 150, 162r
Lubin, L., 235, 247r
Lucas, T., 234, 247r
Lumley, J.M., 177, 184r

Mably, S., 54, 60r
Maccoby, E.E., 4, 6, 10, 18r, 64, 90, 95r, 98, 108r, 175, 182r, 192, 206, 212r, 213r
MacDonald, K., 64, 95r
Macnamara, J., 173, 182r
MacPhee, D., 64, 95r
Mahler, M.S., 120–121, 123, 127, 133r
Main, M., 12, 17r, 127, 133r
Malatesta, C.Z., 128, 133r, 232–233, 238, 247r
Malkin, C., 220, 248r, 261, 263, 267, 269, 272, 279r, 297, 298, 324r
Malpass, R., 87, 95r
Mancuso, J.C., 81, 95r
Mandler, G., 116, 133r
Marcus, J., 228, 246r
Markus, G.B., 65, 88, 96r
Markus, H., 65, 88, 96r
Marquis, D.P., 179, 182r
Martin, J.A., 10, 18r, 64, 90, 95r, 98, 108r, 182r
Martini, M., 274, 276, 278r
Massey, G.C., 48, 59r
Masters, J., 192, 212r
Masur, E.F., 224, 247r, 269, 278r
McBair, M.C., 27, 38r
McCabe, M., 228, 239, 247r
McCall, R.B., 228, 237, 247r
McCartney, K., 46–49, 51, 53, 60r, 61r
McClelland, D.C., 289, 323r
McCord, J., 185, 212r
McCord, W., 185, 212r
McGhee, L.J., 268, 277r
McLane, J.B., 181, 184r, 220, 250r
McLaughlin, B., 173, 174, 175, 182r
McNamee, G.D., 181, 184r, 220, 250r, 264, 278r

Mead, G.H., 118, 134r, 296, 323r

Meadow, K.P., 177, 182r, 184r

Meadows, S., 54, 60r

Mehan, H., 259, 278r

Melbin, M., 288, 323r

Melhuish, E.C., 46, 53, 60r

Meltzoff, A.N., 222, 228, 233, 239, 247r

Merleau-Ponty, M., 121, 134r

Meschulach-Sarfaty, O., 232, 246r

Meseck-Bushey, S., 97n, 109r

Messer, D.J., 170, 182r, 265, 266, 278r

Michalson, L., 79, 95r, 114, 133r, 234, 247r

Milbrath, C., 48, 59r

Millar, W.S., 138, 162r

Miller, B.C., 308, 321r

Miller, J.G., 64, 95r

Miller, L.B., 49, 51, 60r

Miller, P.J., 266, 278r

Minick, N., 242, 250r

Minton, C., 175, 182r

Minuchin, S., 65, 95r

Mischel, W., 115, 134r

Mitchell, G., 27, 37, 38r

Mitchell, R.W., 216, 230, 247r

Moerk, E.L., 262, 266, 278r

Moffatt, S., 46–47, 51, 61r

Moore, M.K., 222, 233, 239, 247r

Morgan, G.A., 283, 323r

Morissette, P.L., 302, 322r

Moss, E., 47, 60r

Moss, H.A., 6, 18r

Most, R.K., 270, 276r

Mowrer, O.H., 191, 212r

Mueller, E., 234, 247r, 310–311, 321r, 324r

Mundy-Castle, A., 241, 247r

Munn, P., 102–104, 108r

Murphy, C.M., 170, 182r

Murphy, L.B., 5, 18r

Murray, H., 47, 51–52, 59r, 237, 246r

Murray, P., 240, 246r

Myers, B.J., 311, 324r

Nadel, J., 235, 248r

Nadel, S.F., 207, 212r

Nadel-Brulfert, J., 234–235, 248r

Nadler, R.D., 32, 39r

Nash, A., 237, 240, 246r

Neff, D.A., 27, 38r

Nelson, K.E., 231, 249r

Nerviano, V.J., 46–47, 51, 61r

Nettles, M., 106, 108r

Newman, D., 253, 278r

Newson, E., 288, 312–313, 324r

Newson, J., 218, 232, 248r, 261, 279r, 288, 312–313, 324r

Newton, D., 52, 58r

Ninio, A., 219, 228, 248r

Norman, W., 78, 95r

Nunes, L.R., 222, 248r

Nye, F.I., 65, 95r

Ochs, E., 241, 248r, 249r, 266, 274, 278r

O'Connell, B., 228, 245r

O'Leary, K., 228, 249r

Olson, D.H., 65, 89, 95r

Olson, G.M., 216, 248r

Orlansky, H., 4, 18r

Painter, M., 48–51, 61r

Papert, S., 272, 278r

Papousek, H., 138, 162r, 224, 232, 248r, 258, 266, 270, 278r

Papousek, M., 224, 232, 248r, 258, 266, 270, 278r

Parisi, S.A., 283, 323r

Parke, R.D., 64, 95r, 96r, 173, 176, 178, 181, 182r, 228, 237, 247r

Parkes, C.M., 201, 212r

Parsons, G., 170, 184r

Parton, D.A., 223, 248r

Passman, R.H., 285, 320r

Patterson, A.H., 48, 60r

Patterson, G.R., 64, 95r, 103, 105, 108r

Pawlby, S.J., 224, 226, 238, 248r

Paxon, L.M., 100, 107r

Peaslee, M.V., 46, 60r

Pellegrini, A.D., 50, 60r

Pence, A.R., 52, 53, 59r

Pepler, D., 100, 107r

Petrovich, S.B., 138, 149, 162r

Philips, J., 51, 54, 60r, 61r

Phillips, D.A., 48, 60r

Phillips, P.J., 285, 288, 293, 324r

Piaget, J., 5, 18r, 98, 108r, 121, 134r, 217, 238, 248r, 284, 324r

Pine, F., 120–121, 123, 127, 133r

Pinkerton, B., 48, 61r

Plewis, I., 51, 61r

Plomin, R., 97, 97n, 100, 106–107, 107r, 108r, 109r

Poe, P., 260, 278r

Policare, H.J., 46, 48, 59r

Polivy, J., 79, 93r

Poortinga, Y., 87, 95r

Poulson, C.L., 138, 162r, 222, 248r

Powell, D.R., 54, 60r

Power, T.G., 64, 95r, 173, 176, 181, 182r

Prescott, E., 48, 50–52, 60r

Price, G.G., 52, 54, 59r

Primavera, L.H., 234, 249r

Provost, M.A., 47, 60r

Quilitch, H., 50, 60r

Radbill, S.X., 3, 18r

Radke-Yarrow, M.R., 127, 134r, 186n, 213r

Raffaelli, M., 97n, 108r

Ragozin, A.S., 311, 324r

Ramer, A.L., 231, 240, 248r

Ramey, C.T., 44, 46–47, 54–55, 58r, 60r, 64, 95r

Ramsay, D.S., 228, 245r

Ratner, A.M., 150, 162r, 219
Ratner, N., 229, 248r, 300, 324r
Rau, L., 192, 213r
Rayner, R., 3, 19r
Ree, M., 50, 58r
Reid, J.B., 64, 95r
Reilly, J., 266, 280r
Reiss, D., 65, 68, 96r
Reuter, E., 176, 182r
Rheingold, H.L., 113, 134r, 179, 182r, 218, 248r, 268, 279r
Ricciuti, H.N., 283, 324r
Richards, M.P., 7, 9–10, 13–15, 18r, 217–218, 248r
Richardson, L., 228, 245r
Richman, A., 274, 277r
Richman, N., 103, 105, 109r
Richters, J., 185, 194, 198–199, 199, 213r
Ridgeway, C.L., 308, 324r
Risenhoover, N., 302, 323r
Risley, T., 50, 60r
Ritz, E.G., 224, 247r
Rivest, L., 48, 58r
Roberts, D., 288, 302, 303, 322r
Roberts, M.C., 235, 249r
Robinson, C.C., 47, 59r
Robinson, H.B., 46, 53, 60r
Robinson, J., 44, 46, 60r
Robinson, N.M., 46, 53, 60r
Rodgers, J.L., 97n, 109r
Rodgon, M.M., 226, 248r
Rogers, P.P., 228, 245r
Rogoff, B., 218–220, 248r, 254, 257–259, 261–263, 263, 267, 269, 271–274, 279r, 297–299, 308–309, 324r
Rohe, W., 48, 60r
Rosche, M., 47, 51–52, 59r
Rosenberg, B.G., 98, 109r
Rosenblum, L.A., 7, 14, 18r, 26, 28–30, 32, 34,

Rosenblum, L.A. (cont.) 36, 38r, 39r, 64, 95r, 113, 133r
Rosenbluth, L., 46, 48, 59r
Rosenfeld, A., 273, 278r
Ross, G., 219, 251r, 264, 280r, 299, 325r
Ross, H.S., 234, 246r, 300, 310, 324r
Roth, S., 54, 58r
Routh, D.K., 138, 163r
Rowe, D.C., 97, 97n, 109r
Rowell, T.E., 35, 39r
Roy, C., 48–51, 61r
Roy, M.A., 149, 163r
Royce, J., 47, 51–52, 59r
Rubenstein, J.L., 46–50, 52, 54, 59r, 60r
Rubinstein, D., 274, 279r
Rudd, C., 99, 109r
Ruddle, K., 271, 279r
Ruopp, R., 48–50, 52, 60r
Ruppenthal, G.C., 27, 37, 39r
Russell, C.S., 65, 89, 95r
Ryan, J., 231, 249r

Sackett, G.P., 27, 36–37, 39r
Sade, D.S., 32, 39r
Sameroff, A.J., 6–7, 18r, 64, 96r
Sanders, L.W., 117, 134r, 178, 183r
Sanford, N., 191, 213r
Sarnoff, I., 191, 213r
Saxe, G.B., 265, 279r, 308, 324r
Scaife, M., 237, 249r
Scarr, S., 46–48, 53, 60r, 61r, 88, 94r, 97, 99, 109r
Schachter, S., 285, 324r
Schaefer, E., 90, 96r
Schaffer, H.R., 2, 6, 18r, 153, 163r, 166, 169–171, 173–175, 179, 182r, 184r, 192, 213r, 218, 237, 245r, 249r, 258, 262, 279r, 285, 324r
Schank, R.C., 117, 134r

Schieffelin, B.B., 241, 248r, 249r, 274, 278r
Schlesinger, H.S., 177, 184r
Schneiderman, M.H., 175, 184r
Schnur, E., 47, 59r, 173, 184r
Schooler, C., 99, 109r
Schubert, D.S., 98, 109r
Schubert, H.J., 98, 109r
Schwartz, G.G., 36, 39r
Schwartz, J.C., 46, 61r
Scipien, G.M., 285, 288, 293, 324r
Scollon, R., 270, 279r
Scott, J.P., 150, 163r
Scribner, S., 272–273, 279r
Sears, R.R., 4, 6, 18r, 150, 163r, 191, 192, 213r
Seay, B., 285, 324r
Seitz, S., 216, 231, 249r
Seitz, V., 223, 251r
Seligman, M.E.P, 141, 163r
Service, E.R., 289, 324r
Sewell, W.H., 4, 18r
Shapiro, B., 181, 184r
Sharp, D.W., 50, 58r
Shatz, M., 173, 184r, 266, 278r
Shaw, M.E., 308, 324r
Sherif, M., 295, 322r
Sherman, T., 216, 248r
Sherwood, V., 229, 245, 300, 321r
Shore, C., 228, 245r
Shotter, J., 261, 279r
Shumaker, S., 77, 93r
Siegal, M., 50, 61r
Sigel, I.E., 52, 61r, 64, 81, 96r
Singer, J.D., 52, 58r
Siqueland, E.R., 138, 163r
Sjolund, A., 46, 49, 61r
Skinner, B.F., 138, 157, 163r
Slobin, D.I., 270, 279r
Smith, A., 288, 293, 295, 324r
Smith, H.T., 5, 18r
Smith, J.M., 52, 58r

Smith, P.K., 48, 49, 50, 61r
Snow, C.E., 228, 231, 249r, 266, 279r
Sorce, J.F., 142, 162r, 259, 279r, 285, 301, 303–304, 323r, 324r
Sostek, A.M., 273–274, 277r, 279r
Spangler, G., 198, 212r
Speidel, G.E., 231, 249r
Spencer-Booth, Y., 293, 322r
Spitz, R.A., 120, 134r, 143, 145, 163r
Spock, B., 285, 325r
Sprenkle, D.H., 65, 89, 95r
Sroufe, L.A., 185, 210, 211r, 213r
Stanger, C., 116, 129, 130, 133r
Stayton, D.J., 170, 172, 182r, 184r
Stechler, G., 178, 182r
Stenberg, C.R., 232–233, 245r, 302, 321r
Stern, D.N., 117, 134r, 232–233, 249r, 308, 325r
Sternberg, R.J., 80, 96r
Stevenson, J., 103, 105, 109r, 226, 244r
Stevenson-Hinde, J., 141, 162r
Stewart, C., 231, 249r
Stewart, E.P., 295, 309, 325r
Stillwell, R., 102, 109r
Stingle, K., 157, 158, 161r
St. John, C., 97n, 109r
Stocker, C., 97n, 109r
Stoke, S.M., 191, 213r
Stokols, B., 57, 61r
Stone, C., 259, 277r
Stone, L.J., 5, 18r
Stoneman, Z., 64, 93r, 97n, 107r
Storey, R.M., 50, 61r
Strayer, F.F., 47, 60r
Strickland, R.G., 46, 61r
Strum, S.C., 289, 325r
Stukat, K.G., 47, 61r
Stynes, A.J., 31, 39r

Suess, G., 198, 212r
Sullivan, H.C., 98, 109r
Sullivan, H.S., 126, 134r
Sullivan, M., 116, 129, 130, 133r
Summers, J.D., 64, 96r
Super, C.M., 179, 184r, 274, 277r
Sutton-Smith, B., 98, 109r
Svejda, M.J., 142, 162r, 302, 304, 323r, 325r
Swartz, K.B., 36, 39r
Sylva, K., 48, 49, 50, 51, 61r

Taylor, D., 272, 279r
Taylor, M.K., 99, 109r
Terkelson, K.G., 65, 96r
Thelen, M.H., 235, 249r
Thomas, A., 6, 18r
Thomas, E.A., 48, 59r
Thompson, M.A., 228, 245r
Thompson, R.A., 285, 288, 323r
Thoreau, H.D., 292–293, 325r
Tiegerman, E., 234, 249r
Tietze, W., 44, 47, 61r
Tiger, L., 288, 325r
Tinsley, B., 64, 96r
Tizard, B., 48, 51, 61r
Torrey, C.C., 28, 39r
Trause, M.A., 99, 109r
Travers, J., 48–50, 52, 60r
Trevarthen, C., 218, 224, 232–233, 237, 246r, 249r
Tronick, E.R., 218, 233, 245r, 249r
Tulkin, S.R., 273, 278r
Turnbull, A., 64, 96r
Turnbull, C.M., 289, 325r
Tyler, B., 48, 51–52, 61r

Ungerer, J.A., 228, 249r
Unzner, L., 198, 212r
Uzgiris, I.C., 216, 218, 220, 222, 224, 226–228, 231, 233, 237–240, 247r, 249r, 250r, 304, 325r

Valsiner, J., 228, 250r, 261–262, 279r, 293, 298–300, 305, 325r
van der Waals, 274, 279r
Vandell, D.L., 54, 61r, 300, 309, 325r
Vasek, M.E., 224, 238, 240, 250r
Vaughn, B.E., 181, 184r
Vietze, P., 273, 274, 277r, 279r, 283, 323r
Voeller, M.N., 65, 93r
von Bertalanffy, L., 64, 93r, 293, 320r
Voss, D., 99, 109r
Vygotsky, L.S., 219, 250r, 254, 258, 272, 280r, 296–297, 305, 325r

Wachs, T.D., 57, 61r
Wadsworth, M.E., 44, 47, 61r
Wagner, M.E., 98, 109r
Wall, S., 150, 159r, 186, 198, 211r, 285, 310, 320r
Wallen, K., 27, 38r
Wallon, H., 121, 134r, 238, 250r
Walters, R.H., 215, 244r
Warren, S.F., 222, 248r
Wartofsky, M., 258, 280r
Waters, E., 150, 159r, 185–186, 193–194, 198, 211r, 213r, 285, 310, 320r
Watson, J.B., 2–3, 18r, 167, 184r, 228, 250r
Watson-Gegeo, K.A., 241, 250r
Waxler, C.Z., 226, 250r
Weakland, J.H., 64, 93r
Weaver, J., 54, 60r
Weber, M., 289, 325r
Webster Jr., M., 295, 313, 317, 325r
Wedell-Monnig, J., 177, 184r
Weinberg, R.A., 88, 94r
Weinraub, M.A., 64, 95r, 133r, 285, 325r
Weinstein, H., 288, 321r
Weisner, T.S., 100, 109r

Weiss, C., 116, 129, 130, 133r
Wentworth, W.M., 190, 213r
Wertsch, J.V., 181, 184r, 219–220, 242, 250r, 254, 257, 262, 264, 280r, 296, 308–309, 324r, 325r
West, D.J., 185, 209, 213r
West, M.J., 228, 246r, 309, 322r
Westheimer, I., 285, 322r
Whatley, J.L., 268, 277r
Wheeler, S.A., 209, 213r
White, B.L., 181, 184r
Whiten, A., 285, 325r
Whiting, B.B., 100, 105, 109r, 262, 274, 280r
Whiting, J.W., 100, 105, 109r, 262, 280r

Wicklund, R.A., 115, 132r
Wilson, J.Q., 198, 213r
Wilson, K.S., 300, 309, 325r
Winnett, R.A., 46, 47, 51, 61r
Winnicott, D.W., 97, 109r
Wippman, J., 185, 213r
Wise, S., 233, 249r
Wittig, B.A., 152, 159r
Wittmer, D., 52, 61r
Wolff, P.H., 324, 325r
Wolfheim, J.H., 293, 325r
Wood, D.J., 219, 250r, 264, 280r, 299, 312, 325r
Wood, G., 74, 88, 94r
Woodson, R., 232, 233, 246r
Wylie, R.C., 115, 117, 134r

Yanagisako, S.J., 66, 96r
Yando, R., 216, 223, 251r
Yarrow, L.J., 143, 150, 163r
Yarrow, M.R., 4, 6, 11, 19r, 226, 250r
Yeates, K.O., 64, 95r

Zahn-Waxler, C.J., 127, 130, 134r, 186n, 213r
Zajonc, R.B., 65, 88, 96r
Zarbatany, L., 283, 302, 325r
Zaslow, M., 274, 279r
Zelazo, P.R., 46–47, 59r, 228, 249r
Zigler, E., 216, 223, 251r
Zimmerman, R.R., 28, 39r
Zukow, P.G., 266, 280r

Subject Index

A Sand County Almanac (Leopold, A.), 291
Abstraction, of rules, 49–50
Achievement, in self-sufficiency perspective, 289–292
Acquisition
  of language: *see* Language acquisition
  in operant learning, 138
Action controls, 171
Activity
  choice of: *see* Structuring situations, for child involvement
  guiding child's participation in: *see* Guided participation
  imitation of: *see* Imitation
  as unit of analysis in Soviet psychology, 219
Activity level, of child, effect on parental control techniques, 176
Adaptation
  mutual, in parent-child interactions, 168; *see also* Mutuality
  observational learning role in, 218
Adult(s)
  and child, differences in communication between, 273–276
  communicating concepts with child, 262
  conversational speaker-switch pauses, 170
  impact on child, 7–8
  influence on child, 13–14
  situations structured by: *see* Structuring situations, for child involvement
Affection, between siblings, 101–102
Affective imitation, 232–234
Affective reactions, in family functioning analysis, 79
Affiliation, and self-sufficiency, 285
Aggression, between siblings, 101–102, 103, 105

Alger, H., stewardship doctrine of, 301
Alice's Adventures in Wonderland (Carroll, L.), 281–282
Aloneness, and self-sufficiency: *see* Self-sufficiency perspective
Altricial species, and precocial species, differences between
  attachment learning and, 149–150
  self-sufficiency and, 285–286
Ambiguity postulate, in social referencing, 302
Anaclitic identification, 192
Anxiety; *see also* Castration anxiety
  and defensive identification
    in boys, 189
    in girls, 189–190
  and negative influence, contrasting views on, 203–204
"Assumptive worlds," 201
Attachment
  attachment learning and, 150–151
  child-parent, 185–186
  contemporary perspectives, 193–197
  crying, cued responding and, 151–154
  to deviant parents, contrasting views on, 208–209
  enduring features of an, 154–155
  Freud's model of, 192–193
  integrative model, 197–209
    and identification, 199–203
    secure attachment, factors influencing, 198–199
  and pervasive imitation relationship, 157–159
  psychoanalytic perspective, 187
  as representation, 127–129
  security of, 286–287
  and Strange Situation, 285
Attachment-dependence phenomena, 158

Attachment figures, 198–199
  in encapsulation period, 201
Attachment learning, 149–150
  in altricial species, 150–151
  in precocial species, 150
Attention, in different child care
    environments
  amount, 47–48
  type, 48–52
Attention controls, 171
Attitudes, individual's, family functioning
    and, 80–81
Autonomy, versus shame and doubt, ego
    development and, 119

Baby and Child Care (Spock, B.), 286
Bathing, maternal interaction with child
    during, 179–180
Behavior
  facilitators and constraints on, 141–142
  family: see Family behavior
  modification of, 3
    challenge to development model, 15
Behavioral similarity, identification and,
    196
Behavioral stability, explanations for, 195
Behaviorism
  and infant competence, 5
  integrating psychoanalytic approaches,
    4; see also Behaviorist-
    psychoanalytic model of
    socialization
Behaviorist-psychoanalytic model of
    socialization
  deficiency of, 11
  different responses to, 10–12
    recent studies, 12–17
  parenting and, 13
  rejection of, 5–8, 8–9
Being alone, in self-sufficiency perspec-
    tive, 285–286
Beliefs, individual's, family functioning
    and, 80–81
Beyond the Dyad (Lewis, M., Ed.), 113
Birth-order
  and family functioning, 88–89
  and firstborn problems, 99–101
  sociability and, 106
Boys, defensive identification in, 189
Bridging, between familiar and unfamiliar
    skills, 258, 259
  social referencing, 259–261
  words as cultural system, 261–262

Caregiver(s); see also Mother(s); Parent(s)
  adjusting conversation with child, 265–
    266
  behavior characteristics influencing at-
    tachment, 198
  effect of child on, 7–8
  emerging self-other distinction and, 122
  in encapsulation period, 201–202
Caregiving, child care center versus
    home, 52; see also Parenting
Castration anxiety
  in defensive identification in girls, 189
  experimental study of, 191
Child care environments
  cause and effect issue, 57
  contributions of child in, 53–55
  differences between children in, 42–47
    causes, 47–55
    home versus center care, 44
    ranked results, 45
    variables to measure, 43–44
  future research implications, 55–57
  nontraditional versus traditional, 41–42
Child development
  attachment as outcome, 195
  guided participation effect on, 269–270
  image of, 15
  interrelated levels of, 257
  nature versus nurture argument in,
    256–257
  role of imitation in, 215–216, 220; see
    also Imitation
  social influence on, 217–221
Child Rearing (Yarrow, Campbell, and Bur-
    ton), 4
Childhood, early and middle, commit-
    ment during, 202–203; see also
    Infancy
Child(ren); see also Infant(s)
  and adults, differences in communica-
    tion between, 273–276
  competence variables, 43–44
  development of: see Child development
  in different environments: see Child care
    environments; Home environment
  parental control techniques and, 168–
    177; see also Social control
  role in social activity, 266–269
Circumplex model, versus GSRI contex-
    tual model, 89–90
Civilizing process, by socialization, 2, 3
Clay-molding model, 2, 166–167
  mutuality and, 7

Cognition
  individual's, family functioning and,
    79–80
  Piaget's stage theory of, 5
  social: *see* Social cognition
  verbal and nonverbal, as child compe-
    tence variable, 43
Commitment
  contrasting views on
    cost-benefit, 206–207
    positive influence, 204–206
    punishment versus penalty, 207–208
  during early and middle childhood,
    202–203
  and mutuality, 7–8
Communication
  as bridge between understandings, 262
  differences across cultures, 273–276
  emotional and nonverbal, 259–261
Communicative modes
  at different developmental levels, 173–
    174
  verbal versus nonverbal, 174
Competence, 5–6
  social and intellectual, assessment vari-
    ables, 43–44
  child-care environment rankings, 45
Competence variables, to measure social
    and intellectual competence, 43–44
"Competent Collaborator" baby, 9, 10, 17
Concurrent (mutual) influence processes,
    in attachment learning, 155–156
Conflict model, of socialization, 167
Confluence model, versus GSRI contex-
    tual model, 88–89
Conformity, to parental control tech-
    niques, 180
Constraints, on behavior, 141–142
Control: *see* Social control
Conversation, speaker-switch pauses in,
    170
Cooperation, as child competence variable
  with examiner, 43
  with unfamiliar peer, 44
Creativity
  as child competence variable, studies
    measuring, 47
  with materials, as child competence
    variable, 43
Criminals, behavior expectations in child,
    209
"Cross-fostering" experiments, 179
Crying, attachment learning and, 151–154

Cued responding
  attachment learning and, 151–154
  and enduring features of an attach-
    ment, 154–155
Cueing, and social learning, 139–140
Culture
  differences in self-sufficiency perspec-
    tive, 289
  and imitation, 215–216, 217–221
  differences, 241–242
  influencing learning, 272
    adult-child communication strategies,
      273–276
    promoting differences in skills and
      values, 272–273
  parent-child separation, 286
  and sociocultural development, 257
  speech patterns and, 274
Curriculum, benefits of, in child care en-
    vironments, 51–52

Deafness, of child, effect on parental con-
    trol techniques, 177
Decision making, family functioning and,
    73–74
  activities in, 74, 75
  individual family member characteris-
    tics, 76–77, 80
  optimal strategies for, 74–76
Defensive identification, in socialization
    process
  boys, 189
  girls, 189–190
Deficiency-motivation conception, operant
    learning and, 145–147
Demonstration
  modeling versus, 219
  role for, 220
"Dependent Resister" baby, 9, 17
Deprivation, stimulus, operant learning
    and, 144
Determinants of Infant Behaviour (Foss,
    B.M., Ed.), 9
Developing alone, in self-sufficiency per-
    spective, 284
Development
  of child: *see* Child development
  of primates: *see* Primates
  proximal, zone of: *see* Zone of proximal
    development
Developmental level, parental control
    techniques and, 172–175
Developmental Psychology, 4

"Developmental relativism," 5
Developmental social psychology, 11
Deviant parents, attachment to, contrasting views on, 208–209
Dialogue, mutual imitation as, 234–235
Differential reinforcement of other behavior (DRO), 138
Dominance, in status relationships among primates, 33–35
Doubt, autonomy versus, ego development and, 119
DRO: see Differential reinforcement of other behavior (DRO)

Education instruction, in child care environments, center versus home, 50–51
Ego; see also Self-awareness
    Erikson's view of, 119–120
    genetic epistemologists and, 121–122
    Mahler's hypothesis, 120
    role in Freudian theory, 119
Electra complex, 189
    resolution of, 190
Embarrassment, emergence of, 130
Emerson, R.W., views on self-reliance, 294
Emotions
    in communication, 259–261
    and meaning: see Social referencing
    self-socialization and, 129–130
    as variable in family functioning analysis, 79
Empathy, emergence of, 130
Encapsulation period
    boundary erosion in childhood, 202–203
    during infancy, 200–202
Enculturation, imitation and, 215
Environmental-shift conditions, operant learning and, 147–148
Environment(s)
    affecting GSRI variables, 85
    for child care: see Child care environments; Home environment, versus other Child care environments
    deficiency in, influencing operant learning, 143–149
    family: see Family environment
    future research implications, 56–57
    influencing learning mechanisms, 140–141
    multiple, operant learning and, 148–149
    physical, parental management of, 181

Environment(s) (cont.)
    structuring of: see Scaffolding; Structuring situations, for child involvement
    Vygotsky's family, 296
Epidemiological studies, of sibling relationship, 103
Epistemologists, theories of, 121–122
Equal-status conceptualization, of infant socialization, 7–8
Equipment, in child care environments, center versus home, 50
Ethological attachment theory, 193–194
    integrative model and, 200–202
Exchange, between individuals: see Social exchange
Expectations, and social influence, 165–166
Experience, associated with skills, 269–270
Explicitness, of verbal requests, 175
Extinction, in operant learning, 138
Eye-hand coordination, child care environment studies measuring, 46–47

Facial expressions
    adult imitation of, 232–233
    child's response to, 233
Facilitation, social: see Social facilitation
Facilitators, for behavior, 141–142
Family
    belief systems, 81
    contributions of, different child care environments and, 53–55
    demands on, affecting GSRI variables, 85
    defined, 66
    environmental and psychological demands on, 85
    functioning of
        goal-related domains, 70
        GSRI elements and; See Family behavior
    profiles of: see Family profiles, using GSRI
Family behavior
    defined, 69
    and functional domains, 69–71
    GSRI elements, 65, 71
        and family outcome relationship, 82–84
    goals, 72–73
    individual life experiences, 78

Family behavior (*cont.*)
  GSRI elements (*cont.*)
    resources, 77–78
    strategies and plans, 73–77
  profiling: *see* Family profiles
Family environment
  analysis of
    individual level, 67
    social subunit level, 67
    whole family group, 67–68
  and behavior: *see* Family behavior
  concepts of, 65–66
  defined, 71
  external and demographic influences
    on, 84–85
  nature of, 64–65
  structural considerations, 66–69
  studies on, 63–64
Family problem, defined, 73
Family profiles, using GSRI, 68–69
  methods, 87–88
  related to family behavior and outcome,
    82–84
  variables generating, 86–87
Family resources, described, 77
Family success
  defined, 82
  GSRI profiles related to, 82
  measurement of, 81–82
Father(s), boys fear of losing love from,
    189
Feeding patterns, adult control over, 178–
    179
Feelings
  dynamics of, psychoanalytic theory
    and, 191
  and meaning: *see* Social referencing
Firstborn
  effect of sibling arrival on, 99–101
  sociability of, 106
Freud, S.
  attachment model, 192–193
  early attachment theories, 186–17
  identification model of, 187–188
    defensive: *see* Defensive identifica-
      tion, in socialization process
    weaknesses in, 190–193
Freudian-Watsonian model of socializa-
    tion: *see* Behaviorist-psychoanalytic
    model of socialization
Functional domains, of family behavior,
    69–71

Games, infant participation in, 229
Gender
  of child, effect on parental control tech-
    niques, 175–176
  in infancy research, 6
Genetic epistemology, 121–122
Girls, defensive identification in, 189–190
Goal-related domains, of family function-
    ing, 70
Goals, as GSRI element, 72–73
GSRI
  acronym decoded, 65
  contextual model and other models
    compared, 88–91
  elements in family behavior, 71–78
    functional consequences of, 68
  profiles, 68–69
    related to family behavior and out-
      come, 82–84
    variables and methods for using, 86–
      88
Guidance: *see* Guided participation; Social
    guidance
Guided participation
  effect on learning and development,
    269–270
  universality of, 271
Guilt
  emergence of, 130
  initiative versus, ego development and,
    119–120

Handbook of Child Psychology, 216
Help, for child: *see* Scaffolding
History, affecting GSRI variables, 85
Home environment, versus other child
    care environments, 44
  attention and stimulation
    amount of, 47–48
    quality of, 53
    type of, 48–52
  family contribution, 53–55
Hostility, between siblings, 101–102

Identification, in socialization process; *see*
    also Defensive identification
  contemporary perspectives, 195–196
  Freud's model, weaknesses in, 190–193
  integrative model for, attachment and,
    199–203
  psychoanalytic perspective, 187–190

Identity: *see* Ego; Self-awareness
Imitation
  developmental perspective of, 215–216,
    217–221
  enculturation and, 215
  in interactive context, 216, 221–223
    affective, 232–234
    during infant-adult interactions, 223–
      230
    in language acquisition, 230–232
    during peer interactions, 234–235
    social context issues, 235–242
  modeling and: *see* Modeling
  and observational learning contrasted,
    236
  pervasive, attachment and, 156–159
  role in child development, 220
  of sibling behavior, 102
  in social context, 235–236
    concept, 236–238
    cultural differences, 241–242
    functions, 238–239
    individual differences, 240–241
    model's relation to infant, 239–240;
      see also Modeling
  in socialization studies, 10
Imitative-identificatory phenomena, 158
Imprinting, 150
"Imps of darkness," 3
Individual
  in family analysis, 67
  life experiences of, as GSRI element, 78
    beliefs and attitudes pertaining to the
      family, 80–81
    cognitive and intellectual abilities, 79–
      80
    emotional and affective reactions, 79
    personality-based orientations, 78–79
Individualism, and self-reliance, 294–295
Individuality
  imitation and, 240–241
  influencing socialization outcome, 6–7
  parental control techniques and, 175–
    177
  sibling influence and, 102–107
  in socialization theories, 3–4
Infancy; *see also* Childhood
  comprehensive social psychological ap-
    proach in, 306–307
  encapsulation during, 200–202
  parental role changes during, 178
  self-sufficiency in: *see* Self-sufficiency
    perspective

Infancy research
  on imitation, 217; *see also* Imitation
  investigating socialization, 4
  rejecting behaviorist-psychoanalytic
    model of socialization, 5–7, 8–9
  different responses to, 10–12
  recent studies and, 12–17
  since 1960's, 1–2
Infant positioning, communication strategies and, 275
Infant(s); *see also* Child(ren)
  attachment behavior of, 192–193
  influence on adult, 7–8
Initiative, versus guilt, ego development
  and, 119–120
Instruction
  and activity structure, 243–244
  in child care environments, center ver-
    sus home, 50–51
  modeling as strategy for, 228–229
Integrative model, in attachment theory,
  197–198
  contrasting views of socialization, 203–
    209
  infancy and childhood, 199–203
  secure attachment correlates, 198–199
Intellectual competence
  child care environment studies measur-
    ing, 46–47
  individual's, family functioning and,
    79–80
  variables to measure, 43–44
Interaction
  and adult-child communication strategy,
    273–276
  ease of, 311–313
  mother-infant, types of, 36–37
  and relationships, self-awareness and,
    126–127
  social product view of: *see* Social
    production
Intergenerational effect
  family belief systems and, 81
  on GSRI variables, 85
Interpersonal exchanges, imitation implementing, 217
Intersubjectivity, social production and,
  313–315
Intra-individual variation, in infancy research, 6
Isolationism, analogy of, 284

Joint socialization: *see* Mutuality

Knowledge
  of physical world, child care environ-
    ment studies measuring, 47
  of self: see Ego; Self-awareness
  social construction of, 219–220

LAD: see Language Acquisition Device
    (LAD)
Laissez-faire model, of socialization, 166
Language acquisition
  function of, 261
  imitation in, 230–232
  maternal language effect on, 262
Language Acquisition Device (LAD), 299
Language Acquisition Support System
    (LASS), 299
Language skills
  acquisition of: see Language acquisition
  measurement variables for, 43
  studies measuring, 47
LASS: see Language Acquisition Support
    System (LASS)
Laterborn
  effect on firstborn, 99–101
  sociability of, 106
Learning
  arranging environments for: see Struc-
    turing situations, for child
    involvement
  attachment: see Attachment learning
  cultural variations in, 272–276
  guided participation effect on, 269–270
  operant: see Operant learning
  pervasive imitative, 156–159
  social: see Social learning
  vicarious, 10
Letters of a Woman Homesteader (Stewart,
    E.P.), 295
Life experiences, of individual, as GSRI
    element, 78–81
Longitudinal studies, of sibling relation-
    ship, 102–103
"Looking glass" self, 117–118
Love, maternal and paternal, boys' fear of
    losing, 189

Manager, parent as, 181
Maternal language, and language acquisi-
    tion, 262
Maternal love, fear of loss in boys, 189
Maturation, mechanisms of, 141
Meaning, guidance through: see Social
    referencing

Messages, referencing, 301; see also Social
    referencing
Microgenetic development, 257
Mirror, recognizing self in, 123–124
Mistrust, trust versus, ego development
    and, 119
Modeling
  versus demonstration, 219
  as effective instructional strategy, 228–
    229
  and imitation, 239–240
Modeling-imitation sequences, 221–222
  language acquisition and, 231–232
  during play, 226
  and socialization relationship, 243
Momentary state, of child, parental con-
    trol techniques and, 169–172
"Motherese" phenomenon, 172
Mother(s); see also Maternal
  child's differentiation of self from, 120–121
  control technique studies, 171–172
  and face-to-face interactions, 232
  and firstborn relationship, effect of sec-
    ond child on, 99–101
  imitation of children's utterances, 231
  and infant positioning, 275–276
  interaction with child
    at bathtime, 179–180
    during play, 227–228
  primates
    influence on development, 36–37
    mother-infant relationship, 36
Multiple environments, operant learning
    and, 148–149
Mutual involvement: see Mutuality
Mutuality, 7–8
  of individual effort and social facilita-
    tion, 256–258
  parent-child interactions and, 168, 182
  of parental control: see under Social
    control
  recent studies on, 14

Narration skills, adult involvement in de-
    velopment of, 264
Naturalness, 311–313
Nature versus nurture, in child
    development
  Piaget's work on, 257
  theories compared, 257–258
  Vygotsky's work on, 256–257
Negative influence, anxiety and, contrast-
    ing views on, 203–204

Non-verbal cognition, as child competence variable, 43
Nonverbal communication, 259–261
Nurture, versus nurture: see Nature versus nurture

Observational learning
  and imitation
    contrasted, 236
    interactive framework for, 218
    pervasive imitation learning and, 157
    role in adaptation, 218
Oedipal complex, 189
Ontogenetic development, 257
Operant learning, 138–140
  social influences due to, 142
    attachment learning, 149–154
    concurrent influence processes, 155–156
    environmental deficiency, 143–149
    pervasive imitative learning, 156–159
    social referencing, 142–143
Orientation(s)
  personality-based, family functioning and, 78–79
  social, for task performance, 316–318
  task, social production and, 315–316
Original Word Game, comments on, 261
Outcome(s)
  attachment as, child development and, 195
  biological factors influencing, 84
  family, evaluation of, 81–82
    GSRI relationships in, 82–84
  social guidance, 305–306
  social production, 318–319
  social referencing, 302
  of socialization, individual differences influencing, 6–7

Parent–child relationships
  early socialization and, 167–168
  sibling impact upon, 99–101
  social control and, 111–115
Parenting
  behavior model, versus GSRI contextual model, 90–91
  in behaviorist-psychoanalytic model of socialization, 13
Parent(s)
  controlling behavior: see Social control
  as manager, 181

Parent(s) (cont.)
  reinforcing behavior, 4
  as teacher, 309
Participation: see Guided participation
Paternal love, fear of loss in boys, 189
Patterns of Child Rearing (Sears, Maccoby, and Levin), 4
Peers
  imitation during interactions with, 234–235
  influence on child's development, 98
Penalty, punishment versus, contrasting views on, 207–208
Penis, girls' desire to recapture, 189–190
Personality-based orientations, in individual's life experiences, 78–79
Pervasive imitative learning, attachment learning and, 156–159
Phenomenon
  attachment-dependence, 158
  imitative-identificatory, 158
  "Motherese," 172
  secure base, 285, 286
Phylogenetic development, 257
Physical environment, child care center versus home, 50
Physical world, knowledge of, child care environment studies measuring, 47
Piaget, J.
  and child's knowledge of self, 121–122
  child's relationship with social environment, 284
  stage theory of cognitive development, 5
  work on nature versus nurture, in child development, 257
  and Vygotsky's work compared, 257–258
Plans, strategies and, as GSRI element, 73–77
Play
  infant-adult interactions, imitation during, 223–230
  modeling-imitation sequences during, 226
  between siblings, 101–102, 104
Positioning, of infant, communication strategies and, 275
Positive influence, commitment and, contrasting views on, 204–206
"Prägung," 150

Precocial species, and altricial species, differences between
  attachment learning and, 149
  self-sufficiency and, 285–286
Precocity, of infant competence, 5–6
Preparedness, learning and, 141
Pride, emergence of, 129–130
Primates
  developmental aspects of, 27–28
    mother's influence on, 36–37
    social status and, 30–32
  mother-infant relationship, 36
  social group components, 28–29
  social nature of, 23–24
  social status of
    behavioral development and, 30–32
    emerging sexual behavior and, 32–33
    social cognition role in, 33–36
  social structure of
    factors influencing, 24–25
    natural variations in, 25–26
    and ontogeny of sexual segregation, 29–31
Privation
  social, effect on macaque babies, 285–286
  stimulus, operant learning and, 143–144
Proactive controls, 172
Problem solving
  child care environment studies measuring, 47
  family functioning and, 73–74
    activities in, 74, 75
    individual family member characteristics, 76–77, 80
    optimal strategies for, 74–76
Proximal development, zone of: see Zone of proximal development
Psychoanalysis, behaviorism approaches integrating, 4
Psychoanalytic theory
  on attachment and identification, 187–190
  language of, 190–191
  operational definitions, 191
  psychoanalysts' resistance to, 191–192
  views on socialization, comtemporary views contrasting with, 203–209
Psychology
  Soviet, activity as unit of analysis in, 219
Punishment, versus penalty, contrasting views on, 207–208

Reasoning, child care environment studies measuring, 47
Reciprocity: see Mutuality
Recognition, of self, 123–124
Referencing messages, 301; see also Social referencing
Regulation, of child care environments, effect on child competence, 53
Reinforcement
  of behavior, by parent, 4
  concept of, 139
  differential, of other behavior, 138
Reinforcer, operant learning and, 139
Reinforcing stimulus, operant learning and, 139
Relationships
  among primates
    mother-infant relationship, 36
    social cognition role in, 33–36
  parent-child: see Parent-child relationships
  self-awareness role in, 125–129
Representation, attachment as, 127–129
Resources, as GSRI element, 77–78
Responding, cued: see Cued responding
Responding alone, in self-sufficiency perspective, 283–284
Responses, operant learning and, 138–139
Responsibility
  dividing, structuring situations through, 264
  for managing situations
    adult's adjustment of support, 265–266
    child's role, 266–269
    effective transfer, 264
Reversal learning, operant learning and, 138
Rewards, 3
Role, assuming in status relationships, 33–34
Rules, in child care environments, center versus home, 49–50

S-R connections, 195
A Sand County Almanac (Leopold, A.), 291
Scaffolding
  guidance-in-development and, 300
  guidance-through-structure and, 299, 300
  revising over time, 265
  social guidance and, 298–299

Secondary emotions, 129
Secure attachment
    deviant parents and, 208–209
    factors influencing, 198
    punishment versus penalty, techniques
        used, 208
Secure base phenomenon, 285, 286
Security, of attachment, 286–287
Selectivity postulate, in social referencing,
    302
Self
    created in social nexus, 117–122
    interpretations of, 115–117
    socialization and, 124–125
Self-awareness; see also Ego
    Cooley and Mead's work, 117–118
    emergence of, empirical support for,
        122–124
    emotions following, 130
    genetic epistemology theories, 121–122
    infant participation before, 125
    Piaget's work, 121
    role in relationships, 125–129
    and self-knowledge relationship, 115–
        117
    socialization promoting, 129–130
Self-conscious emotions, 129
Self-identity: see Ego
Self-knowledge, and self-awareness rela-
    tionship, 115–117
Self-recognition, development of, 123–124
Self-reliance
    Emerson's perspective of, 1
    in self-sufficiency perspective, 294–295;
        see also Self-sufficiency perspective
Self-reliance (Emerson, R.W.), 1, 294
Self-sufficiency perspective, 282
    ecological validity of, 286–289
    prescribed values for, 289
        achievement, 289–292
        self-reliance, 294–295
        solitude, 292–293
    as a trinity, 282–283
        being alone, 285–286
        developing alone, 284
        responding alone, 283–284
Sensitivity, parental control techniques
    and, 170
Sex role, and social control, 112–113
Sexual behavior, in primates, 32–33
    status relationships and, 33–35
Sexual segregation, ontogeny of, and pri-
    mate social structure, 29–31

Shame
    autonomy versus, ego development
        and, 119
    emergence of, 130
Shift conditions, operant learning and,
    147–148
Siblings
    direct effects of, 101–102
    impact on parent-child relationships,
        99–101
    influence on social development, 97–99
        individual differences and, 102–107
    social understanding and, 13
Similarity, behavioral, identification and,
    196
Skills
    associated with experience, 269–270
    familiar and unfamiliar, providing
        bridge between, 259–262
    imitation facilitating, 217
    narrative, adult involvement in devel-
        opment of, 264
    promoting differences in, 272–273
Sleeping patterns, adult control over, 178–
    179
Social assistance, social production and,
    309–311
Social cognition
    as child competence variable, 44
    and primate social status, 33–35, 33–36
Social competence
    as child competence variable, 43
    findings from child care environment
        studies, 46
Social control, 111–115
    during first year of life, 177–181, 182
    joint parent-child involvement in, 111–
        115
    parental techniques, 168–169
        child's developmental level and, 172–
            175
        child's individuality and, 175–177
        child's momentary state and, 169–
            172
Social entities, significance of, 307–309
Social exchange
    imitation implementing, 217
    parental sensitivity in, 170
Social facilitation
    of individual development, 258–270
    mutuality of, 256–258
Social facts, 307
Social groups, of primates, 28–29

Social guidance
in infant development, 297–298
outcomes, 305–306
reason for, 304–305
through meaning: *see* Social referencing
through structure: *see* Scaffolding
Vygotsky's and Mead's work on, 296–297
Social influence
and development, 217–221
expectations and, 165–166
force of, 2–4
in infancy research, 1–2
model of, viii, 12–17
self-knowledge and, 115–117
and social control, 111–115
in social psychology, 11
Social learning
operant learning and, 139–140
in socialization studies, 10
theory of, and contemporary perspectives on attachment, 194–195
Social orientation, for task performance, 316–318
Social privation, effect on macaque babies, 285–286
Social production
intersubjectivity, 313–315
naturalness and ease of interaction, 311–313
outcomes, 318–319
and social assistance, 309–311
social orientation for task performance, 316–318
temporal and task orientation, 315–316
Social referencing, 259–261
ambiguity and, 302
broad versus narrow conceptualization of, 304
defined, 301
operant learning and, 142–143
outcomes, 302
predictions of, 302–303
as reappraisal, 303
social guidance and, 301–304
variations in, 303–304
Social relationships
attachment as representation, 127–129
interactions and, 126–127
levels of, 125–126
Social status, of primates: *see* Primates
Social structure, of primates: *see* Primates
Social subunit, in family analysis, 67

Social understanding, siblings and, 13
Socialization
contrasting views of, 203–209
core issues, 165–166
in infancy research, 1–2
models of, 166–168; *see also* individually named models
contemporary perspective, 193–196
integrative, 197–209
psychoanalytic perspective, 187–193
outcomes, individual differences influencing, 6–7
parent-child attachment and, 185–186; *see also* Attachment
parental control and: *see* Social control
recent studies in, 12–17
Watson and Freud's theories of, 2–4
different responses to, 10–12
research opposition to, 5–8, 8–9
Sociocultural development, 257
Solitude, in self-sufficiency perspective, 292–293; *see also* Self-sufficiency perspective
Soviet psychology, activity as unit of analysis in, 219
Speaker-switch pauses, in adult conversation, 170
Speech, cultural patterns of, 274
Stability, behavioral, explanations for, 195
Standards
adoption of, deviant parents and, 208–209
self-awareness emergence and, 129–130
Status, social, of primates: *see under* Primates
Stewardship, doctrine of, 301
Stimulation
in different child care environments
amount, 47–48
quality, 53
type, 48–52
influencing learning mechanisms, 140–141
Stimulus
aversive, 139
influencing learning mechanisms, 140–141
reinforcing, 139
Stimulus deprivation, operant learning and, 144
Stimulus privation, operant learning and, 143–144
Strange Situation test, measuring attachment by, 285

Strategies and plans, as GSRI element,
    73–77
Structure
    affecting GSRI variables, 85
    guidance through, 298–301; see also
        Scaffolding
    social, of primates: see Primates
Structuring situations, for child
        involvement
    adjusting support, 265–266; see also
        Scaffolding
    and child's participation role, 266–269
    choosing and structuring, 262–263
    dividing responsibility, 264
Struggle, elements in socialization pro-
        cess, 205–206
"Sturm und Drang," 13
Subordinance, in status relationships
        among primates, 34–35
Success, of family: see Family success
Symbiosis, of primate mother-infant rela-
        tionship, 36
Synchrony, 12

Task orientation, social production and,
        315–316
Task performance, social orientation for,
        316–318
Teaching, quality in child care environ-
        ments, center versus home, 51–52
Temperament, in infancy research, 6
Temporal orientation, social production
        and, 315–316
The Child and its Family (Lewis and Rosen-
        blum, Eds.), 113
The Effect of the Infant on its Caregiver
        (Lewis and Rosenblum, Eds.), 7
The Integration of the Child into a Social
        World (Richards, M., Ed.), 9
Thoreau, H.D., views on solitude, 292–293
Thought
    dynamics of, psychoanalytic theory
        and, 191
    Mead's views on origins of, 296
Threats, perceived or real, defensive iden-
        tification and, 189–190
"Touching base," 285, 286
Toy play: see Play
Training, for caregivers, child care center
        versus home, 52
Trust, versus mistrust, ego development
        and, 119

"Ugly individualism," 294–295
Understanding, imitation facilitating, 217
Union of Soviet Socialist Rebublics
        (USSR), activity as unit of analysis
        in Soviet psychology, 219
Universality
    cultural, 270–271
    of guided participation, 271

Valuation, imitation facilitating, 217
Values
    adoption of, deviant parents and, 208–
        209
    promoting differences in, 272–273
Verbal cognition, as child competence
        variable, 43
    studies measuring, 47
Verbal requests
    explicitness of, 175
    preverbal infants and, 180
Vicarious learning, in socialization stud-
        ies, 10
Vygotsky, L.
    joint socialization theory, 254
    nature versus nurture work, in child
        development, 256–257
    and Piaget's work compared, 257–
        258
    personal social environment of, 296
    and zone of proximal development: see
        Zone of proximal development

Waking-sleeping states, adult control over,
        178–179
Walden (Thoreau, H.D.), 292
Words, as cultural system for bridging,
        261–262
"Working models," encapsulation and,
        201

Zone of free movement (ZFM), concept
        of, 299–300
Zone of promoted actions (ZPA), concept
        of, 299–300
Zone of proximal development, 14
    cultural universals and, 270–271
    elaboration of (Rogoff and Gardner),
        255–256
    Vygotsky's concept of, 254–255
    Vygotsky's formulation of, 296–297